D0451583

The United States and the Americas

Lester D. Langley, General Editor

*This series is dedicated to a broader under-
standing of the political, economic, and especially cultural forces and issues that have
shaped the Western hemispheric experience—
its governments and its peoples. Individual
volumes assess relations between the United
States and its neighbors to the south and north:
Mexico, Central America, Cuba, the Domini-
can Republic, Haiti, Panama, Colombia, Vene-
zuela, the Andean Republics (Peru, Ecuador,
and Bolivia), Brazil, Uruguay and Paraguay,
Argentina, Chile, and Canada.*

The United States and the Americas

Cuba and the United States

Louis A. Pérez, Jr.

Cuba and the United States: Ties of Singular Intimacy

Third Edition

The University of Georgia Press
Athens and London

© 1990, 1997, 2003 by the University of Georgia Press
Athens, Georgia 30602
www.ugapress.org

The maps on pages xii and xxiv are from
Cuba: Between Reform and Revolution by Louis A. Pérez, Jr.
Copyright © 1988 by Oxford University Press, Inc.
Reprinted by permission.

Set in 10/14 Palatino by Tseng Information Systems, Inc.
Printed digitally in the United States of America

Library of Congress Cataloging-in-Publication Data

Pérez, Louis A., 1943–
Cuba and the United States : ties of singular intimacy /
Louis A. Pérez, Jr.—3rd ed.
xxii, 336 p. : maps ; 23 cm.—(The United States and the Americas)
Includes bibliographical references (p. 311–326) and index.
ISBN 0-8203-2483-3 (paperback : alk. paper)
1. United States—Foreign relations—Cuba. 2. Cuba—
Foreign relations—United States. 3. Cuba—History—
1810–1899. 4. Cuba—History—1895– I. Title. II. Series.
E183.8.C9 P465 2003
327.7291073—dc21   2002035276

ISBN-13: 978-0-8203-2483-8 (paperback : alk. paper)

British Library Cataloging-in-Publication Data available

To Deborah,
For all the reasons

The new Cuba yet to arise from the ashes of the past must needs be bound to us by ties of singular intimacy and strength if its enduring welfare is to be assured. Whether those ties shall be organic or conventional, the destinies of Cuba are in some rightful form and manner irrevocably linked with our own, but how and how far is for the future to determine in the ripeness of events.

    —William McKinley, State of the Union Message, December 5, 1899

Contents

Preface to the Third Edition   xiii

Preface   xv

Acknowledgments   xxi

1. The Origins of Relations   1

2. A Convergence of Interests   29

3. At the Crossroads   55

4. Intervention and Occupation   82

5. Context and Content of the Republic   113

6. The Purpose of Power   149

7. Stirrings of Nationality   170

8. Twilight Years   202

9. Revolution and Response   238

Notes   283

Bibliographical Essay   311

Index   327

CUBA
and the Caribbean Sea

Preface to the Third Edition

"We will continue to enforce economic sanctions and ban travel to Cuba until Cuba's government shows real reform." With this pronouncement in Miami on May 20, 2002, George W. Bush affirmed North American determination to carry on with the forty-three-year-old U.S. embargo on Cuba and thereby became the twelfth U.S. President to uphold sanctions against the government of Fidel Castro.

While much has remained unchanged in the six years since the appearance of the second edition of this book, it is nevertheless true that portents of change are everywhere to be seen. Certainly, change can be discerned in the climate of popular opinion, change that reveals itself principally in the form of new dispositions for public debate on the efficacy of a policy that previously enjoyed overwhelming and undisputed bipartisan support. In the last six years, public opinion polls have shown repeatedly that a majority of the American people favor expanding contacts between the people of both countries. Important sectors of the business community have raised their voices to question the wisdom of a policy that has placed Cuban markets beyond the reach of U.S. producers. Ever-growing numbers of legislators from both houses of Congress, and particularly representatives from farm states, have been among the most zealous advocates of expanded trade relations between Cuba and the United States. In July 2002, over the strong objections of the White House, the Republican-controlled House of Representatives approved legislation to end the enforcement of the U.S. travel ban to Cuba.

Some of these efforts have borne fruit. In 2001, Cuba purchased $30 million of U.S. agricultural products, the first transaction between both countries in more than forty years. Travel between both countries has increased markedly, allowing Cubans and North Americans to visit each other in growing numbers and with greater frequency. Cultural exchanges have expanded.

Yet it is also true that much of what has changed has occurred within a larger context of changelessness. Political relations and economic ties remain tenuous. North American travel to Cuba remains subject to Treasury Department licensing procedures derived from the Trading with the Enemy Act passed in 1917 as a response to conditions occasioned by World War I. Cuban travel to the United States is subject to the vagaries of political currents in both countries. After September 2001, the appearance of Cuba on the State Department's list of terrorist nations has implications of other kinds. For its part, the Cuban government responded with charges of its own, accusing the United States of state-sponsored terrorism against Cuba and insisting that persons known to have conducted terrorist attacks against the island and its people had obtained support and sanctuary in the United States.

The debate on terrorism is, of course, the most recent phase of the Cuba-U.S. dispute. Until the early 1990s, the United States justified sanctions on Cuba as a measure against a surrogate power for the Soviet Union. After the collapse of the communist systems of Eastern Europe, sanctions were justified through charges that Cuba had established itself as a safe haven for a Caribbean-wide network of narcotrafficking. After September 2001, sanctions found renewed purpose as a measure in the war against terrorism. All the while, the issue of Cuba continued to loom large in domestic politics, made even more dramatic by the role of the state of Florida in the outcome of the 2000 presidential elections.

It is not at all clear how both countries will proceed from this point forward. It is difficult to envision the circumstances under which a sitting U.S. president would travel to Havana to be received by President Fidel Castro. The United States appears to have settled into a policy best characterized as "waiting for Fidel to die." And while much intellectual currency and many public funds have been expended in U.S. official circles to anticipate the form that a post-Castro Cuba will take, the history of past relations suggests that North American policymakers will be utterly unprepared for what happens next in Cuba.

Preface

Relations between Cuba and the United States seemed destined from the beginning to be close and complicated. Before both were separate and sovereign nations, even as they continued as European colonies, circumstances had created needs in each that only the other could meet. Proximity alone explains much, and a great deal can be understood by geography. In the United States control over the island was perceived as a natural and logical extension of boundaries manifestly destined to expand, a way of defending territorial gains of past expansion and the means of future ones. Lying astride the principal sea lanes of the Caribbean and guarding the entrance to the Gulf of Mexico, the island early assumed a strategic significance of looming proportions. It became all but impossible for North Americans to contemplate the future security of southern boundaries and guarantee the well-being of Gulf maritime interests without first disposing of what became known increasingly as the "Cuba question."

Economic factors, too, contributed to the fateful connection and were as much a function of a unique geographical context as of specific historical circumstances. Even as Cuba continued within the Spanish political system, it was passing into the North American economic system, creating an anomaly of far-reaching implications. Certainly this, too, was facilitated by geography. But it was also related to the specific character of Spanish colonial administration and commercial policies, to world market forces and regional political conditions, to unanticipated opportunity and calculated opportunism, to Cuban economic needs and the capacity of the United States to meet those needs, and vice versa. By the latter third of the nineteenth century, the United States had emerged as the principal market for Cuba's exports and was well on its way to becoming the principal source of the island's imports. In the same way that North American political leaders understood the strategic significance of Cuba, Cuban producers understood the economic importance of the United States. This convergence of interests established the context of relations between Cuba and the United States for more than a century. North Americans considered Cuba essential to the politico-military security of the United States; Cubans looked upon the United States as vital to the socioeconomic well-being of the island. Through the nineteenth century, Cubans became increasingly dependent upon the United States as a market, as a provider of consumer goods and foodstuffs, as a source of credit and capital, and as a defender of the status quo.

In the nineteenth century, these conditions underscored the desirability if not perhaps the inevitability of annexation. The logic seemed compelling. And, indeed, certainly in the United States, such a union became almost a foregone conclusion. Possession of Cuba became a national preoccupation, and not always a rational one. Almost from the beginning of the nineteenth century, the United States threatened war to prevent sovereignty over Cuba from escaping its control, and at the end of the century it employed precisely that means to gain control of the island.

Union was not a vision confined to North Americans, however. Annexationism was also a potent political force in Cuba. Throughout much of the nineteenth century, producers and property owners saw in annexation a way of resolving some of the more anomalous conditions of the colonial political economy. It found support too among Creole elites who looked to union with the United States as a means to contain the deepening social tensions in Cuban society, a way of guaranteeing local socioeconomic preeminence without having to share power with rival political contenders.

But annexation was not unopposed. The notion of a separate and independent nationality, in full possession of its own destiny, early took hold of the Cuban imagination. The proposition of *Cuba Libre* passed through several ideological formulations until, by the end of the nineteenth century, it came to represent a movement of enormous vigor, possessed of elements of nationalism, social justice, and popular democracy all having to do with the notion of a Cuba free and for Cubans. For many, this notion of self-determination was a proposition with which there could be neither concession to Spain nor compromise with the United States.

These served as the principal issues of the nineteenth century, the key elements of relations between Cubans and North Americans. They assumed a variety of forms and were played out in a number of guises, and ultimately they came together in a fateful convergence in 1898. But 1898 was not an end at all. It served only to change the form these issues assumed without substantially modifying their content. The imposition of the Platt Amendment in 1901, followed by repeated U.S. armed intervention and political interference and accompanied by a vast expansion of U.S. capital into the island, in combination with a pervasive cultural presence, served to shape the nature of relations between Cubans and North Americans.

The Platt Amendment came to institutionalize the U.S. presence in Cuba. The United States developed early into a power contender in the Cuban polity, with economic interests to defend and political allies to back. But it was no less true that the Platt Amendment acted to preserve Cuban independence, however truncated, and if more in form than function. Relations as stipulated in the 1901 statute were duly ratified and formalized in the Permanent Treaty of 1903, and no longer was annexation necessary, or even desirable, for the issues that had so concerned North Americans during the nineteenth century were adequately satisfied through the Platt Amendment early in the twentieth. At the same time, the Platt Amendment preserved just enough space to keep the *independentista* vision alive. What survived, in fact, was the ideal of independence around which would develop an enduring commitment to its eventual and complete fulfillment.

Relations between Cuba and the United States in the twentieth century were shaped decisively by changing conditions in both countries. United States interests were not static; they changed over time, periodically and significantly between the 1890s and the 1910s, and again between the 1920s and 1950s. In both form and function U.S. policy responded to the changing nature of North American interests in Cuba. These shifts corresponded to changes in Cuban society that were often the product of North American hegemony. Social formations, political structures, economic systems, cultural forms, and, in the end, the very character of the state in Cuba were affected decisively by the North American presence. The social system became more complicated, class structures more clearly defined, and social conflict more distinctly articulated, ultimately altering the character of the national discourse.

These developments profoundly shaped relations between Cubans and North Americans. Cubans and North Americans had good cause to think about each other. Both peoples thought much and long about their relationship, pondered its significance, considered its implications, and otherwise contemplated the meaning of the connection. But Cubans thought more about it, if only because the North American presence on the island was a factor of prepossessing proportions, in ways that Cuba could not have been in the United States. After 1959, North American obsession with Cuba overtook Cuban preoccupation with the United States. For North Americans no less than for many Cubans the revolution was possessed of traumatic content. The sudden end of a historic relationship, in an atmosphere of recrimination and acrimony, had jarring effects on both sides of the Florida Straits.

It is not likely that North Americans were more familiar to any other people in Latin America than Cubans, and vice versa. They came to know each other well. Geography, strategic considerations, and vital economic concerns worked inexorably to link the destinies of both peoples. This was, of course, often more a function of chance than choice, the result of the peculiarity of the historical experiences of each nation. But it is no less clear that once the connections were made, relations between Cubans and North Americans assumed a logic of their own, out of which developed a duality in which a pervasive ambivalence—especially among Cubans—served to define the character of the interaction: between trust and suspicion, between esteem and scorn, between a desire to emulate and a need to repudiate.

For nearly two centuries this clash has persisted, creating in the process the enduring context of relations between Cuba and the United States. North American resolve to control Cuba and Cuban determination to resist control have become part of the national character of each and something of an obsession for both.

II

This study is first and foremost a history of Cuba, specifically an account of Cuba and Cubans in their relations with the United States. Politics and policy are treated, of course, but principally as a function of social, economic, and cultural relations between the two countries. The emphasis, then, is on the manner in which Cuban relations with the United States worked to shape Cuban history and influence Cuban attitudes, values, and behavior, and vice versa. The purpose here is to examine the points and places at which Cubans and North Americans made contact, in Cuba and in the United States, the circumstances of those contacts, and the consequences. Examined too are the geopolitical and historic elements intrinsic to the Cuban experience that made the island particularly susceptible to North American influence.

This book explores the dilemmas that proximity to the United States —its politics, economy, and culture—bequeathed to Cuba and Cubans in their quest for national identity. Cubans yielded to U.S. influence and power, but they adapted and with considerable ingenuity and success learned to manipulate North American policy. In the process, they were active participants in shaping the form and function of U.S. policy to their advantage and for their benefit. Ultimately, the circumstances of the interaction between Cuba and the United States—two nations vastly unequal in size, population, resources, and power— contributed to shaping Cuban national institutions, political culture, social structures, and economic development. In more modest ways, Cubans participated in the social, economic, political, and cultural life of the United States, sometimes with dramatic and lasting effect. That formal relations between Cuba and the United States ended after January 1961 does not suggest that the influence of one on the other has stopped. It has simply taken different forms.

Acknowledgments

The completion of this book leaves me very much in the debt of others, beginning with the staffs at the Archivo Nacional de Cuba and the Biblioteca Nacional "José Martí" in Havana and the National Archives and Library of Congress in Washington, D.C. I am especially appreciative of the efforts made in my behalf by the staff of the Inter-Library Loan office of the University of South Florida Library, particularly Marykay Hartung and Gayle Wozniak. They provided unflagging support through the course of this work, for which I am, once more, in their debt.

No less important to the completion of this project was the assistance provided by the staff of the Information Processing Center of the College of Social and Behavioral Sciences at the University of South Florida. Cecile Pulin worked with this manuscript during the early and most difficult drafts. Carole Rennick was helpful in moving the preparation of the manuscript toward its final form. Nita Desai provided vital assistance on many specific aspects of this project and was ready always to help in all the ways that matter. Sylvia Wood assisted in the completion of this project in ways too many to recount and too many to repay. I am most grateful. As so often in the past, Peggy Cornett made life infinitely easier while this book was in preparation. She has been a constant source of support and assistance, unconditionally and unfailingly.

I am indebted also to friends and colleagues who gave generously of their time and insights while the manuscript was nearing completion. José Keselman provided thoughtful comments on several chapters. K. Lynn Stoner gave a careful reading to a large portion of the manuscript. She made many helpful suggestions and provided additional data to corroborate some of the key arguments of the book. I am indebted also to M. Fraser Ottanelli, who read the full manuscript and made valuable suggestions from a perspective not available to me. Robert P. Ingalls subjected the last draft of the manuscript to a rigorous review, probing arguments here and questioning syntax there. Steven F. Lawson read a late draft of the complete manuscript. I am afraid that the value of some of his comments was lost to me because of his impossible handwriting, but what I was able to decipher was enormously useful and helped me to focus on some of the key issues of the book. Nancy A. Hewitt read most of the manuscript and provided generous comments on both style and substance. Her importance cannot be overstated. Jules R. Benjamin read the completed manuscript and offered thoughtful suggestions and comments. My father provided enormous assistance with information for the section on music. He read and corrected the final manuscript version —and it could not have been done by anybody better. I am grateful also to Trudie Calvert, who subjected the completed manuscript to a thorough final review and in the process eliminated many of the remaining inconsistences and discrepancies. It is a better book for her having read it. I have, finally, appreciated the opportunity of working with Lester D. Langley, who first proposed this study. He has provided encouragement and assistance all along the way, for which I am grateful.

The final moments of the completion of this book have provided me with an occasion for some retrospection, a time to take stock of what else has happened during the time this manuscript has been in preparation. Some things have remained constant, and for much of this I am grateful for the constancy of friends. They know who they are.

This has also been a time of loss. The deaths of Edwin Lieuwen, James W. Silver, and Ramón Pi y Castella have deprived me of friends who by word and deed taught me much about a great deal. They are very much missed.

This has as well been a time of transition. It seems that change has come up suddenly between my daughters and me, although I know that it has been years in the making. Amara's departure for college has created a void that is partially mitigated by the certainty that I would not have had it any other way. Maya occupies a place of singular importance in my life, and this time together has been an occasion of renewal. We are approaching that moment of detachment: it is a good thing that I have had almost two decades to prepare for it.

The United States and the Americas

Cuba and the United States

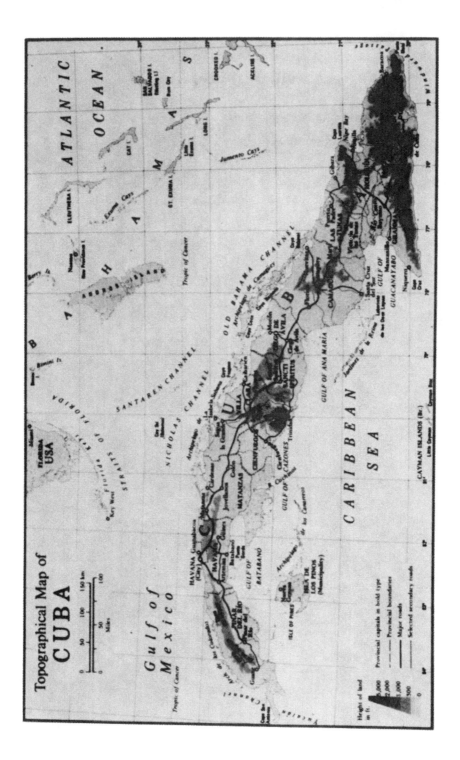

1   The Origins of Relations

Relations between Cuba and the United States began modestly enough through irregular commercial contacts, mostly illicit, between European colonies in the New World, trading to obtain otherwise scarce commodities or to elude exorbitant colonial taxes—and sometimes both. This trade was both practical and logical for each partner, but especially for the Cubans. The eighteenth century brought comparatively good economic times to Cuba, a period of sustained if not spectacular economic growth. Local producers and consumers were in need of wider markets for expanding production and increased imports in response to growing consumption. Much of this expanded trade centered on the production of tobacco commodities, largely in the form of powdered tobacco for snuff, cut tobacco for pipe smoking, and leaf tobacco for cigar manufacturing. The production of hides also expanded, and exports both legal and illicit soared. But it was sugar that registered the more notable advances during the first half of the eighteenth century. The number of mills increased, the cultivation of cane expanded, production modernized. During the 1730s, Cuban annual output reached a record two thousand tons, more than doubling by the end of the 1750s to fifty-five hundred tons. [1]

But the expansion of the Cuban economy was not an unmixed blessing. Its success, especially during the reign of the Bourbons, brought Cuban prosperity to the attention of the always penurious royal exchequer. The Bourbons had introduced a new efficiency to colonial administration, and there was no mistaking the purpose of the policy: it aspired to nothing less than complete control over colonial resources and receipts. The early Bourbons promoted the development of state monopolies, most notably the Factoría de Tabacos (1717), to control production, prices, and distribution of tobacco, and the Real Compañía de Comercio (1740), to regulate trade and commerce between Spain and Cuba. The results were not long in coming. To the dis-

1

may of Cuban producers and consumers, the opportunities to export their goods and the prices paid for their products declined even as the supply of imports diminished and their prices increased.

But Cuban complaints were not confined to state monopoly schemes. No less irksome to local producers and consumers was the endless proliferation of new taxes and the increase of old ones. Indeed, taxation was a central feature of the Bourbon strategy for transferring revenues from the colony to the metropolis. The number of taxes increased and methods of collection improved. Profits went down, prices went up. No sector of Cuban society was immune from taxes, in one form or another, on one product or on one service or another.

There were other problems, most of which had less to do with colonial administration than with economic organization. In fact, rising Cuban production had overtaken existing transportation capacity and available markets. Two developments were occurring at once: increasingly transportation bottlenecks—from production points to ports, but especially from ports to overseas markets—were frustrating Cuban efforts to expand production. Spain could not provide Cuban producers with adequate shipping, on a sufficiently regular basis, to accommodate expanding sugar production, both actual and potential. Increasingly, too, and equally troublesome, Spain was losing the capacity to absorb Cuba's rising production but resisted Cuban demands for free access to wider markets. Spain was not always consistent in these efforts, nor were the efforts always successful. That was part of the problem.

These conditions underscored the growing anomaly of a dynamic colonial economy dependent on a stagnant metropolis. Spanish producers were losing the ability to provide the island with sufficient imports at reasonable prices, both of which were necessary to sustain continued economic growth in Cuba. No less important, Spain's inability to provide Cuban planters with African slaves in adequate numbers, with regularity, and at reasonable prices acted in still one more fashion to thwart the expansion of Cuban production. On all counts, and all at once, Spanish colonialism was straining to accommodate to the changes transforming the Cuban economy and increasingly revealing itself incapable of doing so.

Some of the more opprobrious features of Spanish colonialism were made bearable during the early decades of the eighteenth century by the occasional availability of alternative markets and new sources of imports, principally in the form of trade with North American colonies. Spanish authorities had long looked upon trade between Cuba and British North America with some ambivalence, alternating between passive acquiescence and active resistance. Local officials recognized the logic of this commerce, which provided access to markets new and near and a source of supplies cheap and certain. It promised also to meet some of the more outstanding Cuban demands and even to provide additional sources of revenue in the form of tax receipts and trade duties.

How these commercial contacts, legal and illicit, flourished was often a function of Spain's European diplomacy and depended on whether and when Spain possessed the means to impose its will on the colonists. Sometimes it did, sometimes it did not. The result was a policy characterized by irresolution and unpredictability—trade sometimes sanctioned, sometimes suspended; contraband sometimes permitted, other times prohibited. Periodic attempts to suppress contraband often succeeded only in creating new problems and exacerbating old ones. Occasionally, and especially under the early Bourbons in the eighteenth century, Spain moved vigorously against illicit trade. Smuggling continued, however, though at greater costs to Cubans, if only because risks were greater. Spanish authorities merely disrupted the flow of contraband trade without adequately meeting the ensuing increase in local demand. And the result was hardship. Almost always decisions were made from above and abroad, in the pursuit of policies that Cubans often neither approved nor understood and almost never influenced.

But if Spain often acted to contain the forces of Cuban development, it occasionally if inadvertently also served to release them, and on no occasion more dramatically than in 1762. The entry of Spain into the Seven Years' War (1756–63) between England and France transformed the Caribbean into a zone of military operations and Cuba into a key military objective. In 1762 the British seized Havana.

The British occupation of Havana promoted ties between Cubans and North Americans on a scale hitherto unprecedented. Fully one-quarter of the twenty-two-thousand-man expeditionary force, much of which was outfitted in the thirteen colonies, consisted of North Americans. The opening of Havana revealed to Cubans what was possible under optimal circumstances and that such circumstances were indeed possible. It created opportunities that producers in Cuba previously could only have dreamed about. The port was thrown open to free trade with Great Britain and its New World possessions. Trade taxes were abolished. Vendors and jobbers from England descended upon Havana, offering Cubans a dazzling array of coveted consumer goods, staple items, and industrial wares: linens, textiles, manufactures, and especially sugar machinery. Merchants and traders from the North American colonies established themselves in the Cuban capital, selling grains, tools, and foodstuffs. Also available now in Cuba, and on a scale never before attained, was the most highly coveted commodity of all: African slaves. The Cuban demand for slaves was almost insatiable. Slave traders of all nationalities converged on Havana in a scramble for a share of the newly opened Cuban market. During the ten-month occupation, an estimated ten thousand slaves were introduced into Havana—as many as normally would have entered in ten years.

Producers and traders in Havana prospered through their participation in this expanded commerce. New markets became available for Cuban sugar, tobacco, molasses, and hides. During the ten-month occupation, Cuban merchants in increasing numbers, and with increasing frequency, traveled to North American ports, establishing trade contacts that endured long after the British had left Havana.

The restoration of Spanish authority in 1763 was accompanied by other changes. Between 1764 and 1765 the Bourbons eliminated some of the more restrictive features of previous commercial policies. Cubans were authorized to seek additional markets with their own ships. The old tax structure was dismantled and replaced by a flat

6 percent ad valorem for national products and 7 percent for foreign goods. The state trade monopoly was dismantled. Import duties on slaves were abolished. In 1774 Spain rescinded all duties on Cuban imports. The following decade, Spain opened Cuban ports to un-limited free trade in slaves to all individuals and all companies of any nationality.

II

The rebellion of the thirteen colonies in 1776 provided new trade opportunities between Cubans and North Americans. Spain opened Cuban ports to North American commerce officially in November 1776, with an appropriate mixture of pomp and protocol. The decision was in part inspired by opportunism, in part by self-interest: it was a gesture both to support the North Americans and to settle old scores with the English. Spanish authorities moved with dispatch and pur-pose to aid these new enemies of their old adversary. Access to Cuban ports promised the struggling North Americans a market for their exports and an alternate source of tropical commodities previously obtained from the British West Indies.

It was a very popular decision in Cuba. The opportunity to trade with the North Americans, on a scale reminiscent of 1762–63, was a boon to the local economy. At the time the thirteen colonies rebelled, Cuban producers were in an ideal position to benefit from the revival of North American trade. The North Americans were in need of sub-stitute sources of sugar, and Cuban producers sought new markets for expanding output. The rebellious thirteen colonies lost access to their former supplies of tropical imports from the British Caribbean, and Cuba could partially make up for the loss. No less important, North American producers acquired customers for products previously sold in the English Antilles. North American merchant vessels were again welcomed in Havana harbor, and Cuban producers once more secured access to wider markets for their sugar and molasses and received in return flour, manufactured goods, lumber, and slaves. Spain's official participation in the war against England after 1779 further stimulated trade. Unable to guarantee shipments of foodstuffs and vital provisions to Cuba, Spain sanctioned increased Cuban trade by relaxing, and in some cases removing altogether, old commercial restrictions. Not since the English occupation of 1762–63 had Havana harbor been as crowded with as many foreign merchant vessels, and with similar effects. The economy expanded. Merchants and producers alike prospered during these years, and trade with the North Americans seemed to have no limits. [2]

But the advantages derived from the North American trade again proved short-lived. Once more Spain intruded itself into Cuban affairs. In January 1784 Spanish authorities restored in full former trade restrictions, effectively proscribing Cuban commerce with all countries except Spain. North American commercial houses were closed, U.S. agents and jobbers were expelled, and foreign merchant vessels were barred from entering Cuban ports. The total number of ships voyaging annually between Havana and the thirteen colonies, which had increased from 4 in 1776 to 368 in 1782, dwindled to 10 by 1785. [3]

These policies announced Spanish intentions to restore the old regimen of *peninsular* commercial exclusivity, fully and immediately. Advantages accrued once more to Spanish manufacturers and merchants, to the detriment of Cuban producers and consumers. Cubans were again officially forced to sell cheap and buy dear and otherwise make do with contraband and smuggling as a means of conducting commercial transactions with the North Americans.

For the newly independent North American colonies, however, previously one of the principal collaborators in this clandestine trade, contraband was no longer either a sufficient or a secure means of meeting expanding commercial needs. They soon offset the loss of Cuban markets by increasing trade with the French colony of Saint-Domingue. By 1790, the value of North American exports to Saint-Domingue was more than the combined value of all exports to the rest of the Caribbean, some $3.3 million out of a total $6.4 million. At the same time, Saint-Domingue provided almost the entire stock of sugar, molasses, cocoa, and coffee imports entering the United States. Cubans were the losers. [4]

Once more Cuban producers were rudely reminded of the vagaries to which they were periodically subject and, worse, over which they had little control. These policy reversals were causing havoc in Cuba and becoming increasingly intolerable. Each policy shift produced more disruption than the one before. War between Spain and France (1793–95) resulted in the reopening of Cuba to North American commerce. In June 1796, Madrid closed Cuban ports, only to reopen them the following October, when Spain allied itself with France in a war against England. For the following five years the island was open to the shipping of neutral nations, a condition that especially favored the North Americans. Trade with the United States flourished. Cuba exported sugar, molasses, rum, and coffee; the United States provided food supplies, clothing, furniture, manufactured goods, and slaves. During these years, too, North American vessels were permitted to carry Cuban exports to European markets. In 1798, for the first time —briefly but portentously—the volume of commerce between Cuba and the United States exceeded that between Cuba and Spain. "The wealth and importance of this colony," exulted U.S. consular agent George C. Morton from Havana in 1801, "has increased during the few years that it has been open to the American trade, in almost astonishing degrees with regard to the habits of industry, knowledge of commerce, general civilization, and comforts of life."[5]

Not long thereafter Spain abruptly reasserted commercial exclusivity and suspended Cuban trade with the United States. North American exports to Cuba declined from $8.4 to $5.7 million in 1800–1801, while Cuban sugar exports to the United States dropped from thirty-seven thousand to eight thousand tons and plunged to four thousand tons the following year. The value of North American imports declined to $938,289. A year later Spain and France were again at war with England, and once more North American merchant vessels were a welcome presence in Cuban ports. During 1806–7, the value of North American exports increased to $12 million while Cuban sugar exports increased to forty-three thousand tons.[6]

The Cuban economy expanded during these years, not in a spectacular fashion, to be sure, but in fits and starts, and over time registered discernible gains. Twenty years after the British occupation of Havana, far-reaching changes had overtaken Cuban society. If the availability of new markets had made the expansion of sugar production profitable, the availability of new slaves had made it possible. The slave trade flourished during the latter half of the eighteenth century. Slaves had long been a highly coveted commodity, the stock in the illicit trade that had thrived for almost two centuries. But the contraband slave trade as the principal means of meeting expanded labor needs was neither adequate nor reliable. Vital to the Cuban strategy of expanded sugar production was not only an increase but a guaranteed supply of slave labor. The British occupation followed by the Bourbon liberalization of trade provided a powerful boost to the importation of slave labor. Between 1512 and 1763, an estimated sixty thousand slaves had been introduced into Cuba, but in the succeeding thirty-five years almost one hundred thousand slaves entered the colony.[7] One effect was a rise in the number of sugar mills and a dramatic expansion of the sugar industry. New trade contacts between 1763 and 1783 provided powerful stimulus both for the conversion of old land to sugar and for the expansion of sugar onto new land. The acreage devoted to sugarcane increased spectacularly—from 10,000 acres in 1762 to 160,000 in 1792—and output increased from ten thousand tons annually during the 1770s, to twelve thousand in the 1780s, and sixteen thousand in the early 1790s.

These production advances added new pressure to expand and stabilize Cuban trade relations with markets other than Spain and brought problems of another kind. Prosperity may have freed Cuban producers from some of the more oppressive features of Spanish mercantilism, but it also contributed to subjecting them to a new tyranny of Spanish merchants. Rising sugar production and increasing trade gave new importance to *peninsular* traders and retailers. They dominated the critical import-export nexus around which the Cuban economy was developing. As Cuba moved inexorably toward monoculture in the late eighteenth century, dependence on imports—foodstuffs, clothing, and manufactures—increased, and so did the importance of the merchants. So, too, did the importance of trade with the North Americans, upon whom Cubans were becoming increasingly dependent as buyers and sellers.

Spanish trade policy through the eighteenth century tended un-abashedly to promote Spanish interests over Cuban ones, with impor-tant consequences. Most immediately, it increased the strength of the mercantile/commercial sector, largely Spanish, over the agricultural/ranching sector, mostly Cuban, thereby sharpening the distinction between *peninsular* interests and Creole ones. These developments, in turn, served further to accelerate and accentuate the deepening contra-diction of the colonial political economy. *Peninsular* merchants aspired to nothing less than complete domination of colonial trade, a position from which to exercise strategic control over an economy increas-ingly dependent on imports and exports. They tended to underpay for exports and overcharge for imports. Cuban producers demanded greater freedom to trade directly with foreigners. They intuitively op-posed and consciously resisted the proposition that Cuban production functioned solely for the benefit of Spain and Spaniards.

III

Cuba neared the end of the eighteenth century as the beneficiary of modest economic growth, stimulated largely by expanded sugar pro-duction and increased if erratic trade opportunities. But Cubans were comparative latecomers to sugar production. The opportunity for ex-pansion was limited, and by the end of the eighteenth century Cuba was approaching those limits.

One problem was competition, one competitor in particular. By the late eighteenth century, the French colony of Saint-Domingue was arguably the most prosperous European colony in the New World. An estimated eight hundred estates produced an annual average of seventy-one thousand tons of sugar, and nearly three thousand coffee farms produced more than thirty thousand tons of coffee, account-ing for more than 60 percent of the world supply. Only one-third of this vast production was consumed in metropolitan France; the bal-ance was reexported to other world markets. Cuban producers could not compete. They had increased sugar production in steady though modest increments, but they lacked the means to sustain their expansion and were without the markets to expand into. Costs were higher, customers were fewer, and as a result, Cubans found incentives to expand too few and too uncertain.

The opportunity for Cuban producers came unexpectedly in August 1791, when the slaves of Saint-Domingue rose in rebellion. For the remainder of the decade, the French colony was ravaged by civil strife. Successively, England, Spain, and France attempted to pacify the rebellious colony without any effect other than to prolong the conflict and add further to the widespread havoc and devastation. The results were dramatic and permanent. The plantations were destroyed, production collapsed, and the planters departed. The effects reverberated across the Atlantic. The world supply of sugar declined. Demand for alternative supplies of sugar increased. Prices followed, increasing from twelve *reales* in 1790 to thirty-six in 1795.

As a result of the turmoil in Saint-Domingue, the United States lost its principal trading partner in the Caribbean—a loss partially offset by the sporadic opening of Cuban ports in the decade that followed. After 1791 Cuba stood as the obvious beneficiary of the disruption of production in Saint-Domingue, but Cubans could not reasonably hope to develop and sustain a stable trade relationship with the North Americans as long as the terms and duration of that trade remained subject to the capricious dictates of Spanish authorities.

The need for Cuba to develop new and expanded trade relationships assumed added urgency in the decade immediately following the collapse of Saint-Domingue. Indeed, few other circumstances could have so favored the swift expansion of Cuban sugar production. Cuban producers inherited all at once rising prices, increasing demand, and mounting world shortages. Sugar production expanded in a frenzy, an immediate and improvised response to soaring world prices. Old producers increased production. New ones initiated production. The number of estates increased; the zones of cultivation expanded. Between 1774 and 1827 the total number of mills more than doubled, increasing from fewer than five hundred to a thousand.[8] New acreage passed into sugar production: an estimated average seventeen hundred acres a year in the 1790s, increasing to about thirty-five hundred acres annually by the 1810s, and reaching thirteen

Table 1.1.
Selected Imports, 1790 and 1799*

	French West Indies				Spanish West Indies			
	Sugar	Coffee	Cocoa	Molasses	Sugar	Coffee	Cocoa	Molasses
1790	9,316,834	2,377,584	395,827	5,056,138	529,610	6,314	661	525
1799	3,186,108	2,057,004	123,550	189,383	6,621,337	321,216	92,588	1,715,623

*All units are in pounds except molasses, which is in gallons.

Source: *American State Papers, 1789–1809: Commerce and Navigation* (Washington, D.C., 1832), 1:37, 441.

thousand acres a year by the 1840s. Production soared from an annual average of twelve thousand tons during 1786–90, more than doubling to twenty-six thousand tons for 1796–1800, and more than tripling during 1831–35 to eighty-eight thousand tons. [9]

The opportunity to expand production in the aftermath of the Saint-Domingue rebellion was also aided by timely expansion of trade contacts. As the total value of North American exports to Saint-Domingue declined from $3.3 million to $2.8 million in the 1790s, exports to Cuba increased from $147,807 to $9 million. [10] No less dramatic were the changes in imports from the regions classified by the U.S. Treasury Department as the "French West Indies," principally from Saint-Domingue, and the "Spanish West Indies," principally from Cuba (see Table 1.1).

Cuba's opportunities to expand trade and commerce were, to be sure, more a function of Spanish political requirements than Cuban economic needs, and trade under these circumstances was not an unmixed blessing. Spain devised myriad ways to exploit Cuban prosperity. Exorbitant customs tariffs discriminated against foreign imports carried aboard foreign ships. Cubans protested and Spain relented, if only slightly, and reduced customs between 20 to 36 percent ad valorem. It was not free trade: Cubans paid for it.

Expansion of sugar production and the ensuing prosperity were

themselves cause and effect of other changes in Cuba, and none perhaps as dramatic as the increase in population. Between 1791 and
1817, the total population more than doubled, increasing from 272,300
to 553,000 and increasing again to 704,000 by 1827. Changes in the size
of the population were accompanied by changes in its composition.
Between 1792 and 1827, the white population more than doubled,
from 134,000 to 311,000. But it was the population of people of color
that registered the most dramatic gains. The vast labor requirements
to meet expanded sugar production led to a new demand for African slaves. Between 1792 and 1817, the slave population more than
doubled, from 85,000 to 199,000, and by 1827 it increased again by
almost half to 287,000. By 1841, the slave population had increased
again and now represented about 45 percent of the island's total population (436,000 out of 1 million). At the same time, the number of free
people of color more than doubled, from 54,000 in 1792 to 106,000 in
1827, and to 153,000 in 1841.[11] Through the first half of the nineteenth
century, the combined population of slaves and free people of color
accounted for more than half the total number of inhabitants on the
island. The implications were not lost upon whites.

IV

Changes no less far-reaching were also transforming the organization and orientation of Cuban foreign trade. The rise of sugar exports
signaled the decline of other sources of foreign exchange, for the expansion of the former came at the expense of the latter. Steadily and
inexorably, Cuba developed into an export economy dependent on
the production of one crop, and increasingly the production of one
crop for one market. In 1761, Cuba was still an exporter of jerked beef.
By 1792, Cuba was importing thousands of pounds of jerked beef.
Through the first half of the nineteenth century, sugar accounted for
an increasing proportion of total Cuban export earnings: 60 percent in
1840, 68 percent in 1850, 74 percent in 1860, and increasingly a greater
share of Cuban sugar exports was expanding into North American

markets. These trading patterns were fixed early. The United States was an ideal trading partner: it was near, with a dynamic merchant marine, a growing population, rising demand, and an expanding economy.

The United States was as important a source of Cuban imports as it was a market for Cuban exports, a situation that figured prominently in Cuban production strategies. After 1818, with the opening of the island to world trade, the Cuba–United States trade nexus began to replace Spanish commercial connections, creating for Cuban producers new prospects but also new problems. For Cubans to expand production for export at the expense of production for consumption was both a practical and a profitable strategy because they could easily remedy local shortages with foreign supplies. Indeed, it was more cost-effective to rely on imported food for the local market than to sacrifice sugar exports for foreign markets. That the United States could meet these needs, as well as provide Cuba with necessary industrial and manufactured supplies, from a comparatively short distance, in a relatively short period of time, and at reasonably low transportation costs, both encouraged and facilitated the expansion of Cuban sugar production.

It also increased the importance of trade with the United States. The number of North American ships arriving at Cuba increased from 150 in 1796, to 606 in 1800, 783 in 1826, 1,702 during 1846–50, to 2,088 during 1851–56.[12] Commerce flourished. Trade contacts expanded steadily. North American ships originated from Boston, New York, Philadelphia, Savannah, and New Orleans and provided Cubans with box shooks, staves, caskets, barrels, hoops, nails, tar, textiles, salt, fish, corn, lard, flour, and rice. They returned loaded with sugar, cocoa, tobacco, molasses, and coffee.

The United States gradually became Cuba's single most important trading partner. In 1850, Cuban trade with the United States represented 39 percent of the total, followed by England (34 percent) and Spain (27 percent). Five years later, the North American share increased to 42 percent, and it rose to 48 percent in 1859 (see Table 1.2). In the following decades, Cuban trade patterns were even more strik-

Table 1.2.

Cuban Trade with the United States, England, and Spain, 1846–1859
(in pesos)

	United States		England		Spain	
	Imports	Exports	Imports	Exports	Imports	Exports
1846–50	27,838	37,426	21,682	35,105	27,210	16,957
1851–55	35,978	61,817	31,991	42,388	44,729	17,727
1856–59	40,308	68,339	29,406	37,294	31,042	20,974

Source: José R. Alvarez Díaz et al., A Study on Cuba (Coral Gables, 1965), p. 129.

ing. In 1865, the island exported 65 percent of its sugar to the United States and 3 percent to Spain. By 1877, the United States accounted for 82 percent of Cuba's total exports, followed by Spain (5.7 percent) and England (4.4 percent). In some sectors, Cuban dependency on North American imports was especially striking (see Table 1.3). The implications of these trade patterns were far-reaching, and observers, local and foreign alike, were immediately sensible to their meaning. "The trade of the country is falling into the hands of foreigners," commented traveler Anthony Trollope from Cuba in 1859, "into those principally of Americans from the States. Havana will soon become as much American as New Orleans."[13]

The importance of Spanish participation in the Cuban economy was diminishing. Spain could neither offer Cuban producers adequate markets nor guarantee Cuban consumers sufficient supplies. The United States promised both. Spain had lost the capacity to consume all of Cuba's sugar exports and without refinery capabilities lacked the means to reexport Cuban sugar to other markets. Cuba developed economic needs distinct and increasingly divergent from those of Spain.

By the mid-nineteenth century, Cubans were arriving at the conclusion that they could not achieve the full potential of their productive

Table 1.3.
Value of Selected Imports for Cuban
Domestic Consumption, 1852

Product	Total value	From the United States
Fish	$668,425	$152,171
Rice	1,046,604	811,462
Grain and pulse	320,212	115,991
Lard and butter	948,144	902,635
Lumber	2,042,187	1,864,997
Specie	989,424	532,468

Source: Alexander von Humboldt, *The Island of Cuba,* trans.
John S. Thrasher (New York, 1856), p. 302.

capabilities within the traditional framework of empire. The anomaly
was not lost on them. And, indeed, the Cuban economy had already
expanded beyond the restrictive framework of existing colonial structures. But trade with Europe and the United States was still subject to
the constraints of Spanish policy. Spain could not supply the goods,
or the shipping, or the markets demanded by Cuba but persisted in
obtruding itself between Cuba and world markets. Spain was super-
fluous to the Cuban economy in every way but one: it regulated the
terms of the exchange, and increasingly this was a point of contention
between Cubans and Spaniards. Official efforts to promote Spanish
exports and encourage the use of Spanish carriers cost residents in
Cuba dearly. To the mounting chagrin of consumers and producers in
Cuba, the island was subjected to a series of discriminatory customs
duties. By the terms of the 1853 tariff law, foreign products shipped on
Spanish carriers paid 21.5 to 25.5 percent ad valorem and on foreign
carriers 29.5 to 35.5 percent. *Peninsular* products carried by national
shippers paid 6 percent ad valorem; for products carried by foreigners,
the duty increased to 19.5 percent. So too with island exports: goods

Table 1.4.
Tariff Rates on Selected Items (in pesos)

Product	Spanish		Foreign	
	Spanish carrier	Foreign carrier	Spanish carrier	Foreign carrier
Flour (100 kilograms)	Free	.81	2.44	3.26
Tallow (50 kilograms)	1.05	1.95	2.60	3.90
Fish (100 kilograms)	.38	.76	1.14	1.91
Lard (50 kilograms)	.65	1.30	2.60	3.90
Fuel oils (50 kilograms)	.42	.85	1.72	2.60
Rice (50 kilograms)	.26	.42	.80	1.35
Vermicelli (50 kilograms)	.80	1.50	2.00	2.62

Source: Spain, Minister of Colonial Affairs, *Tariff Rates of Duties Payable on Goods, Wares, and Merchandise Imported into the Island of Cuba* (Havana, 1867), pp. 4–6.

shipped by foreigners paid 7.5 percent, Spanish carriers 3 percent. The 1867 schedule provided a representative price listing of basic commodities (see Table 1.4). Colonial authorities levied custom duties on imports, imposed taxes on exports, and assessed freight charges on foreign carriers, all of which served to lower profits for Cuban producers and raise prices for Cuban consumers. By the middle of the nineteenth century, these duties were particularly odious, for the vast majority of Cuban imports originated from foreign producers and were carried by foreign shippers.

A 35 percent ad valorem was only the beginning. Added to this levy were a series of other surcharges, including port appraisals, tonnage duties, municipal and provincial surcharges, and retail taxes. Not infrequently, consumers in Cuba paid more than double the original market price for U.S. imports. One midcentury estimate calculated that approximately $15 million worth of North American textiles, agricultural goods, furniture, and tools was resold in Cuba for more than

$30 million. A total of $73,000 in duties was paid on $91,000 worth of U.S. flour. [14]

The colonial tariff schedule, revised upward and modified periodically, had the net effect of increasing significantly the cost of living for residents of Cuba. And nowhere were costs as high as in the city of Havana. Observed tourist James E. Alexander during his travels through Cuba in 1833: "I was surprised at the enormous duty on American flour. A barrel of it is purchased at New Orleans for five dollars, if shipped in a Spanish bottom, it pays seven dollars of duty; if in a foreign vessel, ten; it afterwards sells for fifteen or sixteen; so that the price obtained for this necessary article covers the duty and freight, and remunerates the importer, though it will be evident from this that living is not cheap in Havannah." Almost twenty years later traveler Edward Sullivan noted that "the great disadvantage of the Havanna is the expense of living and house-rents, which exceed either London or Paris." [15]

V

Exorbitant customs duties and discriminatory tariff rates did not, however, interrupt the expansion of trade. Indeed, so vital was the North American connection in Cuba that local producers grudgingly accepted colonial taxes as part of the normal cost of doing business with the United States. Despite these patently specious surcharges, ties between both countries continued to deepen. Through the first half of the nineteenth century, North Americans in increasing numbers successfully integrated themselves into strategic sectors of the Cuban economy. North American traders shrewdly and effectively pursued the Cuban market, providing slaves and manufactured goods at reasonable prices, often extending generous credit arrangements, and accepting in return sugar and molasses as payment.

United States interests in Cuba increased as the North American capital and commercial stake on the island expanded. Direct U.S. investments in Cuba increased in value and variety. North American merchants, bankers, and shippers established commercial houses in the principal seaports, most of which played the dual role of trading establishments and moneylenders. Trade companies established themselves in Havana, Matanzas, Cienfuegos, Cárdenas, Sagua la Grande, Trinidad, and Santiago de Cuba, and soon they became a ubiquitous presence across the island. North American trading houses, including the Vernon Brothers of Newport, Perkins and Burling of Boston, and Gardner and Dean of Newport, maintained representatives in Havana and accounted for an increasing share of the African slave trade. Others included Moses Taylor & Co., Charles Tying & Co., Martin Knight & Co., Storey & Co., George Harris & Co., Drake Brothers & Co., Howland Brothers & Co., Dudley Selden & Co., Safford, Smith & Co., and Moreland & Co. They provided credit, purchased the sugar crops, and supplied vital imports. Increasingly, the trading companies expanded their control over the carrying trade and augmented their shipping lines to handle the coastwise traffic of Cuba. But more important, they controlled the service linking Cuban trade with New Orleans, Savannah, Charleston, Baltimore, Philadelphia, New York, and Boston.

From these positions, North American capital expanded into other sectors of the local economy, including sugar plantations, mills, and coffee farms. The Cuban properties of Samuel Shaw Howland (Howland Brothers) included El Dorado sugar plantation and the Ontario and Mt. Vernon coffee *fincas*. North American investments in mining increased. As early as 1833, U.S. investors acquired interests in the Juraguá iron mines near Santiago. Other North American claims followed in quick succession: copper mines in El Cobre, iron mines in Daiquirí and Manicaragua, and the Bayestabo mines in Nuevitas (American Mining Company).[16] Thomas B. Smith and Hezekiah Bradford operated the Compañía de Minería Cubana near Cienfuegos. The New York Ore Dressing Company owned mines in El Cobre. Other North American enterprises secured concessions to work bituminous coal deposits near Havana.

The establishment of these operations further stimulated the value and volume of the Cuba–United States trade. More and more, too, U.S. capital goods became a vital factor in the expansion of the industrial and transportation infrastructure of the island. As early as 1819, a North American–built steamship took up the coasting trade between Havana and Matanzas, becoming one of the first steam vessels employed outside the United States. During these years, planters in growing numbers introduced steam power in the mills. The first successful steam-powered mills began operation after 1817, principally with machinery imported from Great Britain. As the popularity of steam power increased, North American manufacturers displaced English producers. Between 1834 and 1838, engineers from the United States, supervised by Alfred Cruger of South Carolina, using North American supplies and equipment, completed the construction of a fifty-one-mile rail line between Havana and Güines—the first railroad in Latin America and decades before the completion of the first track in Spain. Sugar machinery and equipment, railroad cars, and especially locomotives, as well as iron rails, became the stock in trade around which the commerce between Cuba and the United States subsequently expanded and around which the Cuban economy organized.[17]

In the process, North Americans began taking up residence in Cuba, largely in or near the principal port cities—from 1,256 in 1846 to almost 2,500 in 1862.[18] The defeat of the Confederacy at the end of the U.S. Civil War brought a wave of immigration to Cuba—former Confederate officers and politicians, as well as planters, merchants, and professionals, together with their families and personal slaves. For a brief period immediately after Appomattox, ranking representatives of the defeated Confederacy crowded into Havana hotels, among them Generals John C. Breckinridge, Robert A. Toombs, Birkett D. Fry, John B. Magruder, Hamilton P. Bee, William Preston, Jubal A. Early, Commodore John N. Maffitt, Colonel Wood Taylor, and former governor of Louisiana Thomas Overton Moore. Some eventually returned to the United States, but many remained and joined the growing ranks of North American planters and property owners in Cuba. Eliza McHatton-Ripley, her husband, and two personal slaves emigrated from Louisiana to Matanzas, where they purchased the debt-ridden, mismanaged Desengaño sugar plantation and a contingent of forty slaves from the Royo family. Louis Lay emigrated from New Orleans and soon owned a trading company and hotel in Havana. A year after the end of the Civil War, the U.S. consul in Havana reported on the large numbers of "refugees from New Orleans," who, together with their personal slaves, had taken up residence in Havana. [19]

Most North American residents of Cuba were connected with trade, commerce, shipping, and agricultural production. Despite their small numbers, in some regions their participation was vital to the local economy. In 1828 a local North American planter, D. B. Woodbury, in need of a convenient port from which to export his sugar, and merchant William F. Safford (W. Safford & Co.), founded the city of Cárdenas, which soon became known as an "American city" because of its large North American population. By the latter part of the nineteenth century, more than 90 percent of Cárdenas's trade was with the United States. "From day to day the colonies of the Americans on the island increase," Captain General Conde de Alcoy reported with some concern in 1850, "as can be seen in the increases registered in Sagua la Grande, Cienfuegos, Matanzas, Cárdenas, etc. Daily the Americans purchase extensive territories and under their auspices Cárdenas is being reborn into a new city." [20]

North Americans settled everywhere in Cuba but tended to favor the north coast, particularly Havana, and as far east as Gibara. "Havana is crowded with *Americanos*," observed George W. Williams in 1855. The *Mercantile Weekly Report* was published in Havana expressly for the North American colony. In 1855 a new hospital was established in Havana exclusively to serve the needs of the North American community in Cuba. The prominent North American presence along the north coast between Havana and Sagua la Grande prompted English traveler Richard R. Madden to observe in 1849 that "some districts on the northern shores of the island, in the vicinity, especially, of Cárdenas and Matanzas, have more the character of American than Spanish settlements." This view was echoed more than ten years later by R. W. Gibbes, who visited Matanzas: "Matanzas being mainly settled by citizens from the United States, our language is more common there than in any other Cuban city, and the customs of the place are more Americanized." John Glanville Taylor observed that the "district of Holguín, of which Gibara is the port of entry, can boast of more English-speaking society, than any other foreign place, of equal size and note."[21]

A network of boardinghouses developed along the north coast, operated principally by North Americans, mostly women, catering to residents and travelers from the United States. They sponsored social functions and operated evening card games; on occasion they provided theater productions and cabaret entertainment and housed foreign dignitaries. United States national holidays were celebrated with festivity and the obligatory mixture of speechmaking and merriment. Local Cubans and Spaniards were frequent participants in these functions. In their modest way, the boardinghouses served as centers of cultural diffusion, a point at which North Americans and Cubans converged socially, talked politics, trade, and commerce, and gradually came to know each other.[22] Around the boardinghouses and inns on the north coast developed a variety of other establishments, owned by North Americans and catering to the needs of both North American travelers and local residents. Along the principal bay streets of the port cities bars, brothels, and restaurants grew up. Billiard rooms were especially popular, providing still one more point at which Cubans and North Americans converged to socialize.

As their numbers increased and their roles expanded, the importance of North Americans also increased. Many married into prominent Creole families. The Phinney family of Rhode Island married into the Quintanas of Matanzas. North Americans in growing numbers were arriving to operate the expanding Cuban industrial manufactures imported from the United States, especially modern steam-powered mill machinery and railroad locomotives, and to service the tracks and rail lines. North American *maquinistas* (machinists) arrived late in the fall and remained in Cuba through June, the duration of the sugar harvest, for which they were typically paid $2,500, plus room and board. In Regla, the great depot of the molasses trade, the foundry vital to the maintenance of local molasses tanks was constructed and managed by North American engineers. The island's coastwise shipping was handled increasingly by steam vessels manufactured in the United States, which were often piloted by North Americans. During the late 1850s, as railroad building expanded across the island, hundreds of North Americans were employed in construction, repair, and maintenance capacities. In 1858 alone, more than 1,800 workers from the United States, principally engineers, mechanics, and artisans, arrived in Cuba under contract to work on the railroads. The following year, 5,034 North American travelers arrived in Cuba, 3,106 of whom remained to work. [23]

Cuban producers early developed both a dependence on North American machines and reliance on North American technicians to service them. "American steam-engines are fast taking the place of animal power," observed Maturin M. Ballou in 1854, "and more or less are monthly exported for this purpose from New York, Philadelphia and Boston. This creates a demand for engineers and machinists, for whom the Cubans are also dependent upon this country; and there are said to be at this time two hundred Bostonians thus engaged at a handsome remuneration, upon the island." Visiting in Cuba several years later, Richard Henry Dana, Jr., met a North American engineer on a Matanzas plantation, "one of a numerous class, whom the sugar culture brings annually to Cuba," observed Dana, and added: "They leave home in the autumn, engage themselves for the sugar season, put the machinery in order, work it for the four or five months of its operation, clean and put it in order for lying by, and return to the United States in the spring. They must be machinists, as well as engineers; for all the repairs and contrivances, so necessary in a remote place, fall upon them." Carlton H. Rogers, also traveling in Cuba during the late 1850s, observed: "The cars on this [Havana-Güines] road are of American manufacture (that is, built in the United States), are drawn by American-built engines, and conducted by American engineers." [24]

Spanish colonial authorities were not insensible to the implications of this expanded U.S. presence. As early as 1843, the Ministry of State created a high-level commission to determine the size and distribution of the North American population on the island and calculate the extent of its property holdings. Concern was growing in Spain that U.S. influence in local affairs was also increasing. Although no action was taken, many in Spain and Cuba were already urging restrictions on North American acquisition of property on the island. [25]

Authorities understood too the meaning of Cuba's deepening reliance on technology and technicians from the United States. Governor General José G. de la Concha complained in 1853 that the number of Cuban students graduating as lawyers was far out of proportion to local needs, to the neglect of professions and occupations essential to the well-being of the island. "Ever since the introduction of steam-powered machinery in the sugar mills and the construction of the first railroad," de la Concha observed, "the need for Spanish *maquinistas* increased, for the consequence of giving foreigners, mostly North Americans, access to the mills was foreseen." De la Concha complained that though the island had five educational institutions offering full curriculum for law studies, it lacked even one school to train *maquinistas*, sugar masters, and engineers—"all so necessary for the principal industry of the country." [26] This trend continued through the end of the nineteenth century. Of the 846 students enrolled in the University of Havana during the academic year 1887–88, 280 were in law, 250 in medicine, 234 in pharmacy, 44 in philosophy, and 38 in science. [27]

Cuban imports of U.S. machinery increased through the nineteenth century, the sugar industry expanded around these imports, and the relationship between the two was at once obvious and compelling. Clear, too, were the implications of these developments. The relationship was fixed early in the nineteenth century, and attempts to disengage Cuba from U.S. markets, or restrict imports from the United States, or in any other way interrupt the transactions upon which Cubans depended more and more, from whatever source, threatened the island with dire consequences. Cuban prosperity developed around and increasingly depended upon the North American connection, and as this dependency increased, so did North American influence. "The prosperity of the island," observed Richard Madden during his travels in Cuba as early as the 1830s, "has derived no small advantage from those numerous American establishments. Improved modes of agriculture, of fabrication, of conveyance, were introduced by the Americans." Madden added:

> The substitution in Cuba of the old grinding-mill, rudely constructed of wood, by steam-engine machinery, is also chiefly due to the Americans. To them, therefore, Cuba is indebted for the various improvements in the fabrication of sugar, and modes of conveyance of the produce of its plantations, which enable the proprietors to compete so successfully with those of the English colonies. Cuba, ever since I knew it, has been slowly but steadily becoming Americanised. [28]

Through the first half of the nineteenth century, North American capital and credit and North American investments and imports shaped the course of Cuban economic development. Although comparatively few in number, North Americans were active in strategic points in the economy. Increasingly, too, they were property owners, adding further to the potency of the U.S. presence. As early as 1823, as many as fifty North Americans owned plantations valued at $3 million in Matanzas. Merchant Frederick Freeman established himself in Trinidad and acquired several sugar estates in the surrounding countryside. Not far away were the sugar properties of George Dewolf. William Stewart of Philadelphia acquired La Carolina estate near Cienfuegos, a plantation of about two thousand acres, worked by 500 slaves. Augustus Hemenway of Boston purchased the San Jorge estate near Sagua la Grande in 1840, a property of more than twenty-five hundred acres with 160 slaves.[29] Other North American proprietors included George K. Thorndike, the owner of the Santa Ana plantation in Sagua la Grande; J. W. Baker from Philadelphia, who owned the twelve-hundred-acre San José estate near Cienfuegos, worked by 700 slaves; the Phinney family, who owned La Palma, Roble, and La Sonora, all near Cárdenas; and the Russell Jenks family, who owned extensive holdings in the Yumurí valley of Matanzas.

That so many North American plantation owners in Cuba were northerners and held large numbers of slaves did not pass unnoticed by southern observers. Traveling to Cuba from South Carolina in 1856, George W. Williams observed: "I find quite a number of planters from the United States residing here, and they nearly all hail from the Northern States."[30]

North Americans continued to acquire estates, purchase slaves, and otherwise increase their participation in the expanding sugar industry. Observed one traveler in the mid-nineteenth century: "The great amount of American capital invested in slave property in Cuba, and the energy with which the new American settlers have entered on the cultivation of new land (the establishment of new American plantations averaging during the last three years, twenty a year), have largely contributed to give an impetus to the trade which has been fatal for the efforts for its suppression."[31]

The North American presence presaged a new order. Its influence knew no boundaries and expanded in many directions at once. A predominantly Catholic society opened up to a Protestant migration that although comparatively small was nonetheless associated with modernity and progress. Wrote Richard Davey of these years: "During the last seventy years . . . the country has been overrun by Americans, who have introduced every form of Protestantism, from Episcopalianism to Quakerism, and even Shakerism."[32]

North Americans were moneylenders and shippers, buyers and sellers, engineers and machinists. Cubans, in turn, were becoming increasingly dependent on U.S. technology and technicians, U.S. markets and imports, U.S. capital and credit. Above all, this relationship served to foster and facilitate the integration of the Cuban economy into the North American system. The presence and growing importance of the North American connection worked to weaken Cuban cultural and institutional ties to Spain, with far-reaching consequences. "The Anglo-Norman and Spanish races here meet," observed Fredrika Bremer during a midcentury visit to Cuba, "for good and for evil, secretly and openly combating for dominion; and in the midst of this wonderfully beautiful scenery, . . . beneath the tropical sun, among the palm-trees and coffee plantations, one sees already the homes of the North American, rail-roads, and shops. The Anglo-American 'go-a-head' here comes in contact with the motto of the Spanish Creole, *poco-a-poco;* and—will run it down sooner or later, that is not difficult to foresee."[33]

As the Cuban economy continued to organize around the expanding North American presence, changes of other kinds, affecting other aspects of Cuban society, were set in motion. The expansion of the Cuban–North American trade connection meant a commensurate increase in shipping between the countries, and especially passenger service, with a proportional decrease in maritime traffic between Cuba and Spain. Side-wheel ships of the Atlantic Mail Steamship Company sailed every Thursday and Saturday for Havana and Philadelphia. The Baltimore-Havana Steamship Company operated passenger and freight service on the first and fifteenth of every month. The French Imperial Mail Steamship Company sailed between Havana and New Orleans monthly.

These developments, to be sure, reflected mid-nineteenth-century commercial realities. But they had other effects, many of which had little to do directly with trade and commerce. The decline of commercial maritime activity between Cuba and Spain also reduced the only means of travel between the island and the peninsula. As passenger travel between Cuba and the United States expanded and improved, transatlantic maritime service between Cuba and Spain became increasingly irregular, infrequent, and unreliable. As the number of vessels in service declined, the quality of passenger travel deteriorated. At the same time, the U.S. merchant fleet expanded, service improved, and steamships replaced sailing vessels, thereby reducing travel time. A voyage to New York was completed in less than four days; to New Orleans in half that time. Passage to Spain often took two weeks and, given the infrequency of shipping and unreliability of service, often two and three times that long. For the same reasons, wealthy Cubans in growing numbers were using North American shipping to travel to Europe. It was easier and more reliable to travel to England or France via New York than Spain. North American carriers provided faster service, more frequently, more reliably. Indeed, by the 1850s, Cubans were almost totally dependent on North American carriers for the movement of mail in and out of the island, with the United States, with Europe, and with Spain. [34]

The results were both effects of changing economic conditions and causes of other changes. The failure of colonial authorities to provide adequate educational facilities, and especially the backward condition of higher education, obliged wealthy Cuban families to seek schooling for their children outside the island. If colonial authorities provided Cubans with better educational facilities, observed Abiel Abbot during his visit to Cuba in the early 1820s, "the rich would have less occasion to send their sons abroad for education." [35] Improved transportation service to the United States increased the appeal of North American educational institutions. Schools were near, travel was convenient, costs were lower. Colonial authorities understood well the meaning of these developments. "The remoteness of the Peninsula," warned the Ministry of State as early as 1843, "the infrequent communications with the Metropolis as compared with that which [Cubans] have with North America, the decline of our maritime power . . . have contributed to undermining the spirit of nationality, providing powerful encouragement to the youth of the island . . . to obtain their education in the United States, where they acquire habits pernicious to the constituted government." [36] A similar warning was sounded ten years later by Governor General José G. de la Concha. "The lack of communications," de la Concha complained in 1853, "and the failure to allocate to Cuba sufficient resources for the education and instruction of the well-to-do youth, has meant that rather than coming to Spain, as in other times . . . they have gone to foreign countries, and principally the United States for their education." Proximity to the United States was producing the "most baneful consequences," especially with regard to the "preservation of the national spirit." De la Concha urged Madrid to improve transportation to and from the island and to modernize its maritime fleet with new steamships. Improved transportation between Spain and its Caribbean possessions, he predicted, promised not only "to strengthen the ties between the metropolis and the Antilles, but provide additional indirect means to promote immigration from Spain to the islands without the inconveniences of breaking relations and weakening family ties."[37]

2   A Convergence of Interests

The expansion of the Cuban economy in the nineteenth century created new problems and exacerbated old ones. The rise of sugar production transformed Cuban society and announced the emergence of new social classes and new class tensions. A Creole propertied elite acquired its distinctive features during these years, shaped as much by its frustrations with colonialism as by its function in the colony. Creole elites constituted a majority of sugar planters, coffee growers, tobacco farmers, and cattle ranchers. They controlled much of the real property. They possessed wide-ranging power over the population in their domains as slave masters, employers, and rentiers. But their power was not unlimited. Cubans demanded greater control over resources and commerce—control, in short, over all areas of vital importance to their interests. As producers of commercial export crops, Creoles demanded direct access to foreign markets and cheap prices for foreign imports. They resented *peninsular* control of overseas trade and resisted Spanish taxes on foreign commerce.

The clash of rival economic interests between planters and merchants served to exacerbate political tensions between the colony and the metropolis. Spanish customs duties on foreign imports upon which Cubans were becoming increasingly dependent, foodstuffs no less than agricultural and industrial equipment, combined to raise the cost of living and increase the cost of sugar production. Creole property owners demanded not only economic policies to protect and promote their interests but political positions so they could implement the policies to meet their needs. Cubans demanded freedom to promote their own interests, arrange their own taxes, regulate their own economic growth. They demanded freedom to expand, to develop resources according to their needs on their terms, to earn more by producing more, and to expand more by exporting more. They

29

needed, above all, access to political power to protect their economic interests.

At the same time, however, Creole elites were mindful of the constraints their social reality imposed on their ambitions. They were required to press for their demands with circumspection, and always with moderation. They understood, most of all, that their local preeminence was to a large extent dependent on the very source of their discontent. Certainly the colonial system obstructed their political ascendancy, and it limited economic expansion. But it also acted to contain the social forces that threatened their socioeconomic prominence. And therein lay the singular contradiction of the colonial political economy in the nineteenth century. The spectacular expansion of Cuban sugar production and the consolidation of the Cuban planter class occurred against a backdrop of political unrest and social upheaval. An economy largely dependent on slavery came into existence at the precise moment when slavery was under attack from many quarters abroad and meeting growing resistance among many groups in Cuba. The slave trade was on the decline, and pressure for the abolition of slavery was on the rise. As early as 1792, Denmark banned the slave trade in its Caribbean territories. England and the United States abolished the slave trade in 1808, followed by Sweden in 1813 and Holland in 1814.

One other consideration preyed on the minds of local elites. The island was filling with new slaves even as slave rebellion was succeeding in the neighboring colony of Saint-Domingue and as slave uprisings were spreading elsewhere in the Caribbean: in Jamaica in 1795, 1824, and 1841, in Barbados in 1804 and again in 1824, in Demerara in 1808, and in Antigua in 1831. Even in the United States slave conspiracies and rebellions occurred periodically: in Virginia in 1800, New Orleans in 1811, South Carolina in 1822, and again in Virginia in 1831.

Indeed, both the opportunity and the occasion for slave uprisings increased markedly in Cuba during the nineteenth century, largely as a result of the rapid expansion of slavery across the island and the sudden surge of recently arrived adult slaves. The island filled with vast numbers of African-born slaves—intractable, undisciplined, resentful, and with a memory of their lost freedom: 385,000 slaves were imported between 1790 and 1820, 272,000 more between 1820 and 1853, another 175,000 between 1853 and 1864. By the early nineteenth century perhaps as many as 75 percent of all those in bondage in Cuba had been born in Africa.

Creole fears were not unfounded. Social unrest and slave uprising cast a long shadow over Cuban prosperity. Slave rebellions occurred with increasing frequency as the discontent of free people of color fused with the disaffection of blacks in bondage: in 1811 and 1812, in 1825, 1830, and 1837, again in 1840 and 1843. All failed in the end, but all served to remind local elites of the fragile balance of social forces, in and out of Cuba, to which colonial government was given to defending. The specter of slave rebellion in Cuba dampened planters' enthusiasm for an independent nation, especially one without adequate resources to suppress the dreaded slave uprisings. After 1822, Cuban planters, particularly those in the eastern zones, had one more worry. Haiti's invasion of Santo Domingo raised fears among eastern elites that Haitians would march westward into Cuba and launch a war of emancipation against the island.

It happened, too, that prosperity on the island was beginning as colonialism on the mainland was ending. From Mexico to Argentina, Spain's New World empire was in varying degrees of disarray and disintegration. The cost of independence was high, as civil war fused inexorably with social strife and both combined to disrupt production and paralyze local economies.

Political discontent was also on the rise in Cuba. A small but growing Creole middle class, based in the liberal professions, salaried personnel, and small farmers, found the *peninsular* rule increasingly odious. They were joined by urban artisans, peasants, and growing numbers of free people of color, who also found their condition in the colony daily less satisfactory. Their antipathy toward Spanish administration transferred easily into antagonism toward Creole elites who defended Spanish administration and just as easily generalized into misgivings about the slave system upon which the privilege and property of local elites rested.

Hence the anomaly of the position of the Creole elites: the very social forces required to dislodge *peninsular* elites could just as easily displace Creole ones. There was, thus, ample reason for Creoles to look upon the Spanish regime with ambivalence. They were dependent on the very colonial structures they resented. That the scattered and short-lived separatist conspiracies that did occur in Cuba in the early nineteenth century also had abolitionist objectives all but guaranteed elite defense of Spanish rule. In no other Spanish colony was the local economy so totally dependent on slavery; in no other Spanish colony did African slaves constitute so large a part of the population; in no other Spanish colony did the total population of color constitute a majority. Creole elites presided over a plantation economy based on a vast slave labor force, a production system that engendered at least as much antagonism between whites and blacks as the political system had produced between Creoles and *peninsulares*. Cubans could not reasonably challenge the assumptions of Spanish primacy without inviting slaves to challenge the premises of their subjugation. They were, further, enjoying the first flushes of a dazzling prosperity. Sugar production was increasing, exports were expanding, profits were on the rise: this was not the time for revolution. And for all their complaints against the colonial regime, they understood well that, for the time being, Spain represented their best, and only, guarantee of social order and economic well-being.

II

Cuban support of Spanish rule was not without misgivings and reservations. Certainly local elites believed Spain capable of defending Creole interests from internal challenge, and this of course met one important Cuban concern. They were not, however, as confident about Spain's ability to defend their interests from external challenges.

It was a weak Spain to whom Cuban elites had entrusted their collective fates. These were tumultuous decades in Spain, years of inter-
mittent civil war at home, military defeats abroad, chronic political
instability, periodic foreign intervention, and always the threat of se-
cessionist strife—all of which made Spain immensely vulnerable to
foreign pressure.

Cubans' worst fears were soon realized. Slavery and the slave trade
were under assault in the New World and the Old. Most of the re-
belling Spanish colonies in the New World had enacted abolitionist
measures during the 1810s and 1820s. For a moment, in 1810–11, it
appeared that the liberal Spanish parliament (Cortes) in Cádiz would
proclaim an end to slavery in all Spanish territories.[1] Nothing became
of Spanish abolitionist projects, and within several years liberals in
Spain were in disarray and out of power and the threat of abolition
passed. That authorities in Spain even debated ending slavery, however, had a chilling effect in Cuba and again reminded Cubans of the
uncertainties associated with Spanish colonialism.

English abolitionist policies worried Cubans the most, and for good
reason. In 1817 Spain acquiesced to British pressure and agreed in a
treaty to end the colonial slave trade effective May 1820. In fact, the influx of slaves into the island continued, almost without interruption,
henceforth more or less in the form of a vast contraband network, for
the trade in slaves obeyed the logic of market forces in Cuba and not
political pronouncements from Europe.

The suppression of the slave trade drove planters from the open
market to illicit trade, where risks were commensurately higher and
demands on available supply correspondingly greater, and prices were
inevitably steeper. The proscription of slave trading, further, struck
at the very sources of the slave system in Cuba and presaged the
end of slavery. Fear increased among Cuban producers that abolition
was Spain's ultimate objective. Spain appeared to have arrayed itself
against Cuban interests. This was nuisance enough, but it did not fundamentally or alone threaten the system whose survival was the principal reason Creoles had opted to remain under Spanish rule. After
the 1830s, when Britain ended slavery in its Caribbean territories, mat-

ters assumed a new gravity as English pressure on Spain for abolition increased markedly. Alarm and apprehension spread in Cuba, for few believed that Spain possessed the will or the wherewithal to resist the British.

III

Not all Cubans were reconciled to the idea of the end of slavery, and indeed some contemplated an alternative to the uncertainty of independence and the unreliability of colonialism: annexation to the United States, a notion that gained proponents and enthusiasm among many important sectors of the Creole patriciate through the first half of the nineteenth century. Annexation offered Cubans a marvelously simple and sensible solution to many of their most pressing problems. In the short run, union with the United States promised to guarantee the survival of slavery and the salvation of the plantation economy. Slavery was flourishing and expanding in the United States, which gave Cubans comfort and confidence. By joining the North American slave system, Cubans would obtain sanction and security for local slave institutions. Union with the United States, further, offered Cuban planters the opportunity to participate in the flourishing internal slave trade, without risks and at competitive prices. The outbreak of slave rebellions in Cuba during the early 1840s, moreover, raised questions about Spain's capacity to maintain social control over the expanding population of color. Annexation thus promised not only the salvation of slavery but security from slaves.

Annexation also promised to resolve some of the more anomalous features of the mid-nineteenth-century colonial political economy. Buyers and sellers, consumers and producers everywhere in Cuba had developed an important stake in the North American connection. Certainly annexation would simplify Cuban commercial relationships. Sugar, molasses, tobacco, coffee, and hides went out; vital foodstuffs, sugar machinery, and, increasingly, capital came in. The ban on the legal slave trade had increased the participation of North

Americans in the local economy, and Cubans were becoming increasingly dependent on that connection for their supply of illegal slaves, no less than for capital, shipbuilders, and crews. Havana was crowded with North Americans, merchants such as Paul Febre from Pennsylvania and J. Morland of New York, who participated in a brisk trade in slaves from Africa and ships from the United States. The special sea vessels required by Cuban slave-trading houses, possessed of ample cargo dimensions to underwrite profits and of speed and maneuverability to elude British patrols, were available only from the United States, principally from the shipyards of Baltimore. The transactions typically involved merchants in Havana, trading houses in New York, and shipbuilders in Baltimore. In what was no doubt one such routine transaction in 1823, Captain George Coggeshall piloted the schooner *Swan* to Cuba for G. G. & S. Howland of New York, laden with an assorted cargo. Both cargo and ship were sold in Havana, and Coggeshall returned to New York with funds in gold aboard another Howland vessel loaded with hogsheads of molasses and barrels of sugar. Perhaps as much as 90 percent of the merchant vessels engaged in the illicit slave trade in Cuba were constructed in the United States, sailed under the U.S. flag, and were operated by North American crews.[2]

Annexation seemed a logical political outgrowth of this deepening economic relationship. At a time when almost 50 percent of Cuban trade depended on access to North American markets and manufacturers, few among Cuba's elites could fail to appreciate the virtue of annexation. Union would eliminate the onerous Spanish taxation on foreign imports and remove North American tariffs on Cuban products, both of which would contribute to increased profits on exports and reduced prices on imports. Slavery would survive, markets would expand, tariffs and discriminatory duties would disappear. In exchanging colonial status under Spain for expected statehood in the United States, Creole elites understood that they would gain at once local political ascendancy and the backing of the federal government to contain any internal political challenge to property and privilege.

More than economic self-interest or political ambition motivated Cuban elites. Many had developed an admiration for North American institutions, in which democratic ideals seemed to coexist congenially with slave institutions. "It is an irrefutable fact," wrote annexation-ist Domingo del Monte in 1838, "that the United States of America [has] enjoyed the greatest political liberty since its founding, and they still have slaves."[3] Cubans frequently traveled to the north on business trips and family vacations. Many had sent their children to North American schools to complete their education. Many had de-veloped extensive commercial contacts and social ties in the United States. They had come to know the United States well and looked upon union as an important step in the direction of modernity and progress. Annexation found brisk support during the 1820s from the eastern planter class, for all these reasons and one more: local elites continued to dread the possibility of an invasion from Haiti.

Annexationist stirrings began as early as 1810 in response to aboli-tionist debates in the Cortes of Cádiz. Creoles thus gave early form to what was to characterize elite strategies for the remainder of the nineteenth century: a willingness to separate from Spain as a means to protect local interests. Determined to resist the abolition of slavery, planter elites authorized José de Arango y Núñez del Castillo to pre-sent the Cuban case for annexation to U.S. Consul William Shaler. Arango presented himself as a representative of "the great many of the wealthy landed proprietors" who were prepared to act to "save the country." He alluded to Cuban determination to break with Spain, stressing that "all the men of influence here are rich, and when a crisis arrives great confidence may be placed on their own private interests, which will necessarily lead them into the right course." Separation from Spain, Arango acknowledged, was not without risks. Cubans were particularly concerned over the prospects of success against Spain, only to see the island seized by England. Antipathy against Britain ran deep and wide, for Cubans understood correctly that under British rule the days of the slave trade, no less than slavery itself, would be numbered. Arango continued:

> Against the United States no such unfriendly sentiments . . . exist here: we admire your institutions, your laws, and your form of government;

we see that they procure your prosperity and your happiness. Now such being the circumstances of our situation there is naturally but one course for us to take, which is to solicit union with you. . . . It appears to me that such a measure must be equally interesting to both parties. Our situation means we guarantee the navigation of the Mississippi; and our harbors, our soil, our climate, offer incredible resources to commerce and agriculture, and when these advantageous qualities of our Island came to be developed by such a government as yours, they would besides making us rich and happy, add incalculably to your national wealth and political importance. [4]

Arango's mission was to secure a North American commitment to assist the Cubans, if necessary, to maintain internal order and aid in the defense of the island against an anticipated British invasion.

Consul Shaler was enthusiastic about the project. "I observed," he reported, "that in case of the event he dreaded, it would be the policy of the United States to give them the necessary aid, and I added, 'Your friends should rely with confidence on the American people. We are able to support and protect you in all cases, if you are true to yourselves.' " [5] But officials in Washington were cautious and slow to respond. Eventually Shaler's activities in Havana aroused Spanish suspicions, and in November 1811 he was arrested and subsequently expelled from the island.

During the 1820s and 1830s annexationist sentiment increased, in large part as confidence in Spain's ability to defend elite interests decreased. Creoles used their growing contacts with North Americans to expound on the virtues of annexation. They met surreptitiously with North American diplomats, proselytized among U.S. merchants and traders, and appealed privately to North American travelers, always with the same exhortation to annexation. In 1822, a group of Creole planters appointed Bernabé Sánchez to travel to Washington and personally solicit support from the Monroe administration for an annexationist conspiracy. [6]

IV

Annexation sentiment was also increasing in the United States. It was a sentiment possessed of distinct symbiotic properties: Cuban advocacy of annexation to the United States encouraged North Americans' territorial acquisitiveness and vice versa. North Americans had long coveted Cuba, and they never concealed their commitment to its eventual possession. To many, the destinies of the two countries seemed not merely intertwined but indissoluble. Cuba was so near as to confer on geographical proximity incontrovertible sanction for political intimacy. Cuba was fated to be part of the North American Union. So powerful a hold did this proposition have over U.S. calculations that it soon became an axiomatic imperative. Just as there were incontrovertible laws of nature, North Americans posited, so too were there self-evident truths of politics. "There are laws of political as well as of physical gravitation," John Quincy Adams suggested in 1823, "and if an apple, severed by a tempest from its native tree, cannot choose but fall to the ground, Cuba, forcibly disjoined from its own unnatural connection with Spain, and incapable of self-support, can gravitate only towards the North American Union, which, by the same law of nature, cannot cast her off from its bosom."[7]

North American designs on Cuba became a fixed feature of U.S. strategic objectives early in the nineteenth century. The acquisition of the Louisiana territory (1803) and Florida (1819) expanded U.S. borders to the Gulf, conferring on Cuba a new and special geopolitical significance. The island lay astride the two maritime approaches to the Gulf, the Florida Straits to the north and the Yucatán Channel to the west. It commanded the principal shipping lanes in and out of the Caribbean. Henceforth it became all but impossible for the United States to contemplate the expansion of commercial and strategic interests in the region without pausing first to consider the status of Cuba. "Let us look at Cuba," Daniel Webster exhorted in 1826. "It is placed in the mouth of the Mississippi. Its occupation by a strong maritime power would be felt in the first moment of hostility, as far up the Mississippi and the Missouri. . . . It is the commanding point of the

Gulf of Mexico. See, too, how it lies in the very line of our coastwise traffic; interposed in the very highway between New York and New Orleans." [8]

Annexation was the obvious solution to North American concerns. "Cuba, almost in sight of our shores," wrote John Quincy Adams, "from a multitude of considerations has become an object of transcendent importance to the political and commercial interests of our Union." Adams surveyed Cuba's commanding position with "reference to the Gulf of Mexico and the West Indies seas," the "safe and capacious harbor of Havana," the vast potential of Cuban markets, and the nature of its production, and concluded: "It is scarcely possible to resist the conviction that the annexation of Cuba to our federal republic will be indispensable to the continuance and integrity of the Union itself." [9]

These views were reiterated often, sometimes with a slight change of emphasis, but always with the same attention to commercial objectives and strategic concerns. "I candidly confess," Thomas Jefferson wrote, "that I have ever looked on Cuba as the most interesting addition which could ever be made to our system of States. The control of which, with Florida Point, this island would give us over the Gulf of Mexico, and the countries and the Isthmus bordering on it, as well as all of those whose waters flow into it, would fill up the measure of our political well-being." James Buchanan insisted that possession of Cuba offered unlimited trade possibilities and promised to relieve the United States "from the apprehensions which we can never cease to feel for our own safety and the security of our commerce whilst it shall remain in its present condition." [10]

North American designs on Cuba were not unopposed, however. Certainly Spain was one obstacle in the way of annexation, and at no point in the nineteenth century did Madrid express a willingness to relinquish its sovereignty over Cuba. A more formidable opponent to annexation, however, was Great Britain, which, it was generally known, stood prepared to oppose U.S. expansion into the Caribbean. [11] The forceful acquisition of Cuba, North Americans understood, risked war, certainly with Spain and probably with England—a prospect that dampened the ardor of even the most zealous annexationist. For all his enthusiasm on the question, John Quincy Adams was eminently sensible of risks attending annexation and counseled prudence and patience. "Numerous and formidable objections to the extension of our territorial dominations beyond the sea," he cautioned, "present themselves to the first contemplation of the subject."[12] England loomed large over cabinet deliberations in 1822, as members of the Monroe administration considered the Cuban request for annexation. Adams recorded in his diary:

> The question was discussed what was to be done. Mr. Calhoun has a most ardent desire that the island of Cuba should become part of the United States, and says that Mr. Jefferson has the same. . . . Calhoun says Mr. Jefferson told him two years ago that we ought, at first possible opportunity, to take Cuba, even though at the cost of a war with England; but as we are not now prepared for this, and as our great object must be to gain time, he thought we should answer this overture by dissuading them from their present purpose, and urging them to adhere at present to their connection with Spain.[13]

Unable to acquire Cuba from Spain and unwilling to risk war with England, the United States adopted an alternative approach to annexation: Cuba could remain outside the North American Union as long as it remained within the Spanish Empire. This principle of "no transfer" occupied a position of central importance in North American thinking about Cuba for much of the nineteenth century. The proposition rested on a number of corollary tenets, central to which was a U.S. commitment to the defense of Spanish sovereignty. Annexation would be fulfilled eventually, even inevitably, North Americans were certain, as long as sovereignty over Cuba did not pass to a third party. This notion of colonial succession, whereby the United States would replace Spain in Cuba, required the defense of the status quo and the maintenance of Spanish rule. Until such time as Spain proved incapable of maintaining its authority over Cuba, Spanish sovereignty over the island would be supported as the most desirable alternative to annexation. Guaranteeing Cuba's "independence against all the world *except* Spain," Jefferson reasoned, "would be nearly as valuable to us as if it were our own." United States minister in Spain John Forsyth assured Spanish authorities in 1822 that U.S. "interests required, as there was no prospect of [Cuba] passing into our hands, that it should belong to Spain."[14]

The defense of Spanish sovereignty had more immediate objectives however, chief of which was to foreclose any possibility of the island falling under the control of a potentially hostile power. The presence of a powerful and menacing European power so near to the United States, at the very crossroads of the Gulf and Caribbean waterways, was an eventuality the United States was prepared to avoid at all cost. The prospect of war may have forestalled U.S. efforts to acquire Cuba but did not prevent North Americans from threatening war to stop someone else from acquiring the island. As early as 1823 Jefferson counseled James Monroe to "oppose, with all our means, the forcible interposition of any power, either as auxiliary, stipendiary, or under any other form or pretext, and most especially, [Cuba's] transfer to any power, by conquest, cession or in any other way." "In the hands of a powerful and active nation," U.S. minister in Spain Alexander H. Everett warned two years later, "[Cuba] would carry with it complete control over the commerce of the Gulph [sic] of Mexico, and over the navigation of the River Mississippi, as to endanger very much the intercourse of our country in that quarter. . . . It has been viewed by all as a settled point that the American Government could not consent to any change in the political situation of Cuba other than one which should place it under the jurisdiction of the United States." John Forsyth made a similar warning in 1823 as minister to Spain—"We desire . . . no other neighbor in Cuba but Spain. . . . The United States would do everything in their power, consistent with their obligations to prevent Cuba from being wrested from Spain"—and again in 1840 as secretary of state—"In case of any attempt, from whatever quarter, to wrest from [Spain] this portion of her territory, she may securely depend upon the military and naval resources of the United States to aid her in preserving or recovering it." Secretary of State John M. Clayton stated U.S. policy succinctly in 1849: "The news of the cession of

Cuba to any foreign power would in the United States, be the instant signal for war. No foreign power would attempt to take it, that did not expect a hostile collision with us as an inevitable consequence."[15]

But North Americans understood that the challenge to Spanish sovereignty was not confined to external sources. No less a threat originated from within, from among Cubans themselves and their efforts to end the colonial connection and establish an independent nation. Independence also signaled a modification of sovereignty over Cuba, to which the United States was no less opposed. That a large portion of the Cuban population consisted of people of color persuaded North Americans that independence would be the prelude to chronic social strife and political disorder.[16] Haiti was the most oft-cited example of the fate awaiting a free Cuba. "If Cuba were to declare itself independent," warned Henry Clay, "the amount and character of its population render it improbable that it could maintain its independence. Such a premature declaration might bring about a renewal of those shocking scenes, of which a neighboring island was the afflicted theatre." That a large portion of the population of color consisted of slaves impelled Martin Van Buren to warn in 1829: "Other considerations connected with a certain class of our population, make it the interest of the southern section of the Union that no attempt should be made in that island to throw off the yoke of Spanish independence, the first effect of which would be the sudden emancipation of a numerous slave population, the result of which could not be very sensibly felt upon the adjacent shores of the United States."[17]

The prospects of Cuban independence aroused other fears. Few North American officials believed Cubans capable of self-government. Indeed, the central premise of Adams's "law of political gravitation" rested on the proposition that Cubans were "not competent to a system of permanent self-dependence." Henry Clay gave explicit and enduring form to North American opposition to Cuban independence in 1825, suggesting obliquely that the United States would consider intervention to help Spain defend its sovereignty against Cubans. "This country prefers that Cuba and Porto Rico should remain dependent on Spain," Clay insisted. "This Government desires no political change of that condition. The population itself of the island is incompetent at present, from its composition and amount, to maintain self-government." And if Cubans rebelled against Spain, Clay warned, the "possible contingencies of such a protracted war might bring upon the government of the United States duties and obligations, the performance of which, however painful it should be, they may not be at liberty to decline." [18]

Through most of the nineteenth century, and at several critical junctures, the attitudes of Cuban elites and North American officials converged and reinforced each other. Both feared social strife, racial disorder, and political instability. They were pessimistic about the Cuban capacity to sustain sovereignty and preside over successful self-government. They opposed independence. Both favored annexation, in the long run, but were committed, in the short term, to the defense of Spanish rule—the Cubans because it guaranteed order and defended property and privilege, the North Americans because it assured the presence of a weak European power and one easy to replace eventually. And for both, the continued presence of Spanish rule, as objectionable and odious as it may have been, was still the best available guarantee against disorder and disruption. Spain would have to do either until it proved unable to discharge this responsibility or the responsibility could be better discharged by someone else, or both.

V

Annexationist stirrings peaked and subsided in both countries during the 1840s and 1850s. In the United States, expansionist elements were in political ascendancy and pursued the acquisition of Cuba with new vigor. In 1848, President James K. Polk offered Spain $100 million for Cuba, without success. Six years later President Franklin Pierce raised the offer to $130 million, also without effect. The 1850s generally were years of strident expansionist activism. The Young America movement summoned young political leaders to advance the cause of freedom and democracy in the New World. William Walker planned to seize Nicaragua, and John Quitman dreamed of Cuban annexation to maintain southern parity for the slave states. In 1854, the U.S. ministers to Spain, France, and England met in Ostend, Belgium, and publicly urged the United States to renew its offer to purchase Cuba. The Ostend Manifesto warned that if Spain refused to sell, "then, by every law, human and divine, we shall be justified in wresting it from Spain if we possess the power." [19]

These were also years of rising annexationist activity in Cuba—in part a response to the increase of expansionist rhetoric and deeds in the United States and the new possibilities that both foretold for Cuba. North American efforts to purchase the island raised Cuban expectations, as did the Ostend Manifesto, and all served to encourage hope in Cuba that annexation was imminent. Similarly, Cubans must have been heartened by the Texas experience, when slaveowning settlers seceded from Mexico in defense of slavery and subsequently joined the North American Union. [20]

The resurgence of Cuban annexationist sentiment was also a product of renewed discontent with Spanish rule, principally new grievances over old problems. In 1834, Spain again disrupted Cuban commerce by raising duties on North American flour imports. The United States reacted immediately by assessing higher tonnage duties on goods imported aboard Spanish carriers and imposing a special duty on Cuban coffee. Cubans were once more the principal casualties of the continuing tariff skirmishes between Spain and the United States.

Hard times arrived in Cuba. Prices increased as import inventories decreased. Trade declined immediately, and coffee exports declined precipitately—from thirty-two thousand tons in 1833 to eighteen thousand tons in 1835. A newly organized Cuban merchant marine, dependent almost entirely on the carrying trade between the island and the United States, collapsed, and with it disappeared the shipbuilding industry on the island. In 1835 the abolitionist specter again passed over the island, this time in the form of a new treaty whereby Spain conceded to Britain wider authority to search and seize vessels suspected of transporting African slaves. New Spanish efforts in 1848 to promote *peninsular* flour exports prompted Spain again to raise duties on North American flour. The United States responded by raising duties on Cuban coffee, thereby dealing coffee growers another terrible blow. This time coffee growers did not recover, and Cuban coffee production dwindled to near insignificance.

To promote the cause of annexation in Cuba and the United States, Cuban exiles established the Consejo de Gobierno Cubano in New York. One of the founders and early presidents of the Consejo de Gobierno was Cristobal Madán, a wealthy Creole planter, who was married to the sister of John L. O'Sullivan, author of the phrase "Manifest Destiny." Others included property owners José Aniceto Iznaga, Alonso Betancourt, Gaspar Betancourt and novelist Cirilo Villaverde. The Consejo de Gobierno published a weekly newspaper, *La Verdad*, which was circulated widely in the United States and distributed clandestinely in Cuba and served as the principal means to disseminate annexationist propaganda.

The Consejo obtained wide support among Cubans in exile. Many were Creoles who had run afoul of Spanish authorities in Cuba and sought safety abroad. This community consisted principally of planters, businessmen, property owners, and intellectuals. Others were the sons and daughters of Cuban elites, large numbers of whom had come to the United States to study and travel and subsequently developed a powerful attraction to North American institutions and culture and for whom annexation was as desirable as it was logical. Indeed, so politically significant had the student population become that in 1849 Spain denied exit permits to all Cubans desiring to study abroad. Creoles now had one more complaint to add to their growing list of grievances.

The Consejo de Gobierno also disseminated annexationist propaganda among North Americans. Its members lobbied congressional representatives, spoke at public functions, and distributed information to the principal newspapers. These activities may well have been the Consejo's most important political function, for they bolstered annexationist sentiment in the United States. Circulating freely and actively among prominent North Americans were large numbers of Cubans, mostly white, many wealthy and fluent in English, familiar with and devoted to things North American, and passionately devoted to union with the United States. It was, of course, the highest form of flattery that so many Cubans, and of such high social standing, desired union with the United States, and one to which North Americans were eminently susceptible. Cuban proselytizing confirmed the belief that annexation was at least as popular in Cuba as it was in the United States and that the desire for union was the prevalent political sentiment in Cuba, at least among those classes who mattered most. Thus subsumed into U.S. expansionism was a mission of liberation—annexation as an act both of manifest destiny for North Americans and self-determination for Cubans.

Annexationist activity had, indeed, increased inside Cuba as well, most notably with the establishment of the Club de La Habana in 1847. The membership roster of the annexationist club read like a registry of the Creole patriciate and included property owners Cristobal Madán, Domingo del Monte, Miguel Aldama, Anacleto Bermúdez, José María Sánchez Iznaga, José Aniceto Iznaga, Francisco de Frías (Count of Pozos Dulces), José Luis Alfonso, and Gaspar Betancourt Cisneros.

During the late 1840s and early 1850s, the Club de La Habana developed into a center of annexationist conspiracies. In 1848 a delegation of planters, including José Aniceto Iznaga, Alonso Betancourt, and Gaspar Betancourt Cisneros, appealed to President Polk to support an annexationist plot in Cuba. Polk eventually declined to aid the Creole conspiracy, but these contacts, as well as propaganda from the Consejo de Gobierno, reinforced the cause of those who advocated annexation of separatist Yucatán (briefly considered by the Polk administration after the defeat of Mexico) and further inspired a generation of southern dreamers of tropical empire.

The activities of the Club de La Habana peaked during the late 1840s in its support of filibustering expeditions under Narciso López. A former officer in the Spanish army, López was related to two important annexationist families—he was the nephew of José María Sánchez Iznaga and brother-in-law of Pozos Dulces—and moved freely among annexationist elements in both Cuba and the United States. With financial assistance from Cuban and North American supporters, and under the unfurled banner of a newly designed flag—a tricolored lone star, inspired by the Texan flag—López struck three times and failed each time: a filibustering expedition to Manicaragua in 1848, an invasion of Cárdenas in 1849, and an expedition to Bahía Honda in 1851. The ill-starred expeditions originated in the United States and consisted mostly of North Americans. Of the six hundred expeditionaries who invaded Cárdenas, only five were Cuban. North Americans were also in the majority among the four hundred men who attacked Bahía Honda, where López was captured and subsequently executed. [21]

Other annexationist risings followed in quick succession during the 1850s, and all failed. Several conspiracies were uncovered in Camagüey, the most prominent of which was the short-lived rebellion led by Joaquín de Agüero in 1851. In the same year, another uprising was organized by planter Isidro Armenteros of Trinidad. One year later Spanish authorities uncovered another annexationist plot in Pinar del Río. In 1854, a far-flung annexationist conspiracy in Havana was discovered and dissolved.

VI

Annexationist activity waned on both sides of the Florida Straits at about the same time and for related reasons. The United States became increasingly absorbed with complicated domestic issues, many of which had direct implications for Cuba. Eventually the debate over slavery in the United States all but foreclosed any possibility that new slave territories would be admitted into the Union. In midcentury the Cuba issue intruded itself into U.S. domestic politics and in ways that increasingly boded ill for Cuban prospects for annexation. The last two López expeditions originated from the South, financed largely by southern sponsors, for whom annexation of Cuba would have represented a triumph for the slave system. For these reasons, annexationist projects aroused widespread suspicion among abolitionist elements in the North. Within the decade, the United States was embroiled in civil war.

Conditions were changing in Cuba, too. A new ministry in Spain announced its determination to resist British antislavery pressure, thereby allaying some Cuban misgivings. The illegal slave trade continued and for a short while expanded in spectacular fashion. Annexationist sentiment in Cuba was also on the wane—for some an idea whose time had not come, for others an idea whose time had passed. Some had supported union with enthusiasm, others with resignation, but by the late 1850s and early 1860s, nearly everyone was having second thoughts. Certainly the Emancipation Proclamation in the United States in 1863 had a chilling effect among planters, many of whom had earlier looked to annexation as the salvation of slavery in Cuba. They now derived some solace from their failed efforts. Those who previously advocated annexation as the best defense of slavery now opposed it—for the same reason.

Spanish authorities had become aware of the nature of the annexationist threat to colonial rule and moved with dispatch and purpose to crush suspected centers of annexationist conspiracies. Arrests and deportations increased in numbers and frequency. Authorities took especially vigorous measures in Camagüey province, a center of strong annexationist sentiment. The provincial military commander assumed supreme authority over the district, and army units were reinforced. The *ayuntamiento* (city council) of the provincial capital was suppressed. In perhaps the most radical measure contemplated by Spain, colonial authorities warned Creole elites that an annexationist challenge to Spanish rule would be met immediately with a decree of emancipation. "Emancipation would be the ruin of the proprietors and merchants of the island," Governor General Federico Roncali informed Madrid in 1849 in a communication subsequently published in the Havana press. "It would put an end to the only means of preventing the island's falling to annexationists. . . . The terrible weapon could, in the last extreme, prevent the loss of the island, and if the inhabitants convince themselves that it will be used, they will tremble and renounce every illusion before bringing upon themselves such an anathema."[22] The Spanish maneuver was ingenious. The scheme was designed to array the slave population on the side of Spain by giving slaves a stake in colonial rule: emancipated slaves would defend their newly acquired freedom under Spain against Cubans seeking to perpetuate slavery through annexation to the United States.

During the mid-nineteenth century, Spain also displayed an increasing inclination to settle differences with Cubans through concession and compromise. A new liberal ministry in Spain inspired the belief among Creole elites that some of the more pressing grievances of the colony could be resolved through negotiation. These were promising developments, and almost immediately Creole political activism moved away from annexationist plots to reformist politics. Many of the very planters who had previously advocated annexation to the United States, including Miguel Aldama, Pozos Dulces, and José Luis Alfonso, reaffirmed their allegiance to Spain. In 1865 the Reformist party was founded and gave new political form to old Creole demands for sweeping changes in the colonial regime, including the relaxation of trade restrictions and reform of tax and tariff structures.

Hopes for change proved illusory and short-lived, however, and within two years liberals in Spain and reformists in Cuba were on the defensive and in disarray. The liberal ministry was overthrown and the Reformist party was dissolved, and in both Spain and Cuba reaction was in the ascendancy. Repression increased. The opposition press was silenced, critics were exiled, political meetings were banned, and opponents were imprisoned. Spain chose this moment to raise old taxes and introduce new ones. In March 1867, Spain imposed a new series of protectionist duties on foreign products, four times the amount charged for Spanish goods—a particularly severe burden on a population utterly dependent on foreign imports. The United States responded in kind and raised tariffs on Cuban products by 10 percent. Once more, Cubans were caught up in a situation not of their making but with potential for their undoing.

A new round of tax increases would have been ill-conceived at any time. On this occasion it was also ill-timed. Tax increases coincided

with and contributed to economic dislocation. The economy plunged
into a deep recession. Sugar production was in decline. So were prices,
which by 1866 had fallen to their lowest point in almost fifteen years.
In December 1866, the principal banks on the island suspended pay-
ments and brought to a momentary halt all sugar transactions, adding
to the general climate of uncertainty.

Reactionary policies, retrogressive taxes, and recession, all at once,
served to give dramatic form to the aspects of Spanish rule that many
Cubans found most objectionable. Discontent spread anew, and, with
no prospect of obtaining relief through reform, Creoles in growing
numbers were inclined to seek remedy through revolution. Conspiracies increased in numbers and scope, especially among Creole elites
in the eastern provinces, the most disaffected sector of the Cuban
patriciate. By 1868, ranking representatives of the eastern Creole bourgeoisie, cattle barons from Camagüey and sugar planters from Oriente—Carlos Manuel de Céspedes, Salvador Cisneros Betancourt,
Francisco Vicente Aguilera, Bartolomé Masó, Pedro Figueredo, and
Ignacio Agramonte—were deep in conspiracy against Spain.

VII

The "Grito de Yara" on October 10, 1868, announced revolution
on the island and the call for independence from Spain. The rebellion expanded quickly in the eastern provinces—first across Oriente,
westward into neighboring Camagüey, and eventually if only briefly
into the eastern regions of Las Villas. By the early 1870s, the separatist
uprising had attracted more than forty thousand supporters.

That Creoles changed the means of opposition from the political
to the military did not signify a fundamental change in the reformist
character of Cuban ends. The uprising was reformism by another
means. The separatist program-manifesto gave new expression and
renewed vigor to the central tenets of Creole reformism. Once again
annexationism surfaced as an expression of Creole disaffection with
Spanish rule. Independence from Spain was envisioned principally as

a transition to union with the United States. The annexationist tendencies of the rebellion were fixed early. Only weeks after the "Grito de Yara," Carlos Manuel de Céspedes, Pedro Figueredo, and Bartolomé Masó petitioned Secretary of State William Seward to consider Cuban admission to the Union. A year later the constituent assembly of Guáimaro explicitly proclaimed annexation as the ultimate purpose of the Cuban rebellion. Soon thereafter, the representative assembly of the provisional government petitioned President Ulysses S. Grant for recognition of belligerency as prelude to admission into the Union.

But annexation as a function of Cuban initiative had never elicited a favorable response in the United States. On several previous occasions, most notably in 1822 and 1848, Creole annexationist efforts were rebuffed. It happened again during the 1860s and 1870s. In fact, North Americans had from the outset conceived of annexation principally in one of two ways: either as an outright act of colonial succession, in much the same fashion as the acquisition of Louisiana and Florida, or as a spoil of war, much in the manner in which the Mexican territories were seized. When John S. C. Abbott traveled through Cuba in 1859, he envisaged only two ways the island would join the Union: "There are but two conceivable measures of annexation, namely *purchase* or *seizure*." [23]

Not contemplated, however, was for the United States to deal with a successful Cuban separatist movement, presided over by a Cuban provisional government, negotiating the terms of union as a more or less sovereign entity. Cubans who were encouraged by the Texas experience failed to note one important distinction: Texans were, in fact, North Americans. Thus, whereas Cubans anticipated statehood from union with the United States, which would guarantee their own local political ascendancy, North Americans alluded more to the acquisition of a territory. As early as 1822, the U.S. commercial agent in Havana reported that "the natives which amount to three-fourths or ⅔ of the white inhabitants of the Island are decidedly in favor of this Island being attached to the U.S.—as a *state* not as a *colony*." [24] Even as late as the turn of the century, the issue continued substantially unchanged. "The most enthusiastic advocates of annexation among intelligent Cubans," Forbes Lindsay concluded after his travels in Cuba, "would not be willing to come under the American flag with anything less than the status and rights of a state. . . . [They] would not be content with a territorial position." Lindsay noted, however, that "a large majority of the native population of Cuba have negro blood in their veins. Practically one hundred percent of the people confess the Roman Catholic faith and Spanish is the mother tongue of the same proportion. Would the American nation agree to the construction of a sister state out of such material?"[25]

The issue of status was a major concern among Creole elites throughout the nineteenth century. Indeed, among the reasons that annexation sentiment waned in Cuba during the 1850s and 1860s was growing fear that union with the United States would create more problems than it solved. Annexation as a territory, not a state, would subject the island to direct administration by North Americans: officials appointed by Washington, no doubt in the form of patronage for the ruling party, who would arrive to administer Cuba in behalf of a distant government. Cuba would enjoy no more right of self-government as a territorial possession of the United States than it had as a colony of Spain. Cubans feared, too, that they would share the fate of the Hispano-Mexican population in the territories seized from Mexico in 1848, when longtime residents were displaced and dispossessed of their homes and property by a myriad of bewildering new laws and legal proceedings rigged to favor Anglo-American litigants. Some feared that the island would soon be overrun by North American settlers, who eventually would eclipse Creoles altogether. There was, thus, a darker side to the Texas experience, and not a few in Cuba were sensible to its implications. In his travels across the western provinces during the late 1850s, Richard Dana learned that Creoles "fear that the Anglo-Saxon race would swallow up the power and property of the island, as they have done in California and Texas, and that the Creoles would go to the wall." Antonio Saco, an otherwise staunch and steadfast defender of Creole property interests, demurred on the issue of annexation. Cuba lacked sufficient population

and educational levels, Saco warned in 1848, to withstand the anticipated influx of North American migrants. The issue for Saco was the
survival of culture and the defense of national identity. If the island
had a larger white Cuban population of 1.5 million, Saco argued, instead of a mere five hundred thousand, annexation would pose little
threat to the survival of Cuban culture. [26]

The Cuban initiative for annexation during the Ten Years' War met
no more success than had previous ones. And there were other problems in 1868. Cubans' continued defense of slavery remained an in-
surmountable obstacle to annexation. The destruction of foreign property by Cuban insurgents and disrupted trade created havoc for North
American interests and aroused ill-will in the United States toward
the Cuban cause. Other considerations—some historic, others pragmatic—also contributed to U.S. opposition to the Cuban uprising.
Once annexation appeared unlikely—as was settled early in the conflict—Washington took a dim view of Cuban efforts to free themselves
from Spain. Rather, the United States invoked two of the central elements of its long-standing Cuba policy: opposition to independence
and support of Spanish sovereignty. Cuban requests for recognition
of belligerency, a status that would enhance the insurgents' ability to
wage war, were denied. Recognition of Cuban independence, Grant
responded, "was impracticable and indefensible"; belligerent status
was "unwise and premature." [27] The notion of Cuban incapacity for
self-government persisted. Secretary of State Hamilton Fish held the
intellectual and moral quality of Cubans in low esteem, believing a
population consisting of Indians, Africans, and Spaniards incapable
of self-government. Cuban separation from Spain was no doubt inevitable, Fish thought, but that independence from Spain signified
sovereignty for Cuba was a different matter and was resisted in Washington. [28]

Through the better part of the Ten Years' War, the United States continued to proclaim its commitment to Spanish rule. The United States
urged Spain to introduce reforms as a way both to mollify disgruntled
Cubans and to end the war, leaving its rule intact. At one point, Grant

offered to mediate the dispute, with the United States brokering an agreement between Spain and the insurgents that would guarantee colonial rule in exchange for colonial reform.

The United States may have been unwilling to negotiate annexation with the Cubans, but it was willing to discuss the acquisition of the island with the Spaniards. Indeed, many in Washington were hopeful that the war would create conditions encouraging Spain to sell the island. Secretary of State Fish was optimistic that a prolonged and costly war in Cuba would force Spain to part with the island. The Cuban insurrection, Fish commented at a cabinet meeting in April 1869, promised to expose the "madness and fatuity" of Spain's continued sovereignty over Cuba; ultimately, the war would produce "a condition of affairs, a state of feeling that would compel all the civilized nations to regard the Spanish rule as an international nuisance, which must be abated, when they would all be glad that we should interpose and regulate the control of the Island."[29] Indeed, at several points during the war, the Grant administration explored the idea of purchasing the island from Spain.

By the late 1870s, the war was coming to an end. Spain had established its military superiority and was now prepared to discuss with Cubans the terms of political reconciliation. In the end Spain promised reform, and this pledge served as the basis of the peace settlement with the rebellious Cubans. By the terms of the Pact of Zanjón of February 1878, Spain committed itself to a wide range of political reforms and economic concessions. Cuban insurgents received amnesty, and most laid down their arms.

3   At the Crossroads

The Ten Years' War marked a transitional point for Cuba in the nineteenth century. After 1878, Spain remedied some of the structural sources of Cuban discontent, with varying degrees of success. Slavery was abolished within a decade. Trade policies were modified. In 1884 and again in 1886, Spain negotiated limited reciprocal trade agreements with the United States, eliminating the differential flag system and abolishing some of the more onerous import duties and taxes. Political concessions began auspiciously enough, and early indications suggested that this time Spain would make good on its commitment to colonial reforms.

Certainly many Cubans believed this, especially Creole elites, who immediately after the Pact of Zanjón organized a new Liberal party (Autonomist). Creole elites welcomed the end of the colonial insurrection in 1878, and they welcomed even more the opportunity to seek political leadership in postwar Cuba. Autonomists were committed to the pursuit of reform and self-rule within existing colonial relationships, representation in the Spanish Cortes, and the expansion of free trade. They opposed independence, fearful that separation from Spain would lead to political instability and social strife and that both would result in economic ruin. They also endorsed the legitimacy of the colonial regime and the primacy of empire as the central and unchallenged tenets of colonial politics. For Autonomists, reforms were the best guarantee of empire, and empire was the best guarantee against revolution.

But also after 1878 some of the more pronounced contradictions of the colonial political economy stood in sharp relief and gave both new form and new direction to the Cuban quest for a separate nationality. The effects of the Ten Years' War continued to influence the course of Cuban internal development and the character of Cuban international relations. The disruption of Cuban sugar production during the

55

war had encouraged the expansion of sugar elsewhere in the world. Cane production increased in Latin America and Asia and beet sugar production expanded in Europe, creating a major challenge to Cuban primacy in world markets. After the Ten Years' War, Cubans not only discovered that they faced new competition and the loss of old markets, but worse yet, a glut in world sugar production depressed the world price of sugar—from 4.6 cents a pound in 1870 to 2.7 cents in 1880. [1]

Crisis was not long in coming. The collapse of sugar prices affected every sector of the local economy and announced calamity for Cuba. By the mid-1880s, the island was in the throes of depression. "Out of the twelve or thirteen hundred planters on the island," the U.S. consul in Havana reported early in 1884, "not a dozen are said to be solvent." [2] Seven of the island's largest trading companies failed; business houses closed and banks collapsed. In the first three months of 1884, business failures totaled over $7 million.

The postwar economic crisis set the stage for a new round of North American expansion into the colonial economy. For nearly a century, the Cuban economy had been organized around commercial relations with the United States, depending increasingly on North American markets and imports. This connection determined Cuban production strategies, influenced local consumption patterns, and shaped the character of the Cuban political discourse. After 1878, the North American presence in the Cuban economy assumed new forms and functions. Cuban producers were in desperate need of new capital and fresh sources of credit, neither of which was readily available within the existing framework of Spanish colonialism. Increasingly, they turned to the United States, and the consequences were far-reaching and permanent. Credit transactions increased in value and volume through the 1880s and for many staved off bankruptcy. But redemption was short-lived and costly. For many others, economic conditions did not improve, and increasing numbers of Cuban planters failed and lost property to North American creditors. During the last decades of the nineteenth century, North American ownership of property in Cuba expanded, initially through foreclosure and subsequently by purchases from planters in distress. Many planters survived the crisis of the 1880s but at the cost of their traditional supremacy over production. The price of solvency was increasing displacement and eventual dependency. Across the island the Cuban grip over production slipped, announcing the demise of the Creole planter class.

Developments in the jurisdiction of Cienfuegos, once a center of the Cuban patriciate, gave dramatic expression to the displacement of the Creole bourgeoisie. As early as 1883, the local U.S. consular agent reported that all the mills in the region had changed ownership at least once as a result of indebtedness and foreclosures.[3] During these years Boston banker Edwin Atkins foreclosed on the Juan Sarria family estate, Soledad. Atkins subsequently acquired the Carlota plantation from the Ramón de la Torriente family, the Caledonia estate from the heirs of Diego Julián Sánchez, the Guabairo property from Manuel Blanco, the Limones farm from the Vilá family, and the Brazo estate from the Torre family. From the declining Carlos Iznaga family Atkins acquired Vega Vieja and Manaca and obtained a long-term lease on Algoba. The Santa Teresa estate was purchased from Juan Pérez Galdós and Veguitas acquired from José Porrúa. From the Barrallaza family Atkins secured the Vaquería property. Atkins also purchased the San Agustín estate, formerly owned by the Tomás Terry family. The Rosario estate, owned by the Sarrias, was later attached to Soledad. The Atkins interests also secured long-term leases on several other estates, including San José, Viamones, and San Esteban. The New York banking firm Eaton Stafford and Company also acquired a number of sugar properties in the Cienfuegos-Trinidad region. The E. & L. Ponvert brothers of Boston expanded their holdings around the four-thousand-acre Hormiguero estate in Palmira, buying out or foreclosing on the smaller properties of local insolvent Cuban planters.[4]

The Creole bourgeoisie survived the crisis of the 1880s, but in a different condition. Many planters were obliged to exchange titles of property for ownership of stocks in U.S. corporations and relinquish their positions as landowners for places on corporate boards of directors. Many became administrators and lived off salaries rather than rents and profits. Planters would henceforth function increasingly as agents of North American interests and instruments of U.S. economic penetration of Cuba. Their well-being depended on the success of North American capital in Cuba, guaranteed access to U.S. markets, and the policies to facilitate both.

The transfer of property was accompanied by a transformation of nationality. Through the latter half of the nineteenth century more and more planters found it expedient to acquire U.S. citizenship. Cubans used U.S. nationality as an instrument to defend their economic interests, a hedge against local instability and a means to enlist the support of the North American government in the defense of local privilege and property. Through naturalization planters sought to acquire a powerful foreign backer, a patron to be summoned when Spanish colonial authorities demonstrated inefficiency or indifference to the needs of local property interests. Equally important, as U.S. citizens, planters were in a position to request reparation and receive indemnification for property losses resulting from political disorders. As naturalized U.S. citizens, Cubans obtained exemption from military service, an important consideration.

These developments internationalized Cuban politics and provided the United States with another entrée into the internal affairs of the island. In the closing decades of the nineteenth century, as the Creole bourgeoisie sought to adjust its strategies to changing economic conditions, the transfiguration of planters' nationality placed the object of their allegiance above national interests and located the sources of their patronage outside the island. The Cuban citizen seeking naturalization during the Ten Years' War, James W. Steele observed derisively in 1881, "preferred joining his brigade in New York, staying a few months or years, getting his documentary evidence of United States citizenship, and coming back again exempt from any and all military service on either side, and thereafter fighting his battles with the Spaniard in a consulate of his adopted country."[5] A new habit developed in Cuba, a practice that endured into the twentieth century, in which the local bourgeoisie, possessed with the sanction to petition the United

States in its behalf in disputes with local political authorities or when challenged by rival social forces, looked to Washington for the defense and settlement of local disputes.

Planters may have had special reasons for acquiring U.S. citizenship, but Cubans in increasing numbers, and from all classes, were becoming naturalized U.S. citizens. A survey of U.S. citizens in 1881 registered with the consulate in Havana revealed a total of 2,492 citizens, of whom 1,502 were born in Cuba. A year later consul Adam Badeau complained of a lack of adequate staff and noted: "The number of naturalized American citizens, mostly of Cuban birth, residing here, amounts to several thousand, and these are constantly making demands upon the time and attention, and claiming the protection, of the Consulate General. This alone renders the employment of additional service desirable."[6]

II

Through the latter decades of the nineteenth century the Cuban economy moved toward greater integration into the North American system. The economic crisis of the 1880s served in other ways to facilitate North American expansion into the Cuban economy. The decline in the world price of sugar, the rise of new competitors, and the loss of old markets underscored the urgency of guaranteeing Cuban sugar a secure and stable place in the North American market on as favorable terms as possible. Cuban dependence on North American markets increased markedly during the 1870s and 1880s as beet sugar growers in France, Austria, and Germany expanded production and displaced Cuban exports from European markets. Beet sugar, accounting in 1853 for only 14 percent of total world production of sugar, had by 1884 come to represent 53 percent of the international supply. Cuba's combined sugar exports to France, England, and Germany declined from 232,682 metric tons in 1868, to 57,649 in 1878, and to 4,446 in 1893. For the same years, Cuban sugar exports to Spain declined from 29,273 metric tons to 16,785, and then to 10,324.[7] By the end of the 1880s

Table 3.1.
Estimated U.S. Investment in Cuba, 1896

Jurisdiction	Amount
Cienfuegos	$12,000,000
Matanzas	9,000,000
Sagua la Grande	9,229,000
Santiago de Cuba	15,000,000

Source: Richard Olney, "Report of the Secretary of
State," December 7, 1898, in U.S. Department of State,
Papers Relating to the Foreign Relations of the United States
(Washington, D.C., 1897), p. lxxxv.

it had become apparent that the United States was the only market
with the capacity to absorb Cuba's expanding production. These circumstances underscored the urgency of promoting close commercial
ties between the countries, with Cubans especially mindful of the
heightened importance of the North American market.

During these years, North American capital expanded into other
sectors of Cuban property and production. United States companies
operated the utilities in the principal Cuban cities. By the latter decades
of the nineteenth century, a North American printing firm was producing most of the currency used in Cuba. During the 1880s, Havana cigarette manufacturers reorganized production for automation around
U.S. machines. North American control over Cuban mineral resources
expanded. The Bethlehem Steel Corporation organized the Juraguá
Iron Company, Ltd., and the Ponupo Manganese Company, both near
Santiago. The Spanish American Iron Company (Pennsylvania Steel
Company) operated manganese and nickel mines near Daiquirí. The
Sigua Iron Company established control over mining activities near El
Caney. In one year, 1892, more than $875,000 worth of iron ore was
shipped to the United States from the port of Santiago de Cuba.

These developments were both products and portents of shifting

Table 3.2.
Value of Cuban Trade with the United States,
1885–1890

Year	Exports	Imports
1885	$42,306,000	$9,006,000
1886	51,110,000	10,409,000
1887	49,515,000	10,546,000
1888	49,319,000	10,053,000
1889	52,130,000	11,691,000
1890	53,801,000	13,084,000

Source: Susan Schroeder, *Cuba: A Handbook of Historical Statistics* (Boston, 1982), p. 432.

colonial relationships. In one decade, the Cuban economy revived with U.S. capital, came to rely on U.S. imports, and reorganized around U.S. markets. By the 1890s, North American investment in Cuba was calculated at the $50 million mark and in fact was probably far greater (see Table 3.1). During the late 1880s, trade between Cuba and the United States increased steadily (see Table 3.2). By the 1880s Cuba was functioning almost wholly within the North American economy. Nearly 94 percent of Cuba's total sugar production was exported to the United States. "*De facto*, Cuba is already inside the commercial union of the United States," commented U.S. Consul Ramon O. Williams in 1882. "The whole commercial machinery of Cuba depends upon the sugar market of the United States. . . . A large portion of the planters, merchants, bankers, and white working population in the Island, begin to perceive that if other countries . . . interpose themselves between Cuba and the sugar market of the United States, that the plantations, rail-roads, banks and all the other parts of Cuba's commercial machinery must stop." Increasingly, the greater share of Cuban exports were destined for and the bulk of its imports originated from the United States (see Table 3.3). Williams reported in 1886:

Table 3.3.
Value of Cuban Trade with the United States, 1893

Exports		Imports	
Sugar	$60,637,000	Lard	$4,023,000
Tobacco	8,940,000	Wheat flour	2,822,000
Cigars and cigarettes	2,766,000	Machinery	2,792,000
Fruits and nuts	2,378,000	Lumber	1,410,000
Honey	1,081,000	Ham and bacon	1,377,000
Iron ore	641,000	Corn	582,000
Hides	279,000	Potatoes	554,000

Source: U.S. Department of the Treasury, Foreign Commerce and Navigation of the United States (Washington, D.C., 1893), pp. 557–560.

The Island is now entirely dependent upon the market of the United States, in which to sell its sugar cane products; also that the existence of the sugar plantations, the railroads used in transporting the products of the plantations in the shipping ports of the island, the export and import trades of Cuba based thereon, each including hundreds of minor industries, such as the agricultural and mechanical trades, storehouses, wharves, lighters, stevedores, brokers, clerks and bankers, real estate owners, and shop-keepers of all kinds, and holders of the public debt, are now all directly related to the market of the United States to the extent of 94 percent for their employment.[8]

Trade ties were strengthened further in 1891, when Spain and the United States negotiated the Foster-Cánovas agreement giving Cuba preferential access to U.S. markets in exchange for Spanish tariff concessions to North American imports. The effects were as dramatic as they were far-reaching. Sugar production expanded spectacularly. From some 632,000 tons in 1890, sugar production approached 976,000 tons in 1892, reaching for the first time the 1-million-ton mark in 1894.

The 1891 agreement further stimulated North American investment in Cuban sugar production. A new round of U.S. expansion in the Cuban economy began soon thereafter. In 1892, the American Refining Company obtained the Trinidad Sugar Company. A year later, a group of New York sugar merchants organized the Tuinucú Cane Sugar Company and established operations in Sancti Spíritus. Also in 1893, and in Sancti Spíritus, a group of New Jersey investors acquired control of the three-thousand-acre Mapos estate. By far the most spectacular acquisition during these years was registered in 1893, when a New York firm headed by Benjamin Perkins and Osgood Walsh obtained control of the Constancia estate in Cienfuegos. The sixty-thousand-acre Constancia plantation was the largest sugar property in the world.

Trade statistics underscored the dimensions of Cuba's economic ties to the United States. In one decade, the Cuban economy had taken a giant stride toward deepening its dependence on the capital, imports, and markets of the United States.

These were indeed good years in Cuba. Pressure on the cost of living eased as the reduction of duties lowered prices on foreign imports. The sugar system, in a central and strategic relationship to all other sectors of trade and commerce, prospered and expanded, and with it the entire economy.

III

Even as the predominant sugar interests of the island acted to integrate the Cuban economy further into the North American system, developments elsewhere and of other types were fostering ties no less binding. In different ways, but for similar reasons, other sectors of the Cuban economy also developed vital linkages to the United States, and none more than tobacco manufacturers. During much of the early nineteenth century, cigar producers in Cuba had enjoyed almost uninterrupted expansion into the U.S. market. Indeed, by midcentury, North Americans were among the most important customers of the coveted Havanas.

Table 3.4.
Cuban Cigar Exports, 1889–1891
(in number of cigars)

Year	Total cigar exports	Cigar exports to the United States
1889	250,467,000	101,698,560
1890	211,823,000	95,105,760
1891	196,644,000	52,115,600

Source: *Diario de la Marina*, August 16, 1892.

This situation changed after the 1850s. First, the Panic of 1857 in the United States created pressure for protection and eventually led to higher customs duties on foreign manufactures, including cigars. During the U.S. Civil War, a new round of tariff increases raised duties on Cuban cigars almost 45 percent. The effects were immediate: Cuban cigar exports declined by nearly one-third.[9]

North American protectionism precipitated a major reorganization of the Cuban cigar industry. Several resourceful manufacturers, seeking to penetrate the North American tariff wall, relocated their factories in the United States, first in Key West during the late 1860s and then in Tampa in the 1880s.

The U.S. tariff policy had devastating consequences in Cuba. Cigar exports declined further and faster. What had been one of Cuba's principal manufacturing activities, a major source of foreign exchange and domestic employment, was relocated outside the island and inside the tariff walls of its principal market. Once in the United States, manufacturers were able both to obtain tobacco leaf from Cuba cheaply enough and enjoy the benefits of protectionist duties levied on cigar imports from Cuba. Whereas Cuba had previously exported a manufactured product, the cigar, it was reduced to exporting the raw material, the leaf. Between 1846 and 1859, the number of cigar factories in Cuba declined by half, from a thousand to five hundred. Conditions worsened thereafter. In 1859, the value of cigar exports was twice that of leaf; by 1890, the total value of leaf was twice that of cigars.[10] The decline of cigar exports was striking (see Table 3.4).

The decline of the cigar industry during the worst days of the 1880s depression made a difficult situation almost impossible. The cigar industry had employed more than one hundred thousand workers in agriculture and manufacturing, half of whom were cigarmakers. As cigar exports decreased, more cigar factories closed. By the early 1890s, some thirty-five thousand cigarmakers were unemployed and the balance were reduced largely to part-time work.[11]

IV

Unsettled political conditions during the 1860s and 1870s and difficult economic times during the 1880s contributed to promoting the Cuba-U.S. connection in ways profound and permanent. There was perhaps no more dramatic sign of troubled times in Cuba than emigration, an exodus that assumed the proportions of a diaspora. Over the latter half of the nineteenth century, more than one hundred thousand men, women, and children, almost 10 percent of the population, took up residence abroad—in Europe, in Latin America, but especially and mostly in the United States.[12]

The unemployed and the unemployable, political dissidents, Cubans of all occupations and professions, of both sexes and all ages, from all classes and all races, resettled in the United States. This vast Cuban emigration influenced and was influenced in many ways by North Americans, their culture, their institutions, and their politics. Local economies in Florida were transformed as capital from Cuba assembled the material and human resources upon which the future growth of Key West and Tampa would depend. A symbiotic cycle was set in motion that was to endure well into the twentieth century. The Florida cigar factories expanded in numbers and production, and so did Cuban emigration; as the Florida cigar industry flourished, Havana production languished: the pattern was of prosperity and expansion in Florida, depression and contraction in Cuba. Factories closed in Havana and unemployment increased; emigration increased, new factories in Florida opened, and local Florida economies expanded. By the turn of the century, the total value of the cigar industry in Tampa had surpassed $17 million, employing a labor force of 10,500 workers, generating an average weekly wage of $200,000, approximately 75 percent of the total city payroll. The expansion of the cigarworkers' payroll created other opportunities. A tertiary service economy developed around the expanding cigarworkers' community: barbershops, cafés and restaurants, retailers, and artisans. The population of Key West increased from twenty-eight hundred to eighteen thousand. Tampa grew from two thousand to twenty-three thousand.[13]

At the same time, thousands of Cubans were settling along the Atlantic seaboard in Boston, New York, Philadelphia, Wilmington, and Baltimore. In part, this was a continuation of the Creole migration that began earlier in the nineteenth century. Planters, merchants, and businessmen traveled freely and frequently between Cuba and the United States, maintaining dual citizenship and dual residences. "There is something strangely cosmopolitan in many of the Cuban families," observed Richard Dana during his travels through Cuba, "where are found French origin, Spanish and American intermarriage, education in Europe or the United States, home and property in Cuba, friendships and sympathies and half a residence in Boston or New York or Charleston, and three languages at command."[14] Creole elites migrated northward during the summer months to vacation in Saratoga Springs, Sharon Springs, and Niagara Falls. They traveled to the United States to obtain medical attention, to shop, to vacation, to study. Increasingly, too, they developed business interests and acquired property in the United States. Fearful of political turmoil and haunted by the specter of race war and social chaos at home, Cuban elites in increasing numbers took to investing abroad. The Diago family, Juan Pedro Baró, Carlos Drake, and the Iznaga family, among others, owned portfolios thick with North American stocks, securities, and bonds. By 1880 planter Tomás Terry had amassed a fortune valued at $13.7 million, of which $9.3 million was invested in the United States and distributed in such varied enterprises as the Morris & Essex Railroad Company, Jersey City Water Works, Central Pacific Railroad, Forest Improvement Company, Pennsylvania Coal Company, and U.S. government securities. By 1895, an estimated $25 million from Cuba was on deposit in U.S. banks. [15]

North American educational institutions continued to attract the children of Creole elites. Education in Cuba continued to suffer from chronic neglect. Only 10 percent of the 357,000 children under ten years of age attended school. Secondary and higher educational facilities were all but ignored. The city of Pinar del Río, with a population of thirty thousand, a flourishing commercial center surrounded by rich tobacco *vegas*, had but one school with a total enrollment of forty boys. Creole elites lacked adequate educational facilities for their children and continued to send their children abroad to complete their education. Colonial authorities were mindful of the implications but lacked either the resources or the resolve to make any changes. As early as 1853, Governor General José G. de la Concha warned that "many families have sent and continue sending [their children] to foreign schools, and especially to those in the neighboring American Union, and with grave damage to ties of family and nationality, and with no less harm to the country to which they generally return with new habits, ideas, and dangerous affectations." The absence of adequate educational facilities, de la Concha stressed, was forcing Cubans to emigrate "to receive abroad an education inconsistent with the sentiments of nationality and devoted to the formation of men for societies governed by institutions completely different from those of his country." "Almost all of the new generation," observed traveler Nicolás Tanco Armero in 1861, "go to the land of Washington, and there take in new customs that they are unable to abandon upon their return to the island." Traveling through Cuba decades later, Maturin M. Ballou arrived at substantially the same conclusion: "No matter in what political faith these youths had left home, they were sure to return republicans." [16]

In the United States, Cubans found an array of educational institutions to meet their needs. Many Cuban children were educated in private primary and secondary institutions. Traditional families enrolled their children in Catholic institutions in Baltimore. The upwardly mobile petit bourgeoisie enrolled their sons in business and commercial schools in New York. Still more Cubans completed their educations in traditional colleges and professional schools in the United States. Others opened private schools in the United States, providing primary, secondary, and professional programs for the children of their compatriots.

The enrollment of Cubans in North American institutions was only in part the result of inadequate public instruction on the island. Education abroad was also possessed of an internal logic of its own. It served to affirm status and proclaim privilege, and elites and would-be elites alike understood its social value. Education outside Cuba, and particularly in the United States, reflected prevailing bourgeois ideology. For those members of the Creole elites who envisaged close relations with the United States, enrolling their children in U.S. schools was a way to prepare for and promote a North American future for Cuba. Some of Cuba's most passionate advocates of annexation included men who had been educated in the United States—Francisco de Frías (Count of Pozos Dulces) was educated in Baltimore, and Gaspar Betancourt Cisneros and Ricardo del Monte attended school in Philadelphia. Sailing from New York to Cuba in 1873 L. de Hegermann-Lindencrone met one of the Iznaga sons, "who has just come from Harvard College . . . and was now returning to his native land to help his father on the plantation."[17]

The Cuban expatriate community in the United States also included growing numbers of the Creole petite bourgeoisie, Cubans forced to emigrate as a result of economic dislocation and unemployment. Countless numbers of Cuban professionals, including attorneys, physicians, journalists, teachers, pharmacists, engineers, educators, and writers, emigrated to the United States. They were distressed over the economic circumstances that forced their expulsion abroad but resented more the political conditions that perpetuated their exclusion at home. An export economy, based traditionally on slave labor, and in which trade and commerce were controlled by *peninsulares*, continued to be incapable of accommodating the needs of the growing Cuban middle class. Cuban workers and artisans, principally cigarmakers, arguably the most politically active sector of the Cuban proletariat, idled by the declining Havana cigar factories, were also well represented among the thousands forced to emigrate in search of work.

Vast numbers of Cubans, from all sectors of colonial society, came into close and prolonged contact with North American culture, institutions, and values. This community represented a cross section of Cuban society—the Creole petite bourgeoisie and bourgeoisie as well as the expanding ranks of the Cuban working class. Their experiences guaranteed that North American influences would penetrate Cuban society deeply and indelibly. Many Cubans were educated and trained by North Americans. Thousands acquired U.S. citizenship. Many abandoned Roman Catholicism, associated with Spanish rule, and became Methodists, Baptists, and Quakers. Many took North American spouses. Their children were often born and reared in the United States and received North American given names, although none perhaps as striking as Henry Lincoln de Zayas. In habits, tastes, preferences, and too many other ways perhaps to appreciate fully, with consequences impossible to measure, Cubans partook freely of North American culture. Included in this émigré population were future opinion makers and power brokers: presidents, vice-presidents, senators, and cabinet ministers; Cubans who were later to become newspaper publishers, ambassadors, professors, labor leaders, a future rector of the University of Havana, an archbishop of Havana, a Nobel prize nominee.[18]

That so many traveled so often between Cuba and the United States was still one more way by which North American influence was diffused and disseminated through the island. They returned to Cuba clothed in North American attire, with tastes for things North American. Many decorated their homes with North American furnishings. The houses of the *habaneros*, observed William Cullen Bryant as early as 1850, "are filled with rocking-chairs imported from the United States."[19] No self-respecting well-to-do Havana household was without the fashionable New York coupe. Many retained the services of North American governesses to teach their children English and provide them with the basis of a U.S. education.[20] Some came home as preachers and ministers of Protestant denominations and representatives of North American religious organizations. Itinerant missionaries ranged across the island, especially in the eastern provinces, spreading as much a cultural ethic as a religious message. A Presbyterian church and an Episcopal mission operated in Matanzas. A Baptist church was established in Havana under the direction of Reverend Alberto J. Díaz during the 1890s. Díaz had migrated to New York to recover from wounds suffered in the Ten Years' War. During his convalescence he joined the Baptist church and enrolled as a student for the ministry. Supported by the American Board of Missions in the United States, Díaz returned to Cuba and established a Baptist mission, described in 1897 as "the largest and most influential Protestant mission in Cuba, having preaching halls and schools in several parts of Havana and its suburbs."[21]

Progress arrived to Cuba in the form of North American technological advances great and small, innovations lasting and ephemeral, the newest and the latest. Cubans could not help but stand in awe at the prodigious accomplishments of North American material culture, many of which were already transforming the way Cubans were living in their own country. The Spanish-American Light and Power Company of New York illuminated the nights of Havana with gas light to the wonderment of *habaneros*. North Americans built the railroads that connected the cities and constructed the electrical rail systems within the cities. A North American firm obtained the telegraph concession in 1849, and between 1851 and 1862 the principal towns of the island were joined together. Modernity meant also that as early as 1867 a U.S. submarine cable company, the International Ocean Telegraph Company, linked Cuba first with the United States (Havana–New York and Havana–New Orleans), and not Spain, serving in still another fashion to foster and facilitate wider commercial and cultural contacts. Telephone service was inaugurated in 1889. Increasingly, too, Cubans became dependent upon the United States for news concerning market trends, price fluctuations, and trade developments. North American bicycles appeared on Havana streets in growing numbers. Iron arches manufactured in the United States boosted bridge construction. At about the same time, the Bessemer steel process reduced substantially the cost of railroad construction and encouraged a new round of rail expansion based on expanded U.S. imports. Havana hotels were transformed as electric lights and elevators of North American origins were introduced. The best horses in Cuba, for transportation and sport, for work and pleasure, were imported from the United States. Woven wire mattresses, postal lock-boxes, calendar clocks, cameras, and plated cookware were only some of a vast array of North American consumer goods that found widespread popularity and a ready market on the island.

North American influences found other expressions. By the 1870s, baseball had taken hold among Cubans. The sport was originally associated with the Creole elites, many of whom had taken up the game during their residence in the United States. They played among themselves and paid for their own uniforms and equipment. It spread into Cuba during the late 1870s and 1880s, largely brought back to the island by returning Creoles but also introduced by the crews of North American merchant vessels that docked in Cuban port cities. In December 1874 the first interprovincial competition was organized, and Havana defeated Matanzas. Four years later, the Cuban League of Professional Baseball was organized—the second professional baseball league in the Western Hemisphere, three years after the establishment of the National League in the United States. [22]

The Cuban attraction to baseball was not only for play and recreation, however. It also represented a cultural statement that had political implications. Cubans were turning their backs on bullfighting, the pastime of Spain, and embracing baseball, the sport of North Americans. It was seen as a gesture of enlightenment and above all modernity: a way to express growing Creole nonconformity with things Spanish. During the 1880s and 1890s, Cubans in Key West and

Tampa used baseball for another purpose: they organized into local leagues, and receipts collected at the gate were donated to the cause of Cuban independence.[23]

Through the latter half of the nineteenth century, as Cuban migration expanded throughout Mexico, Central America, and the Caribbean, Cubans themselves became transmitters of North American cultural forms. North American religious organizations found Protestant Cubans' bilingual skills especially useful in evangelical activity in Mexico and Central America. Cubans assumed positions with North American mercantile establishments and shipping firms with trade interests in Latin America. And wherever a Cuban expatriate community formed, baseball followed.

It would be difficult if not impossible to assess fully the impact of the myriad ways in which Cubans responded to North American society and how those responses influenced behaviors and attitudes in Cuba in later years. Cubans came to know the United States intimately. They understood its political culture. They participated in local politics, and in Florida many held state and local public office.[24] Cubans participated directly in the North American economy as investors, manufacturers, managers, and workers. These contacts, which often lasted for decades, could not but have affected the way Cubans came to perceive their own society and influenced their attitudes toward the United States.

But familiarity also created ambivalence. Certainly for many Cubans their experiences in the United States enhanced their admiration for things North American and confirmed the logic of close relations. Producers saw economic advantage, liberals admired the democratic institutions, and the upwardly mobile middle class looked upon North American material progress and the promise of its vast productive capabilities with awe and expectation.

But there were doubters and dissenters, Cubans for whom familiarity with the United States served to strengthen their resolve to pursue a separate nationality. Cubans of color suffered from racist policies and practices. Afro-Cuban labor organizers, including Guillermo Sorondo, Francisco Segura, and Martín Morúa Delgado, all residents in the United States, were only among the most prominent Cubans of color to embrace the most exalted visions of Cuban independence. Cigarworkers and labor leaders witnessed, and in some instances experienced firsthand, the heavy hand of North American antilabor activity. In Tampa and Key West, Cuban workers were subject to periodic abuse and mistreatment. The predominant Latin component of the local population could not change the central reality that Florida was, in the end, still the U.S. South. Antilabor attitudes fused with racial hostility and nativist sentiment and erupted periodically in Ku Klux Klan violence against Cuban communities. Midnight marches, cross burnings, and floggings made deep impressions on Cuban émigrés. "One of my earliest memories of Key West," recalled retired cigarworker Tomás Mayet seventy years later, "was a Ku Klux Klan march through our neighborhood, lighting the night with blazing torches, and sowing terror in the workers' households."[25]

Other doubts created growing skepticism among Cubans about the promise of North American culture. Many recoiled in horror at the violence of Haymarket and Homestead. Some were troubled by what they saw as excessive North American preoccupation with material culture. There were, to be sure, class correlates to this dichotomy, as indeed there would be class dimensions to the competing constructs of *Cuba Libre*. And no doubt, too, the varieties of Cuban experiences in the United States reinforced existing political tendencies. If this was the only result, however, it would not have been inconsiderable, for henceforth the course and character of the Cuban struggle for sovereignty and the ideal of a separate nationality were to be influenced decisively by the Cuban expatriate population residing in the United States.[26]

V

Political discontent was only one aspect of colonial disaffection. In 1894, Cubans had new but not unfamiliar problems, and again they involved the complicated issue of Cuba's economic relationship with the United States. In 1894, the United States rescinded its tariff concession to Cuban exports. By imposing a new duty of 40 percent ad valorem on all sugar entering the United States, the Wilson-Gorman Tariff Act dismantled the cornerstone of Foster-Cánovas reciprocal trade arrangements between Washington and Madrid. Spanish authorities responded swiftly and in kind by canceling duty concessions to North American imports. A full-fledged trade war seemed imminent and inevitable.

The sudden disengagement of Cuba from its prosperous but brief and privileged participation in the U.S. market had jolting consequences for the island. Cuba lost preferential access to the only market with the capacity to absorb its expanding sugar production and insulate the island from the uncertainties of world competition. The restoration of Spanish tariffs, further, raised the specter that the United States would retaliate by banning Cuban sugar from North American markets.

Profits declined immediately. Production dropped. Sugar exports valued at $64 million in 1893 plummeted to $45 million in 1895 and $13 million a year later. The 1-million-ton sugar harvest of 1894 collapsed to 225,000 tons in 1896. No less daunting to sugar producers, they also faced after 1894 the grim prospect of losing preferential access to the equipment, machines, and spare parts around which the sugar industry had reorganized after midcentury. New duties on North American materials after mid-1894 raised the prices of all imports. The loss of preferential access to the U.S. market, moreover, occurred simultaneously with a sudden drop in world sugar prices. For the first time in the history of Cuban sugar production, the price of sugar dropped below two cents a pound.

The impact of the crisis of 1894, however, went far beyond the sugar system. No facet of Cuban society was unaffected. Merchants, traders, and retailers who had replaced their traditional commercial ties with suppliers in Spain for dealers in the United States faced ruin. Unemployment rose, the supply of commodity goods decreased, prices increased. The prices for foodstuffs imported from the United States, upon which large sectors of the population depended, soared.

Table 3.5.
Prices for Selected Foods Imported from the United States,
1893–1895 (in 100 kilos)

Food	1893–1894	1894–1895
Wheat	$ .30	$3.95
Flour	1.00	4.75
Corn	.25	3.95
Meal	.25	4.75

Source: Ramon O. Williams to Edwin F. Uhl, January 5,
1895, Despatches from U.S. Consuls in Havana, 1783–
1906, General Records of the Department of State, Record
Group 59, National Archives, Washington, D.C.

Government duties were passed directly on to consumers, and prices
reached unprecedented heights. Higher duties led to increased prices.
The restoration of colonial custom duties meant that all Cubans would
henceforth pay higher prices for vital food imports (see Table 3.5). As
costs increased, higher-priced goods became scarce. North American
imports dropped, and shipping declined. By October 1894 half the
U.S. steamers serving Santiago had been withdrawn from service. [27]

The implications of the events of late 1894 were apparent to all
Cubans. The passage of a decade had not dimmed Cuban memories
of the economic crisis of the 1880s. A unanimous outcry of indignation and protest against Spain rose across the island. "The worst of all
is that we have to go against our Government and take sides with the
yankees," *La Lucha* complained. "We need, in effect, American flour
entering Cuba under reasonable conditions and Cuban sugar entering
American ports under similar conditions. . . . It is out of order for
us to be the ones to launch a tariff war, for our sugar has no market
other than the United States. Every one of our tariff measures should
have the dual purpose of facilitating the entrance of American goods
into our ports and doing nothing to encourage our neighbor from
impeding the importation of our sugar." [28]

Frustrated by their inability to influence policy decisions in Madrid, planters, merchants, and businessmen in Cuba sought to enlist U.S. assistance. Cubans appealed directly if only privately to North Americans to intercede with Spanish authorities in Washington on their behalf. United States consular agents in Cuba were approached by planters soliciting Washington's support in their struggle against Spanish colonial policy. Cubans "are slowly accustoming themselves to think that their capital is not at Madrid but at Washington," *La Lucha* discerned perceptively. "And once such a belief takes hold, the effects of such a shortsighted [tariff] policy will be such that appeals to patriotism will no longer be able to alter the course of events."[29]

Once again the question of Cuba's status and the nature of its relationship with Spain became topics of political debate and public discussion. An enormous sense of uncertainty and uneasiness settled over the island. "The residents and commercial interests here," the U.S. consul in Santiago reported, "are protesting loud and strong against being thus summarily cut off from their natural commercial allies, and this action on the part of the home government adds greatly to the feeling of unrest that pervades all classes."[30] Prosperity required the expansion of trade, which required the reduction of Spanish control over the Cuban economy. The brief cycle of prosperity resulting from close economic ties with the United States made the prospect of returning to the regimen of Spanish exclusivity as inconceivable as it was inadmissible.

There was an element of familiarity to these events, and Cubans were growing weary of it. "Here we are tired of protesting against the exorbitant levies used to keep yankee goods out of Cuba," *La Lucha* lamented in Havana. "In vain, too, have been our efforts against the imposition of prohibitive duties on American goods. We have not been heard in Madrid; because we are miserable and long-suffering colonists, our clamors are undeserving of the attention of those who govern and misgovern."[31]

VI

Among the Cuban émigré communities the idea of *Cuba Libre* persisted, was reborn, and eventually transformed into an ideal of immense popular appeal. For decades, *Cuba Libre* had remained an essentially undefined and wholly ambiguous formulation. Most agreed that free Cuba meant separation from Spain. In the 1880s, largely through the efforts of José Martí, *Cuba Libre* came to mean something more. Martí was himself an émigré, having fled from Spanish authorities to New York in 1880. There he quickly distinguished himself as an outstanding orator and gifted writer, and by the mid-1880s he had attracted considerable support from the expatriate population.

Martí was an indefatigable political activist. He understood the necessity of organization and in particular the need to establish a revolutionary party to give *Cuba Libre* ideological substance and institutional structure. The party would act to unify all sectors of the separatist polity along democratic lines, in and out of Cuba, and develop the political, social, and economic principles upon which to base the revolution. Martí worked initially with the Cuban émigré community in New York but soon found it hostile to his plan to organize a broad-based, democratic, revolutionary party. The proposition of a political party, however, found widespread support among the cigarworker communities in Florida. Martí's organizing activity subsequently centered on the émigré proletariat in Florida and culminated in 1892 with the formal establishment of the Cuban Revolutionary party (PRC) in Tampa. The central goal of the PRC, Martí proclaimed, was to promote "common revolutionary action" to liberate Cuba and organize all Cubans for war. The PRC pledged its commitment to armed struggle by uniting Cubans in exile with patriots on the island for the common purpose of waging a war for independence and providing moral and material support in exile for the revolution in Cuba. [32]

These developments changed permanently the character of *Cuba Libre*. Collaboration with the émigré cigarworkers broadened the social base of the separatist movement and expanded the social content of separatist ideology. Martí denounced racism and committed *Cuba*

Libre to racial justice. He supported women's political participation and personally encouraged the organization of women's revolutionary clubs. He censured privilege and condemned the concentration of wealth and property. But above all, Martí was passionate and uncompromising in defining the goal of Cuban arms: independence, full and complete sovereignty, from both Spain and the United States. After nearly fifteen years of residence in the United States, Martí realized that the North Americans represented the greatest threat to Cuban independence. Increasingly, annexation was the eventuality that Martí feared most. For the last decade of his life, Martí was as active an opponent of annexation to the United States as he was an advocate of independence from Spain.

Martí's experiences in the United States, especially his views on the relationship of Cuba to the United States, contributed to shaping separatist ideology. His experience strengthened his resolve to resist Cuba's absorption by the United States. Profoundly dismayed by Haymarket, he wrote a passionate indictment of North American capitalism:

> The worker thinks he has a right to certain security for the future, to a certain well-being . . . to feed without anxiety the children that he raises, to a more equitable part in the products of labor in which he is an indispensable factor, to some time in the sun in which to help his wife sow a rose-tree in the patio of the house, to some corner to live that is not a fetid tenement where, as in cities like New York, one cannot enter without feeling sick. . . . And each time the workers in Chicago asked for this in some form, the capitalists join together and punished them by denying them the work which for them is meat, hearth, and light. They set the police on them, always willing to use their clubs on the heads of the people shabbily dressed. On occasion the police killed a bold person who resisted them with stones, or some child. They reduced them in the end to returning sullenly to work because they were hungry, with their wretchedness inflamed, their dignity offended, considering vengeance. [33]

Martí understood the political implications of dependent economic relations such as those that had come to characterize Cuban-U.S. trade during the 1890s. "Economic union means political union," Martí warned in 1891. "The nation that buys, commands. The nation that sells, serves. It is necessary to distribute commerce in order to guarantee liberty. The nation that wishes to die, sells to only one nation, and the one that wishes salvation, sells to more than one. The excessive influence of one country in the commerce of another is converted to political influence." Martí concluded: "The first step taken by a nation to dominate another is to separate it from other nations."[34]

Martí was also critical of North American culture. "The North had been unjust and greedy," he wrote in 1893:

> It has thought more about assuring the fortune of a few than about creating a nation for the good of all; it has brought to the new American land all the hatreds and all the problems of the old monarchies. . . . In the North the problems are becoming worse, and the charity and patriotism which could solve them do not exist. Here men do not learn to love one another, and neither do they love the soil where they were born, and where they toil tirelessly in brute struggle and exhausted by their efforts to exist. Here a hungry machine has been constructed that can satisfy the universe saturated with products. Here the land has been badly distributed; and the unequal and monstrous production, and the inertia of monopolized land, leave the country without the safeguard of shared harvests, which feed a nation even if they do not make a profit from it. The North is closing itself off and is full of hatreds. We must start leaving the North.[35]

Martí also wrote of the "North where we came to live out of fantasy and imprudence, and through deception arising from taking people at their word." He characterized the United States as a culture that had "no bond other than that of interests," surrounded by "sordidness and bestiality," a society made up of a "mass of beings without means of support who divide, and flee, at the moment when the community of profit does not bind them together." Only a day before his death in Cuba in May 1895, he reaffirmed his dedication to the defense of Cuban independence from the United States: "What I have done up to now, and shall do, is to . . . block with our blood . . . the annexation of the peoples of America to the turbulent and brutal North that despises them. . . . I lived in the monster, and know its entrails:—and my sling is that of David's."[36]

The extent to which Martí was influenced by his years of residence in the United States is, of course, a matter of conjecture, but the experience must have played an important part in his intellectual development. Not all of what Martí observed of North American society, of course, repelled him. There was much about life in the United States that he admired, and he often wrote of North Americans with esteem and affection, especially during his early years of exile in New York. But he was also aware of the class tensions and racial antagonisms of North American society and understood their implications for Cuba. Union with the United States, Martí wrote, "would be death for me and our country."[37]

At the time of Martí's death in 1895, *Cuba Libre* had come to signify more than separation from Spain. It had expanded into a social movement of enormous appeal. By the 1890s, dissatisfaction with colonialism had become as much a dispute between Cubans themselves as between Cubans and Spaniards. Inequity in Cuba by the 1890s had a peculiarly home-grown quality. That the sources of oppression in Cuba were more internal than external, more social than political, served as the central premises around which armed separatism took definitive shape during the 1880s and 1890s. Cubans continued to speak of independence, but now they spoke of war as a method of redemption and a means of social revolution. A new constituency had formed around *Cuba Libre:* the politically displaced, the socially dispossessed, the economically destitute—Cubans for whom armed struggle offered the means to redress historic grievances against the colonial regime and its local defenders. Martí mobilized support from those sectors of Cuban society most susceptible to appeals for a new order: the dispossessed and the poor, both black and white. He transformed rebellion into revolution, subsuming a social imperative into the struggle for national liberation, thereby transfiguring the very character of separatism.

Armed struggle was a means of redemption and redistribution. Martí fashioned *Cuba Libre* into a movement committed not only to free Cubans from the old oppression but to give them a new place in society. The new Cuba, shorn of its economic debilities and social inequities, would bring forth a new society.

Two obstacles stood in the way of independence: *peninsulares* and planters. There was also a third: the United States. So profoundly did the new formulation of *Cuba Libre* challenge the system of colonialism, both at its external source and in its internal effects, and so unyieldingly did it proclaim the primacy of Cuban interests, that it placed separatists squarely on a collision course with the United States. The *independentista* formula was simple: Cuba for Cubans—the one eventuality which nearly one hundred years of North American policy had been dedicated to preventing.

4   Intervention and Occupation

The new separatist war began in February 1895, in much the same fashion as others before it, with localized skirmishes, mostly in remote mountain folds of eastern Cuba, initially too distant to cause planters and politicians in western Cuba much concern. Rebellion in eastern Cuba was not uncommon, and no one in power or with property had any reason to believe that the "Grito de Baire" of February 24 would end in any way other than its countless predecessors: a matter of no consequence.

But in early summer matters assumed a sudden gravity, and what began as a local affair became national. The insurgent armies marched out of the eastern mountains into the rich cattle-grazing ranges of Camagüey in the summer, through the fertile sugar land of Matanzas and Havana in the autumn, and into the lush tobacco fields of Pinar del Río by winter. In the course of ten months, the insurrection had reached regions never before disturbed by the armed stirrings of nationality. The presence of separatist armies in the west, coincident with preparations for the 1896 sugar harvest, stunned local elites, *peninsular* and Creole alike. Prospects for the harvest were bleak, and when it was completed, even the pessimists were shown to have been overconfident: from a record 1-million-ton crop in 1894 the harvest fell to 225,000 tons in 1896. Not since the 1840s had Cuban sugar production been so low. And in 1897 it dropped again, to 212,000 tons.

Indeed, the purpose of the uprising was to disrupt the sugar economy. As early as July 1895, insurgent General Máximo Gómez proclaimed a moratorium on all economic activity—commerce, manufacturing, agriculture, ranching, but most of all and especially sugar production. There was to be no planting, no harvesting, no grinding, no marketing. Any estate found in violation of the ban, Gómez vowed, would be destroyed and its owner tried for treason. "All sugar plantations will be destroyed, the standing cane set fire and the factory buildings and railroads destroyed," the decree warned. "Any worker assisting the operation of the sugar factories will be considered an enemy of his country . . . and will be executed."[1]

The attack against property set the stage for the redistribution of property as a design for peace and gave decisive expression to the social content of *Cuba Libre*. The insurgent leadership committed itself to a nation of small landowners, each farmer to enjoy security derived from direct and independent ownership of land. In 1896 the insurgent army command issued an expropriation decree, pledging at the end of the war to redistribute among defenders of *Cuba Libre* all properties belonging to *peninsulares* and Creoles who supported Spanish rule. The war thus provided more than the opportunity to end colonial rule: it created the occasion to destroy one social class to benefit another.

II

Creole elites held few illusions after 1896. For decades local property owners had clung to the colonial regime for protection, and now in the waning years of the nineteenth century, Spain was at the verge of defaulting on the sole raison d'être for its existence in Cuba. Members of the beleaguered bourgeoisie contemplated their impending extinction with despair. Growing more certain in their conviction that Spain's hold over Cuba was slipping, they were now prepared to sacrifice traditional colonial relationships for an alternative source of protection and patronage. They confronted what they had feared most through the nineteenth century—a successful uprising of the underclasses— and they needed assistance quickly.

Only U.S. intervention, many concluded, might end the insurrectionary challenge and redeem the beleaguered social order. As early as June 1896, nearly one hundred planters, lawyers, and industrialists petitioned President Grover Cleveland for North American intervention to end the crisis. "We cannot," the petitioners wrote, "express our opinion openly and formally, for he who should dare, whilst living in Cuba, to protest against Spain, would, undoubtedly, be made a victim, both in his person and his property, to the most ferocious persecution at the hands of the government." Spain, the petition continued, could offer Cuba nothing for the future except continued destruction and ruin. Nor did property owners find comfort in the thought of independence. If continued Spanish rule threatened to re- sult in ruin, independence promised to lead to havoc. "Can there be no intermediate solution?" the petitioners asked. Without confidence in Spain, and uncertain about the future under Cuban rule, property owners asked Washington to intercede in their behalf: "We would ask that the party responsible to us should be the United States. In them we have confidence, and in them only."[2] "The worst thing that could happen to Cuba," another planter wrote a year later, "would be independence." Cubans, he added, "cannot bring a firm and stable government to the island."[3] In early 1897, a U.S. correspondent in Havana reported that planters, merchants, and businessmen had con- cluded that Cuba was lost to Spain and hoped for U.S. intervention and, ultimately, annexation of the island.[4] Later that year, William H. Calhoun, a special agent in Cuba, commented that "Cuban planters and Spanish property holders are now satisfied that the island must soon slip from Spain's grasp, and would welcome immediate Ameri- can intervention."[5]

III

From the outset of the war, the Cleveland administration upheld the government's long-standing policy toward Cuba: opposition to in- dependence and support of Spanish sovereignty. The reasons were familiar: Cuban independence would result in political instability, social conflict, and economic chaos. That Afro-Cubans in such num- bers and with such prominence filled insurgent ranks and that arms had been distributed so widely to the population at large were further reasons to fear the end of Spanish rule in Cuba. Even the "most de- voted friend of Cuba" and the "most enthusiastic advocate of popular government," Secretary of State Richard B. Olney insisted, could not look at developments in Cuba "except with the gravest apprehension":

> There are only too strong reasons to fear that, once Spain were withdrawn from the island, the sole bond of union between the different factions of the insurgents would disappear; that a war of races would be precipitated, all the more sanguinary for the discipline and experience acquired during the insurrection, and that, even if there were to be temporary peace, it could only be through the establishment of a white and black republic, which, even if agreeing at the outset upon a division of the island between them, would be enemies from the start, and would never rest until the one had been completely vanquished and subdued by the other. [6]

The United States quickly proclaimed its support of Spanish sovereignty. As early as 1895 Cleveland demanded adherence to U.S. neutrality laws and vigorously pursued their enforcement. Washington also cooperated with Spain to combat Cuban filibustering expeditions organized from the United States. Between 1895 and 1896, North American authorities intercepted more than half the Cuban expeditions fitted in the United States and vigorously prosecuted offenders. Only one-third of the seventy expeditions organized in the United States during the war reached Cuba. [7]

But the United States was also certain that Spanish military efforts to end the insurgency—even if Madrid possessed the means, and especially because it did not—were doomed to failure. "While the insurrectionary forces to be dealt with are more formidable than ever before," Secretary of State Olney wrote in September 1895, "the ability of Spain to cope with them has visibly and greatly decreased. She is straining every nerve to stamp out the insurrection within the next few months. For what obvious reason? Because she is almost at the end of her resources." Olney concluded: "Spain cannot possibly succeed." [8]

The expansion of the insurgency westward confirmed North Americans' worst fears. "It can hardly be questioned," Olney explained to Spanish Minister Enrique Dupuy de Lôme in April 1896, "that the insurrection, instead of being quelled, is today more formidable than ever and enters upon the second year of its existence with decidedly improved prospects of success."[9] Only a political solution, Washington insisted, based on reforms and including autonomy in some form, held any promise of ending the insurrection with Spanish sovereignty intact. The United States advocated reform as a means to end the revolution and supported autonomy as an alternative to independence. "It would seem," Cleveland predicted in 1896, "that if Spain should offer to Cuba genuine autonomy—a measure of home rule which, while preserving the sovereignty of Spain, would satisfy all rational requirements of her Spanish subjects—there should be no just reason why the pacification of the island might not be effected on that basis."[10] The administration offered the good offices of the United States to mediate a settlement based on reform. "What the United States desires to do," Olney assured the Spanish minister, "is to cooperate with Spain in the immediate pacification of the island on such a plan as, leaving Spain her rights of sovereignty . . . shall yet secure to the people of the island all such rights and powers of local self-government as they can reasonably ask."[11]

But Spain was confident that repression, not reform, was the way to settle Cuban disorders. Speaking for the Spanish court, the Duke of Tetuán rejected Washington's offer, arguing that the island already enjoyed "one of the most liberal political systems in the world." An end to the Cuban rebellion based on anything other than a triumph of Spanish arms, Tetuán suggested, would doom all future efforts to establish peace on a long-standing basis and condemn the island to a recurring cycle of periodic uprisings. Moreover, Tetuán added tersely, if conditions in the future warranted the introduction of new reforms, Spain was fully capable of meeting its responsibilities without assistance from the United States.[12]

IV

Certainly not all North Americans shared the opinion of the administration. On the contrary, the cause of *Cuba Libre* found widespread support in the United States. Not a few North Americans, like Frederick Funston, rushed to volunteer their services to the insurgent forces in Cuba. Many more participated in fund-raising activities and lobbying efforts in the United States. The cause of *Cuba Libre* also found widespread support in Congress, and very early the course for collision was set between the legislature and the executive.

In 1897 a new Republican administration in Washington under William McKinley pressed colonial reforms with new vigor and a new Liberal ministry in Madrid under Praxedes Mateo Sagasta ceased to oppose reforms, both for the same reason: to prolong Spanish sovereignty. The war had stalled into a campaign of attrition that Spain could not win. The Spanish army was on the defensive and confined to the principal cities; the Cuban army was on the offensive and controlled the countryside. The economies of both Cuba and Spain were approaching collapse.

In the autumn of 1897, in part because of U.S. pressure, in part as a response to deteriorating conditions in Cuba, the new Liberal ministry undertook a series of far-reaching reforms. In October, Madrid appointed moderate Ramón Blanco as governor general. Amnesty was issued and political prisoners were released. In December, Spain announced a new Autonomist constitution and on January 1, 1898, installed a liberal Creole government.

Colonial reforms had the net effect of sealing the doom of Spanish rule in Cuba. Indeed, had the United States been deliberately seeking to dislodge Spain from the island, it could not have come upon better means. For the defenders of *Cuba Española* reforms assumed the proportions of treason. Loyalists denounced the establishment of a Creole autonomist government, insisting that reforms served only to open the back door to power for Cuban subversives. Radicals would quickly overrun moderates, revolution would overtake reform, and autonomy would become independence.

That resident Spaniards lost exclusive control over colonial administration was cause enough to arouse *peninsular* ire and indignation. It mattered little that autonomists were politically moderate, often men of means, and ideologically allied to Spain. The Creole-*peninsu-*

lar schism persisted unabated to the very end of the colonial regime. *Peninsulares* now became advocates of North American intervention, preferring rule by the United States to government by Cubans. "All classes of the Spanish citizens," U.S. Consul Fitzhugh Lee reported in late 1897, "are violently opposed to real or genuine autonomy because it would throw the control of the island into the hands of the Cubans and rather than that, they would prefer annexation to the United States or some form of an American protectorate." [13]

But it was not only a question of nationality. The establishment of a liberal government convinced loyalists, *peninsulares* and Creoles alike, that Spain had lost the will to defend its sovereignty in Cuba. Many detected in this changed attitude evidence that Spain was preparing to abandon the island. The more thoughtful among *peninsulares* and Creoles understood, too, that the new autonomist government lacked the means to wage war and was without authority to make peace. The establishment of a government of Creole moderates dealt the final body blows to conservative resolve in Cuba. Events in late 1897 and early 1898 undermined the morale of the only forces in Cuba who, except for the insurgents, still retained the loyalty and will to win.

Certain now that Spain no longer controlled events at home or abroad, convinced that Madrid possessed neither the means nor— after 1897—the will to defend the status quo, local elites acted to shed a metropolis incapable of protecting their interests. Loyalists found themselves caught between the ebbing of metropolitan authority and the advancing tide of colonial rebellion. Political separation from Spain became necessary to forestall independence under Cubans.

Rallies and mass meetings across the island denounced the new autonomist government. Appeals for U.S. intervention increased. In November 1897, the U.S. vice-consul in Matanzas reported that "nearly all Spaniards, businessmen, and property holders in this province wish and pray for annexation to the United States." [14] "Property holders, without distinction of nationality, and with but few exceptions," Consul Pulaski F. Hyatt cabled from Santiago, "strongly desire annexation, having but little hope of a stable government under either of the contending forces."[15] Fitzhugh Lee reported similar sentiments in Havana. "A large majority of the Spanish subjects," he wrote in November 1897, "who have commercial and business interests and own property here will not accept Autonomy, but prefer annexation to the United States, rather than an independent republic or genuine autonomy under the Spanish flag."[16]

By the end of the year sentiment for U.S. intervention had become public. In December 1897, a statement published in Havana and signed by businessmen and property owners claiming to represent 80 percent of the island's wealth denounced the autonomist regime.[17] In the same month, a meeting of property owners in Cienfuegos concluded with a resolution urging President McKinley to establish a protectorate over Cuba. In February 1898, leading *peninsulares* established a formal commission for the purpose of securing North American assistance. "The Mother country cannot protect us," one spokesman insisted. "Blanco will not protect us. If left to the insurgents our property is lost. Therefore, we want the United States to save us."[18]

V

Reforms that were excessive for loyalists were not enough for separatists. Insurgent Cubans denounced autonomy and rejected accommodation with Spain based on anything less than complete independence. "It is the firm resolution of the army and people of Cuba," vowed General Máximo Gómez, "who have shed so much blood in order to conquer their independence, not to falter in their just cause until triumph or death crowns their efforts."[19] Two weeks later, Gómez reiterated the Cuban position: "We no longer ask concessions. . . . Even were Spain's proposals bona fide, nothing could tempt us to treat with her. We are for liberty, not for Spanish reforms."[20]

Rather than making Cubans more conciliatory, reforms actually made them more intransigent. Separatist morale soared. Spanish concessions were evidence of Spain's impending defeat, Cubans were certain. "Spain's offer of autonomy is a sign of her weakening," Provisional President Bartolomé Masó proclaimed.[21] General Calixto García agreed: "I regard autonomy only as a sign of Spain's weakening power and an indication that the end is not far off."[22]

Reforms had failed. As a last resort, Spain had made the ultimate concession to empire and found it wanting. Spanish sovereignty over Cuba was coming to an end. Cubans now prepared for the final campaign. A new optimism lifted insurgent morale to an all-time high. Never before had separatists been so certain of triumph as they were in early 1898. Preparations for the last desperate battles began. In eastern Cuba General Calixto García prepared to lay siege to Santiago. In the western zones, insurgent commanders began to encircle the larger inland provincial cities. Máximo Gómez now wrote confidently about preparations for the final assault against Spanish strongholds. With "cannons and a great deal of dynamite," Gómez predicted, "we can expel them by fire and steel from the towns."[23]

The United States also understood that the failure of reforms ended any reasonable likelihood that Madrid would reestablish sovereignty over the island. Cuba was lost to Spain. Cuban successes had all but nullified Spanish claims to sovereignty and thus neutralized North American efforts to underwrite that sovereignty. "Spain will lose Cuba," Secretary of State John Sherman concluded bluntly. "That seems to me to be certain. She cannot continue the struggle."[24] Assistant Secretary of State William R. Day concurred. "The Spanish Government," he wrote in March, "seems unable to conquer the insurgents."[25] In a confidential memorandum, Day went further:

> To-day the strength of the Cubans [is] nearly double . . . and [they] occupy and control virtually all the territory outside the heavily garrisoned coast cities and a few interior towns. There are no active operations by the Spaniards. . . . The eastern provinces are admittedly "Free Cuba." In view of these statements alone, it is now evident that Spain's struggle in Cuba has become absolutely hopeless. . . . Spain is exhausted financially and physically, while the Cubans are stronger.[26]

Against the landscape created by the receding tide of Spanish sovereignty, Washington confronted in Cuba the anathema of all U.S. policy makers since Jefferson—the specter of Cuban independence. The implications of the "no transfer" policy were now carried to the logical conclusion. If the United States could not permit Spain to transfer sovereignty over Cuba to another power, neither could it permit Spain to cede sovereignty to Cubans.

VI

The lapse of Spanish sovereignty in 1898 released the United States from any further obligations to Spain. But if Spanish sovereignty was untenable, Cuban pretensions to sovereignty were unacceptable. Washington now applied pressure on Madrid to settle the status of Cuba politically with the United States before Cubans settled it militarily with Spain. A sudden urgency now drove the North American purpose. A settlement had to be reached before summer, the onset of the rainy season, when Cuban military operations would intensify. The summer of 1898, everyone sensed, would be decisive. Cubans were preparing for the final offensive, and no one doubted that they would succeed.

Efforts to negotiate a settlement with Spain were based on a transfer of the island to the United States. In January President McKinley appointed Whitelaw Reid to undertake private negotiations with Madrid and a month later informed ranking members of the Senate of administration plans to purchase the island. In Spain, Ambassador Stewart L. Woodford concluded that the transfer of the island had to be made as soon as possible—peacefully if possible, with Spanish honor preserved if it could be, but above all quickly and absolutely.[27] On March 17, Woodford reported on a lengthy discussion with Colonial Minister Segismundo Moret. Spain had lost Cuba, Woodford stressed to Moret, but Cuban independence was not acceptable. Woodford doubted that the "insurgents can secure peace and good order in Cuba under a free or independent government" and concluded: "Some way must be found by which Spain can part with Cuba without loss of self-respect and with certainty of American control so

that we may give that protection to loyal Spaniards and rebels alike."
The United States was prepared to purchase the island for "a fixed
sum," Woodford indicated, part of which would be retained as a fund
to settle war claims. [28]

Spain equivocated and delayed, and increasingly it became apparent in Washington that Madrid had little intention of transferring the
island to the United States. On March 27, Washington delivered a
three-part ultimatum to Spain demanding an armistice until October 5, an end to resettlement programs and permission to distribute
relief supplies, and the participation of President McKinley as mediator to end the dispute. In return, the United States promised to use its
"friendly offices to get insurgents to accept the plan." [29] After another
ten days of frantic negotiations, Spain capitulated. On April 5, the
queen regent personally interceded and proclaimed a unilateral cease-
fire in Cuba, effective immediately and lasting through October. On
April 10, Washington received Spain's formal acceptance of the essential provisions of McKinley's March 27 ultimatum.[30] On the same day,
in Havana, Governor General Blanco ordered all Spanish forces to
halt operations. [31]

McKinley had scored a diplomatic victory on all fronts but one—
he failed to make good on the North American part of the March 27
ultimatum: to use U.S. "friendly offices to get insurgents to accept the
plan." Indeed, the collapse of the North American proposal was due
less to Spanish equivocation than to the U.S. inability to obtain Cuban
acquiescence to the cease-fire. In early April, McKinley summoned
Horatio Rubens, the Cubans' legal counsel in New York, to the White
House to discuss the terms of the impending settlement. Rubens later
recalled the meeting:

> "You must," he clipped out at me, "accept an immediate armistice with
> Spain."
> "To what end, Mr. President?"
> "To settle the strife in Cuba," he cried.
> "But is Spain ready to grant Cuba independence?" I asked.
> "That isn't the question now," he exclaimed, his voice rising. "We may
> discuss that later. The thing for the moment is an armistice."

Rubens rejected the cease-fire on the grounds that it promised to bene-fit only Spain and would have calamitous consequences for the Cuban war effort:

> The reason is a practical one, Mr. President. Nothing you could propose would be so beneficial to Spain and so detrimental to Cuba as an armistice. If an armistice is carried out in good faith, it means the dissolution and disintegration of the Cuban army. There is no commissary for it even now; it must live, poorly and precariously, on the country. If armistice is accepted the army cannot obtain its food supplies; it will starve. Further-more, in the natural uncertainty pending negotiations, the men would scatter, going to their homes. . . . If, on the other hand, having accepted the armistice, the Cubans continued to live on the country they would be loudly charged with breach of faith. [32]

In Cuba, separatist army chieftains denounced the cease-fire and ordered the insurgent forces to continue operations. "They have to be hit hard and at the head, day and night," General Calixto García exhorted his troops. "In order to suspend hostilities, an agreement is necessary with our Government and this will have to be based on independence." "More than ever before," Máximo Gómez proclaimed, "the war must continue in full force." [33]

Cuban rejection of the Spanish cease-fire ended hopes in the United States that the dreaded summer campaign could be averted. Spain had attached only one condition to its agreement: that Cubans observe the cease-fire. Spain now had no choice but to resume field operations and face inevitable military defeat.

At the same time, events in Cuba and U.S. policy response were in-creasingly the object of conflict between Congress and the president. Partisan politics was one source of conflict. Another was competition for control over foreign policy. Clashing points of view transformed a difficult situation into a nearly impossible one between legislators sympathetic to the Cuban cause and the executive hostile to *Cuba Libre*.

In the early spring, events were being shaped by forces beyond the control of the United States and Spain: Cubans were determining the course. Once Spain refused to transfer sovereignty over Cuba to the United States, and once Cubans rejected the continuation of

Spanish sovereignty in any form, North Americans faced two prospects: Cuban independence or U.S. intervention.

The Cuban revolution threatened more than the propriety of colonial rule or property relations in the colonial regime. It also challenged the U.S. expectation of colonial succession, for in ending Spanish sovereignty in 1898, Cubans endangered the North American claim of sovereignty. Acquisition of Cuba was envisaged always as an act of colonial continuity, formally transferred and legitimately ceded by Spain to the United States—an assumption of sovereignty over a territory presumed incapable of a separate nationhood. The success of the Cuban rebellion changed all this. The United States prepared for intervention as alarmed at the prospect of a Cuban victory as it was exasperated at Spain's inability to end the war. Neither the force of Spanish repression nor the concession of Spanish reforms had checked the advance of Cuban arms. Spanish sovereignty was beyond recovery. In 1898 Cuba was lost to Spain, and if Washington did not act, it would be lost to the United States.

VII

In April 1898 President William McKinley requested of Congress authority to intervene militarily in Cuba. Ostensibly the war was against Spain, but in fact it was against Cubans.

The president's war message provided portents of policy: there was no mention of Cuban independence, nothing about recognition of the Cuban provisional government, not a hint of sympathy with *Cuba Libre*, nowhere even an allusion to the renunciation of territorial aggrandizement—only a request for congressional authorization "to take measures to secure a full and final termination of hostilities between the Government of Spain and the people of Cuba, and to secure in the island the establishment of a stable government, capable of maintaining order and observing its international obligations." The U.S. purpose in Cuba, McKinley emphasized in his war message, con-

sisted of a "forcible intervention . . . as a neutral to stop the war."
McKinley explained: "The forcible intervention of the United States
. . . involves . . . hostile constraint upon both the parties to the contest."[34] The war was to be directed against both Spaniards and Cubans
to establish the grounds upon which to neutralize the two competing
claims of sovereignty and establish by superior force of arms a third.
This was the outstanding virtue of the "neutral intervention" to which
the United States had committed itself by April. "We have already can-
vassed recognition of independence," the State Department reported
on April 7, "with an adverse conclusion." The "neutral intervention"
would effectively concede to the United States control of the island.
"It would make a notable difference in our conduct of hostilities in
Cuba if we were to operate in territory transiently ours by conquest,
instead of operating in the territory of a recognized sovereign with
whom we maintain alliance." Nor was the State Department unmind-
ful of the long-term advantages of transient conquest: "We would be
free, if successful, to dictate the terms of peace and control the organization of an independent government in Cuba. We could hold the
Cuban territory in trust until, with restored tranquility a government
could be constitutionally organized which we could formally recognize and with which we could conclude a treaty regulating our future
relations to and guarantee of the Republic."[35]

McKinley's proposed intervention was immediately denounced by
the Cuban junta in the United States. What possible reason could
the administration have for withholding recognition of independence,
Cubans asked, unless its goal was annexation? "We will oppose any
intervention which does not have for its expressed and declared object
the independence of Cuba," junta spokesman Gonzalo de Quesada
proclaimed.[36] Speaking in behalf of the insurgent provisional government and the Liberation Army, counsel Horatio S. Rubens announced
the necessity of having "to go a step further" and bluntly warned that
intervention as suggested by McKinley would be regarded as "nothing less than a declaration of war by the United States against the
Cuban revolutionists." He added:

If intervention shall take place on that basis, and the United States shall land an armed force on Cuban soil, we shall treat that force as an enemy to be opposed, and, if possible, expelled, so long as the recognition of a free Cuban republic is withheld. I do not mean to say that the Cuban army will assemble on the coast to resist the landing of Federal troops, but that it will remain in the interior, refusing to cooperate, declining to acknowledge any American authority, ignoring and rejecting the intervention to every possible extent. Should the United States troops succeed in expelling the Spanish; should the United States then declare a protectorate over the island—however provisional or tentative—and seek to extend its authority over the government of Cuba and the army of liberation, we would resist with force of arms as bitterly and tenaciously as we have fought the armies of Spain. [37]

Administration opponents in Congress also made repeated attempts to secure recognition of the Cuban provisional republic, and by mid-April McKinley yielded to compromise. Congress agreed to forgo recognition in exchange for the president's acceptance of a disclaimer. Article IV of the congressional resolution, the Teller Amendment, specified that the United States "hereby disclaims any disposition of intention to exercise sovereignty, jurisdiction, or control over said island except for pacification thereof, and asserts its determination, when that is accomplished, to leave the government and control of the island to its people." [38]

The Joint Resolution calmed Cuban misgivings. Satisfied that the intervention made common cause with separatist goals, Cubans prepared to coordinate joint military operations with their allies. It did not matter that the North Americans refused to recognize the republic, as long as Washington endorsed the goals for which the republic stood. "It is true," Calixto García conceded, "that they have not entered into an accord with our government; but they have recognized our right to be free and independent and that is enough for me." [39]

VIII

The intervention transformed a Cuban war of liberation into a U.S. war of conquest. And it was the victory to which the United States first laid claim and from which so much else would flow. The Cuban war for national liberation became the "Spanish-American War," nomenclature that in more than symbolic terms ignored Cuban participation and announced the next series of developments. The construct legitimized the U.S. claim over the island as a spoil of victory. The North Americans had not arrived as allies of Cubans or as agents of Cuban independence. They had gone to war, as they always said they would, to prevent the transfer of sovereignty of Cuba to a third party.

The exclusion of the Cubans began early. North American commanders moved insurgent forces behind front lines, principally in support roles. Cuban commanders were ignored. Negotiations for the surrender of Santiago de Cuba in July were conducted without Cuban participation, and by the terms of the surrender Cubans were barred from entering the city. Cuban commander Calixto García was astonished and asked U.S. army leader William R. Shafter for clarification of the agreement. He learned that Santiago was now considered territory conquered by the United States and "part of the Union."[40] The decision to deny Cubans access to the city, General Shafter explained publicly, was based on the fear that insurgents could not be restrained from attacking unarmed Spanish soldiers, abusing women, and plundering the city.[41]

Indignation swept across Cuban camps. General García denounced the idea that Santiago was "part of the Union." "I will never accept," the Cuban commander vowed, "that our country be considered as conquered territory."[42] García bristled at the charge that the Cuban army could not be trusted to enter Santiago. "Allow me to protest against even a shadow of such an idea," García wrote Shafter; "we are not savages who ignore the principles of civilized warfare. We respect too much our cause to stain it with barbarity and cowardice."[43]

This conflict gave early form to the fundamental cross-purposes at which Cubans and North Americans found themselves in 1898. Cuban suspicions deepened, and by war's end the estrangement was all but complete. Insurgent commanders became sullen and noncooperative. Some withdrew from joint operations and broke off relations with North American forces. Calixto García resigned, proclaiming that he was "no longer disposed to continue obeying the orders and cooperating with the plans of the American Army," and warned his comrades against relinquishing any authority to the "army of the intervention."[44]

Cuban actions, in turn, antagonized North Americans. When Cubans balked at assignments of menial tasks behind the lines, they were denounced as shirkers and slackers. When they repudiated the terms of the Santiago surrender, they were portrayed as willful and arrogant. Resentment spread among the North Americans. By late summer, contempt for Cubans had become commonplace behind U.S. lines. "The Cubans are a dirty filthy lot," one officer complained.[45] Cuban insurgents "hear nothing but words of scorn from our men as they pass," the Associated Press correspondent in Santiago de Cuba reported. "Even our officers no longer conceal their disgust for their allies, and it is understood that the warm friendship displayed toward them at first has now turned into contempt."[46]

Exclusion from the negotiations for the surrender of Santiago in July was only the first in a series of rebuffs to Cubans. The terms of the peace protocol in August were also negotiated without Cuban participation, as was the peace treaty in Paris later that autumn. Nor did it take long for the North Americans to come around to the views of the old colonial elites. United States authorities came into direct contact with those social groups most hostile to *Cuba Libre*, and they confirmed the North Americans' worst impressions of insurgent Cubans. Contemptuous of the *insurrectos*, often hysterical in their opposition to Cuban independence, local elites denied that Cubans possessed the aptitude for self-government. They warned that pillage, race war, and endless vendettas by vengeful Cubans were certain to follow in the wake of independence. Businessmen, merchants, and landowners flocked around the newly arrived North Americans hoping for salvation from Cuban independence.

Their views quickly gained currency among North Americans. The "higher classes," a *New York Times* reporter wrote, "are opposed, above all things, to an out and out Cuban Government. . . . If the Cuban revolutionists get control, there will be a long reign of terror in which all who have opposed the insurrection will suffer greatly." Another correspondent predicted that independence "would mean to turn over the island to a worse condition of anarchy from which we are seeking to rescue it." The Associated Press correspondent wrote of the "dread" in Santiago de Cuba at the prospect of independence and concluded that the "better classes . . . fervently hope that the United States will retain the reins of government in the island, as the only guarantee of stability and prosperity." [47]

In fact, North Americans needed little encouragement to oppose Cuban independence. Nearly a century of maligning the Cuban capacity for self-government had more than adequately prepared the United States to believe the worst about its erstwhile allies. That persons in a position really to know—residents with property and prestige, senior Spanish civil and military authorities, church officials, newspaper editors—also opposed independence corroborated North American suspicions.

Almost from the outset of the intervention, the proposition of independence was scorned and its proponents discredited. Cuban motives for independence were suspect, almost as if opposition to the North American presence was evidence enough that self-serving if not sinister motives lurked behind separatist strivings. Cubans were not inspired by love of liberty but by the lure of looting. "From the highest officer to the lowliest 'soldier,'" one traveler wrote, "they were there for personal gain." [48] The Cuban desire for independence, North Americans concluded, was motivated by a wish to plunder and exact reprisals. Cubans were possessed, one observer reported, by the "sole active desire to murder and pillage." [49] "If we are to save Cuba," a New York journalist exhorted, "we must hold it. If we leave it to the Cubans, we give it over to a reign of terror—to the machete and the torch, to insurrection and assassination." [50]

This was a proposition from which the North Americans drew

a number of inferences: first, Cubans were not prepared for self-government. Again, again, and again they struck the same theme. The ideological imperative of empire took hold early and deeply. The consensus was striking. Admiral William T. Sampson, a member of the United States evacuation commission, insisted that Cubans had no idea of self-government—and "it will take a long time to teach them."[51] Some North American officials believed Cubans incapable of self-government at any time. "Self-government!" General William R. Shafter protested. "Why those people are no more fit for self-government than gunpowder is for hell."[52] General Samuel B. M. Young concluded after the war that the "insurgents are a lot of degenerates, absolutely devoid of honor or gratitude. They are no more capable of self-government than the savages of Africa."[53] A similar note was struck by Major George M. Barbour, the United States sanitary commissioner in Santiago de Cuba. The Cubans, he insisted, "are stupid, given to lying and doing all things in the wrong way. . . . Under our supervision, and with firm and honest care for the future, the people of Cuba may become a useful race and a credit to the world; but to attempt to set them afloat as a nation, during this generation, would be a great mistake."[54]

Independence was as implausible a proposition as its proponents were unfit to govern, and in the North American mind both were linked. Only the "ignorant masses," the "unruly rabble," and "trouble makers"—"the element," Governor General Leonard Wood warned, "absolutely without any conception of its responsibilities or duties as citizens"—advocated independence. "The only people who are howling for [independence]," Wood concluded with undisguised contempt, "are those whose antecedents and actions demonstrate the impossibility of self-government at present."[55]

IX

The *independentista* ideal was popular, however, and most North Americans in Cuba conceded, if only in private, that a majority of

Cubans were devoted to *Cuba Libre*. But numbers alone, they were quick to counter, could not be permitted to determine the fate of Cuba—particularly when the sentiment of the majority was identified with disruption, disorder, and chaos. That large numbers of Cubans opposed annexation was cause enough to distrust and discredit independence sentiment. If there were people who opposed U.S. rule, they were probably led by wicked men, or knew no better. In either case, opposition to the United States from this source served only to confirm Cuban incapacity for self-government.

If the United States found no support in the *independentista* majority, it derived some consolation in the quality of the anti-independence minority. The "better classes," the propertied, the educated, the white —those sectors, in short, most deserving of North American solicitude —were desirous of close and permanent ties with the United States. "The real voice of the people of Cuba," Governor General Leonard Wood reassured the White House in late 1899, "has not been heard because they have not spoken and, unless I am entirely mistaken, when they do speak there will be many more voices for annexation than there is at present any idea of." There was, certainly, "much plausibility," correspondent Herbert P. Williams learned during his travels in Cuba, that the large majority of the "half-barbarous rabble in a vote would request us to leave the island." It was "probably true," too, that "the Cubans who want us to go outnumber those who want us to stay." But mere numbers were inconsequential, Williams insisted. Conceding that the United States "ought not go into the business of government without the consent of the governed," Williams nevertheless concluded: "The point is that if all, or nearly all, the people whose convictions deserve respect are on one side, mere numbers should not be allowed to decide the matter."[56]

These were considerations of great concern to North American authorities. Indeed, a political eclipse of the representatives of the "better classes" was no less a threat to U.S. interests, for it was upon the political ascendancy of the local elites that U.S. hopes for sway over Cuba rested. Both opposed Cuban independence. Both opposed Cuban government. Policy makers needed supporters, property own-

ers needed security. North Americans searched for a substitute for independence, local elites sought a substitute for colonialism. The logic
of collaboration was compelling and compulsory. Old colonial elites
in need of protection and new colonial rulers in need of allies arrived
at an understanding. Indeed, the political ascendancy of the "better
classes" promised not only to obstruct the rise of *independentismo* but
also to institutionalize U.S. influence from within. It mattered slightly
less if Cuba were independent, if that independence was under the
auspices of a client political class whose own social salvation was a
function of and dependent on U.S. hegemony.

X

North American efforts centered initially on fostering the ascendancy of the old colonial elites as political surrogate in opposition to
the *independentista* polity. Preparations for municipal elections in June
1900 required first the restriction of suffrage to exclude, in the words
of Secretary of War Elihu Root, the "mass of ignorant and incompetent" so as to promote "a conservative and thoughtful control of Cuba
by Cubans" and "avoid the kind of control which leads to perpetual
revolutions of Central America and other West India islands."[57]

Having limited the franchise, the United States next turned its attention to organizing its local political allies. Governor General Leonard
Wood labored diligently in behalf of conservative candidates, seeking
to forge the "better classes" into a political coalition capable of competing electorally with the "extreme and revolutionary element." He
gave private encouragement to conservative candidates, repeatedly
reassuring them of U.S. support while seeking to neutralize the opposition. "Of course," Wood acknowledged, "the usual opposition party
will gradually develop, but I shall endeavor to give them as slender a
foundation as possible to stand on."[58]

The balloting in the 1900 municipal election dealt U.S. efforts a
rude blow. Almost everywhere U.S.-backed candidates went down to

defeat. *Independentistas* triumphed and, flushed with victory, stepped up their demands for U.S. evacuation of the island.

Disheartened but undaunted, Wood turned his attention to preparations for the next round of balloting, elections scheduled for December 1900 to select a constituent assembly. This time Wood participated more actively in behalf of conservative candidates. In August, he undertook an arduous tour of the island to campaign for the election of the "better classes." In Santiago de Cuba, Wood publicly appealed for the election of the "best men" and drew his moral with a familiar metaphor: "Bear in mind that no constitution which does not provide for a stable government will be accepted by the United States. I wish to avoid making Cuba into a second Haiti." In Puerto Príncipe, Wood warned that if Cubans elected delegates who failed to support order, the United States would not withdraw its military forces. In Cienfuegos he reported confidently that the "better class of men [are] coming to the front daily for candidates to the convention." In his final pre-election report to the White House, Wood detailed the achievements of his travels around the island. "I have seen most of the prominent men," he explained, "using every effort to have them send the best and ablest men to the Constitutional Convention without consideration to political parties. Some of the men nominated are excellent, others are bad. I hope, however, that the latter will be defeated." Nevertheless, he struck a note of caution and appealed to McKinley to proceed slowly with plans for evacuation "until we see what class are coming to the front for the offices called for under the Constitution."[59]

Independentistas prevailed again. "I regret to inform you," a disappointed Wood wrote Senator Orville H. Platt in December 1900, "that the dominant party in the convention to-day contains probably the worst political element in the Island and they will bear careful watching." He lamented:

The men whom I had hoped to see take leadership have been forced into the background by the absolutely irresponsible and unreliable element. . . . There are a number of excellent men in the Convention; there are also some of the most unprincipled rascals who walk the Island. The only fear in Cuba to-day is not that we shall stay, but that we shall leave too soon. The elements desiring our immediate departure are the men whose only capacity will be demonstrated as a capacity for destroying all hopes for the future.

And he made his point: "The class to whom we must look for the stable government in Cuba are not as yet sufficiently well represented to give us that security and confidence which we desire." [60]

Wood shared his despair with the secretary of war. "I am disappointed in the composition of the Convention," he confided ruefully to Root. The responsibility of framing a new constitution had fallen to some of the "worst agitators and political radicals in Cuba." Wood questioned again the wisdom of proceeding with plans for evacuation. "None of the more intelligent men claim that the people are yet ready for self-government," Wood wrote plaintively. "In case we withdraw," he warned, the members of the convention represented "the class to whom Cuba would have to be turned over . . . for the highly intelligent Cubans of the land owning, industrial and commercial classes are not in politics." Two-thirds of the convention delegates were "adventurers pure and simple," not "representatives of Cuba" and "not safe leaders." [61]

XI

As 1900 drew to an end, the United States found itself in possession of an island that it could neither fully retain nor completely release, confronting the imminent ascendancy of the very political forces that the intervention had been designed to contain. The way Cubans had responded to democratic elections, North American officials concluded, confirmed Cuban incapacity for self-governance. By failing to elect the candidates acceptable to the United States, Cubans had demonstrated themselves ill-suited to assume the responsibility of independence. Cubans' judgment was flawed; they simply could not be trusted to elect the "best men." Some conclusions seemed in order.

The elections revealed Cubans to lack political maturity. They were swayed easily by emotions and led readily by demagogues, which to North Americans meant that they were not ready to assume full responsibility for sovereignty. Under the circumstances, the United States could not withdraw from Cuba without reserving for itself some means through which to guarantee order and stability.

The rationale for a continued exercise of U.S. authority found sanction in revised interpretations of the Joint Resolution. If the principle of the Teller Amendment could not be repudiated, its meaning would be revised. "The United States," the Teller Amendment stipulated, "hereby disclaims any disposition or intention to exercise sovereignty, jurisdiction, or control over said island except for pacification thereof." The new official interpretation of the Teller Amendment insisted that the "pacification" required conditions of stability. But "stability" and "stable government," too, were many things to many people. "What does 'pacification' means in that clause?" Senator Platt asked rhetorically in mid-1900. "We became responsible for the establishment of a government there, which we would be willing to endorse to the people of the world—a stable government, a government for which we would be willing to be responsible in the eyes of the world."[62] And at another point, Platt insisted: "'Pacification' of the 'island' manifestly meant the establishment in that island of a government capable of adequately protecting life, liberty and property."[63]

Once stability was subsumed into the meaning of the Joint Resolution, independence became a condition which the United States claimed authorization to recognize, or restrict, or revoke—however circumstances warranted. Stability, like pacification, however, also underwent repeated ideological transformations, and it soon became clear that in its final form it was not a condition unlike that of a protectorate to the United States. When asked during congressional hearings if Cubans should be "entirely independent in the administration of their own local affairs," General James H. Wilson answered unequivocally: "Only so far as they are willing to bind themselves to manage their own affairs, in a way that would be acceptable and agreeable to us."[64] Wood agreed: "When the Spanish-American war was declared the United States took a step forward, and assumed a position as protector of the interests of Cuba. It became responsible for the welfare of the people, politically, mentally and morally." [65]

XII

By the third year of the military occupation, the United States had failed to diminish the appeal of *Cuba Libre*. *Independentismo* persisted as a potent political force. The inability of the old colonial elites to win political control required the United States to seek alternative means of hegemony. The "better classes" had shown themselves to be of limited political value. They had fared poorly at the polls, and no amount of North American backing, it seemed, could elevate them to power. "I think we are in great danger of finding ourselves in a very awkward and untenable position," Root warned in early 1901. The administration was prepared, even anxious, to end the occupation, but not without first securing guarantees necessary to U.S. interests. Root sought to give U.S. authority legal form, something in the way of binding political relations based on the Monroe Doctrine. [66]

In January 1901, Root outlined four provisions he deemed essential to U.S. interests. First, that "in transferring the control of Cuba to the Government established under the new constitution the United States reserves and retains the right of intervention for the preservation of Cuban independence and the maintenance of a stable Government adequately protecting life, property and individual liberty." Second, that "no Government organized under the constitution shall be deemed to have authority to enter into any treaty or engagement with any foreign power which may tend to impair or interfere with the independence of Cuba." Root also insisted that to perform "such duties as may devolve upon her under the foregoing provisions and for her own defense," the United States "may acquire and hold the title to land, and maintain naval stations at certain specified points." Last, that "all the acts of the Military Government, and all rights acquired thereunder, shall be valid and be maintained and protected." [67]

These were not entirely new policy formulations. They had been discussed earlier in one form or another. Root acknowledged that his proposals owed some inspiration to England's relations with Egypt, which seemed to allow "England to retire and still maintain her moral control."[68] His urgency, however, was new. New, too, was the means by which Root proposed to fix the terms of political relations. Only eighteen months earlier he had envisioned the question of political relations between Cuba and the United States as a proper subject of future negotiations. "When that government is established," Root had asserted in 1899, "the relations which exist between it and the United States will be a matter for free and uncontrolled discussion between the two parties." After 1900, however, Root decided to impose unilaterally on the Cuban constituent assembly the formal terms of Cuba's relations to the United States as part of the "fundamental law of Cuba."[69]

In large measure, the decision to fix the nature of relations between Cuba and the United States even as the island was occupied militarily and governed by the United States signaled the failure of U.S. designs. The *independentista* ideal proved stronger than North Americans had anticipated, and once it assumed institutional forms, principally through political parties, party programs, and duly elected officeholders, it expanded into a force of even greater popular appeal. The decision to press for binding relations, even while the island remained under military occupation, further underscored the realization in the United States that once achieving independence Cubans would not acquiesce to the proposed limitations upon their sovereignty. The original expectation in 1899 that political relations would be the subject of "free and uncontrolled discussion" between both governments rested on the assumption that the United States would be negotiating with representatives of the old colonial elites who depended on North American hegemony as the source of their local ascendancy. After 1900, however, the results of local elections raised the real possibility that the island would pass wholly under the control of the *independentista* coalition, ill-disposed to compromise national sovereignty to accommodate North American needs.

It was thus necessary to use the military occupation as the means to exact Cuban acquiescence in U.S. demands. Otherwise, North Americans faced the improbable situation of having to negotiate with Cuba on a parity of sovereignty the restriction of its national sovereignty. This was the "great danger" to which Root alluded that would place the United States in "a very awkward and untenable position." The "most obvious meaning" of the Joint Resolution, Root conceded confidentially in early 1901, called first for the establishment of an independent government in Cuba, followed by the negotiation of a treaty of relations between Cuba and the United States. "Yet," Root hastened to add, "it is plain that such a course would leave the United States in a worse position as to her own interests than she was when Spain held the sovereignty of Cuba and would be an abandonment both of our interests and the safety of Cuba herself." United States interests required "constitutional limitations which would never be put into the [Cuban] Constitution except upon our insistence or suggestion." Senator Platt agreed. To defer the issue of relations until the inauguration of a Cuban government, he warned, risked surrendering "any right to be heard as to what relations shall be" and further risked having to be "contented with nothing at all."[70]

Wood responded to the proposed relations with enthusiasm. The stipulations, he was certain, would over the long run serve to promote the political ascendancy of the better classes. The relationship between the poor political showing of local elites in Cuba, on one hand, and the lack of a stated U.S. policy, on the other, Wood argued, was self-evident. "Our policy towards Cuba," he complained, "has rendered it impossible for business and conservative elements to state frankly what they desire, they fearing to be left in the lurch by our Government's sudden withdrawal." Wood returned to his enduring concern:

> It must not be forgotten for a moment that the present dominant political elements are not representative of the Cuban people as a whole. In general terms they are a lot of adventurers and to turn the country over to them before a better element has come to the front will be nothing more

or less in effect than turning the island over to spoliation. It would be a terrific blow to civilization here. I believe in establishing a government of and by the people of Cuba and a free government, because we have promised it, but I do not believe in surrendering the present Government to the adventurers who are now in the Convention and in many of the municipalities. Let Congress set a definite date of withdrawal provided a suitable government exists and I will make every effort to bring the conservative and representative elements to the front. . . . I have started the new year with a systematic policy of urging and encouraging by all proper means, the conservative element to come forward and interest themselves in the political situation. [71]

XIII

In its essential features, the Platt Amendment, enacted into law by Congress in February 1901, addressed the central elements of U.S. objectives through the course of the nineteenth century. An adequate if imperfect substitute for annexation, it served to transform the substance of Cuban sovereignty into an extension of the U.S. national system. Restrictions imposed upon the conduct of foreign relations, specifically the denial of treaty authority and debt restrictions, as well as the prohibition against the cession of national territory, were designed to minimize Cuban international entanglement:

I. That the government of Cuba shall never enter into any treaty or other compact with any foreign power or powers which will impair or tend to impair the independence of Cuba, or in any manner authorize or permit any foreign power or powers to obtain by colonization or, for military or naval purposes or otherwise, lodgment in or control over any portion of said island.

II. That said government shall not assume or contract any public debt, to pay the interest upon which, and to make reasonable sinking fund provision for the ultimate discharge of which, the ordinary revenues of the island, after defraying the current expenses of government shall be inadequate.

III. That the government of Cuba consents that the United States may exercise the right to intervene for the preservation of Cuban independence, the maintenance of a government adequate for the protection of life, property, and individual liberty, and for discharging the obligations with respect to Cuba imposed by the Treaty of Paris on the United States, now to be assumed and undertaken by the government of Cuba.

IV. That all Acts of the United States in Cuba during its military occupancy thereof are ratified and validated, and all lawful rights acquired thereunder shall be maintained and protected.

V. That the government of Cuba will execute and as far as necessary extend, the plans already devised or other plans to be mutually agreed upon, for the sanitation of the cities of the island, to the end that a recurrence of epidemic and infectious diseases may be prevented, thereby assuring protection to the people and commerce of Cuba, as well as to the commerce of the southern ports of the United States and of the people residing therein.

VI. That the Isle of Pines shall be omitted from the proposed constitutional boundaries of Cuba, the title thereto being left to future adjustment by treaty.

VII. That to enable the United States to maintain the independence of Cuba, and to protect the people thereof, as well as for its own defense, the government of Cuba will sell or lease to the United States land necessary for coaling or naval stations at certain specified points, to be agreed upon with the President of the United States.

VIII. That by way of further assurance the government of Cuba will embody the foregoing provisions in a permanent treaty with the United States. [72]

The failure to install the better classes in power meant an uncertain future in the organization of the new republic. Clearly if the authority and resources of the United States could not contain the potency of the revolutionary ideal during the occupation, what would follow the evacuation? Elections had underscored the uncertainty if not inefficacy of democratic process, and the point was not lost on North Americans. The Platt Amendment rested on the central if not fully stated premise that the principal danger to U.S. interests in Cuba originated with Cubans themselves, or at least those Cubans in the *independentista* camp. Whether in the direction of foreign affairs, or in the management of public funds, or in the conduct of national politics, government by Cubans remained always a dubious proposition, an enterprise as unsound in its premises as it was uncertain in its permanence. Root was blunt. The proposed relations represented "the extreme limit of this country's indulgence in the matter of the independence of Cuba." The political leadership emerging in Havana did not inspire confidence in the United States. "The character of the ruling class," Root acknowledged, "is such that their administration of the affairs of the island will require the restraining influence of the United States government for many years to come, even if it does not eventually become necessary for this government to take direct and absolute control of Cuban affairs."[73]

XIV

News of the Platt Amendment provoked widespread popular protests in Cuba. Anti-U.S. demonstrations were held across the island. Former insurgent chieftains denounced the proposed relations and alluded to the necessity of returning to the field of armed struggle to vindicate the *independentista* ideal. Municipal councils, civic organizations, and veterans associations cabled protests to North American authorities in Havana and Washington. This show of popular opposition encouraged the constituent assembly to balk at enacting the amendment as part of the new constitution. Apprehension increased among North American officials. A naval squadron was prepared for a "courtesy call" to Havana. Yet Wood fretted and cabled Root: "Can you indicate our action in case Convention should refuse to accept Platt Amendment?"[74]

Root was unmoved. There would be neither compromise on the congressional amendment nor concession to Cuban independence, he warned, until Cubans ratified the proposed relations. He was adamant. "Under the act of Congress they never can have any further government in Cuba, except the intervening Government of the United

States, until they have acted." The members of the constituent convention "should have sufficient intelligence to understand that they cannot escape their responsibility except by a refusal to act, which will necessarily require the convening of another Convention which will act." "No constitution can be put into effect in Cuba," Root warned directly, "and no government can be elected under it, no electoral law by the Convention can be put into effect, and no election held under it until they have acted upon this question of relations in conformity with this act of Congress." Continued resistance to U.S. demands, Root warned ominously, would have dire consequences. "There is only one possible way for them to bring about the termination of the military government and make either the constitution or electoral law effective; that is to do the whole duty they were elected for."[75]

In early June, Cubans ceased to resist. It was apparent that the choice before the convention was limited sovereignty or no sovereignty. It accepted the Platt Amendment as an appendix to the new 1901 constitution by a sixteen-to-eleven vote.

5   Context and Content of the Republic

The military occupation ended on May 20, 1902, with an appropriate mix of ceremony and celebration and with much made about the successful transition from colony to republic. But the stunted Cuban republic fashioned by the U.S. proconsuls had little relevance to Cuban social reality. Cuba's war of liberation had produced foreign intervention, not independence, and when the U.S. military occupation ended, the conditions imposed on the exercise of national sovereignty had rendered meaningless all but the most cynical definition of independence.

The intervention shattered the polity that had formed around *Cuba Libre* and in the process diffused the vigor of Cuban nationalism and dispersed its exponents. Backed by a vast army of occupation, and in control of government and public administration, the North Americans proceeded to dismantle *independentista* structures. That the United States succeeded was in large measure made possible by the very heterogeneity of the separatist amalgam, specifically the presence of large numbers of Cubans within the revolutionary coalition who inhabited that dual world of devotions divided between Cuba and the United States. Many were dedicated to the ideal of *Cuba Libre* but also cared for the United States. They were reasonable men and women with an abiding belief in North American institutions. They believed especially in the promise of the Teller Amendment and exhorted other Cubans to believe. The danger to the Teller pledge, they argued, lay with Cubans themselves, who in their impatience for independence, in their justifiable eagerness to be free and sovereign, might act precipitously and induce the United States to nullify its commitment. They were not unaware of the slurs and slanders made by North Americans against Cubans and charges of Cuban incapacity for

113

self-government; many were mortified by the cruel characterization of the men and women who for so long had toiled and sacrificed to make Cuba free. They attributed U.S. opinions to ignorance and were certain that in time, as the North Americans came to know Cubans better, their views would change. In the meantime, however, Cubans were exhorted to display good judgment, demonstrate self-restraint, and prove themselves worthy of North American trust. They counseled cooperation and collaboration. In the face of charges of incapacity for self-government, they urged Cubans to serve in the military government and demonstrate their worth and not to challenge North American rule. Opposition to the U.S. presence, many feared, threatened the independence to which they believed the United States was committed. Cuba would receive its independence, predicted Gonzalo de Quesada in New York, but whether independence arrived sooner rather than later depended on the "behavior of Cubans." To challenge North American authority and resist the occupation promised "only to delay independence."[1] The anomaly did not pass unnoticed: independence now became a function of Cuban acquiescence to North American rule.

Separatists who occupied this world of dual loyalties played a crucial role in interpreting North Americans to Cubans, and vice versa. They were instrumental in reducing Cuban opposition to the military occupation, persuading many of the more intransigent separatists of the wisdom of concession, compromise, and collaboration.[2] Certainly they facilitated the consolidation of North American control, but only up to a point—and at that point they acted to guarantee the survival of a separate nationality. They were instrumental in preventing outright annexation, conveying to North Americans the vigor of *independentismo*. Their prominence in separatist circles made North American reconciliation with the *independentista* polity possible. United States misgivings were calmed by the presence of this ideologically congenial sector of the most politically potent force in Cuba. They made palatable to North Americans the possibility of an independent republic and in their person and through their prudence succeeded in persuading the United States that self-government was perhaps, in fact, a tenable proposition.

They were, after all, very much like North Americans, from whom they derived their ideological bearings and cultural preferences. They had served the cause of *Cuba Libre*, mostly as civilians in the provisional government or in the party, but some also in the army. Many had lived in the United States, with origins in the colonial petite bourgeoisie, been educated in North American schools, and held U.S. citizenship. They moved freely among the North Americans and gained access to positions of public office and administration early in the military occupation. In a larger sense, their response was more complicated than an act of collaboration in exchange for patronage. Among the most prominent of them were Civil Secretary of Finance Pablo Desvernine, holder of a law degree from Columbia University; José Ramón Villalón, civil secretary of public works, who held a civil engineering degree from Lehigh University; General Pedro Betancourt, civil governor of Matanzas, and Perfecto Lacosta, mayor of Havana, both with degrees from the University of Pennsylvania; General Mario G. Menocal, chief of police, who had attended the Chautauqua Institute in New York State and graduated from Cornell University; Demetrio Castillo Duany, civil governor of Oriente, a naturalized U.S. citizen, who had attended the New York School of Commerce; Alcides Betancourt, secretary of the provincial government of Camagüey, who had studied commerce in New York; and José Eliseo Cartaya, inspector of Havana customs, a naturalized U.S. citizen. Fernando Figueredo was also a U.S. citizen and had attended the School of Engineers in Troy, New York, and subsequently accepted an appointment as chief of the Cienfuegos customs house. Federico García Ramis, chief clerk of the Cuban Supreme Court, studied law in the United States; General Emilio Núñez, civil governor of Havana, obtained his dentistry degree in Philadelphia; Carlos M. Rojas, mayor of Cárdenas, studied poetry at Harvard under Henry Wadsworth Longfellow; Carlos Zaldo, civil secretary of justice and state, studied at Fordham. Tomás Estrada Palma, installed by the United States as the first president of Cuba, was fluent in English, a converted Quaker, and a naturalized U.S. citizen.

Familiarity with North American methods and the English language also allowed Cubans to obtain employment in service to the expanding North American economic presence on the island. Indeed, the speed with which U.S. investments expanded in the early 1900s owed much to Cuban cooperation. Cubans served North American enterprises as local managers and administrators; they acted as purchasing agents and middlemen, negotiators and brokers, overseers and advisers. They served as legal representatives and provided vital information about local economic conditions and technical assistance with land surveys, local regulations, and property appraisals.

There was an element of choicelessness about these developments. Postwar Cuba was in ruins. In this capital-starved economy, only North Americans, it seemed, possessed the resources to promote national reconstruction and economic revival. North Americans provided employment when there were few other alternatives; North Americans offered security in an environment of uncertainty.

The idea took hold early and endured long that national goals and economic well-being could best be fulfilled through cooperation with North Americans. Collaborating with the United States offered a means of political ascendancy and individual mobility. Cubans sympathetic to North Americans obtained political positions and the emoluments of public office. In control of the perquisites of government, they obtained the wherewithal to develop institutional advantage in the competition for political power. In the end, collaboration with the United States became a central element of Cuban political culture and a key strategy of virtually all aspirants to political office.

There were, of course, class-color correlates to the Cuban accommodation to the North American presence. Not all Cubans were reconciled either to the restrictions on national sovereignty or the nonachievement of the social objectives of the struggle for independence. Cubans had been summoned to dramatic action but failed to produce dramatic change. The inequities of colonial society survived into the republic, giving renewed vitality to the historic sources of Cuban discontent and revived vigor to the traditional causes of Cuban dissatisfaction. For Cubans who had aspired to independence as formulated by Martí, the Platt Amendment was a bitter denouement indeed. For the countless tens of thousands of Cubans of color who had sacrificed for a new society, the republic was a fraud; for the vast numbers of poor and landless, the promise of *Cuba Libre* proved a lie.

The North American intervention thwarted more than the triumph of Cuban nationalism. Because *independentismo* had subsumed into its vision of *patria* elements of social justice, racial equality, and material well-being, the United States placed itself directly in the way of the Cuban quest for self-determination and self-fulfillment. Indeed, in its fullest meaning, national sovereignty represented the means of collective mobility. An obstacle for the former signified an obstruction to the latter. There was more than bluster to General William R. Shafter's startling pronouncement in late 1898: "As I view it, we have taken Spain's war upon ourselves."[3] The moral was not lost on Cubans.

After 1902, Cubans discovered that old grievances had assumed new forms. The real significance and the lasting effects of the intervention passed virtually unnoticed. The United States had not only rescued and revived the moribund colonial order, it had assumed responsibility for its protection and preservation. In all its essential features and in its principal functions, the new republic served to give different political form to the socioeconomic content of the old colony. The Platt Amendment complicated matters, for henceforth Cuban attempts to resolve the surviving anomalies of the colony and redress the continuing inequities of the colonial system inevitably involved confrontation with the United States. The course was set for collision.

II

The extensive destruction of property during the war followed by U.S. occupation after the war inaugurated a new and decisive phase in North American economic penetration of the island. Cuban property owners emerged from the war in debt, without either available capital or obtainable credit. The total urban indebtedness of some $100 million represented more than three-quarters of the declared property value of $139 million. A similar situation existed for rural real estate, the total value of which was set at some $185 million with a mortgage indebtedness of $107 million.[4]

The principal beneficiaries were North Americans, who swarmed to Cuba after the war in search of bargains in the form of defunct plantations and abandoned estates. Such opportunities were manifest. "Nowhere else in the world," exulted one U.S. investor in 1904, "are there such chances for success for the man of moderate means, as well as for the capitalist, as Cuba offers today. . . . I advise the capitalist to invest in Cuba, and seriously suggest to the young and ambitious man to go to Cuba and cast his fortune with those of the island."[5] "It is simply a poor man's paradise and the rich man's mecca," proclaimed the *Commercial and Financial World*.[6] "Land, at this writing," two former U.S. consular agents reported in 1898, "can be bought in unlimited quantities at from one-half to one-twentieth of its value before the insurrection. For the ordinarily prudent man with some capital, who is willing to work, the island has opportunities for success and wealth through safe and profitable investments, the equal of which can be found in no other place."[7]

United States control over sugar production expanded during and immediately after the occupation. As early as 1899, R. B. Hawley organized the Cuban-American Sugar Company and acquired possession of the seven-thousand-acre Tinguaro estate in Matanzas and the Merceditas mill in Pinar del Río. The same year, the company organized the Chaparra sugar mill around seventy thousand acres of land in Puerto Padre. In 1899 a group of North American investors acquired the eighty-thousand-acre Francisco estate in southern Camagüey province. The American Sugar Company acquired damaged estates in Matanzas. In 1901, the Nipe Bay Company, a subsidiary of United Fruit Company, acquired title to forty thousand acres of land also in the region of Puerto Padre. Later that year, United Fruit purchased two hundred thousand acres near Banes, a vast tract of land that included scores of partially destroyed and defunct estates. Within a decade of independence, almost the entire Oriente north coast, from Baracoa on the east to Manatí on the west, had passed under North American control. During these years also the Cuba Company completed the construction of the Cuban Railway through the eastern end of the island, acquiring in the process some fifty thousand acres of land for rail stations, construction sites, towns, and depots and a right-of-way 350 miles long. The Cuban Central Railway purchased the Caracas estate in Cienfuegos from Tomás Terry. The Cape Cruz Company acquired the estates of Aguda Grande, Limoncito, and San Celestino, a total of sixteen thousand acres near Manzanillo. Joseph Rigney, an investment partner with United Fruit, acquired the San Juan and San Joaquín estates and the damaged *ingenio* (mill) Teresa, all in the region around Manzanillo. [8]

North American capital expanded into other sectors of the economy, including mining, banking, utilities, and transportation. Monopoly capital established control over tobacco production and cigar manufacturing immediately after the war. In 1899, the newly organized Havana Commercial Company, under New York promoter H. B. Hollins, acquired twelve cigar factories, one cigarette factory, and scores of tobacco *vegas* (farms). As early as 1902, the newly organized Tobacco Trust in the United States controlled 90 percent of the export trade of Havana cigars. Four years later, the Tobacco Trust owned a total of 225,000 acres of tobacco land in Pinar del Río. [9]

North American control over mining also expanded. The principal mineral deposits were located in Oriente and included iron, manganese, copper, and lead, distributed in two principal regions in the north and south. Mines in the south, located in the districts of El Caney, Firmeza, Daiquirí, Ponupo, El Cristo, and Bayamo, were controlled by Juraguá Iron Company (Pennsylvania Steel Company and Bethlehem Iron Company), the Spanish-American Iron Company, Sigua Iron Company, the Eastern Steel Company, Cuban Steel Ore Company, and the Ponupo Manganese Company. The principal mining zone in the north was located in Mayarí and was owned almost entirely by the Spanish-American Iron Company. Copper deposits around El Cobre were worked by the San José Copper Mining Company. Other copper deposits in Puerto Príncipe, Santa Clara, and Matanzas were owned by the Cuban Copper Company. Between 1899 and 1902, the military government issued a total of 218 concessions, 134 of which were located in Oriente province. The 21 claims of the Juraguá Iron Company in El Caney totaled an estimated 1,140 acres of land. In 1905 the Spanish-American Iron Company acquired 28,000 acres in Mayarí. Spanish-American Iron, the largest holder of iron property, owned a total of 134,569 acres of surface options and an additional 150,986 acres of mining rights. In all, nearly 500,000 acres were distributed among approximately two thousand mine operations. [10]

North American capital also moved into transportation. The Santiago Railroad Company, the Cuba Railway, the Cuban Eastern Railway, and the Guantánamo Railroad were only the most prominent rail lines owned by U.S. investors. The electric transportation of the island was also dominated by North American capital. The Havana Electric Railway Company, a New Jersey corporation, established control of the capital's transportation system during the occupation. The Havana Central linked the capital to Marianao and Mariel.

Foreign capital controlled utilities. The Spanish American Light and Power Company of New York provided gas service to major Cuban cities. Electricity was controlled by two U.S. corporations, the Havana Central and Havana Electric. In Caibarién, electrical power was provided by the Caibarién Electrical Company, owned by P. B. Anderson. United States contracting companies established branch offices in Havana and competed for government projects. The Havana Subway Company acquired monopoly rights to install underground cables and electrical wires. United States capital controlled telephone service in the form of the Red Telefonica de La Habana, which ultimately was absorbed by the Cuba Telegraph and Telephone Company. United States investors controlled the Cárdenas City Water Works as well as the Cárdenas Railway and Terminal Company. The Havana Electric Railway Company provided trolley service in the capital.

North American contractors, employing mostly North American builders, constructed the public buildings, roads, and bridges of the early republic. North American engineering firms constructed the major port works in Havana and other large coastal cities. The T. L. Huston Contracting Company secured the government contract for dredging the principal ports and constructing concrete and pile wharves in Havana and Santiago de Cuba. The Huston Company also received the concession to build the highway network from Havana west to Pinar del Río. A subsidiary firm, the Huston Concrete Company, obtained the contract for constructing a new sewer system in Havana. The Snare and Triest Company of New York constructed steel bridges, drawbridges, and a fixed bridge for several railroad lines, several lighthouses along the south coast, and a power plant outside Havana. The Tropical Engineering and Construction Company constructed the water supply system of Havana and several power plants in Matanzas.

Some three-quarters of the cattle ranches, with an estimated value of $30 million, were owned by North Americans, principally the Lykes brothers. Sisal farms were owned by International Harvester and banana lands by United Fruit, Standard Fruit, and DeGeorgio Fruit.[11] The firm of Harris Brothers Company provided the government with its principal source of stationery, office supplies, and paper products. The Havana Advertising Company controlled the key advertising contracts and billboards across the island.

United States capital overwhelmed the local economy. As early as 1911, North American capital in Cuba had passed over the $200 million mark and by the early 1920s had increased more than fivefold.[12]

III

The Reciprocity Treaty of 1903 served to revive economic ties between both countries. The tariff schedule conceded to Cuban agricultural exports a 20 percent tariff reduction. In return, Cuba granted the United States a 20 percent concession on most items, with 24, 30, and 40 percent on selected categories. Most imports within the 20 percent category were products that had previously controlled the Cuban market, and hence a tariff reduction was not expected to affect trade. The higher reductions were obtained for goods for which U.S. officials anticipated competition from either other Western Hemisphere nations or European producers, including glassware, earthen and stoneware, cotton and linen goods, boots and shoes, chemicals, paper, dyes, soap, rice, butter, preserved fish and fruits, canned vegetables, and perfumes.

Reciprocity accelerated the integration of the Cuban economy into the North American system. The elimination of the old Spanish colonial trade restrictions, most notably the abolition of discriminatory tariffs and differential flag duties, immediately opened the Cuban economy to North American penetration. Reciprocity discouraged diversification and perpetuated local reliance on imported foodstuffs. Preferential access to U.S. markets deepened Cuban dependency on sugar production and increased North American control over this strategic sector of the economy. As early as 1902, 55 of the total 223 mills were owned by North Americans, accounting for 40 percent of Cuban sugar production. By the mid-1920s, of the total 184 mills, North Americans owned 41, producing 63 percent of the total crop.[13] The Reciprocity Treaty, a U.S. Commerce Department publication stated years later, granted "a practical monopoly of the Cuban import market to the United States and [provided] the stimulus, as well as much of the capital, for the development of the Cuban sugar industry."[14]

The reduction of Cuban duties opened the island to United States imports on highly favorable terms. The privileged access granted to North American products created a wholly inauspicious investment climate for Cuban capital. Even before 1903, the dearth of local capital and depressed economic conditions combined to thwart the development of local industry. After reciprocity, prospects for local enterprise diminished further. United States manufactures saturated the Cuban market and hindered the development of local competition. Reciprocity not only deterred new industry, it also had a deleterious effect on existing enterprises. Many could not compete with U.S. manufactures. Some cut production, others reduced operations, still others failed.

IV

Opportunities in Cuba were not limited to powerful capitalists and large corporations. North Americans of more modest means also looked upon Cuba as a place of new possibilities, a chance to begin anew. The vision was irresistible, and the timing was propitious: Cuba offered a new frontier at about the time Frederick Jackson Turner was lamenting the passing of the old one. It was described variously as "virgin land" and a "new California." [15] "Americans . . . have on their southern seaboard another California," observed traveler Isaac N. Ford as early as 1892. "Indeed," exulted Leonard Wood in 1901, "the island may be called a brand-new country." [16] Cuba offered opportunity in the form of cheap land and new hope for a people with industry and ingenuity—for farmers, miners, ranchers, and small investors, precisely the kind of people who had settled the last North American frontier.

They arrived by the thousands, this new generation of self-styled pioneers, consciously reenacting the drama of taming the wilderness, only this time in the tropics. They arrived as carpetbaggers and gamblers, brokers and vendors, homesteaders and settlers. Mostly they were small farmers and colonists, drawn to Cuba by the availability of land and the hope that tariff concessions on Cuban agricultural exports would create new business opportunities for industrious and enterprising settlers. They saw in the Reciprocity Treaty incentive to emigrate: North American settlers would grow citrus fruits, pineapples, and vegetables for export to North American markets.

No less than the powerful capitalists and large corporations, they displaced Cubans and quickly claimed possession of countless thousands of acres of farms and estates that were either defunct or in default. They were preceded by land speculators and real estate agents, who overran war-torn Cuba looking for bargains and cheap public land and resold tracts in subdivisions to North American settlers, colonists, and farmers.

These transactions announced the onset of large-scale colonization schemes. Through the early 1900s, hundreds of North American families emigrated to Cuba to establish agricultural colonies. By the early 1910s, no less than thirty-five North American agricultural settlements had been established across the island, including in Pinar del Río province, Ocean Beach, Paso Real, Palacios, Herradura, Candelaria, San Cristobal, and Bahía Honda; in Matanzas province, Matanzas, Ceiba Mocha, and Itabo; in Santa Clara province, Riverside, Manacas and Sancti Spíritus; in Camagüey province, Camagüey, Placetas, Florida, La Gloria City, La Atalaya, Port Viaro, Garden City, Boston, City of Piloto, Palm City, and Columbia-on-the-Bay; in Oriente province, Bartle, Las Tunas, Omaja, Cacocum, Holguín, Pedernales, Sabanso, Guanmo, Mir, Paso Estancia, Bayate, and Ensenada de Mora. By 1905, an estimated thirteen thousand North Americans, in Cuba and the United States, had acquired title to more than $50 million worth of land on the island. An estimated 60 percent of all rural property in Cuba was owned by foreigners, with another 15 percent controlled by resident Spaniards. Cuban ownership was reduced to 25 percent of the land.

North American migration was especially significant to the Isle of Pines. By the terms of Article VIII of the Permanent Treaty, the Isle of Pines was excluded from Cuban territorial boundaries pending future negotiations between the two countries. Washington contended that the Isle of Pines was simply another island in the Caribbean archipelago and by implication a U.S. possession by virtue of the treaty with Spain. Indeed, as early as 1899, the U.S. Department of the Interior was publishing maps of the United States and its possessions and designating the Isle of Pines as a North American possession. North American officials originally hoped to use the island as the linchpin in the expanding network of naval stations in the Caribbean and thus insisted that the status of the Isle of Pines be treated differently from that of Cuba.

During the years of subsequent negotiation, even as the Isle of Pines continued under nominal Cuban administration, it filled with North American colonists. As many as a thousand North Americans emigrated to the small island during the early years, acquiring nearly

$22 million in property holdings, certain that the U.S. claim over the island would eventually prevail. An estimated ten thousand people in the United States speculated in land development schemes or otherwise invested in Isle of Pines development projects. Land companies proliferated: Isle of Pines Company, Santa Fe Land Company, the Isle of Pines Land Development Company, the Almacigos Springs Land Company, the Fruit Culture Company, the Canadian Land and Fruit Company, the San José Company. North American settlers organized new towns, including Los Indios, Brazo Fuerte, Columbia, McKinley, and Santa Rosalia. They soon made up the majority of residents in the older towns of Nueva Gerona and Santa Fe. They organized separate schools, taught in English, and hired North American teachers. English soon became the predominant language and U.S. currency the medium of exchange. They established a North American bank and opened several hotels. Two weekly newspapers, the *Isle of Pines News* and the *Isle of Pines Appeal,* were published in English. A variety of social organizations, including the American Club, the Pioneer Club, the Santa Fe Social Club, the Card Club, and the Hibiscus Club, served as centers of social activity. Colonists banded together into the American Settlers' Association and the American Federation, lobbying associations to represent their interests directly to the Cuban government and Washington. North American clannishness was both cause and effect of scorn and disdain toward Cubans, who in their person and policies stood between the new settlers and their claim over the island. Cubans "are sometimes referred to as *spics,*" wrote one observer, "because the ignorant among the populace are wont frequently to say, 'no spickite Englese'—I don't speak English."[17] On several occasions during the early 1900s North American settlers, impatient with the slow negotiations to resolve the status of the island, plotted to arrest local Cuban government officials, seize control of the island, and establish a provisional government to negotiate union with the United States.[18] Visiting the island in 1908, Irene Wright observed that "American residents there have made the Isle of Pines an American community in everything except political status" and predicted confidently:

As surely as now we own California, political recognition must follow international law being, like other law, simply a statement of what is. Americans are in the majority of the population; American money is not only the official, but the actual currency of trade; the prevailing architecture outside the towns is unreasonably American; American ministers preach from the pulpits; American automobiles and spring wagons have replaced the clumsy oxcart . . . to facilitate shipments of fruits from orchards and gardens owned by Americans, producing for American markets. There are maps published, on which lands whose proprietors are American are colored red; these maps show that, literally, Americans own the Isle of Pines. [19]

The ratification of the Hay-Quesada Treaty in 1925 was a bitter blow to North American *pineros*. Surveys and maritime reconnaissance of the Isle of Pines and the surrounding waters had revealed the island to lack suitable harbors and the waters to be without sufficient depth and hence of little strategic value to the United States. By the terms of the Hay-Quesada Treaty, the United States relinquished to Cuba sovereignty over the island. With hopes of U.S. rule dashed, most North American settlers eventually departed, reducing the U.S. presence on the island to a handful of embittered residents. A decade later Sydney A. Clark toured the island and observed that the "small towns, such as Columbia and Santa Fe, once eager and flourishing, are now like the ghost towns of California's Mother Lode, populated by a scattered number of North Americans: still bitter at the action taken by the United States Senate on Friday, March 13, 1925, when it ratified the Hay-Quesada Treaty." Clark found Nueva Gerona to look "like a small town of Georgia or Tennessee that broke its tether, strayed to a strange pasture and became a stranger's property." [20]

North American colonies in Cuba during the early years of the republic announced the first wave of a vast and steady U.S. immigration. Not a few looked for the day when Cuba, filled with North Americans, numerically strong, strategically placed, and having discharged their civilizing mission, would lead the island into the North American Union. The agricultural colonies were to serve as the vanguard of this movement. Leonard Wood wrote wistfully about a future in which Cuba's population would reach 12 million, made up in the main of "industrious and enterprising planters and developers, a large proportion of whom will probably come from our own country." Historian Irene Wright, herself a North American resident of Havana, wrote exuberantly about the new generation of intrepid pioneers in Cuba, who struggled "to give final shape to that which they have taken in hand. Arrayed against them are the rigors of a southern, not northern, climate; and the dangers of contact with decadent, not savage, contestants with them for control." For many, it was Texas all over again. Others saw Hawaii. "It is not difficult to imagine," commented Lindsay Forbes in 1911 about the U.S. presence in Cuba, "a coup d'etat, resulting in a government in the hands of Americans."[21]

V

The growing U.S. presence in Cuba was accompanied by the expansion of North American cultural forms. Nowhere were these efforts better organized or more sustained than in education. The reorganization of the public school system during the military occupation created opportunities to transmit the ideological assumptions of U.S. hegemony and promote emulation of North American cultural forms. Particular attention was given to teaching the English language. Indeed, as early as 1899, journalist Charles M. Pepper could write of a "wave of English teaching that has swept over the island." These language skills, North Americans understood, provided the single most important cultural element linking Cuba to the United States, a skill that once mastered would allow Cubans to move with ease within the larger North American cultural framework. "The importance of teaching English in all Cuban public schools," U.S. Special Commissioner Robert P. Porter stressed in 1899, "must not be overlooked, because the Cuban people will never understand the people of the United States until they appreciate our institutions." In 1899, one observer reported, public schools in Santiago de Cuba were teaching English, "in all the grades for the purpose of its Americanizing effect."

In Matanzas, provincial governor James H. Wilson sought to purchase North American books for the municipal library. "The people here are anxious to learn English and read and study American books," he explained. "Unquestionably our literature will promote their knowledge, improve their morals and give this people a new and better trend of thought."[22] Not a few Cubans understood early that to be educated by the people who had conquered them was the extension of conquest, only by another name.

English also offered practical and immediate advantage. English was the language of the future, North Americans proclaimed, and few Cubans disagreed. The *Manual para maestros*, prepared by Superintendent of Education Alexis E. Frye, underscored the importance of English in the anticipated expansion of commercial and mercantile relations between the two countries. "All the Cubans," Frye asserted, "recognize the fact that the commercial language of the future in Cuba will be English. We have no wish to affect or change the language of the island, which must continue to be Spanish, but by teaching . . . English we will give them a better chance to understand us and do business with us."[23]

The relationship between the expanding North American political and economic presence and the growing ubiquity of the English language, on one hand, and command of English as a requisite for upward mobility and individual success, on the other, was manifest early. Indeed, English-language skills emerged as a distinctive cultural component of the new republican elite. Theory mirrored reality. Cubans observing even casually the ordering of the military occupation after 1899 understood these relationships as both a denouement and a portent. Among the principal beneficiaries of the North American presence were those Cubans who had previously studied and lived in the United States and were thus fluent in English and familiar with North American methods. The narrator in Carlos Loveira's novel *Los inmorales* (1919) describes how protagonist Jacinto Estébanez endured bitter experiences in New York and in the process "went about acquiring something invaluable in our latitudes for the struggle to earn a living: the English language." And to the point: "To know English is to have a guarantee of never being without a job."[24] The implications were not unambiguous. If relations with the United States did indeed continue to expand, it required little prophetic gift to appreciate the importance of English: success in Cuba would come to those who were prepared to meet the future. Across Cuba during the 1910s and 1920s, experimental schools were established to teach English to children and adults. "Many forward-looking Cubans," observed one traveler in 1920, "have come to realize that Spanish is no longer the chief language of commerce and that the inability of people to speak English is a barrier to progress."[25]

North American educational programs established one ideological framework within which the universality of U.S. culture emerged as the central theme and reduced Cuban aspiration for upward mobility to individual rather than collective terms. During the early years the United States sponsored teacher education programs for Cuban instructors to study English, geography, and the history of Cuba and the United States in North American educational institutions during the summer. Residence in the United States, North American authorities hoped, would have a salutary effect on Cuban teachers. Officials expected that after experiencing North American life directly, the teachers would return to Cuba favorably disposed to extol the virtues of North American values and cultural forms. The importance of this educational sojourn, Leonard Wood understood, was "not so much from what they learned from books and lectures, as from what they saw and absorbed from observation."[26] Cubans were escorted on field trips to New York, Philadelphia, and Washington for the purpose, reported one observer, of securing "glimpses into American life and activities." Visits to factories and industrial plants were used to demonstrate "the manifold manufacturing undertakings that underlie the material greatness of the American people."[27] Through the early years of the republic, 90 percent of Cuba's teachers participated in these summer programs, and they educated the first republican generation of Cuban schoolchildren.

Programs were also established for Cuban students. During the early 1900s, several North American organizations were formed to promote education in Cuba. The Cuban-American League of New York subsidized the cost of translating North American books into Spanish for classroom use in Cuba, and the Cuban Educational Association offered scholarships and financial support to deserving Cuban students to study in the United States. As Gilbert K. Harroun, the director of the association, explained, Cubans arrived "with an honest desire to study the American methods and return[ed] to their own land." Harroun exulted privately: "If [we] could dispose of a thousand children yearly we could gain in one half of the hundred years which otherwise will take us to Americanize this place."[28] By the early 1900s, the Cuban Education Association had assisted more than twenty-five hundred Cubans to study in various colleges and universities in the United States.

In lesser numbers but perhaps with greater consequences, North American teachers traveled to Cuba. Typically associated with the growing Protestant missionary presence on the island, they functioned as a religious counterpart to political, economic, and cultural penetration of the island. Catholicism was one more facet of Cuban culture targeted for extinction by North Americans, who saw it as simply another obstacle in the way of reshaping Cuban society into the image of the United States. "Three results of Romish domination are everywhere in evidence," moaned missionary J. Milton Greene in 1910: "an uncultured intellect, a perverted conscience, and a corrupt life," mandating "our evangelical missions [to] withstand and offset those influences which made U.S. government intervention necessary."[29] A Baptist minister reinforced his judgment: "The future of Cuba is unalterably bound up with that of the United States. We have made ourselves responsible in the eyes of the world for her political destiny, and the Christian people of America, whether they would or not, are responsible for the spiritual destiny of the Cubans."[30]

The Catholic church itself had more than adequately prepared the way for Protestant inroads. The colonial church had been inattentive if not indifferent to Cuban spiritual and material needs. Outside of Havana and the larger provincial cities, the church was all but a non-presence. Indeed, vast areas of the island, and especially the eastern jurisdictions, had virtually no contact with Catholic clergy. The end of Spanish rule in 1899 reduced even further the numbers of Catholic clergy. Many returned to Spain at the end of the war. Scores of others departed during the military occupation, after the United States separated church and state and halted state stipends to the clergy.

North American missionaries arrived during the military occupation in scattered numbers and subsequently in successive waves, representing the principal Protestant denominations of the United States: Northern and Southern Baptists, Southern Methodists, Lutherans, Episcopalians, Presbyterians, Friends, and Congregationalists. They staked out spheres of influence in Cuba and partitioned the island, more or less formally, into specific denominational zones. Northern and Southern Baptists divided the island in half, with the Northern Baptists claiming Camagüey and Oriente and Southern Baptists located in Las Villas, Matanzas, Havana, and Pinar del Río. The Friends and Methodists divided eastern Cuba between them; Presbyterians and Congregationalists settled in the western zones; and Episcopalians were active in Matanzas and Santiago de Cuba. The Episcopal church proclaimed the island a missionary diocese with a resident bishop. At an interdenominational conference in Cienfuegos in 1902, Protestant missionaries ratified a comity plan to guide North American evangelical activity in Cuba. Cities with populations of six thousand or more were open to all denominations. To avoid the appearance of interdenominational rivalry and conflict, however, smaller cities were assigned formally to the first denomination to establish itself in the vicinity.

Missionary activity in Cuba expanded in several directions at once. Churches and chapels expanded across the island. Between 1900 and 1910, Baptists in eastern Cuba established forty-four churches, sixty-eight chapel stations, and forty-six Sunday schools in forty-two towns and cities and claimed a membership of more than twenty-two hundred Cubans. By the early 1900s, several hundred Protestant ministers, *curas americanos* as they were called in Cuba, had taken up residence on the island. By 1901, one observer commented, "every considerable village in Cuba had at least one Protestant minister . . . with, generally, two or three women auxiliaries."[31]

Both the pedagogical content and the evangelical message of Protestant education promoted appreciation for North American values and institutions, expressions of the "civilizing mission" and universality of North American culture. Missionaries subsumed into their evangelical message a cultural component, different and distinct from the religious content, through which a sense of individual self-worth and collective esteem was attainable only by emulation of North American methods. "In the missionary work represented by Protestant missions is the best hope for the future of Cuba," proclaimed one missionary in 1910. "There must be a great deal of uplifting, of change, of improvement. The moral standards must be raised, and new ideals must be introduced. The Cuban people have . . . new habits to form, new customs to adopt, before they can reach the condition of civilization which they ought to have."[32] Cuba was in need of "the introduction of a new religious system," wrote the Reverend J. Milton Greene in 1907, and therein was "the real pacification of Cuba, her internal development and her stable prosperity."[33]

Their gains were statistically impressive—especially in rural communities outside Havana. Baptists established a day school in Santiago in 1901, another one in Manzanillo four years later, followed by others in Guantánamo, Baracoa, and Bayamo. With the help of a donation from John D. Rockefeller, they organized a boarding school for boys and girls at El Cristo, "where the pupils would be constantly under formative Christian influences for the development of their spiritual as well as their intellectual natures."[34] By the early 1900s, Protestant missionaries operated a total of one hundred schools (colegios) across the island. In addition to the traditional classroom curriculum, students obtained vocational and technical training in a variety of fields. Education was only one service provided free of charge. No fees were imposed for baptisms, marriages, and funerals. A variety of medical services were also made available at no charge. So, too, were tools and supplies, seeds, and agricultural equipment. Farmers received technical assistance, housewives received domestic advice, and children received education—all at no cost. Protestant programs expanded beyond Sunday services, Sunday school, and summer Bible camps to sponsorship of plays and dramas, community agricultural fairs, women's clubs, community night programs, and vaccination campaigns.

Through educational programs the missionaries recruited Cubans into future evangelical work and as support staff. Asserted one Baptist missionary: "It was most evident to us that some educational work should be undertaken by us if our churches and Sunday schools were to have intelligent native leaders in the future."[35] "It is essential," explained one Protestant teacher, "that the very best school training be given to the rising generation, under missionary auspices. This is necessary, not only for the raising up of a native ministry thoroughly equipped for a ministry that will command respect and a hearing, but also for those who are going to lead in public affairs and in business."[36] By the 1920s, much of the Protestant evangelical activity was in the hands of a Cuban ministry, in contrast to the Catholic church, where Spaniards continued to dominate the ranks of the clergy. This in turn facilitated missionary work. By the 1950s, as many as four hundred thousand Cubans belonged to one of the many Protestant congregations in Cuba, and by that time Protestant ministers outnumbered Catholic priests and Protestant churches and chapels outnumbered Catholic churches.

Increasingly North Americans directed a greater portion of their activities to recruiting the elites. Public schools were in deplorable condition, and Catholic schools were insufficient. Other factors were at work, Protestant educators discerned, and offered missionary schools ready access to local elites. One was "the mixing of the races," wrote the Reverend D. W. Carter, superintendent of Methodist missions in Cuba, "for which cause many of the well-to-do white people are not availing themselves of the public schools." These conditions created "a demand for first-class private schools on the part of persons who are able to pay for the education of their children, thus being opened up a way of access for the missionary to a large and influential class of people." [37]

Many Protestant schools soon assumed the appearance of preparatory schools, designed to meet the needs of the "very best people," principally the children of provincial and municipal elites.[38] For those elites who lacked sufficient resources to send their children to study abroad, the missionary programs offered acceptable alternatives. Children could learn English, acquire familiarity with North American methods, and complete a curriculum that would enable them to enroll in U.S. schools. That public education in the early republic continued to suffer from inattention and inadequate funding enhanced the appeal of private Christian schools. Certainly Protestant officials appreciated the superiority of missionary schools and were not slow to exploit their advantage. "Many of the more intelligent and cultivated people," wrote one missionary, "patronize private schools, both for social reasons, and because of more efficient teaching. The government system of education is unfortunately greatly hampered because of lack of trained teachers. . . . [Cuba] looks to the Christian mission school for her best-trained teachers." [39]

Protestant educational programs reinforced and expanded the influence of North American economic interests in Cuba. Mission educational and vocational programs were often conceived in conjunction with and subsidized by local U.S. corporations and property owners or dependent on donations provided by the U.S. Chamber of Commerce, U.S. corporations, and a variety of civic organizations, including the Rotary and Lions. The Candler school in Havana was named after and in part funded by the founder of Coca-Cola. The Methodist Agricultural and Industrial School in Preston, Oriente, was located on three hundred acres provided rent-free by the United Fruit Company, and the American Friends Board of Foreign Missions operated a school in cooperation with United Fruit. Hershey sponsored an agricultural school in Aguacate.

Christian education facilitated the integration of Cubans into local North American capitalist structures. That U.S. enterprises were favorably disposed toward the mission programs was in no small way a function of the collaborative relationship between North American businessmen and Protestant educators. Missionary schools often developed curricula, taught skills, and provided technical and professional preparation desired by U.S. enterprise. By training students for employment with North American companies, the mission schools discharged important social functions. Theology and ideology fused indistinguishably into North American pedagogy.

Cubans were thus socialized to view as normal, and to succeed in, an economic environment dominated by foreign capital. Local elites often identified their self-interest with the well-being of the North American presence. As early as 1910, the Candler school expanded its business curriculum in response to a call from U.S. investors and became the premier business school of Cuba, supported by donations and grants from local business interests and fully accredited by most universities in the southern United States. Similarly, the Methodist school in Preston developed educational programs to meet the needs of United Fruit, providing instruction, observed Irene Wright in 1911, "directed toward making the girls intelligent and cleanly homekeepers" and the boys "competent employees." The Agricultural and Industrial School was organized as a boarding school, accommodating approximately eighty Cuban students between the ages of fourteen and thirty, all of whom were on scholarships. United Fruit donated the land and provided water and electrical power free of charge and offered scholarship stipends. Additional donations were received from Bethlehem Steel Company and the Atlantic Gulf Sugar Company. Half the members of the board of directors, responsible for admissions, curriculum, and general school policy, were United Fruit and Bethlehem Steel officials. The school offered Cubans an opportunity for upward mobility by teaching English, introducing them to North American ways, and, most important, future employment with United Fruit. The students came to know officials of United Fruit, recalled Edgar G. Nesman, former director of the school, and "were looked upon kindly because they had graduated from the United Fruit–sponsored school."[40]

North American schools developed into important educational institutions on the island, offering a curriculum that spanned from elementary school to college. Inadequate public funding of education during
the early decades of the republic continued to enhance the appeal of
Protestant schools, which soon expanded beyond the basic curriculum
and religious training to include business programs, teacher education, agricultural programs, and professional preparation. Methodists
established some of the most prestigious schools in Cuba, including
Candler and Buenavista in Havana, the Irene Toland School in Matanzas, the Eliza Bowman School in Cienfuegos, and the Pinson School
in Camagüey. Many thousands of Cuban students graduated from
church-supported institutions and subsequently assumed positions of
responsibility in government, education, and business.

VI

The North American presence in Cuba expanded rapidly during the
early decades of the twentieth century. This presence included many
temporary and seasonal residents, mostly wealthy North Americans
who established winter homes along the north coast. They found in
Cuba a pleasant health resort, and they took advantage of the spas
and mineral springs. Many North Americans became permanent residents. By 1910, nearly seven thousand North Americans lived in Cuba
as farmers in agricultural colonies and as professionals in the trades,
commerce, and manufacturing. Many continued in the familiar role of
technicians to service the Cuban economy. The 1907 census identified
the greatest number of North Americans as agriculturists (724), clerks
and copyists (479), merchants (381), engineers and surveyors (171),
mechanics (146), and teachers (141). [41]
But numbers alone belied the function and importance of the North
American presence. Nowhere was this influence more keenly felt
than in the cities and towns located near the large North American sugar corporations. Such powerful enterprises as Hershey (Santa
Cruz del Norte), North American Sugar Company (Yaguajay), Ameri-

can Sugar Refining Company (Esmeralda), Atlantic Sugar Company (Tánamo), Cuban-American Sugar Company (Puerto Padre, Abreus, Perico), Cuba Cane Corporation (Morón, Ciego de Avila, Nuevitas, Alacranes, Sancti Spíritus), and United Fruit Company (Banes, Mayarí), to cite only the largest, emerged as states within a state.

The sugar companies established within their corporate confines U.S. communities, populated and managed principally by North American technicians, chemists, agronomists, managers, administrators, and their dependents. These North American enclaves developed into exclusive neighborhoods, recreating the social and racial patterns of life in the United States. They maintained separate social clubs, post offices, hospitals and clinics, religious and educational institutions, and power plants, and often private police forces. Many communities were reminiscent of neighborhoods in the United States. Wrote one observer of the Hershey community in Santa Cruz del Norte: "[It] is a Cuban rival of the famous Chocolate Town in Pennsylvania, with telephones, electric lights, clubs, theaters, dancing pavilions, an amusement park, a good baseball field, an excellent company hotel . . . and all the requisites of a modern American town."[42] The United Fruit community in Banes resembled a small New England town. "I was proud of Preston for various reasons," wrote traveler Sydney A. Clark of the United Fruit town, "all summed up in one, namely, that the community was *kept up*. The streets were in repair, the dwellings neat and well painted. Each dwelling had a lawn and the grass was cut, the hedge trimmed."[43] The sugar plant (*batey*) of the Cuban-American Sugar Company mill in Puerto Padre consisted of six hundred houses, with its own electrical plant and water supply, three social clubs (two for whites, one for blacks), and private schools built and staffed by Cuban-American Sugar.[44]

In a myriad of ways, these corporate entities dominated the social, economic, cultural, and political life of the *municipios* in which they were located. They provided the employment and payrolls upon which local communities depended, often totally. In rural zones without even rudimentary health facilities, access to modern company hospitals and clinics served as another source of dispensation available to local corporate officials. In everything but name these Cuban towns were company towns. North American corporations were actively if not always visibly involved in Cuban national, provincial, and municipal politics. Indeed, it was all but impossible for local politicians to succeed without support from the local sugar mill and, of course, vice versa. In some of the *municipios* there were few government officials who were not somehow associated with or dependent on the local sugar company. The mill administration was an important constituency, a source of campaign funds, an important source of tax revenue, and a powerful economic presence in the community. It was a political force to be reckoned with, and most local officials made their peace with the corporations on the most advantageous terms. From mayors and local aldermen, to provincial governors and provincial councils, to congressional representatives and senators, U.S. sugar corporations influenced the course and outcome of local politics. The sugar corporations delivered the votes of employees and indulged in varieties of graft and bribery. Children of local elites were admitted to local U.S. schools. United Fruit established a special fund to provide the children of exemplary employees with tuition support to study in the United States and hired friends and relatives of deserving local politicians.

Many national political leaders were directly linked to North American corporations. Some were tided over temporarily with employment after political setbacks. Many political careers were launched by the corporations. Scores of local government officials in the *municipios* of northeastern Cuba were former employees and functionaries of United Fruit.[45] President Mario G. Menocal (1912–20) previously managed the Chaparra mill (Cuban-American Sugar Company). Senator Luis Fernández Marcané served as attorney for United Fruit even as he chaired the Senate Committee on Immigration. Liberal vice-presidential candidate Miguel Arango in 1920 served as the manager of several estates owned by Cuba Cane Corporation. President of the House of Representatives Orestes Ferrara and Senator Antonio Sánchez de Bustamante sat on the board of directors of the Cuba Cane Corporation. Senator José Miguel Tarafa owned shares in the

Central Sugar Company. In return, of course, sugar corporations received a wide variety of concessions and special considerations. They obtained favorable court rulings in litigation, dispensation from local ordinances, police and military assistance to break strikes, favorable tax policies, import-export licenses, waivers of port regulations, and just about anything else they asked for.

In Havana, where the concentration of North Americans was greatest, they organized into social clubs and civic associations. The Jockey Club, the Havana-Biltmore Yacht and Country Club, the Cuban Athletic Club, the Havana Yacht Club at Marianao Beach, the Vedado Lawn Tennis Club, and the American Club of Havana emerged as centers of social life in the capital. Membership served as a means through which to recruit members of Cuban elites into North American circles. A YMCA was established in 1902. The Country Club was founded in 1912 by a small group of North Americans. By the 1920s, it claimed a membership of fifteen hundred and a long waiting list, composed mainly of North Americans but also many prominent Cubans. Every Sunday afternoon, after the races, the Country Club served as the rendezvous point for Havana society, as members and their guests competed on the croquet lawn and on clay and grass tennis courts, relaxed on the eighteen-hole golf course, lounged in the smoking room and bar, and enjoyed the bathing and boating facilities of the club. The American Club, founded in 1902, claimed a membership of seven hundred and was especially active in sponsoring banquets and lawn parties to commemorate U.S. national holidays. The clubs provided an important point of contact between ranking North American officials, merchants, and investors and their Cuban counterparts.

A variety of civic, social, and professional associations also served to institutionalize the North American network in Cuba—the Women's Christian Temperance Union, Rotary and Lions, Knights of Columbus, and the American Legion. The Sugar Club was an exclusive association of North American executives of sugar companies. Other organizations included the Women's Club of Havana, the University Club, Daughters of the American Revolution, United Spanish War Veterans, the Book and Thimble Society, and the Mothers'

Club. The Chamber of Commerce (organized in 1919) represented the interests of the more than 250 North American enterprises in Cuba and served as the principal lobbying organization of U.S. capital in two distinct capacities. Most directly, the Chamber represented North American interests to agencies of the U.S. government by maintaining contact with members' congressional delegations and key congressional committees as well as the Department of Commerce and the Department of State. These contacts were used to seek legislation and favorable policies from Washington for U.S. interests in Cuba, including tariff rates, commercial regulations, and tax supports. The Chamber used these channels to protest Cuban policies by appealing to Washington to intercede in behalf of U.S. interests. The Chamber of Commerce also lobbied the Cuban government directly, maintaining liaisons with the Cuban Congress and the various agencies of the Cuban government. The influence of the Chamber in official circles was considerable, for it was commonly known that as a last resort, North American capitalists were not slow to appeal directly to Washington for support.

North American influence was also disseminated through various English-language publications, including the periodicals the *Cuba Review and Bulletin,* the *Monthly Bulletin of the American Chamber of Commerce,* and the *Cuba Magazine* and three daily newspapers, the *Havana Daily Telegram,* the *Times of Cuba,* and the *Havana Post.* The *Post* was by far the most important. Strident in its defense of U.S. interests in Cuba, often openly scornful of Cuban government, the *Post* emerged as the principal organ of the North American colony in Cuba and something of a quasi-official outlet for U.S. government opinion. *Post* editorial positions seemed always to carry official authority, an ambiguity that served North American interests well and conferred on the *Post* an influence out of proportion to its circulation.

During the 1920s Cuba also emerged as a popular center of North American tourism. An estimated 173,000 tourists during 1910–15 increased to 187,000 in the next five years, rose again to 250,000 between 1920 and 1925, and nearly doubled to half a million in the next five years. During the tourist season in the 1920s, an average of twenty steamers a week and as many ferries traveled between Cuba and the United States, including Havana–New York (New York and Cuba Mail Steamship Company, Peninsular and Occidental Steamship Company), Havana–Key West and Havana-Jacksonville (Peninsular and Occidental Steamship Company), Havana–Key West (Florida East Coast Ferry Company), and Havana–New Orleans (Standard Fruit Company).

A distinctive pace of North American tourism was set by visitors drawn from the social register of U.S. high society. The DuPont family purchased a vast portion of premier beach on the Varadero peninsula and established a private residence and the exclusive DuPont Country Club. The Oriental Park racetrack in Marianao was opened in 1915 by H. T. Brown. Thereafter, the Havana racing scene became one of the highlights of the social circuit. The season extended from November to March, with many of the best horses from the United States racing in Havana during the winter. The opening of the Havana Yacht Club and the Casino Nacional in Marianao earned the Havana suburb the title of "the Monte Carlo of the Western Hemisphere."[46] Havana "is a city of definite attraction where smart people go to be amused," observed one traveler during the late 1920s. And further: "Havana is becoming a second home for that section of the smart set which formerly spent its winters on the Riviera. People whose names mean front-page as well as society page news are returning winter after winter."[47]

Havana was a place for North Americans to enjoy themselves, to do things they would not—or could not—do at home. In Havana, commented Sydney A. Clark, "conscience takes a holiday."[48] Tourism boomed, particularly during Prohibition, as North Americans flocked to Cuba to gamble but especially to drink. Bars in Havana multiplied prodigiously—to more than seven thousand as every restaurant and grocery store competed for the opportunity to quench North American thirst. During the height of the tourist season, Havana bars and clubs were crowded with North Americans. La Florida on Montserrat Street, the Plaza Bar, the Cafe Sazerac, the Inglaterra Bar and Patio, Donovan's, the Paris Bar, the Winter Garden, Sloppy Joe's, Ambos Mundos, Jigg's Uptown Bar—all became favorite haunts of vacationing North American patrons. For "serious drinkers," one traveler reported in 1928, Havana "is only overnight from Miami, a few hours' sail from Key West. It is hot, it is 'wet,' it is, in its easy tropical way, Wide Open."[49]

Tourism of this nature and magnitude, moreover, served in still one more fashion to increase the importance of mastery of English as a means of local well-being. With so much of the Havana economy dependent upon the expanding North American tourist trade, English-language skills soon became a requirement for employment in a wide variety of jobs—in hotels, restaurants, nightclubs, cafés, and casinos, and as bus drivers, cabbies, and telephone and telegraph operators. In Havana a special squad of English-speaking policemen was organized and deployed in the tourist zones. English-speaking taxi drivers were given preference in the lucrative tourist traffic areas.

VII

During the early decades of the twentieth century, the North American influence expanded in Cuba almost unchecked. And though it is impossible to assess its impact with any precision, it must be presumed to have been significant and in some situations and under certain circumstances all-encompassing. North American ways did indeed expand and take hold among Cubans, if only because for so many Cubans these ways were the only ones available. Cubans seeking a better life for themselves and for their children found choices limited and options fewer. As North American control expanded over every vital sector of the island economy, it was hardly possible for vast numbers of Cubans to find alternatives to working for the *yanqui.* That this was the overriding social reality of the early republic required Cubans to seize advantage and opportunity wherever found. This necessarily required Cubans not only to master North American methods but also to adopt the larger ideological and cultural assumptions upon which they were based—to become, in short, "*americanizado.*" Remarked one of Loveira's characters in *Los inmorales:* "From my time in the United States, I acquired one North American virtue, which is a pity that we have not imported to Cuba in our unlimited fondness to imitate everything *yanqui:* it is the virtue of work."[50]

In its multiple cultural expressions, ubiquitous economic forms, and ranging ideological assumptions, the North American presence assumed prepossessing dimensions. In some instances, the signs of this influence were striking. English became the means of the ascendancy for an upwardly mobile elite, and more: English words passed directly into Spanish, especially in sports, commerce and finance, and popular culture of all types. Given names changed, too, and Charles replaced Carlos, as did Henry for Enrique and Frank for Francisco, while Antonio became Tony and Eduardo passed as Eddy. North American parlor games, including bridge and Mah Jong, took hold over a widening cross section of the population. Cuban architecture borrowed freely and unabashedly from North American forms—in the Calixto García Hospital, the Institute of Secondary Education, and nowhere more obviously than in the construction of the Capitolio, a smaller but otherwise faithful replica of the U.S. Capitol building in Washington. The National City Bank building in Havana was designed by the New York architectural firm of Walker and Gillette and built by the Starrett Brothers of New York. "Office buildings . . . seem to have been bodily transported from New York," observed one traveler.[51] During the 1920s, films from the United States displaced European movies and all but arrested the development of a national cinema. "The moving picture industry," commented one traveler as early as 1920, "had been brought entirely from America, the theatres plastered with Douglas Fairbanks' set grin, William Farnum's pasty heroics, and Mary Pickford's invaluable aspect of innocence. Never, in the time I was in Cuba, did I see a Spanish actor or film announced."[52]

Geography, of course, facilitated this process, and once the political obstacles of Spanish colonialism were removed little remained to insulate the island from the United States. This U.S. dominance was underscored by the British vice-consul's observations in 1923 about conditions in the motion picture industry:

The proximity of the United States is almost fatal to the films of other countries. Not only are all the American film stars well known to the

Cuban public, but both the Spanish and American papers in Havana constantly grant publicity and a number of American cinema magazines are in circulation. Advertising is intense. Theatre owners and others have only to run over to Florida (some 96 miles) or even up to New York (60 hours) to see the latest films and purchase them on the spot, and most of them have agents and correspondents in the United States who send particulars of all new films and report on their suitability for the Cuban market. [53]

The Reciprocity Treaty also facilitated the expansion of U.S. cultural forms. North American values penetrated Cuban society deeply, at all levels, but especially at the top. The process began while the island was still a Spanish colony, during the middle years of the nineteenth century, and gained momentum in the early years of the twentieth. North American culture provided the standards by which to measure modernity, and hence the model to emulate. The living standard in the United States served as the basis by which to judge material well-being in Cuba, and hence the one to aspire to. And, indeed, under the circumstances, it could hardly have been otherwise. The sheer magnitude and robust productivity of North American capitalism, as well as the vast overflow of U.S. material culture, all but guaranteed that the island would be saturated with U.S. consumer goods. By the early 1920s, 75 percent of all Cuban imports originated from the United States. "The present-day Cuban is rapidly becoming Americanized," commented one observer in the late 1920s. "Thousands act, think, talk, and look like Americans; wear American clothes, ride in American autos; use American furniture and machinery; oftentimes send their children to American colleges; live for a time in the States themselves or expect to, and eat much American food." [54] This view was reiterated several years later by U.S. Ambassador Harry F. Guggenheim:

> There is first of all, the English language which has spread to such an extent in Cuba that most Cuban businessmen of standing have learned to speak it; the American press exercises a very great influence on the Cuban press—two press associations, the United Press and the Associated Press, supply Cuban papers with a large part of their foreign

news; American movies, American sports, particularly baseball, American dance music, American victrola records and last, but by no means least, American radio and broadcasting programs have made a very definite impression on the Cuban mind. [55]

Indeed, so rapid and so extensive was the expansion of the U.S. presence as to be all but overwhelming. It was above all a visible presence: social clubs, civic organizations, newspapers and magazines, the endless stream of tourists, diplomats, missionaries, and sailors. In the short space of several decades, North Americans all but controlled every major sector of the national economy: sugar, tobacco, the mines and ranches, trade, the utilities, the banks, and the railroads. They owned a vast portion of the national territory. They operated the better schools and presided over the most prestigious social clubs. They lived in privileged circumstances, in Havana and on the great sugar estates. They were moneylenders, landowners, and power brokers. They bought and sold Cuban politicians, policemen, and soldiers the way they bought farms and factories. It did, indeed, appear that the future belonged to the North Americans, and who among the Cubans could risk being left in the past?

The North American presence worked as an insidious and, on occasion, a destructive force. In its ubiquity and pervasiveness, it deprived Cubans of the opportunity to establish the primacy of their needs. This presence encouraged dependence on North American tutelage and largess and most of all relieved Cuban elites of public responsibility.

And because the North American presence in Cuba was so visible, and so visibly privileged, it aroused hostility and antagonism. Cuban efforts at collective mobility assumed increasingly distinct hues of anti-U.S. sentiment, for defense of the status quo had become one of the principal functions of the North American presence. Hostility spread among nationalists, intellectuals, and opponents of local elites, whose own local political ascendancy was often largely a function of North American hegemony. That vast portions of the Cuban working class formed around those sectors of the Cuban economy most heavily capitalized by North Americans meant that workers' efforts at increasing wages and improving working conditions created still another context for Cuban confrontation with the United States. Class conflict in Cuba thus acquired distinct elements of nationalism, anti-imperialism, and anti-U.S. sentiment. The Platt Amendment continued to rankle Cubans, an enduring source of injury to those who aspired to untrammeled national sovereignty. "Cuba hates the United States," one traveler in Cuba wrote as early as 1910. "The Cubans cordially despise the Yankees."[56] Traveling in Cuba the same year, Herbert G. de Lisser observed that the Cubans had begun to face "the sober reality of American domination." The "people who fought for their freedom and who hoped for complete independence fear now that they have but made an exchange of masters." Concluded de Lisser: "It is America who is the enemy, in the mind of the average Cuban—between American and Cuban no love exists."[57]

These circumstances profoundly influenced the character of Cuban nationalism. To all the other sources that propelled the Cuban quest for nationality in the nineteenth century was added a deepening hostility toward the United States in the twentieth. Many believed that national self-fulfillment could be attained only by ending the North American hold over Cuba, past and present, at its sources, and in all its forms. Enrique Collazo, in *Los americanos in Cuba* (1905), was among the first to dispute the importance of North American assistance in the war for independence. The defeat of Spain had been a Cuban victory, Collazo insisted, one stolen by the United States for the purpose of depriving Cuba of its sovereignty. Several years later Julio César Gandarilla returned to this theme in *Contra el yanqui* (1913). Gandarilla denounced the United States as duplicitous and the republic as a hoax. "Cuba struggled not only to shake off the Spanish yoke," Gandarilla insisted, "but so as not to live under any yoke, to achieve absolute independence. What amendment is contained in the American constitution, imposed by a foreign power that annuls and negates the sovereignty and prerogatives of the Federation of the United States?" Gandarilla denounced the "pessimists" in Cuba who by accommodation to the North American presence aided and abetted the debasement of *patria*.[58]

For many the expansion of North American control over the national economy raised another source of concern. The arrival of North Americans in such numbers, with capital resources of such magnitude, gaining control of strategic sectors of the economy with such ease, boded ill for the future of the republic. The unchecked expansion of foreign capital did not mean it was unopposed. As early as 1903, Senator Manuel Sanguily decried the loss of Cuban ownership of land and recommended legislation to restrict future sales of land to North Americans. "Every day they leap ashore from the steamers coming from the North," warned Sanguily, "these men of magnificent race, arrogant, their faces tanned by the cold north winds, with only a satchel but with wallets full of banknotes and their hearts aburst with impetuous blood; striding through our narrow streets with calculating eyes. . . . Ready to buy at low prices our immense lands. Favored by the thoughtlessness or the dire needs of the present owners who quit their patrimony without knowing what they do. And soon they will have everything. . . . And what of us? We shall be powerless."[59] In 1909, the issue came up again, when Congressman Emilio Arteaga introduced another bill to restrict the purchase of property by foreigners. Two years later, the gentle philosopher-educator Enrique José Varona exhorted Cubans to "wage war on the foreign capitalist" to recover control over the national patrimony.[60]

By the early decades of the new republic, a situation not unlike that in the closing decades of the old colony had developed in Cuba. The new republican elite drew its members from diverse origins. In part, it originated from the shattered colonial elites, who had found redemption in the U.S. intervention but in return ceased to function as an independent dominant social class. The trade-off was simple: they survived socially but were eclipsed economically. They were integrated into the structures of North American capitalism, in whose behalf they henceforth functioned. A second component of the republican elite consisted of representatives of an upwardly mobile middle class: thousands of Cubans who early and easily accommodated themselves to and benefited from the expanding North American role in Cuba. They ratified the North American presence and served as the middle persons between the new metropolis and the island. They served as an integrating force, providing North Americans with entrée in Cuba and were themselves, in turn, assimilated, as employees and partners, through ties of sentiment and persuasion, by habits and self-interest, into the structures of North American culture and capitalism.

Greater participation in the North American system was accompanied by other changes. Cuban elites increasingly staked their wealth and welfare on the United States. They looked to the United States to assist in the solution of Cuban problems, and more and more they became one with their patrons. They dwelled in two worlds, tied ideologically to one, linked culturally to the other. "To our wealthy people Gringo is a synonym for Order, Technique, Progress," rues the protagonist of Alejo Carpentier's *El recurso del método*. "The sons of the family who are not studying with the Jesuits of Belen are at Cornell, Troy, when not at West Point. We are being invaded—and you know it—by Methodists, Baptists, Jehovah's Witnesses and Christian Scientists. North American Bibles are part of the furniture of our rich houses, like Mary Pickford's photograph in a silver frame, rubber-stamped with her familiar 'Sincerely yours.' We are losing all our character." [61]

Not all Cubans benefited from the North American presence, of course. Afro-Cubans failed to achieve positions of security and status in the republic they had sacrificed to create. Local manufacturers and industrialists suffered at the hands of reciprocity and the failure of the Cuban government to protect national producers. Peasants, farmers, and small *colonos* were displaced and despoiled of their land by large U.S. sugar corporations and small North American agricultural colonists. Workers suffered from labor policies designed to satisfy foreign capital. Nor could the ruled reasonably look to the rulers for remedy, for ruling was itself a function of North American hegemony. Rarely did the North American presence in Cuba become a political issue. Government in Cuba served the interests of foreigners, as did local elites—just as before. So it was that the notion of transition from colony to republic had little relevance to the Cuban social reality.

6   The Purpose of Power

Relations between Cuba and the United States after 1902 tended to reflect accurately the anomalous constraints under which the republic was created. The Permanent Treaty guaranteed the United States an institutional presence in Cuban internal affairs. Increasingly the ubiquity of North American capital on the island created its own set of imperatives, around which the Cuban economy acquired its principal characteristics and from which political structures were to derive their primary purpose. Taken together, the multiple forms of U.S. hegemony in Cuba functioned as a system and affected profoundly the institutional character of the republic. Political culture, social formations, economic structures, and, in the end, the very function of the state were shaped by and around the expanding North American presence in Cuba.

Old contradictions from the colony passed directly and intact into the republic, and these were compounded by new ones that developed from Cuban treaty relations with the United States. The result was disarray and dysfunction in republican institutions, expressed most commonly in chronic political dislocation and skewed economic development. North American military, political, and economic intervention to remedy the consequences of these conditions made a Cuban solution all the more remote and unobtainable. Instability could not be resolved by North American efforts because it was in large part a function of the North American presence. State structures designed to accommodate U.S. political control, economic relationships created to facilitate foreign penetration, and a clientele political class organized to defend North American interests could hardly be expected also and at the same time to serve Cuban interests well, if at all. North American influence expanded over republican institutions, transforming them in the process into extensions of the U.S. national system to function more to meet North American than Cuban needs. Repeated

149

Cuban efforts to make republican institutions serve primarily national interests brought the deepest dislocation to the republic.

II

Economic well-being in the early republic became defined principally in political terms. Cuban politics developed into competition for control of the government primarily as an economic entity and public office as a form of employment. Politics symbolized opportunity in an economy in which opportunity was limited to outsiders with capital or insiders with power. It provided Cubans with the means of livelihood, mobility, and security. The overwhelming presence of foreign capital all but totally excluded significant Cuban participation in production and control over property. With so much of national wealth beyond the immediate reach of Cubans, public administration and political position guaranteed officeholders, their families, and their supporters access to the levers of resource and benefit allocation in the only enterprise wholly Cuban—government.

Politics assumed an internal logic of its own. Cuban demands on public administration were one manifestation of chronic unemployment and persisting underemployment, an outgrowth of a political economy unable to satisfy the primacy of national needs. The system functioned through a vast network of patronage, sinecures, and spoils of office—jobs, in other words. By 1910, more than thirty-one thousand Cubans were on the national payroll, accounting for nearly two-thirds of national expenditures. By 1915, the total number of public employees increased to forty-five thousand. Countless thousands of others were employed at the municipal and provincial levels and hired by private contractors engaged in government work. The expanding ranks of the civil service served to alleviate unemployment, creating jobs for the otherwise unemployed and work for the unemployable—for Cubans of all classes, but especially the middle class. The process relieved potential political pressure resulting from joblessness and provided a measure of social equilibrium to a political economy very much out of balance.

The system was driven principally by Cuban needs, obedient to an internal logic understood by key players, and transacted through traditional political activities that were economically motivated and socially determined. Politics in the early republic was serious business, if only because it was the only business Cubans controlled. "The true middle class," social commentator Miguel de Carrión observed in 1921,

> in possession of money and the resources of the Republic was not Cuban.
> . . . Thus, we had to pursue an abnormal course in the building of our
> country: instead of bringing to public power a proportion of wealth, we
> brought wealth to the hands of representatives of public power. . . . We
> made politics our only industry and administrative fraud the only course
> open to wealth for our compatriot. . . . This political industry . . . is
> stronger than the sugar industry, which is no longer ours; more lucra-
> tive than the railroads, which are managed by foreigners; safer than the
> banks, than maritime transportation and commercial trade, which also
> do not belong to us. It frees many Cubans from poverty, carrying them to
> the edge of a future middle class, which is still in an embryonic period,
> but that will necessarily form. [1]

That the Cuban electoral system appeared to conform to conventional political behavior tended to obscure the socioeconomic content of republican politics. Appearances were deceptive. Cuban politics observed all the proprieties of idealized electoral competition. Certainly the trappings were present and indeed served as the medium of the Cuban exchange: elections, political parties (Liberal and Moderate/Conservative), and nominating conventions, among others. But in practice, the function of republican politics had little to do with the form. Power contenders observed the protocol and rituals of political competition, and they understood the limits of acceptable conduct.

Political institutions conformed to social reality, which meant that the function they discharged often had little relevance to the one for which they were created. Wide-scale coercion against the electorate was routine; electoral fraud was common. Election rigging all but neutralized the value of the ballot as a means of political change. Political parties were only vaguely possessed of ideological content. Rather, they typically functioned as loose coalitions from election to election, organized around a dominant personality, a mixture of pragmatic calculation and self-serving opportunism. Manuel Márquez Sterling saw this as the absence of "intellectuality" (*intelectualidad*), bemoaning that "the political parties of Cuba lack intellectuality. Politics among us is dominated by men of action."[2] Political ceremony was dutifully observed and on occasion properly celebrated, but what mattered more was politics as a means of economic well-being and social security.

III

The presence of the United States introduced one more demand on an already overworked political structure. By claiming a general proprietary authority over the republic and a specific responsibility for "the maintenance of a government adequate for the protection of life, property, and individual liberty," the Platt Amendment established the United States as a potent political actor on the island. The consequences were far-reaching. That the United States claimed authority to intrude itself in the internal affairs of the republic and regulate the conduct of Cuban politics and the character of public administration, even as it continued to expand its control over the Cuban economy, placed insupportable pressure on the national system.

The resulting dynamic assumed a logic of its own. United States treaty constraints loomed large over the republic and provided the parameters around which national politics developed. Cuban power contenders accepted the reality of U.S. hegemony and on occasion reinforced it through collaboration. Just as often, however, and at every opportunity possible and expedient, they exploited the North American presence to their own advantage. They competed with each other for the benefits of that presence and in so doing served further to give legitimacy and institutional form to U.S. hegemony. Local political contenders learned to share power with the North Americans, more as a function of local ascendancy than ideological preference. Within that framework, however, they never renounced the primacy of Cuban interests, even if only defined narrowly to mean individual mobility and personal enrichment.

The North American presence influenced the strategies of all power contenders, incumbents and aspirants alike. That political rivals could draw different inferences of the meaning of North American treaty obligations underscored the degree to which the U.S. presence was subject to manipulation in local politics. In 1905, incumbent Moderate party president Tomás Estrada Palma obtained a second term through wholesale fraud and coercion. That Moderates undertook reelection in the first place and that they pursued a second term with unabashed ruthlessness was in no small way owing to their belief that treaty obligations required the United States to defend an incumbent president. As Moderates understood the meaning of the Platt Amendment, Washington was treaty-bound to assist constitutional government in the face of internal political disorders. How else could Moderates have interpreted Elihu Root's pronouncement in 1904: "No such revolutions as have afflicted Central and South America are possible there [Cuba], because it is known to all men that an attempt to overturn the foundations of that government will be confronted from the overwhelming power of the United States."[3]

The opposition Liberal party had a different view. Liberals insisted that Article III of the Platt Amendment committed the United States to the "maintenance of a government adequate for the protection of life, property, and individual liberty." Government violence, they argued, had deprived some Cubans of their lives; government fraud had deprived all Cubans of their liberty. Under the terms of Article III, hence, the United States was treaty-bound to install a government "adequate for the protection of life, property, and individual liberty." When Washington turned a deaf ear to Liberal appeals, party leaders undertook armed rebellion. If Washington was unwilling to meet its treaty obligations in behalf of Cuban lives and liberty, Liberals reasoned in 1906, it would certainly intervene to protect North American property.[4] Liberals were among the first in the republic to understand that an incumbent regime could be challenged by the destruction of foreign property—property that was all but impossible for Cuban authorities to defend: miles of unprotected rail lines, vast expanses of cane fields, the long stretches of unguarded telegraph and telephone wires.

In September 1906, Liberal strategies were successful. President Estrada Palma appealed to the United States for assistance to crush the uprising. "Government forces unable to quell rebellion," Consul Frank Steinhart cabled from Havana on September 8. "Government forces unable to protect life and property." A week later Estrada Palma again appealed for intervention, acknowledging bluntly that he had neither the strength "to prevent rebels from entering cities and burning property" nor the means "to protect North American lives and property."[5]

In 1906, political rivals arrived at similar objectives if for different reasons: both parties sought U.S. intervention, both believing they would benefit from intervention. Liberals, unable to undo political defeat at the polls, set out purposefully to create military conditions requiring North American intervention. Moderates, in turn, unable to forestall military defeat in the field, just as purposefully prepared to create political conditions requiring North American intervention.

The United States also had interests to defend, and by early fall it appeared in Washington that only armed intervention offered any prospects of meeting North American needs. The strategic and political implications of the Cuban conflict weighed heavily on the minds of U.S. officials. So, too, did the well-being of North American property interests on the island. In late September the United States intervened to end political disorders and replaced the Moderate government with a provisional occupation government, which lasted from 1906 to 1909.

Not for the last time political rivals in Cuba brought havoc on U.S. interests in pursuit of political objectives. Power contenders derived one important lesson from 1906: when all else failed, or did not succeed quickly enough, the destruction of North American property could serve as the continuation of Cuban politics by other means.

That the United States intervened in 1906 to displace a government held in disfavor by the opposition served to vindicate Liberal strategy. That in elections conducted under U.S. supervision in 1908 Liberals triumphed, moreover, suggested that there was more than one way to redress grievances and obtain political ascendancy.

The Cuban readiness to appeal to the United States, to be sure, had antecedents early in the nineteenth century. It was, in part, shaped by geographic proximity, in part ideological preference, in part desperate opportunism. It reflected also a persistence of colonial habits —Cubans subject to political authority from above, economic forces from without, and social rivals from below—and a perception of themselves powerless to affect the terms of any of these relationships. Cubans with grievances at home increasingly turned abroad for remedy. By appealing to the United States to intervene in their behalf, Cubans found a way to redress these imbalances. It began as early as the 1820s, when slaveholders looked to Washington for protection against the threat of social disorder. It continued through the 1890s, when property owners appealed for North American intervention to block the ascendancy of *Cuba Libre*. The United States represented a guarantee of political order and social peace, but most of all it was the keeper of the status quo. The Permanent Treaty served to give this role something of an institutional character and, in the minds of many Cubans, legal force. It was a protection many Cubans believed they were entitled to and upon which they came increasingly to rely. The habit acquired institutional character through the life of the treaty and persisted well after its abrogation.

That the practice endured for as long as it did, however, suggests that it also met North American needs. The recurring invitation to mediate local disputes provided North Americans with almost unlimited entrée into Cuban internal affairs. At the request of Cubans themselves, the United States found itself in an ideal position to resolve Cuban disputes in a manner most beneficial to U.S. interests. Washington could choose to respond to Cuban appeals or not, depending on the requirements of North American interests. This was the principal means by which the United States adapted the exercise of hegemony to changing circumstances in Cuba. Participation in the resolution of Cuban crises allowed North Americans to promote the ascendancy of pro-U.S. persons and parties, foster pro-U.S. policies, and, in general, obtain advantage in all matters affecting the well-being of U.S. interests. The danger to North American interests occurred not when Cubans appealed for U.S. intervention but, rather, when Cubans pursued independent solutions that excluded U.S. participation.

Political disputes in the early republic tended to get caught up in and worked out through existing treaty relations. Increasingly, Cubans developed political responses around treaty linkages to the United States. Afro-Cuban political leaders in 1912 and Liberals in 1916–17 and again in 1920 invoked the Platt Amendment to justify revolution. "Pray tell President Taft," black political leaders petitioned the U.S. minister in March 1912, "to accept our most solemn protest in the name of the 'Independent Party of Color' against outrages against our persons and our rights by armed forces of the Cuban Government. We protest to civilization, and ask for guarantees of our lives, families, interests, rights and liberties. Weary of injustice and abuses, we look to the protection of your Government under article three of the Platt Amendment."[6] A similar situation occurred in 1917. The moment Conservative President Mario B. Menocal secured reelection through electoral fraud, Liberals insisted, there ceased to exist in Cuba a government that guaranteed life, property, and liberty. The 1917 revolution, Liberals argued, sought only to fulfill the requirements of Article III.[7] Similarly, in preparing for national elections in 1920, Liberals again invoked the Platt Amendment, this time not to justify revolution but to demand U.S. electoral intervention. Government abuse and fraud threatened to nullify democratic processes, Liberals charged, and only U.S. supervision of the elections promised to restrain the government. "It is a case," Liberal party chief Faustino Guerra paraphrased Article III in 1920, "of electoral intervention for the maintenance of an adequate government for the protection of life, property, and individual liberty, seriously threatened at the coming electoral period."[8]

Political disorders in the republic assumed a peculiar economic function, one also determined by the treaty context of the early republic. In 1912 and 1917, as in 1906, violence was directed more against property than against government security forces for the specific purpose of creating conditions requiring U.S. intervention. Indeed, the insurgents did not contemplate overturning the government; rather they sought to create conditions that would provoke U.S. intervention, from which they expected to derive redress of their grievances. As the North American economic stake in Cuba increased, so did the demand for order and stability and the vulnerability of foreign property to attack. That the North American commitment to order was specific and explicit, and given treaty form, made the U.S. presence in Cuba all the more susceptible to pressure from local power contenders. The capacity of disaffected factions to inflict extensive property damage in the briefest time preyed on the minds of North American officials. "The great trouble is," William H. Taft wrote of the 1906 uprising, "that unless we assure peace, some $200,000,000 of American property may go up in smoke in less than ten days." Taft was determined to settle the crisis quickly to "avoid great disaster to business and property interests of the Island."[9] In 1912, Consul Ross E. Holaday in Santiago warned that without a quick political settlement, the government was powerless to prevent determined "incendiaries" from destroying "in an hour property representing millions of dollars in value and that has taken years to construct."[10] The 1917 revolution occurred at the height of the harvest and resulted in more than $200 million in property damages.

These conditions imposed on Cuban governments two mandatory but often conflicting missions. The defense of foreign property was at least as important as the defeat of insurgent forces. A government could deploy its security forces either in the pursuit of rebel bands or in the defense of property, but resources rarely permitted both. Pressure to protect foreign property threatened to leave the government without the means to defend itself. The decision by Estrada Palma in 1906 to deploy the armed forces on foreign property allowed insurgent Liberals to overrun government positions. The U.S. consul in Santiago understood that insurgent tactics in 1912 were designed to "compel the Government to detach soldiers for the protection of foreign property, thereby impairing the effectiveness of the military forces, enabling them to continue indefinitely."[11] When Washington insisted that Cuban authorities do more to protect foreign property, President José Miguel Gómez protested that such use of his military would require his "best troops for the protection of one group of foreign properties in one part of the disaffected district," and inevitably, Gómez insisted, his "entire army of regulars and volunteers would not suffice for police work alone without considering the prosecution of a campaign against the insurrectionists."[12]

Several corollaries developed from these circumstances. First, the greater the inability of a government to protect foreign property, the more vulnerable it was to political violence and the more susceptible to U.S. intervention. For these reasons, disaffected political groups could pursue no more effective means to create pressure on an incumbent regime than to attack foreign property. Indeed, the U.S. treaty commitment to maintain order was virtually an incentive to disorder. More than two years before the 1917 revolution, Liberals were already planning recourse to arms. "The prevailing popular idea," Minister William E. Gonzales reported as early as October 1914, "that the United States would take charge here at the outbreak of disorder is encouraging opponents of the administration to inaugurate disorders." "This idea of being able to upset an administration," Gonzales warned, "by securing intervention by the United States . . . is leading opponents of the Government to inaugurate disturbances."[13]

IV

If the U.S. treaty presence influenced the form and function of political protest, it also influenced state response to political disorders. Cuban officeholders understood well the meaning of the Platt Amendment, especially after 1906, when the United States removed a government unable to discharge its treaty obligations to foreign property.

Cubans were sensible to the necessity of tending to the well-being of foreign interests to ensure their political survival. The degree to which Cubans protected foreign lives and property became the principal measure by which North Americans determined whether or not Cuba possessed a government capable of meeting treaty responsibilities. On occasion Washington was blunt. In 1912 Secretary of State Philander Knox warned that "continued failure on the part of [the Gómez] administration adequately to protect life and property will inevitably compel this Government to intervene in Cuba under and in response to its treaty rights and obligations."[14]

Defense of foreign interests thus became the means by which officeholders retained U.S. backing. Indeed, one of the enduring features of the Cuban political reality was fixed early: a regime in Havana enjoyed U.S. support in direct proportion to its capacity to protect North American property. This situation had consequences of other kinds. Cuban interests were subordinated to foreign ones. During the 1912 uprising the U.S. minister reported that "Cuban interests in Oriente are receiving practically no protection because of the fact so much pressure is being brought to bear in behalf of foreigners."[15]

Government in Cuba continued to be more responsive to foreign needs than national ones. Cuban property owners found in this situation renewed incentive to obtain U.S. citizenship through naturalization and thereby qualify for priority protection from the Cuban government. Cubans now had one more reason to look to the United States for protection of their interests. The protection of foreign interests became an intrinsic and central character of the Plattist state, for it provided the means by which incumbents retained power against internal opposition and averted pressure from abroad.

V

The threat to U.S. interests was not limited to disputes among rival political contenders. It also came from the swelling ranks of the Cuban trade union movement. From the establishment of the republic, the

Cuban labor market displayed several notable features very much in demand by foreign capital. Liberal immigration policies served to provide an abundant supply of cheap foreign labor. Low wages and weak labor organizations, persisting legacies of the colonial system, offered additional inducements to North American investment. These were not preferred conditions for foreign investors—they were requisite ones, and as such they formed part of a total economic environment which the United States was committed to creating and maintaining. It was not sufficient to have preferential access to local markets and local resources. It was necessary also as a corollary condition to depress wages, prevent strikes, and discourage labor organizing.

In fact, Cuban workers registered steady gains during the early decades of the republic. Crafts and trades unionized, and the regional and national federations increased in size and power. The expansion of unionization was both cause and effect of growing labor militancy. Strikes, work stoppages, and boycotts announced the growing power of Cuban trade unionism.

That North American capital so thoroughly dominated production and so largely controlled property meant that attempts to improve working conditions ultimately involved labor confrontation with the United States. Indeed, the most conspicuous labor advances of the decade were registered in the sectors most heavily capitalized by foreign investment, including shipping, railroads, sugar production, and construction. Strikes against shipping and wharf facilities halted trade, interrupted sugar exports, and suspended delivery of vital machinery, equipment, and spare parts. Rail stoppages paralyzed the internal movement of supplies and crops. Strikes against sugar mills threatened the harvest. In fact, so thoroughly had U.S. capital penetrated the Cuban economy that it was not likely that a strike in any sector of agriculture, commerce, manufacturing, communication, transportation, mining, and utilities would not somewhere, somehow, adversely affect North American interests.

Foreign capital perceived the growing strength of labor with no less repugnance than political disorders that destroyed property. Strikes suspended normal business activity, and it mattered not whether they

were wholly peaceful or frequently violent; in either case they interrupted production, endangered property, and threatened profits. A
strike among stevedores in Havana in May 1912 led to sympathy
strikes in Santiago de Cuba, Guantánamo, Manzanillo, and Cienfuegos and ultimately to the suspension of all shipping along the south
coast. North American interests were among the principal casualties. "Present strike," Minister Arthur M. Beaupré cabled Washington,
"seriously damages horticultural interests, which are almost entirely
American, and important American shipping interests."[16] A strike
among sugar workers during the 1919 harvest interrupted the harvest
and resulted in the loss of millions of dollars.[17] Another strike on the
Havana docks in 1920 paralyzed all maritime traffic, causing damage
to North American interests estimated conservatively at $300,000 a
day.[18] In 1922, the Department of Labor estimated that strikes and
work stoppages in Cuba resulted in a loss of $200 million to U.S.
investors. [19]

The growing strength of labor unions was a matter of grave concern to North American capitalists. At issue were the very assumptions upon which foreign capital operated in Cuba. Workers' demands
for increased wages and improved working conditions and calls for
the right to organize found expression in strikes, boycotts, and, increasingly, violence and sabotage. North American capitalists looked
first and immediately to Cuban authorities to protect property against
labor. Ultimately, however, investors relied on Washington to hold the
Cuban government to the task of defending their interests. Havana
was held directly responsible for the actions of Cuban workers, and
if local governments proved unable or unwilling to end the threat to
property, U.S. military intervention to restore order to the workplace
would be necessary. And, inevitably, the inability of Cuban authorities to provide the assistance deemed adequate for the protection
of foreign property created conditions that justified the invocation
of Article III and the threat of armed intervention. By challenging
foreign capital, labor indirectly threatened incumbent officeholders.
If indeed the defense of national sovereignty turned on security to
foreign property, per the requirement of Article III, labor strikes no

less than political disorders threatened national sovereignty. Workers threatened to create the conditions inviting armed intervention and, ultimately, the displacement of Cuban government.

Labor-management relations had direct implications for Cuban–United States relations. "The political problem Spain failed to solve in Cuba," Special Representative Enoch H. Crowder asserted in 1922, "was intimately connected with an economic problem, and this in turn depended upon social and industrial conditions closely connected with the labor question." Crowder drew an obvious moral: "If the above is true, then we can assume that the maintenance of the Government and the protection of property in the country is, to a certain degree, in the hands of the labor elements. For this reason, beside the economic one, our Government had a direct interest in labor conditions because of article three of the Platt Amendment."[20]

Thus the United States included workers as a threat to property and their actions a justification of armed intervention. Labor threatened foreign property, and the United States demanded that local authorities protect property from all sources of danger. The Cuban government was enjoined to oppose labor militancy with as much vigor and force as it would employ to combat armed rebellion. The distinction between politicians organizing an uprising and the proletariat organizing a union, on one hand, and sedition and strike, on the other, was a moot point, a subtlety too fine to distract Washington from the larger task of protecting foreign capital. And, in fact, no such distinction was made. In both cases the effects were similar: profits declined, production diminished, and property values decreased. Indeed, the link between political disorder and labor unrest was itself a policy construct that enlarged the sanction for U.S. intervention. A railroad strike in early 1919, Minister William E. Gonzales informed Washington, "by paralyzing railroads is curtailing sugar production and causing tremendous losses to American interests." This "menace to property interests . . . is as great as would be active revolution." Gonzales urged the State Department to issue a public manifesto directly to the Cuban people stating that "the Government of the United States has therefore determined in exercise of its treaty rights to suggest to the Government of Cuba, if work on the railroads, in the harbors and in other essential industries is not resumed within twenty-four hours, the adoption of certain drastic and thorough-going measures to enforce such resumption, and to lend the Government of Cuba the necessary moral and material aid and support to carry out these measures."[21]

On occasions when local authorities revealed themselves incapable of controlling labor demonstrations, the United States stepped into the breach. A general strike in 1919 prompted the mobilization of some six thousand marines in Philadelphia and Quantico for deployment in Cuba. An additional thousand marines arrived in Cuba to reinforce the garrison at the Guantánamo naval station. Warships made "friendly visits" to port cities affected by strikes in the hope, the secretary of the navy wrote, that they "might have a good effect in easing the condition brought about by a number of strikes now going on."[22] Naval vessels visited the stricken cities of Havana, Cienfuegos, and Gibara, and their presence intimidated workers and forced them to return to their jobs.[23] Marine units stationed in eastern Cuba after the 1917 revolution were also used to combat labor activity. The marine command organized "practice marches" and reconnaissance patrols to provide a military presence in districts affected by strikes. The movement of marines from Santiago de Cuba to Camagüey in one "practice march" was organized in such a manner as to give the deliberate impression that U.S. armed forces had arrived to crush a local strike.[24]

VI

It was not only that the United States opposed organized labor. Washington also opposed Cuban efforts to enact labor reforms and social legislation. North Americans opposed efforts to legislate hours of work and compensation, to provide for pensions and insurance, and to extend state sanction for unionization. Foreign capital resisted most labor legislation, for in one form or another these efforts threatened to impinge on foreign property interests and interfere with foreign investments. Washington opposed attempts to "nationalize" Cuban labor, a requirement that employers hire 51 percent Cuban workers, for such a law would signify the end of cheap immigrant labor. Indeed, liberal immigration policies and unlimited access to contract labor from Haiti and Jamaica long had been central elements of North American efforts to depress wages and discourage unionization. As early as 1900, U.S. officials understood the relationship between immigration and cheap and unorganized labor. "The Cubans learn early the power of combinations," observed Colonel Samuel M. Whitside, "and when they believe that their labor is indispensable, strikes are very liable to follow, but if a foreign element is present, which will not unite in such movements, besides having the idea instilled in their minds that if they are not satisfied they may go and their places will be filled by foreigners, no trouble is encountered."[25]

Legislative efforts to improve the condition of workers also met active North American opposition. Legislation in 1910 proposing an increase of the national minimum wage to $1.25 a day for public employees at national, provincial, and municipal levels was opposed. North American contractors immediately denounced the proposed guidelines.[26] "If the bill becomes law," Assistant Secretary of State F. M. Huntington Wilson protested, "various complications will arise between the Government and those who have made contracts based upon the conditions of the labor market heretofore existing." Washington instructed the legation "to present this matter informally, but correctly, to the attention of the Cuban Government, and to indicate clearly to that Government that the enactment of such legislation is all but certain to bring both Governments difficulties and entanglements of a serious character."[27] The bill was defeated. In 1927 another bill recognizing trade unions and establishing compulsory arbitration also met opposition from foreign capital and failed.[28]

VII

Expanding North American claims over the internal affairs of the republic placed impossible demands on state structures, leading to grotesque distortions of national institutions and exacerbating social tensions. The issue was a conflict over whether the state would serve the interests of the United States, for whom the defense of foreign property was synonymous with security requirements, or Cuban officeholders, for whom defense of self-government was a function of the distributive nature of public administration. In short, the question was who would control the state, who would benefit by such state policies as tariff regulations and tax measures, labor laws and land policies, public franchises and revenue disbursement. Occasions did arise, of course, when the needs of North American capitalists and Cuban officeholders converged and were satisfied at one and the same time. But just as often they did not. The United States demanded unlimited sanction to regulate public administration and supervise internal affairs in Cuba as the means to protect and promote North American property interests. Cubans defended their prerogative over government to expand their interests.

To a large degree, politics in the early republic eluded U.S. efforts at regulation precisely because it was driven by nonpolitical issues. With each political crisis the United States moved to expand its authority over government in Cuba and thereby added new pressure on state structures. North American efforts to remedy the causes of Cuban instability led to the reorganization of Cuban agencies and the adoption of procedures and practices based on North American models and methods. Inevitably, the more the Cuban system was forced to discharge North American functions, the less it served Cubans. Efforts by the United States to make Cuban politics work according to some prescribed and culturally determined version of how politics should work resulted in the creation of institutions with little relevance to the Cuban social reality, creating new sources of instability.

In 1906 this signified nothing less than the complete abrogation of Cuban sovereignty. The United States seized the island anew and ruled through a provisional government and military occupation. Between 1906 and 1909, U.S. efforts centered on reorganizing political and administrative procedures and developing new institutional guarantees of order and stability. The electoral code was revised. A new population census was prepared. New laws dealt with municipal administration, local election boards, judicial reform, and civil service reorganization. A new army was created to assist in the preservation of order. For the North Americans, these were the minimum conditions to guarantee "good government." For the Cubans, they were the minimum conditions to guarantee sovereignty.

The election dispute in 1916 and the revolution in 1917 provided another occasion to expand U.S. control over the island. In March 1919, Washington dispatched General Enoch H. Crowder to supervise political reorganization in Cuba. The electoral code was rewritten and entrusted to judicial agencies greater responsibility for resolving electoral disputes; the authority of the local appellate system over election procedures was expanded. Additional U.S. reforms included the issuance of new voter registration cards, improved communications to relay outlying returns to Havana, and safeguards against the padding of voter registration lists. Another census was completed, followed by a period of party registrations and distribution of new voter identification cards. In the end, the United States took direct charge of supervising the conduct of the 1920 elections, claiming this authority under the terms of Article III. "Experience in the past has shown very plainly," Secretary of State Bainbridge Colby suggested, "that free and honest elections are essential 'to the maintenance of a government adequate for the protection of life, property, and individual liberty.'" Treaty obligations thus made it "incumbent on the Government of the United States to use all available means to observe the conduct of the electoral procedure in Cuba, as well as the spirit in which the electoral law is being enforced."[29]

VIII

The problem with U.S. intervention in all its multiple forms was that it exacerbated the very problems it sought to remedy. More intervention seemed to require more intervention, and there seemed to be no end to the process. The belief that honest elections offered a solution to chronic electoral violence prompted the United States to establish new Cuban agencies, rewrite electoral codes, reorganize balloting procedures, and revise voter registration rolls by updating censuses. But this was not enough. To make certain new agencies operated efficiently, that new codes were enforced impartially, and that censuses were taken accurately, the United States had to oversee these operations. This oversight was still not sufficient. To guarantee the integrity of balloting at the polls and provide credibility of the counting of the ballots obliged the United States to dispatch North American election supervisors in the field. And this was still found wanting. Once in the field, North American agents were called upon to mediate the slightest dispute between a voter and the local election agency. Despite these efforts, elections in 1920 ended in a stalemate, with both sides charging fraud and each threatening rebellion.

These conditions reached a denouement in 1920. Government in Cuba was paralyzed as a result of the disputed election, and the island edged toward civil war. General Enoch H. Crowder returned to Cuba, this time as "Special Representative of the President." For the better part of the next three years, Crowder functioned as something of a proconsul, governing Cuba in every way except in name.

The Crowder appointment reflected growing U.S. disinclination to undertake armed intervention. It suggested, too, the conviction that political intervention, undertaken by the U.S. diplomatic representative, would remedy past problems and prevent future ones. The emphasis was on reform, and the means was not politics but administrative management.

This intervention signified nothing less than a North American moratorium on Cuban politics. Crowder asserted sweeping authority over Cuban administration, including supervision over the pending partial elections, reorganization of national, provincial, and municipal government, budget, loan negotiations, and management of the Cuban economy. For the previous two decades, Washington had moved inexorably toward replacing politics by Cubans with administration by North Americans: prescribing acceptable policies, prohibiting unacceptable ones. In 1920, the United States (as it was doing elsewhere in the Caribbean) adopted unabashedly a management mode of supervising Cuban affairs—not unlike previous military occupations, except that in 1920 the United States did not displace Cuban government; rather, it simply ruled through Cubans.

The Crowder appointment signaled more than a new form of intervention. It represented the most sweeping sanction for the appropriation of Cuban administration ever derived from treaty rights. It was not necessary—or desirable—to suspend Cuban sovereignty as long as the exercise of that sovereignty did not obstruct the exercise of U.S. hegemony. The invocation of treaty rights did not require the displacement of Cuban government, only Cuban acquiescence, and as long as the Cuban government heeded the advice of the special representative there would be no "intervention."

Crowder lost no time exercising this authority over the new Alfredo Zayas government. He pursued the most far-reaching reorganization of Cuban government since the military occupation of 1899–1902, an attempt to eliminate what was perceived as the defects and deficiencies accruing in the two decades of self-government. The time was right, Crowder counseled, to proceed "with the necessary justification to employ the ultimatum in demanding of the Zayas Administration the accomplishment of certain essential reforms."[30]

But, in fact, it was to be more than the adoption of "certain essential reforms." Crowder aspired to nothing less, in his words, than an "era of moral readjustment in the National Administrative life of the Cuban Government," to be accomplished by "coercive influence" and "insistent advice, recommendations, and finally the virtual demands of the United States through my Special Mission." In March 1922, Crowder dictated the first of a series of memorandums—fifteen in all, ultimatums directed to the Cuban government demanding reforms and reorganization of virtually every key aspect of national, provincial, and municipal administration.[31] Crowder also claimed authority to appoint cabinet members. In June 1922, he concluded that members of the Zayas cabinet could neither inspire confidence in nor induce compliance with the moralization program. He insisted upon a cabinet reorganization and the selection of new ministers, especially for the departments of treasury, public works, and *gobernación*. The new secretaries were to be selected, in Crowder's words, for "the purpose of waging a relentless war on the graft, corruption and immorality especially prevailing in these three departments." The appointments, he further stipulated, would be made "only after conference with me as to their availability to carry out these important reforms."[32]

The Zayas administration became quickly and directly the means through which the United States governed the island. Crowder presided over the executive and prevailed over the legislature. He appointed and dismissed officials at all levels and reorganized cabinet departments. He met regularly with congressional leaders, lobbying legislators in behalf of reform measures. Just as often, he protested bills incompatible with the moralization program. When the Cuban Congress balked at reform legislation, the State Department publicly rebuked its "obstructionist action." By early 1923, Crowder had become the Cuban government.

7   Stirrings of Nationality

By the 1920s, the contradictions of U.S. hegemony in Cuba had overtaken the republic. For more than two decades the United States had endeavored to create conditions in Cuba in which North American interests—political, economic, strategic—could flourish and prevail, not only against the interests of other foreigners but against Cuban ones as well. Increasingly, Cubans were reduced to marginal participation in the conduct of the affairs of their own state, operating at the edge in pursuit of their interests, in ways common to all marginalized cultures—through wile, cunning, and opportunism. They exasperated their North American patrons, outwitted them on occasion, and effectively if irregularly thwarted the expansion of North American influence over the island. They neither directly challenged the North American presence in Cuba nor refuted the assumptions upon which U.S. hegemony rested, but through resourcefulness and subterfuge they achieved no small amount of success. Cubans understood well North American power, its limits, and the character of its use, and through this knowledge achieved over time a measure of autonomy. The United States demanded unobstructed scope of action. As Cuban autonomy and local initiative diminished, so did the prestige of national leaders. The Crowder mission was the culmination of this trend.

As the scope of North American intervention widened and its authority penetrated deeper into Cuban internal affairs, the very exercise of that control served to sharpen the contradictions of Cuban political economy. The United States could not preempt Cuban government on the scale it had during the late 1910s and early 1920s without inflicting irreparable damage on the ability of Cuban officeholders to rule internally. What was not perhaps entirely evident to North Americans in the early 1920s was that these were the rulers to whom the United States looked for the defense of its interests, and to deny Cubans the authority to rule was effectively to undermine their capacity to govern. By preempting Cuban rule so blatantly, in plain sight of a national audience, the United States exposed Cuban sovereignty as a fiction, revealing Cuban rulers as little more than instruments of North American interests, incapable of defending national interests and unable to preserve national sovereignty—and thereby serving to set in motion demands for another kind of *patria* and stirring the embers of Cuban nationalism.

Economic and social circumstances of the client state changed in the 1920s. The prosperity of the war years stimulated economic development and released new social forces that changed the character of Cuban society, revealing a more complicated social system, more clearly defined class structures, and more distinctly articulated social conflict. New social groups emerged as aggressive political contenders, seeking change and reform. But they rejected more than the old politics; they also challenged the premises of North American hegemony and denounced U.S. influence over the political system and the national economy.

One sign of the changing times was the emergence of a new Cuban entrepreneurial bourgeoisie, shaped by conditions created during World War I and the development of an import-substitution industry at the consumer-goods level. Local manufacture and light industry expanded during the war years, providing new opportunities for local capital. Land speculation and a building boom in Havana boosted Cuban construction-related enterprise. By the mid-1920s, Cuban capital dominated some thousand factories and businesses across the island.

The emergence of this Cuban entrepreneurial bourgeoisie gave form to a new political constituency, representing capital largely local, advocating goals entirely national, but most of all demanding state support of interests wholly Cuban. These were the groups most susceptible to the appeals of economic nationalism and for whom North American intervention on behalf of foreign capital was becoming increasingly noxious and unacceptable. Their most prominent demands included state protection from foreign competition, reduction of the role of foreign capital in the national economy, state-supported development projects, technical assistance, and subsidized loans and low-interest credit. They called for probity and honesty in public office and demanded increased state intervention in education, medical care, and housing.

Developments in the 1920s galvanized the new entrepreneurial bourgeoisie into political action. These were years during which Cuban property owners became alive to the necessity for greater political involvement in public affairs in defense of local economic interests. In the early 1920s, key sectors of the local bourgeoisie organized into associational pressure groups to defend their interests. The emergence of interest groups created new political pressure for policies in behalf of national needs, including state intervention in the defense of local interests, currency stability, fiscal reform, administrative integrity, and political order. In January 1920, Havana merchants organized into the Asociación de Comerciantes de La Habana to press for improved trade conditions. Their principal concerns centered on the demand to negotiate a more favorable trade relationship with the United States. In 1922, the prestigious Committee of One Hundred was established. Made up of young businessmen led by Porfirio Franca, the committee demanded an end to political misconduct and public malfeasance and the adoption of a merit system in government. Later in 1922, industrialists organized in the Asociación Nacional de Industriales de Cuba, joining all national industry in one organization. The Asociación Nacional de Industriales urged the adoption of strong protectionist policies to defend national industry. Merchants organized into the Federación Nacional de Detallistas and added their voice to the growing clamor for favorable government policies, including the establishment of a merchant bank and the abolition of the monopoly enjoyed by company stores on the large foreign sugar estates.

These new social forces represented first and foremost pressure groups committed to the defense of national interests. More than this, however, they provided a constituency for a new political movement, one that challenged traditional power contenders. In a larger sense, and of far greater significance, they challenged the premises and practice of North American hegemony. Indeed, the United States now faced new political and economic rivals within Cuba, demanding that local government assume a much more active role in the defense of national interests and curtailing the presence of foreign ones. The first expression of the new political alignment occurred in January 1922 with the establishment of the Asociación de Buen Gobierno in Havana. A year later, reformism led to creation of the Junta Cubana de Renovación, which called for protection of national industry and commerce, agrarian reform, a new trade treaty with the United States, educational reform, expansion of health services, women's rights, and an end to U.S. intermeddling in Cuban internal affairs. A coalition of progressive social, political, and economic forces, the Veterans and Patriots Association denounced North American intermeddling, demanded the defense of national interests, and called for honesty in government. By 1924, the movement had turned frankly revolutionary and nearly toppled the Zayas government before it eventually collapsed.

Cuban workers, led by cigarworkers, stevedores, carpenters, drivers, mechanics, and railroad workers, also organized and expanded, gained strength, and emerged as agents of change. No less than the entrepreneurial bourgeoisie, the emergence of the Cuban proletariat into a political contender had far-reaching implications for the North American presence in Cuba. Labor activity expanded from initial efforts to improve conditions in local workplaces, to organizing by trade, and to efforts at national federation. Resistance to labor demands and repression of labor demonstrations added to workers' grievances as they called for the right to organize and strike, freedom for imprisoned workers, and an end to deportation of foreign labor leaders. Increasingly, strikes, boycotts, and, most of all, the general strike transformed labor into a political force of formidable proportions.

Through the early 1920s workers continued to organize, culminating in 1925 in the third National Labor Congress, during which Cuban trade unions consolidated into a single national federation. Delegations from eighty-two trade unions attending the congress, with the endorsement of another forty-six others not present, representing an estimated two hundred thousand workers, merged into one national labor union, the Confederación Nacional Obrera de Cuba (CNOC). Within weeks of the founding of CNOC, Partido Comunista de Cuba (PCC) was organized. The PCC developed strategies of organizing political support among unions, rejected electoral politics, established educational programs for workers, and organized a youth movement.

The emergence of new social forces in the republic created additional sources of national tensions. Militant labor was a potential rival to bourgeois reformists, who were unable to forge a strategy of coalition politics with labor. In fact, the terms of North American hegemony were such as to all but preclude middle-class electoral alliances or social democratic pacts with the Cuban working class. Any hope bourgeois reformers had of becoming effective power contenders within the dependent structures of the republic could not be realized as defenders of labor reforms. Even if inclined to act in behalf of Cuban workers, reformist elements recognized the liability of promoting a trade union agenda. Those who held political power did not control the Cuban economy. Thus labor could not reasonably look to the state for aid and relief, for the state was subject to the constraints imposed by the United States government and capitalists. Officeholders could not enact, nor office seekers advocate, labor reforms without risking U.S. opposition. Thus the development of political structures with the capacity to absorb workers into liberal democratic processes was precluded. Shut out, workers sought alternative means of change. That political parties were unwilling to advocate labor reforms and, further, that government was unable to enact social legislation served to promote organizational independence in the trade union movement and to foster strong rank-and-file commitment to unions. Workers came to see unions, not government, as the principal means of achieving collective gains. As the advocates of reform gave way to the agents of revolution, labor was transformed from a potential ally into a probable adversary. Within a decade, bourgeois reformers found themselves isolated and vulnerable and eventually dependent upon the North American treaty presence for protection from new social forces.

In large measure because of client state politics, bourgeois reformers could not rise above their narrow interests and could pursue these interests only insofar as their objectives did not threaten the premises of North American hegemony. It was not coincidence that the reform agenda developed almost simultaneously with U.S. efforts to reform the Zayas administration. Certainly the Cuban version went far beyond the original and limited goals set up by Washington, and the United States was not slow to pull back and denounce the movement. Nevertheless, at some fundamental level, reform derived some of its original legitimacy from the sanction provided by the United States. That it failed in the end was in large measure because of the failure of reformists to forge an effective constituency. But the attempt was not totally without effect, for the reformist effort did release the forces that would push change one step closer to revolution.

II

These internal changes commenced in the Crowder years and marked the high point of North American intervention in Cuban affairs. Never before had the scope of intervention been so broadly interpreted or its exercise so widely practiced, creating a backlash of such proportions as to threaten a crisis in the exercise of U.S. hegemony. The United States was now no longer the only power contender with demands on local officeholders. New social forces—with an anti-U.S. platform and potential to displace unresponsive rulers from power—appeared in Cuba. Washington was perforce obliged to retreat from blatant intervention in local affairs, lest continued intermeddling risk weakening the internal position of local political allies.

Such discretionary powers as the United States claimed also created conditions that weakened North American influence. Overdrawn interpretations of the treaty rights set in sharp relief the feebleness with which the officeholders defended national sovereignty, to the disgust of the newly mobilized sectors of the national polity. Much of the surge of Cuban nationalism during the 1920s derived directly from an abiding abhorrence of the Platt Amendment—a sentiment that translated quickly into revilement of the national political leaders and revulsion for their North American backers. For the first time since the debates in the constituent assembly of 1901, the Platt Amendment had become the object of national discontent and the subject of political debate. Cubans of all political persuasions agreed on the necessity of abrogating the Platt Amendment. Nothing aroused as much collective Cuban indignation as the Platt Amendment. A source of enduring injury to Cuban national sensibilities, it soon became the focal point of growing nationalist sentiment. On few other issues had Cuban public opinion arrived at such unanimity of purpose. Gerardo Machado stood for presidential office in 1924 on a Liberal party platform committed to a "revision of the Permanent Treaty, eliminating the appendix to the Constitution, and winning Cuba an independent place in the world."[1]

The United States could not ignore the passionate debate over the Platt Amendment. Cuban political leaders could neither dismiss rising nationalist sentiment nor remain neutral in the national debate. Nor could they acquiesce to continued U.S. intervention without impairing further their ability to govern. As a corollary imperative, new restraints were imposed on U.S. influence. Intervention in Cuba could not be exercised without causing further embarrassment to the local officeholders and perhaps, ultimately, not without fully undermining their ability to rule.

By the mid-1920s, North American authorities had come to realize, if only vaguely, the necessity to relax treaty constraints on Cuban sovereignty. This was a necessary concession to rising nationalism and the mounting social pressure and required, they understood, some trade-offs, but with confidence that short-term losses would be more than adequately balanced by long-term gains. Nonintervention was the minimum U.S. concession to the rise of new social forces in the republic, an expedient way of resolving some of the more

obvious contradictions of the Cuban political economy by providing
local rulers sufficient autonomy to exercise political initiative and promote national economic development. Concessions had to be made
to Cuban sovereignty as the best means to contain the social pressure
and defend long-term U.S. interests. The new approach responded to
developments in and out of Cuba at a time when dependent structures
in Cuba were under pressure from within and threatened from below.

III

President Gerardo Machado understood the political implications of
national stirrings and the potency of Cuban discontent. He sensed the
importance of affirming national sovereignty and defending national
interests—not only because it was a theme of enormous political appeal, but also because it was necessary to the very legitimacy of Cuban
government. Cuban rulers needed to be free of treaty restraints, to
govern freely and defend national interests. By the mid-1920s, this
was indeed the minimum condition for the survival of dependent
structures.

Those sectors of the entrepreneurial bourgeoisie that demanded
state support for national interests found a champion in Machado.
During the first two years of the new administration, Machado extolled the virtues of national industrial development and the need for
economic diversification. The state became more active in economic
development. By the terms of the Law of Public Works in 1925, the
government inaugurated ambitious building programs in communications, maritime facilities, and transportation facilities, most notably
the Central Highway spanning the full length of the island. Between
1925 and 1929, nearly $80 million were expended in special public
works programs. The government provided agricultural credit and,
most important, tariff support.[2] In 1927, the government enacted the
Customs-Tariff Law, arguably one of the most important pieces of
economic legislation of the early republic. For the better part of a decade, Cuban industrialists had clamored for protectionist measures.

Machado delivered them. The Customs-Tariff Law pursued actively agricultural diversification and industrial development: duties on raw materials were decreased as a means to promote local manufacturing activity; the tariff on crude oil was reduced to encourage the expansion of refining facilities; sisal was exempted from duties to promote local rope and cordage manufacturing; duties on cotton were lowered to encourage textiles; lower duties on machinery and heavy equipment stimulated the expansion of industrial facilities.

The success of the *machadista* experiment depended on one other condition: containment of the forces of radical change represented by the PCC and the CNOC. Machado understood well the nature of the challenge from labor and the issues at stake. He displayed an early preoccupation with these concerns, thereby giving expression to the growing apprehension of property interests, Cuban and foreign alike, and announcing the terms by which the relaxation of treaty constraints on Cuban sovereignty would be reciprocated. During a visit to the United States in 1925 as president-elect, Machado addressed the question of labor directly. To the Bankers Club of New York he pledged:

> I wish to assure the businessmen present here . . . that they will have absolute guarantees for their interests under the administration of Cuba. Among the problems to which I wish to refer is the question of strikes. I intend, as soon as I take office, to send a message to Congress recommending that a law be passed providing for the settlement by means of arbitrators, of all difficulties which may arise between capital and labor, so that neither the interests of capital nor those of the laboring classes may be injured by prolonged strikes, and so that the tranquility of the Government and the peace of the country may not be disturbed by agitations which interrupt the harmony under which industrial activities should be carried. . . . The public forces . . . will lend to capital and the laborers every assistance to which they are entitled.

At a luncheon reception organized by the National City Bank, Machado was blunt: "My administration will offer full guarantees to all business and enterprises which are worthy of the protection of the

Government, and there is no reason to fear that any disorder will occur, because I have sufficient material force to stamp it out."[3]

The coincidence was compelling. Within several months in 1925, Machado was inaugurated, the PCC was founded, and the CNOC was organized. Machado did not hesitate. Immediately upon his inauguration he turned first on the PCC. From the time of its founding, and through the *machadato*, the PCC was a proscribed party, its activities outlawed, and its members persecuted. Machado acted with equal ruthlessness to contain the mobilized and increasingly militant working class. In September 1926 he dissolved the Sindicado de la Industria Fabrica, arrested Federación Obrera de La Habana (FOH) members, and outlawed FOH publications. Efforts were made to dissolve the CNOC. Foreign leaders were deported. Strikes were crushed. And increasingly, terrorist tactics were taken against labor leaders: murder, torture, disappearances. By early 1927, some 150 labor leaders and workers had been killed.

IV

Machado needed optimal circumstances to succeed as well and as long as he did. But circumstances in Cuba rarely remained optimal for any length of time. In fact, the conditions that allowed Machado to succeed at all were unreliable and fleeting. One source of his success was massive subsidies in the form of foreign loans and credits. In all of the first twenty-five years of the republic's existence, and over the four previous administrations, Cuba had contracted loans totaling $153 million from North American banking and finance agencies. In 1927 alone, Machado borrowed $109 million.[4] These loans were used to underwrite many of the ambitious development programs of the mid-1920s, particularly public works projects, and to offset the loss of customs revenues.

The second factor was the high price of sugar. In the year of Machado's election, the world price of sugar stood at 4.19 cents per pound, and this was an auspicious augury. But it was also a short-lived one. In 1926, the price of sugar declined by almost half, to 2.57 cents, and it declined again in 1928 to 2.46 cents. Good times were over.

The Great Depression came early to Cuba. The government responded to the crisis by lowering Cuban production, a strategy designed to raise prices by reducing supplies. The length of the harvest season was shortened from 136 days to 87 days and the 1926 crop was cut by 10 percent from the 1925 harvest.

Cuban efforts to combat declining world prices created severe hardship across the island. The economy slumped and stopped expanding. All sectors of the economy suffered from the decline of sugar production and curtailment of the flow of currency. Imports declined and internal consumption dropped. Hardest hit were sugar workers, for the shortened harvest (zafra) meant less work for tens of thousands of Cubans already underemployed. Professionals lost clients, merchants lost customers, and white-collar employees lost jobs. Impatience with government policies mounted. Social tensions increased. Strikes spread, and confrontations between workers and security forces increased. Political opposition spread. In 1927, Liberal Carlos Mendieta bolted the party and organized La Asociación Unión Nacionalista to oppose Machado.

Machado could not have chosen a worse time to seek reelection. The economy was faltering, the opposition was increasing, and across Cuba the demand for change was spreading. The announcement that he sought reelection had a chilling effect in Cuba. Presidential succession was firmly linked with abuse, fraud, and coercion. No one misconstrued the meaning of Machado's announcement: incumbents did not lose elections.

Through a mixture of bribery and coercion, Machado obtained the nomination of Liberal, Conservative, and Popular parties for a second term. The joint nomination foreclosed any possibility of an opposition candidate. As a final measure, Machado summoned a constituent assembly in 1928 to revise the length of the presidential term. A new amendment was enacted that extended a presidential term from four

to six years. In the process, however, the convention violated proce-
dural requirements. The 1928 amendment, critics charged, was un-
constitutional, and, by extension, the term of any executive serving
under its provisions was illegal.

In November 1928, running unopposed, and with the tacit approval
of the U.S. government, Machado secured reelection to a new six-
year term. To the already dubious proposition of pursuing a second
term and the palpably coercive methods employed in that enterprise
was added a questionable constitutional procedure for presidential
succession. Machado began his second term under the pall of unconstitutionality. The reelectionist proposition that was in principle
politically ill-conceived was now constitutionally illegitimate.

V

The assault on constitutional legality in 1927 and the specious man-
date for a second term in 1928 deepened opposition and gave focus
to dissent, but it was the Depression after 1929 that accelerated political confrontation and intensified the social struggle. The Depression
wrought utter havoc to the already ailing Cuban economy. A second
blow came from Washington. In mid-1930, the United States passed
the Smoot-Hawley Tariff Act, which increased the duty on Cuban
sugar. Domestic producers and island possessions gained an increasing share of the United States market at the expense of Cuba. Cuba's
share of the market declined from 49.4 percent in 1930 to 25.3 percent
in 1933.[5] The cumulative effect of this tariff policy was devastating.
Sugar production, the fulcrum upon which the entire economy balanced, dropped 60 percent. Cuban exports declined by 80 percent,
while the price of the island's principal export, sugar, fell over 60 percent. Sugar producers struggled to remain solvent by lowering wages
and cutting production by laying off workers. The *zafra* was reduced
again, this time to a sixty-two-day harvest—only two months' work
for tens of thousands of sugar workers.

Everywhere profits plummeted. Commerce came to a standstill.

Local industry and manufacturing reduced production in response to the population's diminished purchasing power, setting off a new round of unemployment and wage cuts. The cycle plunged downward. Commercial, banking, and manufacturing failures reached record proportions. Business failures produced another spiral of unemployment and new rounds of shortages and price rises. Salaries and wages were reduced, workers laid off, and businesses and factories closed. Unemployment soared. Some 250,000 heads of families, representing approximately 1 million people out of a total population of 3.9 million, found themselves unemployed. Those fortunate enough to have temporary work encountered depressed wages, which for the urban proletariat decreased by 50 percent. Pay for agricultural workers fell by 75 percent. In the sugar zones, wages were as low as twenty cents for a twelve-hour workday, the lowest since the days of slavery.[6]

Local industry called for government subsidies, relief programs, and economic supports. During the worst days of the Depression, when national need was the greatest, government revenues that had long served as the major source of subsidy of the entrepreneurial bourgeoisie were transferred into foreign hands to service the external debt. Indeed, the Cuban debt actually increased as U.S. lenders sought to bolster the faltering regime. During the bleakest moments of the late 1920s and early 1930s, as the national debt increased and government revenues declined, loans were transacted with almost casual abandon: a $9 million loan from J. P. Morgan and Company in 1927, a $50 million loan from Chase in 1928, a $20 million short-term note from Chase in 1930. And as dreadful conditions worsened, a new series of loans was made to stave off default: an extension of a $20 million credit in 1931. In 1932 Chase advanced Machado another $1.6 million. Chase Bank also had interests in Machado's personal finances: a personal loan of $130,000, an unsecured loan of $45,000 to the president's construction company, and $89,000 to his shoe factory.[7]

The number and activity of opposition organizations increased during the early 1930s. The ABC Revolutionary Society consisted of intellectuals, professionals, and students, organized around clandestine cells. The ABC embraced armed struggle and responded to government violence with reprisal, committing itself to creating conditions of revolution through systematic use of violence against the government. The Organización Celular Radical Revolucionaria (OCRR) also adopted a cellular structure and adopted armed struggle and sabotage as the means to overthrow Machado. Other new antigovernment groups joined the swelling ranks of the opposition. Women's resistance groups, university professors, and normal school teachers and students became part of a vast underground network dedicated to overthrowing Machado.

Through the late 1920s and early 1930s social conflict deepened and confrontations intensified. Communist strength increased. Labor continued to organize, union membership expanded, and strikes became more frequent. So, too, did mass demonstrations and hunger marches. Between 1929 and 1930, strikes halted production in such industries as cigar manufacturing, metallurgy, construction, and textiles. In March 1930, the CNOC, now outlawed, organized two hundred thousand workers in a stunning general strike that ended only after a wave of government violence and repression. [8]

Through the early years of the crisis, Washington maintained its position of nonintervention. Indeed, in the end the position of nonintervention was a policy of intervention. Intent was not as important as effect, and if effect was not disclaimed then intent was assumed. Most Cubans assumed that the United States remained entirely committed to Machado. As early as 1930, U.S. Ambassador Harry Guggenheim informed Washington that the "policy of non-intervention is interpreted as definite support of Machado." [9] And indeed it was. The most efficacious support Washington could have offered Machado was nonintervention, universally interpreted in Cuba as support. [10] During the early 1930s, the United States spoke of the need to respect Cuban national sovereignty as the highest form of respect for the republic. The United States could not disclaim nonintervention without impairing Machado's political authority and weakening the prestige of a government very much in distress and under siege.

By the early 1930s, the moderate opposition despaired of a political settlement to the crisis. An abortive revolt in 1931 led to four hundred arrests, virtually the entire leadership of the mainline opposition. Polarities sharpened, as the elimination of the moderate center set the stage for confrontation between the embattled extremities of the Cuban polity. As economic conditions deteriorated and social unrest spread, the struggle against Machado was assuming daily the character of a revolutionary upheaval. As the prospects of a moderate settlement decreased, the possibilities of a radical solution increased.

The elimination of the moderate opposition, particularly the Unión Nacionalista, left the Cuban bourgeoisie without political representation in the conflict. After 1931, local manufacturers, industrialists, merchants, and landowners, as well as members of the moderate old-line opposition, found themselves economically insolvent and politically impotent, facing repression from above and revolution from below. After 1931, their only hope was relief from without. U.S. intervention, many concluded, offered redemption from repression and rescue from revolution. Many were genuinely repelled by the regime's intransigence and the ferocity of government repression, which, they understood correctly, in the context of economic collapse, was edging Cuba inexorably toward social upheaval. But even as his presence served to exacerbate these conditions, Machado was seen as the only bulwark against radical change. It was thus necessary to remove Machado to reduce mounting social tensions, but in such a way as to avoid releasing the forces of radical change.

By the early 1930s, Cubans who had earlier decried North American interference in Cuban internal affairs now looked to Washington to settle the conflict. Treaty obligations imposed on the United States responsibility for ending the Cuban crisis, antigovernment representatives insisted. As early as 1927, Fernando Ortiz, the leader of the Junta de Renovación in 1923, appealed to the State Department for "moral intervention." Ortiz insisted upon the "obligation" of the United States to guarantee "good government," one based on the right of intervention and a right that could not "exist without a corresponding obligation."[11] Two years later, Octavio Seigle, a founder of the Unión Nacionalista, struck a similar tone. "The United States," Seigle insisted, "is duty bound to see that Cuba does not continue in the hands of a dictator. Under the Platt Amendment, which is the law in such matters, the United States is obliged to see to it that a government is maintained . . . 'capable of protecting life, property, and individual liberty.' . . . There is a direct obligation to protect the Cubans' right to vote for a government of their own choosing and under which their lives and liberties will be safe."[12] Cosme de la Torriente, a member of the Unión Nacionalista, insisted that the Machado government did not meet the treaty terms of Cuba-U.S. relations, namely to protect life, property, and liberty, and called for the United States to mediate the dispute.[13] In fact, so frequent were opposition calls for U.S. intervention that the pro-Machado Congress proposed amending the penal code to provide a penalty of long-term or life imprisonment for "any Cuban who seeks the intervention or interference of a foreign power in the internal or external development of national life"—a measure proposed in the defense of national sovereignty.[14]

Conditions in the early 1930s were similar to those in crises past. In many significant ways, they were a continuation of earlier crises: from the unresolved contradictions accumulating after 1898, which were themselves compounded versions of problems persisting after 1878, ills that traced their origins to the preceding one hundred years of colonialism, foreign intervention, monoculture, slavery, and inequality. The crises in the 1930s were the latest in the series that so often in the past announced Cuban efforts at self-determination and self-actualization. Developments in the 1930s gave new forms to familiar grievances, made particularly desperate by an economic collapse of unprecedented proportions. In the 1930s, as in the 1860s and 1890s, Cubans stood at the threshold of revolution. Vast sectors of the population mobilized for radical change, and new social forces were in competition with each other and bidding for ascendancy even as they challenged the status quo.

In the 1930s, political repression and economic depression combined to set the deficiencies of the republic in sharp relief. The crisis worked its way across class lines, arraying vast sectors of the population against a government that seemed to be supported only by foreigners. Militant workers, radical students, and the disaffected petit bourgeoisie together with elements of the disaffected republican bourgeoisie coalesced into a vast heterogeneous force for change. The contradictions of Cuban political economy stood exposed for all to see.

VI

In the spring of 1933, the United States responded to the Cuban crisis by dispatching Ambassador Sumner Welles to Cuba to negotiate a settlement of the crisis. "You will point out to President Machado in the most forceful terms," Welles's instructions stipulated, "that in the opinion of your Government, there can be expected no general amelioration of conditions in Cuba until there is a definite cessation of that state of terrorism which has existed for so long." Welles was instructed to offer the "friendly mediation" of the U.S. government to Machado and the political opposition for the purpose of obtaining "a definite, detailed, and binding understanding between the present Cuban government and the responsible leaders of the factions opposed to it." [15]

The mediations offered the means through which to obtain the desired political settlement. It was essential to end the threat of social upheaval in Cuba, principally by eliminating its political source. Machado had outlived his usefulness. The order and stability that he had so deftly provided during his first term, the basis upon which he had received U.S. support for reelection, had disintegrated during his second term. Neither the application of repression nor attempts at reconciliation seemed capable of diminishing the resolve of the opposition. After five years of sustained political strife and unrelieved economic stress, it had become apparent that Machado could not restore order. His continued presence was now the central issue for the political opposition and was arguably the greatest single obstacle to the restoration of political peace.

The mediations also provided the forum through which to bring the "responsible leaders" of the opposition from the fringes of illegality into the fold of legality. This signified nothing less than renouncement of revolution and a way to relieve mounting revolutionary pressure by diverting the opposition away from a conspiratorial solution to a constitutional settlement. The mediations provided, too, the means through which opposition groups obtained their objectives and joined the political process in an orderly institutional fashion. More important, the mediations were a way to get Cubans to abandon an independent course of action and subject them to the constraints of U.S. policy needs. Just as important as easing Machado out was the necessity of easing the new opposition in. The mediations conferred on sectors of the outlawed opposition a measure of political legitimacy, providing them with a vested interest in a settlement sanctioned by the United States. This served as a recruitment process, a method by which the United States selected the participants in the mediations, determining in the process which groups were "legitimate" and which were not, determining which groups were compatible with North American interests, and who would make up the subsequent government. Through the mediations the United States selected opposition groups that would secure access to power and subsequently be linked to the United States by ties of gratitude and indebtedness. North American influence over the new government would be preserved and the place of the United States as a power broker among political contenders maintained. This was nothing less than the renewal of hegemony built into the planned changing of personnel in Havana, a method by which the United States established a political lien on a new generation of power holders.

In large measure, the mediation effort originated with the attempts of the Roosevelt administration to avoid armed intervention in Latin America. The Good Neighbor policy did not, to be sure, reject intervention—only the use of military force to intervene. The policy adopted in the 1933 crisis was reminiscent of the one used in 1921, when Crowder arrived in Cuba to remedy serious local problems. Such proconsular politics seemed to work in the 1920s, and indeed Sumner Welles had been in the State Department working with Crowder. There was no reason not to believe that a North American proconsul could make things right again in 1933.

Many Cubans found this a wholly acceptable solution to the crisis. Not for the first time, local power contenders welcomed a North American settlement of an internal dispute, one from which they expected to benefit. North American intervention promised beleaguered elites the redemption that they themselves were powerless to provide, a timely deliverance from the forces of radical change. Machado looked upon the mediations as evidence of North American efforts to shore up his troubled regime. The opposition, on the other hand, had every reason to believe that the mediations were a clever way devised by the United States to remove the regime. In a larger sense, Cuban participation in the mediations was only the latest manifestation of the generally collaborationist posture that power contenders had long employed in the resolution of local political conflicts. Cubans had learned early that cooperation with the United States was not without advantage, often made the difference between success and failure, and could more than adequately offset the lack of political support or absence of legitimacy, or both. Thus the ABC and OCRR, both clandestine urban commando groups, with an unknown membership and an indeterminate number of supporters, by endorsing the North American proposal earned a place in the mediations and ultimately in the subsequent government. So too did the Liberal splinter group Unión Nacionalista, which at the time of its support of the mediations was all but defunct and in disarray.

The result was often grotesque distortions of republican institutions, whereby structures, parties, and persons defending national interests were thwarted in favor of those who supported North American ones. This fatalistic view of affairs was part of a larger malaise in the republic, giving rise to a pervasive sense of futility and impotence that had its origins in the nineteenth century. But it was more a twentieth-century phenomenon, the product of the disappointing denouement of 1898, the Platt Amendment, and unremitting North American intervention in all aspects of the internal affairs of the new republic. In 1916, Manuel Márquez Sterling wrote about a national "pessimism" that had formed "legions of believers" and constituted a veritable "political school." At another point, he alluded to the "doc-

trinc of fatalism," whereby Cubans learned to defend national sovereignty and minimize North American intervention through a modus
vivendi with the United States in which the primacy of U.S. interests was assured.[16] Its most recurring expression was a resignation to
the prevailing fates that nothing would be done, or could be done,
without North American backing. The final corollary of despair: why,
therefore, do anything?

This mentality affected not only the ways many Cubans aspired
to political power; it also influenced the way they opposed political
power. Opposition strategies were often designed more with an eye
to inducing North American intervention than to developing autonomous means of political change. The 1930s protagonist in Manuel
Douglas's novel *The Cubans* laments that "our limitations are inherited,
the limitations of the Platt Amendment," while his activist counterpart, a member of the ABC, vows to rid Cuba of Machado by provok-
ing "the exercise of the Platt Amendment by the United States through
the deliberate creation of utter chaos in Cuba." So thoroughly had republican institutions been penetrated by and placed at the service of
North American interests that the gesture of political change was no
less a potential act of self-determination and always possessed of the
capacity to challenge the premises of U.S. hegemony. Subsumed into
the quest for national sovereignty was an agenda for political, social,
and economic change, for the actualization of nationality remained
identified with expectation of collective mobility. "There were, in addition, the Americans," ponders the narrator in José Soler Puig's novel
Bertillón 166. "A good government meant one that would concern
itself with the eternal problems of Cuba: unemployment, peasants
without land, the public service monopolies, monoculture, the sugar
mills, the reign of the dollar. The land and the monopolies belong
to the Americans."[17] In the end, the advocacy of nationality became
identified with a populist agenda and hence mass-based politics. This
ideological transformation of nationalism had its origins late in the
nineteenth century and in the twentieth century developed into a
force of enormous vitality. North American and local elites shared a
common interest in containing these forces, and, increasingly, respon-

sibility for the defense of the status quo came to reside in the United States.

The 1933 mediations marked a convergence of interests of the power contenders. Representing the opposition were the Unión Nacionalista, the ABC, the OCRR, women's opposition groups, and university and normal school teachers. The government was represented by leaders of the Liberal, Conservative, and Popular parties and Secretary of War Alberto Herrera representing the administration. But not all the opposition groups participated. The ABC split over the mediations, and the dissenting wing reorganized as the ABC Radical. Students rejected the mediations and denounced them as foreign intermeddling in Cuban internal affairs. So too did the Communist party and organized labor, which were not invited to participate.

VII

The mediations began on July 1. Machado readily acquiesced and conceded freedom of the press, release of political prisoners, and revision of the electoral code. The opposition reciprocated and halted antigovernment activities. But the key to a satisfactory and speedy settlement turned on the president's early retirement. When presented with this requirement, Machado balked, then responded with incredulity and ultimately with rage. He convened a special session of Congress to repudiate the request and vowed to remain in power through his full term of office, pledging to accept "any fair solution proposed" but refusing to be "thrown into the street." [18]

In late July Welles and the recalcitrant Machado faced a new problem. Bus drivers in Havana organized a strike to protest a new government tax. The strike quickly spread to other sectors, and within days all movement of people and goods came to a halt. Havana was paralyzed. By the end of the first week in August, the general strike had acquired the full proportions of a revolutionary offensive.

All pretense of mediation ended, and the U.S. request for Machado's early retirement now became an ultimatum. The source of the new urgency was self-evident—if Machado did not quit the presidency, the general strike would sweep aside the entire government, an eventuality, Welles predicted grimly, with catastrophic consequences and requiring United States armed intervention. Cuba confronted the specter of a far-reaching social upheaval. The *New York Times* correspondent described the situation as "a race between mediation by the United States Ambassador and open revolution." On August 7, Welles bluntly threatened Machado with armed intervention. [19]

To the horror of the State Department, however, Machado defied the United States to intervene. "Inform the President of the United States," Machado taunted Welles, "that [I] would prefer armed intervention to the acceptance of any such proposal." Machado seized upon the threat of intervention to appeal for national support for his government and denounced U.S. intermeddling in Cuban internal affairs. He vowed to defend national sovereignty and exhorted Cubans to defend the homeland against armed aggression by the United States. Privately he informed Welles that he would repel with arms the landing of foreign troops on national territory. [20]

But the U.S. pressure was not without its effects. Gradually Machado's support began to crumble around him. The first defections occurred among the *machadista* parties. Progovernment party leaders viewed Machado's defiance with foreboding, sensing uneasily that this was a contest the president could not win. And what, then, would become of them? If the Machado government fell solely through North American pressure, the traditional parties, discredited for their part in the *machadato*, faced the prospect of drastic reorganization, under the best of circumstances, and probably complete dissolution—as opposition groups demanded. Support of the U.S. proposal, on the other hand, and a timely defection from a president facing an uncertain future, had the virtue of aligning the old parties with the new politics, thereby assuring them survival in post-Machado Cuba. If the new opposition factions could obtain legitimacy by participating in the mediations, the old political parties would guarantee longevity by supporting the mediator. In early August, leaders of the Liberal, Conservative, and Popular parties endorsed the proposed early retirement of Machado and began to prepare the legislation necessary to expedite his departure.

The end of the regime came from the armed forces, who, like the *machadista* parties, had ample reasons to desert the beleaguered president. As the balance of power tipped against the government, the armed forces found their vulnerability increasing in the changing political climate. The United States's inclusion of formerly outlawed groups in the political settlement meant that those factions toward whom army repression had been most severe would soon form the next government. Antigovernment factions had long denounced the military, pledging to reduce the size of the armed forces, restrict military authority, and cut the army budget. For the army to have remained aloof from a political settlement would have placed it at the mercy of a new government composed of its former foes.

But it was the growing fear of U.S. intervention, in the end, that finally moved the army to act. Welles had calculated correctly. Army leaders shrank in horror at the spectacle of Machado defying North American authorities, seeking to mobilize the population in the defense of the island against the threatened U.S. intervention, and appealing to Latin American public opinion to condemn the United States. The "sole purpose" of the military coup, one army representative explained, "was the avoidance of American intervention." [21]

Removal of Machado was a small price to avert that calamity. Too many people had too much to lose not to acquiesce. When Welles publicly withdrew U.S. support of Machado, he set in motion a realignment of the internal balance of power that released Machado's backers to seek a new arrangement with the United States to guarantee their own survival in post-Machado Cuba.

The August 12 military coup provided yet another contortion to the logic by which Cubans defended national sovereignty. Either Cubans removed Machado from government or the United States would act to remove Cubans from government. Acquiescence to U.S. demands thus constituted defense of the nation. Indeed, coup leaders subsequently made much of the "patriotic gesture" of August 12, suggesting that the army, by obviating the necessity of a North American intervention, had preserved national sovereignty. [22]

VIII

A new government under Carlos Manuel de Céspedes assumed power in August 1933. A longtime personal friend of Welles, Céspedes represented an inoffensive compromise to the contentious groupings that were banded together into a provisional government. This was a regime summoned into existence largely in response to North American needs, formed to facilitate Machado's succession and to accommodate the groups of the mediations. It was made up of discredited political parties that functioned under the pall of unconstitutionality and dissident clandestine factions that operated on the fringes of illegality. It neither possessed popularity nor promised a program. And it lasted only three weeks.

The end came from the most improbable and wholly unexpected sources. On the evening of September 3, sergeants, corporals, and enlisted men of Camp Columbia in Havana, meeting to discuss a backlog of grievances, seized control of army headquarters. Under the leadership of Sergeant Fulgencio Batista, the army protesters exhorted the troops to hold the post until the officers agreed to negotiate their demands. Opposition groups, principally university students of the Directorio Estudiantil Universitario (DEU), rallied around the mutinous troops. The "Sergeants Revolt," as the mutiny later became known, originally had modest objectives. The sergeants planned a demonstration to protest deteriorating conditions in the army, not to overthrow Céspedes or oust the officer corps. Having unexpectedly found themselves in mutiny against their officers and in rebellion against the Céspedes government, the soldiers faced the certain prospect of severe disciplinary action, including court-martial and imprisonment.

The antigovernment opposition provided the salvation. Civilian participation transformed an act of insubordination into a full-fledged military coup. It was a coalition of convenience, to be sure, but one that offered rebellious soldiers pardon and dissident civilians power. A political manifesto announced a new Provisional Revolutionary Government, subsequently headed by Ramón Grau San Martín, and affirmed national sovereignty, the creation of a modern democracy, and the "march toward the creation of a new Cuba." [23]

For one hundred days the provisional government devoted itself to the task of transforming Cuba with exalted purposefulness. This was the first government of the republic formed without North American sanction. Under the injunction "Cuba for Cubans," the new government proceeded to enact reform laws at a dizzying pace. On the day of his inauguration as president, Grau unilaterally if only symbolically proclaimed the abrogation of the Platt Amendment. Reforms followed rapidly. The traditional political parties were dissolved. The government lowered utility rates by 40 percent and reduced interest rates. Women received the vote and the university secured autonomy. In labor matters, government reforms included minimum wages for sugarcane cutters, compulsory labor arbitration, an eight-hour day, workers' compensation, the establishment of a Ministry of Labor, a Nationalization of Labor decree requiring Cuban nationality for 50 percent of all employees in industry, commerce, and agriculture, and the cancellation of existing contract labor arrangements with Haiti and Jamaica. In agricultural matters, the government sponsored the creation of a *colono* association, guaranteed farmers permanent right over the land under cultivation, and inaugurated a program of land reform. [24]

Despite the rhetoric of revolution, this was preeminently a reformist regime. It chose regulation over expropriation, the distribution of public lands over the redistribution of private property, the defense of trade union objectives over workers' party objectives. Yet the regime's reformist approach, which eschewed the old collaborationist politics but did not implement a frankly revolutionary program, placed it in an increasingly untenable position. The old politicos, who had been ousted, responded to the coup with unrestrained indignation. They and the army commanders who had deserted Machado as a means to survive the discredited regime once again faced persecution and extinction. But new political groups, including the ABC, OCRR, and the Unión Nacionalista—organizations that earlier had paid dearly to acquire political legitimacy in post-Machado Cuba—were not reconciled to this abrupt and inglorious end to their debut in national politics. Foreign capital recoiled in horror at new laws regulating and restricting freedoms traditionally enjoyed under previous governments.

The regime that was too radical for the organized parties and political factions was not radical enough for workers and communists. Perhaps under normal circumstances, *grauísta* labor reforms might have met many long-standing worker demands, even served as the basis of a social democratic alliance between the labor and middle-class reformers. But neither minimum wages and maximum hours nor compulsory arbitration and workers' compensation mattered for much when there were no jobs. These were the worst times to be implementing reforms. Measures conceived at an earlier time, worthy of pursuit, to be sure, appeared strangely inappropriate and irrelevant during the desperate moments of the Depression. Strikes continued and labor militancy increased. By the end of September, workers had seized control of thirty-six sugar mills, representing 30 percent of the national sugar production.

The most implacable opposition came from the United States. More than constitutionality had perished. The overthrow of the pro-U.S. government, the suppression of the mainline political parties, and the removal of the officer corps represented nothing less than the dismantling of internal structures through which the United States had traditionally underwritten and institutionalized its hegemony. In repudiating the Platt Amendment, further, the new government made its intentions clear.

The implications of Cuban policies were apparent immediately. The defense of Cuban interests jeopardized North American interests. Labor legislation affected North American employers. Agrarian reform threatened U.S. landowners. The reduction of utility rates affected the Electric Bond and Share Company. In fact, so thoroughly had the United States penetrated Cuba that it was hardly possible for any social and economic legislation not to affect U.S. capital adversely. The tempo and tenor of the reform measures persuaded Welles that the provisional government aspired to nothing less than the elimination of U.S. interests and influence in Cuba. "It is . . . within the bounds of possibility," Welles wrote with alarm two weeks after the coup, "that the social revolution which is under way cannot be checked. American properties and interests are being gravely prejudiced and the material damage to such properties will in all probability be very great." The government decrees, he protested, were "confiscatory" in nature and enormously prejudicial to U.S. property interests. "Our own commercial and export interests in Cuba," Welles asserted flatly, "cannot be revived under this government." When in October the government announced an agreement with Mexico to train Cuban army officers, Welles drew immediate conclusions: "In view of the existing situation here and particularly in view of the fact that since the independence of the Republic of Cuba the training of Cuban officers had been undertaken solely in the United States or under the direction of American officers this step can only be construed as a deliberate effort by the present Government to show its intention of minimizing any form of American influence in Cuba." [25]

Welles was neither slow nor unequivocal in his response. For the remainder of his stay in Havana, he pursued a policy calculated to isolate the regime diplomatically and weaken it politically at home. Initially, Welles appealed to Washington for armed intervention—three times in almost as many days. [26] And on each occasion the State Department demurred. Thereafter, Welles pursued alternate forms of opposition. Unable to overthrow the government from without, he sought to undermine it from within. Nothing was as central to this policy as promoting the continuation of conditions of instability and disorder. Three decades of policy imperatives fell suddenly into desuetude—stability and order were now inimical to North American interests in Cuba.

Destabilization required first and foremost the denial of U.S. recognition. Under the best circumstances, nonrecognition promised to lead to the collapse of the government. Failing that, it would force the government into moderation, a way of exacting concessions in exchange for normalization of relations. "If our Government recognized the existing Cuban government before it has undergone radical modification," Welles argued, "such action would imply our lending official support to a regime which is opposed by all business and financial interests in Cuba; by all the powerful political groups and in general . . . all the elements that hold out any promise of being able to govern Cuba. . . . Such action on our part would undoubtedly help to keep the present government in power."[27]

Nonrecognition also served to prolong political turmoil in Cuba. It was a deliberate effort to foster instability, designed to maintain pressure on both the government and the opposition. Nonrecognition obstructed government efforts at reconciliation with its opponents precisely because it offered the opposition incentive to resist the government. Those who otherwise might have supported the government demurred; those who opposed the government were encouraged to conspire and resist.

With the government thus thrown on the defensive, the United States was free to encourage internal subversion. To the deposed political groups, Welles urged continued resistance. To the displaced officers, he counseled a continued boycott of the army. Indeed, nowhere did U.S. policy have as telling results or as lasting effects than with the ousted army officers. Throughout early September the new government urgently sought to reunite the officers with the army. Their resumption of command promised to relieve the noncommissioned officers of the odium of mutiny while strengthening the government internally, validating the September 4 movement in much the same fashion that the officers' participation on August 12 had lent support to the Céspedes government.

The officers' boycott was part of U.S. pressure against the government. The officers were in constant communication with North American representatives, obeying instructions and following advice, certain that collaboration with the United States would lead to a solution of the crisis and a return to their command. As early as September 11, Horacio Ferrer, secretary of war under Céspedes, conferred with Welles and learned that the new government would "continue unrecognized by the United States."[28] Nonrecognition exercised a powerful restraint on the officers, encouraging army leaders to remain away from their commands in the belief that the new government could not long survive without North American support. As long as the new government remained unrecognized, as long as the United States claimed to support the "legitimate government" of Céspedes, the officers could righteously claim to defend legitimacy. On September 9 Welles reported that the officers had entered into a "definite compact" not to support "any government except a legitimate government."[29] Several days later, Ferrer asserted flatly that the officers would never serve under any government not recognized in Washington.[30] The U.S. military attaché reported that many officers were prepared to "pledge allegiance to any government the United States recognizes."[31]

The prospect of U.S. intervention further encouraged the officers to remain away from their commands—in a display once more of a form of fatalism—to await action by the United States. One Cuban officer later recalled that Welles had dissuaded the army commanders "from returning to their commands, which would have strengthened the position of the student government and might have tipped the scales in their favor both with the Cuban public and the American government." The U.S. military attaché advised the officers "under no circumstances to return to their commands," insisting that Washington would not tolerate a revolt by enlisted men, such as had occurred, or permit a change of government, and that "American intervention was undoubtedly the next step."[32]

These were compelling circumstances and, in the context of the U.S. role in Cuban internal affairs, sufficient to persuade the officers of the logic of their decision and the legitimacy of their position. Army leaders were discouraged from supporting a government expected momentarily to be ousted by North American intervention. Their continued boycott was essential, for it was necessary to corroborate the U.S. charge that the new government lacked support and authority. Officers who only three weeks earlier had led the army against Machado to prevent intervention now refused to lead the army under Grau to induce intervention.

In late September, the Grau government abandoned all hopes of reconciliation with the officers. The separated officers were proclaimed deserters and ordered arrested. After a brief siege of the Hotel Nacional in early October, the army leaders surrendered to government authorities. The displacement of the former officer corps also paved the way for a sweeping reorganization of the armed forces. Some four hundred sergeants, corporals, and enlisted men received commissions and filled the newly created vacancies in the army command. Batista was formally promoted to the rank of colonel and ratified in his position as chief of the army. A second blow to antigovernment forces was not long in coming. In early November, a combined force of the ABC and Unión Nacionalista joined with dissident army elements in an abortive uprising. After several days of fighting in Havana, government forces overcame resistance and ended the revolt.

The arrest of the officers and the defeat of the ABC and Unión Nacionalista signaled the collapse of organized resistance to the new government. The principal opposition groups that had formed the previous government, and around which Welles had hoped to reconstitute the "legitimate government," had been defeated and dispersed. North American hopes that antigovernment groups could serve U.S. objectives ended.

Attention next shifted to promoting splits within the government. Certainly the defeat of the organized opposition eased political pressure but in so doing also set the contradictions within the government in sharp relief. Civilians and the soldiers had gone separate ways shortly after September 4. The civilians had carried Cuba deep into the uncertain realm of experimental government, but as they advanced on their "march to create a new Cuba," the army became an increasingly reluctant escort. Military support of the provisional government was always more practical than political, more a form of self-interest than a function of solidarity. This was the government that had sanctioned the sedition and validated four hundred new commissions and from which the new army command derived its putative legitimacy. But military leaders were anxious for a political settlement, if for no other reason than to make permanent their recent promotions. They saw little to be gained by social experimentation, especially if it prolonged the political crisis. It had been from the start only a coalition of convenience, and nothing had changed except that by midautumn the soldiers found themselves increasingly inconvenienced by civilian policies.

These were the fateful flaws, stress points discerned perceptively by Welles. U.S. policy now shifted away from promoting unity among government opponents to encouraging disunity among its defenders. For the second time in as many months, the United States appealed directly to the army to overturn a government that had fallen into disfavor in Washington. Throughout the autumn months Welles maintained close, and increasingly cordial, contacts with Batista. As early as October 4, only days after the arrest of the former officers, Welles reported having held a "protracted and very frank discussion" with Batista. He praised the army chief as the "only individual in Cuba today who represented authority" and whose leadership of the army had earned him the support of "the very great majority of the commercial and financial interests in Cuba who are looking for protection and who could only find such protection in himself." Political factions that only weeks earlier had openly opposed him, Welles disclosed, were now "in accord that his control of the Army as Chief of Staff should be continued as the only possible solution and were willing to support him in that capacity." The only obstacle to an equitable political settlement, diplomatic recognition, and a return to conditions of normality, the ambassador suggested, "was the unpatriotic and futile obstinacy of a small group of young men who should be studying in the university instead of playing politics and of a few individuals who had joined with them for selfish motives." Warned Welles: "Should the present government go down in disaster, that disaster would necessarily inextricably involve not only himself but the safety of the Republic, which he has publicly pledged himself to maintain." [33]

Batista instinctively understood what the U.S. emissary wanted.

In October, Welles reported that Batista had arrived at the conclusion that "a change in government is imperative." By December, he
cabled that Batista was "actively seeking a change in government"
owing to apprehension of army intrigue against him, the constant and
"inevitable" attempts at revolution, and fear of U.S. military intervention.[34] The end came in January, when Batista transferred army support from Grau to the Unión Nacionalista and former Liberal leader
Carlos Mendieta. Within five days, the United States recognized the
new government.

8   Twilight Years

The crisis of the 1930s gradually ended, and many of the conditions that had been at its source were remedied or otherwise adjusted. Relations between Cuba and the United States changed when in 1934 the Platt Amendment was abrogated. The United States retained use of the Guantánamo naval station but agreed to abolish the other clauses of the 1903 Permanent Treaty. Gradually Cuban sugar recovered a larger share of the North American market, although it would never again attain the prominence it enjoyed during the 1910s and 1920s. By the terms of the Jones-Costigan Act (1934), the United States lowered protectionist tariffs on sugar imports. Cuba benefited from this measure, but only slightly. The Jones-Costigan Act substituted quotas for tariffs as the means to protect domestic sugar producers. By the terms of the law, the U.S. secretary of agriculture was empowered to determine national sugar needs, whereupon all sugar-producing regions, domestic and foreign, would receive an annual quota of the total. The assigned quota was based on the participation of sugar producers in the U.S. market for the years 1931–33. The selection of these three years was unfortunate for producers in Cuba, for it was precisely this period—the years of Smoot-Hawley—during which the Cuban share of the North American market was at its lowest.

Nevertheless, Cuban participation in the U.S. market increased gradually through the 1930s, from 25.4 percent in 1933 to 31.4 percent in 1937. During these years, overall sugar production expanded, and the value of the expanded production increased. Between 1933 and 1938, Cuban sugar output rose from 1.9 million tons to 2.9 million tons, with the corresponding value increasing from $53.7 million to $120.2 million.

Also during these years the United States attempted to recover control over the Cuban economy. The U.S. hold over Cuba had slipped.

In the decade between 1923 and 1933, Cuban imports from the United States had declined from $191 million to $22 million and Cuban exports to the United States had decreased from $362 million to $57 million. United States participation in Cuban import trade diminished from 74.3 percent during World War I, to 66.7 in 1922, to 57.4 percent by 1931. Cuba dropped from sixth to sixteenth place as a customer for United States exports. The Department of Agriculture estimated that the loss of Cuban markets for foodstuffs alone meant the withdrawal of some 817,267 acres from agricultural production in the United States. Exports to Cuba of raw materials and manufactured products other than foodstuffs declined from $133 million in 1924 to $18 million in 1933.[1]

Certainly the collapse of the Cuban economy after 1929 contributed to the loosening of commercial ties between Cuba and the United States. But other factors were at work as well. The Customs Tariff Law of 1927 and the subsequent impetus given to the diversification of the economy served to stimulate Cuban self-sufficiency. Because of increased local production, commodity imports formerly supplied by foreign producers, including eggs, butter, and lard, ended altogether or, as in the case of shoes, furniture, and hosiery, diminished markedly. The decline of North American participation in the Cuban import trade also resulted from increased foreign competition. The Depression and the drop of Cuban purchasing power combined to make the island a price market and opened the door to the importation of cheap commodities from Europe and Japan previously supplied by the United States on a quality basis. Mounting tariffs and increased taxes also helped make U.S. imports uncompetitive. Sumner Welles had two missions when he arrived in Cuba in the spring of 1933— one political, the other economic. "First," he recalled later, "to assist the Cuban people themselves to solve the political crisis which had developed and, second, to provide, by cooperation between our two Governments, a means for the rehabilitation of Cuba's national economy, and thereby likewise to reestablish, to the advantage of American agriculture and industry, the market which our own exports had previously enjoyed."[2]

North American plans had been thwarted momentarily by the Grau San Martín government, but with the return to power of pro-U.S. political groups, discussions on a new trade agreement resumed. Under the Mendieta government, the United States negotiated a new reciprocal trade agreement with Cuba. By the terms of the 1934 treaty, Cuba secured a guaranteed market for its agricultural exports. In return, Havana conceded tariff discounts to a large variety of commodity lines and the reduction of internal taxes on U.S. products. North American concessions covered thirty-five articles; Cuban concessions affected four hundred items. Tariff reductions granted to Cuban exports ranged from 20 to 50 percent; tariff concessions to U.S. imports ranged from 20 to 60 percent.

The new reciprocity treaty, to be sure, contributed to Cuban economic revival. Cuba's principal export, sugar, was the item most favored in the 1934 agreement. Reductions were also made on tobacco leaf, as well as cigars and cigarettes, honey, fish products, citrus, pineapples, and other agricultural products. At the same time, however, the 1934 treaty severely hampered Cuban efforts at economic diversification, especially in agricultural and manufacturing enterprises, many of which had developed in the aftermath of the 1927 Customs Tariff Law. Under the new treaty U.S. producers were able to adjust trade strategies to changing market conditions in Cuba and thereby reestablish North American primacy in the Cuban economy.

The new reciprocity treaty was the final blow in a series of adversities that befell the new entrepreneurial bourgeoisie of Cuba. Early in the century foreign capital had expanded at the expense of the old landed elites, principally in agriculture; during the 1930s, foreign capital expanded again, this time at the expense of the new entrepreneurial bourgeoisie, principally in industry and manufacturing. In a curious and fateful fashion, the Customs Tariff Law of 1927, designed originally to promote national industry, served instead to encourage the expansion of foreign manufactures on the island. North American capital expanded directly into those sectors of the economy that Cubans had previously sought to preserve for themselves. One effective method of eluding the Cuban tariff regulations was for foreign manufacturers to establish subsidiary firms on the island. Cuban manufacturers producing commodities originally protected by Cuban tariff regulations received new competition. Many foreign-owned subsidiaries in Cuba secured the participation of local capital. Some local operations were absorbed totally by the new foreign firms, others simply failed. After the 1930s, Cuba was again economically linked closely to the United States, thereby returning the island to the patterns of pre-Depression dependency. The total value of North American imports increased from $22.6 million in 1933 to $81 million in 1940; the U.S. portion of Cuban imports for the same period increased from 53.5 percent to 76.6 percent. [3]

The economy accelerated with Cuban entry into World War II in December 1941. Under the presidency of Fulgencio Batista (1940–44), Cuba negotiated new trade agreements, obtained additional credits and loans from the United States, and profited from the decline of sugar production in war-torn Asia and Europe. Between 1940 and 1944 the Cuban crop increased from 2.7 million tons to 4.2 million tons (the largest harvest since 1930) and the value of Cuban raw sugar production went up from $110 million to $251 million. In 1941, the two countries signed a lend-lease agreement whereby Cuba received arms shipments in exchange for North American use of Cuban military facilities. In the same year, the United States agreed to purchase the full 1942 sugar crop at 2.65 cents per pound. An agreement the following year similarly disposed of the 1943 crop. With the continued revival of sugar production, the economy moved fully out of its slump. Prosperity returned. The virtual collapse of Cuban trade with Europe during World War II also facilitated the expansion of North American goods in Cuban markets.

II

World War II created new opportunities for Cuban economic development, few of which, however, were fully realized. Wartime prosperity coincided with the ascendancy of the Auténtico party, first the presidency of Ramón Grau San Martín (1944–48) and later Carlos Prío Socarrás (1948–52). Funds were used irrationally. Corruption and graft increased and contributed in no small part to missed opportunities, but so did mismanagement and miscalculation. Few structural changes were made in the economy, thus leaving unattended chronic problems of unemployment and underemployment and a flawed agrarian order.

In large measure, this was a result of the historic interrelationship between the Cuban and North American economies. Elsewhere in Latin America, shortages occasioned by the war, and especially manufactures, encouraged new industries and the expansion of old ones. Import scarcities created new local market demands, many of which were met by national producers. Cuba's proximity to the United States meant that import commodities were more readily available on the island, reducing significantly the opportunity for local producers to expand into the domestic market. Import linkages to the United States resulted in wartime shortages in Cuba, especially for goods scarce in the United States, most notably automobile tires, petroleum products and other fuels, chemicals, construction materials, and vegetable oils. In the main, however, the flow of North American imports to Cuba continued with far less interruption than elsewhere in Latin America.

The Cuban economy began to decline by the late 1940s, and only the temporary reprieve of high sugar prices occasioned by the Korean War delayed economic dislocation. The problem of inflation increased throughout the decade. Favorable economic conditions with the potential to enhance Cuban productive capabilities were lost. Capital generated by the postwar prosperity was either invested abroad or mismanaged at home. "Much of the savings of Cubans," wrote the International Bank for Reconstruction and Development of these years, "has gone abroad, been hoarded or used for real estate construction and for speculation."[4] Between 1946 and 1952, the Cuban gross fixed investment as a percentage of gross income was only 9.3 percent, while in Argentina it reached 18.7 percent, in Colombia 18.6 percent, in Brazil 15.7 percent, in Mexico 13.4 percent, and in Chile 13.1 percent.[5]

Such a boom-bust cycle had long been associated with the island's export economy. But in the late 1940s and early 1950s, these conditions had far-reaching implications. The Cuban economy was approaching stagnation, a condition partially obscured by a dazzling postwar prosperity. Sugar continued to drive the economy, which meant that Cuba continued to link its well-being to an export product for which market conditions were uncertain and competition was intense. The decline of rival producers during World War II lulled Cubans into a false sense of security. In fact, most of Cuba's dynamic development had been reached before 1925, during the expansion of the agricultural and industrial phase of sugar production. After the mid-1920s, the Cuban economy made relatively little progress. The symptoms of stagnation were momentarily checked by the booms occasioned by World War II and the Korean War, but the sources of stagnation remained unchanged.

III

Most North Americans—indeed many urban Cubans—were oblivious to these persistent but largely hidden weaknesses in the Cuban economy of the postwar era. Of far greater interest were the increasing contacts between Cubans and the United States in these years. Advances in transportation and telecommunications brought the United States much closer to Cubans, and vice versa. Points always close became closer. Regularly scheduled passenger ship service increased. Air travel expanded. Within months of the end of World War II Pan American World Airways augmented its flights between Havana and Miami, scheduling as many as twenty-eight flights daily. New air routes were inaugurated, including Camagüey–Miami, Havana–New Orleans, Havana–Tampa, and Santiago–Charleston. Sea-train service linked Havana to New Orleans, freight-car ferry service operated between Havana and West Palm Beach, and automobile ferry service linked Havana with Key West.

The establishment of permanent Cuban communities in the United

States, principally in Florida and New York, provided the population centers around which Cuban immigration continued to expand. An estimated ten thousand Cubans lived in Tampa, and at least as many resided in New York. A new generation of Cubans migrated to the United States during the economic hard times of the 1920s and 1930s and continued to do so after World War II and through the early 1950s. By the later years of the decade, an estimated fifty thousand Cubans lived in the United States. Thousands of young men and women arrived in search of jobs and livelihood, most with the intention of returning to Cuba. Many did not. It was the pathos of this emigration to which the title of Pablo Armando Fernández's novel *Los niños se despiden* (1968) referred. Other Cubans arrived as tourists and for family visits. Affluent Cuban families continued to send their children north to complete their education and pursued business interests in the United States. As early as 1924, Cuban businessmen had organized a Cuban Chamber of Commerce in New York to promote and protect their interests in the United States. During the 1940s and 1950s, Cuban investments in the United States expanded. During the mid-1950s, the U.S. Department of Commerce estimated the combined Cuban short-term assets and long-term investments in the United States at $312 million, of which $265 million was in the form of short-term assets. During the 1950s, Cuban investments centered on real estate property, some in Havana, but more in New York and Florida. By 1955, Cuban real estate investments totaled over $150 million, mostly concentrated in property in south Florida.[6]

Proximity and ease of travel had other effects. Cubans developed a particular fixation on New York and Miami: New York simply because it was New York and Miami to shop. "I am obsessed by New York," proclaims Pablo Armando Fernández's protagonist in *Los niños se despiden*. "That city is a state of mind." And at another point: "New York was nothing anyone could imagine. New York was that which was missing everywhere else, that which was only here, in her heart and in her mind: a passion."[7]

Miami was fascinating for its material bounties. Cubans developed an almost insatiable demand for North American consumer goods.

They traveled to Florida to vacation, but mostly to shop. In one four-month period alone between May and August 1948, an estimated forty thousand travelers from Cuba arrived in Miami. By the early 1950s, this number had increased to fifty thousand. During these years Cubans visiting Florida were spending more than $70 million annually. "Besides the vacation," observed one correspondent, "the whole family can be outfitted with new wardrobes at half the cost of clothing in Havana. Electrical household appliances can be bought at prices that astonish Cubans. . . . They stagger under the weight of packages of all sizes and descriptions."[8] Indeed, by the early 1950s Cuban shopping sprees in the United States became so widespread a practice that merchants on the island demanded legislation to restrict Cuban purchases abroad.

North American cultural forms and consumer goods found new outlets and, as in the pre-Depression years, a ready public within Cuba as well. Radio and especially films, and later television, had a powerful impact in Cuba, most pronounced in Havana. The heavy commercial and advertising content of North American radio and television served in still other ways to promote consumption of U.S. products. California, New York, and Florida department stores routinely advertised sales in Havana dailies.

In the aggregate, these developments provided still another means by which North American cultural forms were disseminated through the island. Contacts with North Americans on so large a scale and over such sustained periods of time could not but change Cuban attitudes and behaviors in ways large and small. Movies, television, comic books, novels, and newspapers established Cuban preferences for everything from child-rearing practices to fashions, family planning to family vacations, music to diet, social conventions to entertainment fads, beauty and sex appeal to patterns of courtship and forms of recreation. Adults idolized Bette Davis, Joan Crawford, Gary Cooper, Judy Garland, John Wayne, Clark Gable, Spencer Tracy, Joe E. Brown, Humphrey Bogart, and Guy Madison, while their children were delighted by Popeye, Dick Tracy, Winnie Winkle, Mickey Mouse, and Wonder Woman. Using the 1950s as the setting for the novel *Tres tristes tigres,* Guillermo Cabrera Infante writes of one Cuban woman as "very young and beautiful, a bit like a Cuban Myrna Loy," of Cuban women having a crush on Gregory Peck, of local singers crooning "in the style of old Bing Crosby, but in Spanish."[9] Hollywood largely shaped Cuban standards of beauty, and Cuban magazines, including *Bohemia, Carteles,* and *Vanidades,* disseminated North American movie star culture to every recess of the island. North American affluence and spending habits were daily expressed in film and on television, in the automobile showrooms, and by throngs of free-spending tourists. Like their counterparts in the nineteenth century, wealthy Cubans in the 1940s and 1950s moved through both worlds with ease and often were thoroughly acculturated. Erna Fergusson recalled meeting the Ichasa family in Pinar del Río: "The Ichasas are one of those Cuban families that make you wonder whether you are in Cuba or the United States. Both mother and daughter were educated in the States. . . . With me their talk and manner was altogether Yankee."[10]

Other points of contact between Cubans and North Americans resulted in emulation of other attitudes and behaviors. Cubans working with and for North American enterprises adapted easily to U.S. social and business conventions. The ways Cubans entertained conformed increasingly to North American etiquette. Contact with North Americans at the country clubs changed local recreational habits. Cubans took up golf, tennis, bowling, and handball. Sexual restrictions also relaxed. Consuelo Hermer and Marjorie May wrote in 1941 of the influence of the Havana Country Club: "Cubans, watching the impersonal, between-sexes camaraderie of the Americans, were encouraged to allow their daughters a similar measure of freedom. In this way, the Country Club can really be credited for the relaxation of the hitherto rigid *dueña* system. Today, daughters of Cuba's first families lounge or play on the clubhouse grounds with the same freedom our own girls enjoy, and, to a certain extent, this attitude has penetrated to other social levels."[11]

In fact, Cuba was beginning more and more to sound and look like the United States. At Christmas time, vast numbers of Nordic pines were shipped to Cuba aboard refrigerated freighters. The use of the English language had spread across the island. All aspects of North American culture worked their way into Cuban society, at all levels. Wrote Ruby Hart Phillips of these years:

> The United States is mirrored in every phase of Cuban life. The modern Cuban eats hot dogs, hamburgers, hot cakes, waffles, fried chicken and ice cream. It has become almost impossible today in Havana to find native food such as malanga, yuca or ajiaco. Spanish architecture remains only because of its indestructible bulk. The new apartment buildings could be mistaken for those in any American city, and the new private homes resemble those of Florida. Spanish furniture is rapidly becoming extinct. American-made refrigerators, electric and gas stoves, and kitchen units have changed household customs. [12]

The construction boom of the 1950s provided one more entrée for U.S. influence in Cuba. As in the early 1900s, North American capitalists in Cuba employed architects and engineers from the United States to design and build banks, office buildings, and apartment houses. New exclusive social clubs, most notably the Miramar Yacht Club and the Commodore Yacht Club, no less than the newly constructed hotels, cabarets, and casinos, bore the telling influences of Miami Beach and Las Vegas. The residences of the Cuban bourgeoisie, in such exclusive neighborhoods as Miramar, Kohly, Biltmore, La Coronela, and Alturas del Vedado, imitated unabashedly the mansions of California and Newport, Rhode Island. At the same time, the construction of middle-class housing drew inspiration from North American ranch and cottage styles, introduced into Cuba through *House and Garden, House Beautiful, Architectural Forum*, and *Architectural Record*.[13] Not too many years later writer Pablo Armando Fernández would cast a rueful eye at what the 1950s had wrought in the old neighborhoods of Vedado and lament: "Oh, there were such beautiful houses here, and such great trees! All gone. . . . Even our bad taste was imported. We were not even allowed to discover our own bad taste; it was brought to us from Miami and New York."[14]

Cuban elites participated in and kept abreast of the latest U.S. styles and fashions. North American dancing, including the Charleston, the lindy, and the fox-trot, enjoyed widespread popularity among Cubans of all ages. North American fashion shows were especially popular in Havana and provided local clients with previews of the newest styles in formal evening wear, casual attire, and sports clothes. Nor did Cubans make the slightest concession to the tropics: furs were among the more popular items in fashion shows. Erna Fergusson attended one such event in Havana and observed with a hint of incredulity: "On Monday evening the auditorium offers a brilliant clothes show with imported models, diamonds and emeralds, silver fox and chinchilla. A lady said: 'Americans think we are silly to wear furs, but we like outdoor entertaining—the smartest New Year's party is outdoors at the Country Club—and of course we *need* furs.'"[15] Commented one tourist guide: "Paradoxically enough, there's a big furor over furs in Havana. The great silver-fox plague raging up North has now spread down to the tropics. Cuban women of means adore mink, ermine, sable, fox, all the precious furs, and wear them lavishly. As a matter of fact, Havana seems to be a Mecca for phony-furs among the poorer women. To own a fur-piece is everyone's ambition, even if it's only a skimpy one-skin scarf of dubious ancestry."[16]

The twin themes of North American cultural penetration and politico-economic control long served as the key motifs of Cuban fiction. Writers before and after the revolution, authors in exile, critical of the revolution, and writers in Cuba, sympathetic to the revolution, explored the myriad and complicated ways Cubans were affected by the North American presence. Guillermo Cabrera Infante in *Tres tristes tigres* mocked "Spanglish" and made pointed comments about the ways North American eating habits, work ethic, and courtship patterns influenced Cubans. Nivaria Tejera in *Sonámbulo del sol* used the country clubs as the vehicle through which North American cultural forms permeated Cuban society. In *Gestos* Severo Sarduy indicted the expanding use of English, Protestant missionaries, and U.S. sailors as the symbols of what Cuban society had become. Miguel Cossío Woodward in *Sacchario* looked at the prevalence of North American comic strips, including Mandrake the Magician (Mandrake el Mago),

Donald Duck (el Pato Donald), and the Wizard of Oz (el Mago de Oz), and the popularity of U.S. rock and roll music as still other manifestations of U.S. cultural predominance. Antonio Benítez Rojo (*El escudo de hojas secas*) and Juan Arcocha (*Los muertos andan solos*) ridiculed the Cuban bourgeoisie's slavish adhesion to North American fashions, entertainment, and acquisitiveness.

IV

Influences did not flow only one way. Cubans made contributions to North American culture in sports, and especially in boxing and baseball. Cuban boxers who succeeded in the United States included Kid Chocolate and Kid Gavilán. Among the better-known baseball players were Bert Campaneris, Miguel Angel (Mike) González, Tony Oliva, Cookie Rojas, Diego Seguí, José Tartabull, Martin Dihigo, Conrado Marrero, Orestes (Minnie) Miñoso, Edmundo (Sandy) Amorós, Zoilo Versalles, Miguel (Mike) Cuéllar, Orlando Peña, Pedro Ramos, and Camilo Pascual. [17]

It was in the realm of music, however, that Cubans made their most significant and lasting contribution to North American culture. From the borscht belt in upstate New York to the ballrooms and dance floors of the large cities, Cuban dances worked their way into the repertoire of professional and recreational dancers alike. The *danzón*, the *rumba*, the *son*, the *bolero*, the *mambo*, the *cha-cha-cha*, and the *pachanga* enjoyed widespread popularity in the United States. During the 1920s, the *rumba* gained a large following in clubs, dance studios, and on film, followed the next decade by the *conga*, made popular by a newly arrived Cuban émigré, Desi Arnaz. By the 1940s, according to dance school statistics, the popular demand for *rumba* lessons was second only to the fox-trot. "It is safe to say that *rumba* is no passing fancy," wrote musicologist Earl Leaf in 1948. "*Rumbas* alternate with fox trots at dances in the metropolitan clubs. . . . '*Rumba* matinees' are regular features in the salons of fashionable hotels. A new phrase '*rumba* wives' has been added to the Broadway lexicon to describe the women who haunt the *rumba* dens of the city by day and by night. To them *rumba* is a drug."[18]

Afro-Cuban forms and rhythms fused with jazz and eventually entered the mainstream of North American music. Cuban musicians became key members of many of the most prominent bands in the United States, including those led by Duke Ellington, Stan Kenton, and Louis Armstrong. Drummer Luciano González (Chano Pozo) had a decisive influence on the music of Dizzy Gillespie, and through him, on an entire generation of North American musicians. Trumpeter Mario Bauza worked with Chick Webb and Cab Calloway. It was Bauza who persuaded the more established Cab Calloway to hear a young Dizzy Gillespie—"a trumpeter who knew his Cuban rhythms."[19] After the success of Chano Pozo with Dizzy Gillespie, other established orchestras moved to hire Cuban drummers. Percussionist Armando Peraza recorded with George Shearing, Dave Brubeck, and Cal Tjader. Other orchestras that hired Cuban percussionists included those of Woody Herman, Nat King Cole, Jerry Wald, and Gene Krupa. Trumpeter Arturo (Chico) O'Farrill arranged and played for Benny Goodman, Stan Kenton, and Dizzy Gillespie. Carlos Valdez (Potato) played with Herbie Mann, Art Blakey, and Kenny Dorham. Cuban musicians quickly enjoyed prominence in their own right and included Ernesto Lecuona, Don Aspiazu and the Havana Casino Orchestra, Frank Grillo (Machito), José Curbelo, Candido Camero, Dámaso Pérez Prado, Miguelito Valdés, René Touzet, Xavier Cugat (born in Spain and raised in Cuba), and Arsenio Rodríguez—all of whom, in varying degrees, permanently influenced North American tastes in music and choice of dance.

V

Not all Cuban contacts with the United States were felicitous and of happy portent, however. Many Cubans who migrated to the United States during these decades did not fare much better than their predecessors during the 1880s and 1890s. For countless numbers of Cuban workers, professionals, and intellectuals, life in the United States proved to be a constant struggle against daily adversities and indignities. They, too, experienced discrimination, racial violence, and abuse in the workplace. "The Afro-Cuban has found it difficult to adjust himself to the strict color line in Florida," observed an investigator from the Federal Writers' Project of the WPA.[20] In Tampa (Ybor City and West Tampa) vigilante groups, with the sanction and often participation of local law enforcement agents, attacked union organizers and workers. Labor leaders were beaten, union offices gutted, and strikes broken by violence. Union officials were kidnapped or otherwise forced to flee for fear of their lives. They may have been the fortunate ones, for others were beaten and killed.[21] The Ku Klux Klan continued to visit terror on Cuban communities. Recalled José Yglesias of a cigarworkers' strike in Tampa in 1931: "During the strike, the KKK would come into the labor temple with guns, and break up meetings. Very frequently they were police with hoods. Though they were called the Citizens' Committee, everybody would call them Los Cuckoo Klan. The picket lines would hold hands, and the KKK would beat them and cart them off."[22] In Tampa and Key West class conflict joined with ethnic tensions and racial hostility to make life for many Cubans precarious and uncertain. "Cuban nigger" was an epithet frequently hurled at Latins in Tampa.[23]

Linguistic difficulties and cultural differences produced other problems. Reported one WPA observer in 1936:

Very little has been done toward making the Cuban people . . . feel that they are Americans. Even many of the second and third generations of the Cubans, although born in the United States . . . are not considered as Americans by many of the English speaking Americans. Many of the English speaking Americans (who have never associated with the Latins) are biased against them without any cause whatsoever. Also in many of the American business and commercial enterprises, the Latin American is not given the opportunity to fill a position in those enterprises. Many times a Latin has been fired from one of the American companies to place an English speaking American of less caliber.

In Tampa, public schools posted strict injunctions against children speaking Spanish and punished offenders with reprimands and suspension. Language problems among children often resulted in poor school performance and a high dropout rate. "The Cuban children," observed one WPA investigator in 1936, "could not adjust themselves to the new environment as well as the American children. This proved to be a drawback in their educational advancement. At the age of 15 and 16, many of the Latin boys and girls were still in the grammar schools."[24] Not surprisingly, most Cuban children quit school before finishing.

This was not what Cubans had expected. Embittered by their experiences in the United States and often victims of racial prejudice and ethnic discrimination, many returned to the island and responded to anti-U.S. sentiment. Cuban writer Rogelio Llopis, a former resident of New York, provided a suggestive narrative in his short story "A Horrible Man": "Neither Curbelito nor I knew enough English. . . . For nobody who spoke the language fluently would take much notice of us. Mostly they used to look over our shoulders as if we had the plague and contact had to be avoided at all costs. It was worse still when we spoke our own language in public." And when Mr. Malone confronts Llopis's Cuban protagonist: " 'I really despise you,' his eyes seemed to say as they met mine. 'Lousy spics,' he suddenly grunted." The protagonist's final musings are telling: "Here people find it hard to understand that a foreigner can be proud of being what he is and might not want to adopt the American way of life." Juan Arcocha's protagonist Esteban in *A Candle in the Wind* (1967) has a similar experience. Esteban is chosen by a North American corporation in Cuba to receive managerial training in the United States, but his encounter with North American society provides a rude awakening: "He detested life in that country, where he had to spend his time apologizing for being Latin. Americans look you over coldly from head to foot. When you are outstanding in something, they are surprised, as though they had never suspected you were capable of it. Then they go to the opposite extreme and exaggerate any of your merits that come to their attention." Warren Miller traveled in Cuba in 1960 and recorded the musings of another former resident of the United States:

> I had many unpleasant experiences while I lived in the United States. I don't say that *all* your countrymen believe they are superior to every-

one else. But I think seventy-five per cent of them believe that they are. I spent two years in New York swallowing blood because I could not answer back. My English was not good enough, and I did not want to get into fights. . . . In the United States I once met a man who said to me, "But you can't be Cuban; you are white." How is it you know so little of a country just an hour away from you? I will tell you why. It's because you think you are so superior to us that you don't *have* to know about us. [25]

Cubans in the United States, and especially in Tampa and Key West, whether as permanent residents or new immigrants, maintained close contacts with communities on the island. Certainly proximity and travel had much to do with the persistence of these linkages. But ties of class and nationality also figured prominently. Cigarworkers on both sides of the Florida Straits inhabited a single universe, one in which common interests and similar objectives overcame distances of time and space. This was a world through which Cuban workers in Havana and Tampa traveled freely and frequently, as much catalysts as the consequences of change. Ties were forged and preserved over time and in periods of struggle in both countries. Unemployment in Havana produced migration to Key West and Tampa, and vice versa. Workers on strike in Tampa received moral and material support from unions in Havana, and the other way around. In this manner, Cubans in Florida maintained contact with Cubans on the island, a contact that guaranteed each a measure of continuing participation in the affairs of the other. Cubans in Tampa remained very much engaged in workers' struggles and the revolutionary process on the island.

Thus it was that young Fidel Castro traveled to Tampa in November 1955, in much the same way that José Martí had done almost sixty-five years earlier. "The Republic of Cuba is the daughter of the cigar makers of Tampa," Castro reminded his audience in Tampa. He exhorted local Cubans to provide moral and material assistance to the revolutionary struggle against Batista.[26] They did not disappoint him. Scores of 26th of July clubs were organized in Tampa, and like the patriotic *juntas* of the 1880s and 1890s, the clubs of the 1950s collected supplies, raised funds, and generally made favorable propaganda in behalf of the 26th of July Movement. And during the years that hundreds of thousands of new Cubans emigrated to Miami in opposition to socialism in Cuba, old Cubans in Tampa remained constant in their support of the revolution. "Most Latins in Ybor City were *fidelistas,*" recalled José Yglesias. "For the old timers the [U.S.] embargo was further proof of the barbarity of *americanos*—the 'crackers' with hair on their teeth who once broke up their meetings and called them 'Cuban niggers.' The new Cuban exiles were for them new indeed—they were counterrevolutionary and that . . . makes them untrustworthy. They remember reactionaries who denounced them to the FBI and with impunity, like that of the old nightriders, flung buckets of red paint at their homes."[27]

VI

Patterns first established during the colonial era persisted during the 1950s. The island continued to depend on foreign technicians and professional expertise from abroad, and again mostly North American, to service the sugar sector. Although sugar accounted for fully 86 percent of the value of Cuban exports from 1946 to 1954, more than 32 percent of the aggregate national gross income in 1952, and provided employment for at least 30 percent of the active wage labor force, the study of sugar production was all but ignored by Cuban schools and students alike. "For the current needs of the country," the International Bank for Reconstruction and Development reported in 1951, "there is a very poor distribution of professional graduates turned out by the University. The medical budget is too high; there are far too many lawyers and architects; there are too few chemists and engineers." The bank reported finding "no technical library, in any part of Cuba, which could be considered as even approaching ordinary needs of industrial operation, technical instruction or research."[28] Out of an enrollment of 17,527 students at the University of Havana for the academic year 1953–54, the school of sciences had a total of 1,502 students, out of which only 404 were engaged in the study of sugar

Table 8.1.
U.S. Direct Investments in Cuba
(in millions of dollars)

Sector	1946	1950	1958
Agriculture	227	263	265
Petroleum	15	20	90
Mining	15	70	180
Manufacturing	40	54	80
Public utilities	251	271	344
Trade	12	21	35
Miscellaneous	8	13	7
Total	568	712	1,001

Sources: U.S. Department of Commerce, *Investment in Cuba* (Washington, D.C., 1956), p. 10, Ismael Zuaznabar, *La economía cubana en la década del 50* (Havana, 1986), p. 51.

and agriculture. "The inadequacy of educational facilities in trade, technical, and business fields has long been recognized," commented the U.S. Department of Commerce in 1956, "but few remedial measures have thus far been taken." A familiar condition was described: "Broadly speaking, students desirous of playing a productive role in the development of their country must seek their training abroad." Some years later Theodore Draper would describe this sector of the Cuban middle class as "a rising group of modern technicians, many of them wholly or partially trained in the United States."[29]

North American investments in Cuba continued to expand during the 1940s and 1950s (see Table 8.1). In some sectors, U.S. capital all but eclipsed competitors. North American interests controlled more than 90 percent of telephone and electrical services (International Telephone and Telegraph Corporation and American and Foreign Power Company), 83 percent of the aggregate network of public service railways (Western Railroads of Cuba and Consolidated Railroads of Cuba), and 42 percent of sugar production. Nearly 70 percent of petroleum imported, refined, and distributed in Cuba was controlled by two corporations, Standard Oil of New Jersey and Texaco. North Americans held an additional $211 million worth of portfolio items. The United States government also held an estimated $200 million in Cuban mines. Foreign banks accounted for nearly 40 percent of all Cuban bank deposits. [30]

Cuban commerce with the United States during the 1940s and 1950s continued to account for the larger share of the island's foreign trade, averaging almost 73 percent of the total in the late 1940s and declining slightly to about 68 percent through the mid-1950s. Imports from the United States remained fairly constant, varying from 80.5 percent of the total during 1946–50 to 75.9 percent for 1951–53. Sugar remained the principal export, almost 90 percent during the late 1940s and early 1950s, and the United States continued as the most important single market, consuming approximately 41 percent of Cuban sugar exports. [31]

Overall import-export patterns for the 1940s and 1950s, however, only partially suggest the degree to which Cuba had passed into the North American economy. Increasingly Cubans were depending on imports of consumer goods, durables and nondurables alike. Between 1948 and 1954, Cuban spending on imports of consumer goods increased from $189 million to $226 million, the largest portion of which originated in the United States. Nor does this include the vast amounts of commodities purchased by Cubans making weekend shopping trips to Florida, the full dimensions of which may never be ascertained. "Cuban buying habits," noted the U.S. Department of Commerce in 1956, "ease of communication, prompt deliveries, and excellent transportation facilities give United States merchandise a competitive edge in the Cuban market . . . and assure the United States a high percentage of the Cuban export trade." [32]

Cuban consumption needs were also met increasingly through local production by subsidiaries of North American enterprises. Soap and detergent production was dominated by Cruselles y Cía. (Colgate), Detergentes Cubanos, S.A. (Colgate), and Sabates, S.A. (Procter and Gamble). Cement products were manufactured by Compañía Cubana de Cemento Portland (Lone Star Cement). Burroughs established a flour mill in Regla. Glidden, DuPont, and Sherwin Williams operated the principal paint factories. Automobile tires and inner tubes were produced by Compañía Goodrich Cubana, S.A., and Compañía Goodyear de Cuba, S.A. Glass products were manufactured by Owens-Illinois de Cuba, S.A. Virtually all the fertilizer manufactured in Cuba was by American Agricultural Chemicals. The principal meat producers in Havana were Armour y Cía. and Swift y Cía. A vast retail network was established by F. W. Woolworth ("el Ten Cent"). Metal containers were manufactured by the Continental Can Company in Havana, and soft drinks were produced by Coca-Cola, Pepsi Cola, Canada Dry, Orange Crush, and Royal Crown. Sewing machines were provided by Singer Sewing Machine. Paper products were manufactured by W. R. Grace & Co. Newspaper and publishing ink was manufactured in Havana by Sinclair & Valentine de Cuba, S.A., and H. N. Rosen, S.A. Rubber-soled canvas footwear was produced by the United States Rubber Company. The Cuban Air Products Corporation (Air Reduction Company) manufactured compressed and liquefied gases.

The resident North American community continued to expand, in large part a measure of the increasing U.S. capital stake on the island. An estimated sixty-five hundred North Americans resided on the island, principally in Havana, and many were employed at various strategic levels of the Cuban economy. They obtained medical attention at the Anglo-American Hospital and received prescription medicines from Dr. Lorie's American Drug Store on the Prado. In almost every way, North Americans in Cuba enjoyed a privileged existence. "They live comfortably in beautiful houses," observed Ruby Hart Phillips, "for which they pay high rent of course, employ one to three servants, and belong to one or two clubs, such as the American Club, the Rovers Club, the Country Club, Habana Yacht Club and Miramar Club."[33]

To the resident North American population were added the tens of thousands of tourists from the United States who annually traveled to Cuba. By the mid-1950s, their numbers were approaching three hundred thousand yearly. North American tourism during the 1950s expanded principally around commercialized vice, largely gambling, prostitution, and drugs. Pornographic theaters became one of the new growth industries in Havana during the late 1950s. "Havana flourished as the playground for wealthy Americans and tourists in general," Tad Szulc wrote of these years. "It had spectacular nightclubs, splendid casinos, famous bordellos and every form of street prostitution and vice a visitor's heart could desire."[34]

For all these reasons and others, Havana developed a reputation as a good liberty port for the U.S. Navy. Tens of thousands of North American sailors found ample varieties of recreation during shore leave and spent an estimated $2 million annually, mostly in Havana and Santiago. Pablo Armando Fernández in *Los niños se despiden* could write of a Havana nightclub "smelling of American marines," a mixture of "cigarettes, whisky, Chiclets, Mennen lotion, Lifebuoy soap, khaki, and U.S. Keds."[35] Most of the time Cuban authorities treated North American excesses, drinking sprees, brawls, and minor disturbances with a mixture of indulgence and indifference. In one incident, however, on the evening of March 12, 1949, three drunken North American sailors climbed atop the statue of José Martí in the Parque Central and urinated over the monument. The incident provoked rioting and angry anti-U.S. demonstrations, requiring in the end a formal U.S. apology. What made the event of lasting effect was that it was well photographed by Cubans, and for years thereafter the publication of photos of the North American sailors swinging from the extended arm of José Martí aroused indignation and anti-U.S. sentiment in Cuba.

A building boom during the 1950s was at once cause and effect of the surge of the new North American tourism. Between 1952 and 1958 almost twenty hotels were constructed in Havana. New hotels as well as old ones opened lavish casinos. The Hotel Riviera and the Hotel Capri opened casinos in 1957. The Capri hired North American actor George Raft as the casino host. Other gambling casinos were in operation in Havana, at the Hotel Nacional, Hotel Sevilla Biltmore, Deauville, and Commodore Hotel; in Cienfuegos at the Jagua Hotel;

at Varadero at the Internacional. The Colony Hotel was constructed on the Isle of Pines and joined thirteen brothels and one abortion mill that charged North American visitors $1,500, including the price of the hotel room. Three nightclubs in Havana, the Montmartre, Sans Souci, and Tropicana, also opened casinos. Nightlife in Havana assumed extravagant proportions. Big-name performers from the United States were brought to Havana clubs for North American audiences: Eartha Kitt, Nat King Cole, Lena Horne, Frank Sinatra, Duke Ellington, Sarah Vaughan. Increasingly, however, foreign performers, musicians, and entertainers displaced Cuban artists from work in the principal hotels, nightclubs, and cabarets. As early as 1929, Cuban musicians protested hotels and nightclubs favoring North American bands over Cuban ones. [36]

Increasingly, too, organized crime syndicates from the United States expanded their presence in Cuba. Interest in Cuba began as early as the 1920s and 1930s, during Prohibition, as bootleggers large and small discovered the island to be a convenient and plentiful source of alcoholic beverages. After the repeal of Prohibition, crime interests shifted to gambling. As early as 1937, Meyer Lansky had established control over the gambling casino in the Hotel Nacional. [37] After World War II leading crime figures, including Frank Costello, Lucky Luciano, Alberto Anastasia, Tommy Lucchese, Joe Bonanno, Vito Genovese, Santo Trafficante, and Lansky met in Havana to discuss plans for expanding into Cuba. [38] In 1955 Batista obligingly modified existing gambling laws to permit casinos in any nightclub or hotel worth $1 million or more. Tens of millions of dollars were subsequently invested in luxury hotels, nightclubs, and gambling casinos. Crime figure Norman Rothman operated the Sans Souci and later passed it on to Santo Trafficante, who controlled the Capri. Lansky owned the Montmartre and with his associates acquired interests in the Sevilla Biltmore, the Internacional, the Commodore, and the Havana Hilton. Lansky provided most of the $14 million used to construct the luxurious Riviera Hotel. To staff the expanding casinos and gambling clubs, he established a casino school in his Montmartre Club to teach Cuban youngsters to operate blackjack, roulette, and other games. [39] During the 1950s, gambling receipts surpassed $500,000 monthly. "This is going to be another Las Vegas," an anonymous gambling promoter boasted to *Life* correspondent Ernest Havemann, "only like Las Vegas never imagined." The *Havana Post* concurred and observed that Cuba was bidding for the title of "the Las Vegas of Latin America."[40]

Profits on so lavish a scale could not have been achieved and sustained without close collaboration between organized crime and Cuban officials from presidents to cabinet members, legislators, army and police officers, and city officials. Millions of dollars were distributed among Cuban officials high and low in the form of graft and rake-offs. Criminal activities expanded on all fronts—most notably drugs and prostitution—without the slightest interference from Cuban authorities and wholly free of any fear of local prosecution. Casino and hotel construction proceeded under a wide range of immunities and waivers, from local taxes, from national customs duties, from building code regulations, from gambling licenses.

Plans were under way to develop other sections of the island. During the late 1940s and early 1950s, Lucky Luciano was completing arrangements to transform the Isle of Pines into the "Monte Carlo of the Western Hemisphere." Lavish hotels, gambling casinos, and expanded brothels were to make the small southern island the center of recreational vice. Luciano's plan, former commissioner of the Federal Narcotics Bureau Harry J. Anslinger later disclosed, was to make Cuba the base of international drug trafficking.[41]

During the 1950s, crime syndicates organized auxiliary activities to accompany the expanding gambling operations. Prostitution was upgraded and a first-class call-girl operation was organized with, wrote Lansky's biographer Hank Messick, "a higher class of whores trained or imported." Drugs sales expanded into the local market. Illegal abortion clinics expanded in number and service, and crime syndicates provided capital for clinic buildings where Cuban physicians provided medical services. "In short order," Messick wrote years later, "Havana became the abortion capital of the Western Hemisphere."[42]

This consortium of interests between Cubans and North Americans provided new kinds of policy access to Cuban officials. In 1944, efforts by the United States to persuade President Batista to permit free elections and relinquish power found Meyer Lansky in the improbable role of presidential envoy. In response to a directive from President Franklin Roosevelt, U.S. naval intelligence sent Lansky to confer with Batista and warn the Cuban president against resisting U.S. demands. Batista acquiesed, and in return he was permitted to establish an orange grove near Daytona Beach, not far from the center of Lansky's Broward County headquarters. [43]

That tourism thrived on commercialized vice, sponsored by organized crime, served to introduce into Cuban life one more insidious element from the United States. Arthur M. Schlesinger, Jr., later recalled a visit to Havana during these years: "I was enchanted by Havana—and appalled by the way that lovely city was being debased into a great casino and brothel for American businessmen over for a big weekend from Miami. My fellow countrymen reeled through the streets, picking up fourteen-year-old Cuban girls and tossing coins to make men scramble in the gutter. One wondered how any Cuban— on the basis of this evidence—could regard the United States with anything but hatred." As early as 1952, *Time* magazine could describe Havana as "one of the world's fabled fleshpots." The ubiquity of this North American presence, in its worst manifestations, offended Cuban sensibilities. "Havana has turned into a disgrace," lamented Cuban writer Antonio Llano Montes in 1957. [44]

Havana had come to reflect, in its residents and on its streets, the curious and often incongruous juxtaposition of things of North American, Creole, and African origins: English words interspersed in the Spanish language, African cabarets at the Hilton, blond *mulatas*, Cuban stores stocked with North American manufactures, North American outlets carrying Cuban products. "This must be the only capital city in the world," comments one of Norman Lewis's protagonists in *Cuban Passage*, "where Woolworth's have a counter stacked with charms and voodoo paraphernalia." [45]

VII

Following World War II Cubans were integrated into North American economic structures more fully than ever before. Cuban dependence on U.S. consumer goods had its origins in the previous century, but what was different after World War II was the marked rise in Cuban consumption and the degree to which that increase served to establish new linkages and reinforce old ones. What was different, too, was the extent to which North American enterprises had penetrated the local economy. Not only were Cubans buying more North American imports; they were buying more North American products manufactured in Cuba. Fully 85 percent of North American production in Cuba was sold on the local market.

This close linkage could not but have significantly affected the way Cubans saw themselves, their society, and the relationship of both to everything else. These perceptions were possessed of distinct cultural, political, and ideological dimensions. Cubans in vast numbers came to identify their welfare with the well-being of North American interests. An important sector of the Cuban middle class developed direct ties to and a vital stake in the North American presence. More and more Cubans found themselves working for North American enterprises. By the late 1950s an estimated 150,000 Cubans were employed by North American enterprises on the island. Salaries and wages paid by these firms were considerably higher than those paid by Cuban ones. In 1957, North American enterprises spent $730 million in Cuba: approximately $170 million in salaries and wages, $70 million in taxes, and $490 million on the purchase of local products. Fully 20 percent of the Cuban budget was derived from the taxes paid by these firms.

Cuba developed a consumer culture without counterpart elsewhere in Latin America, underwritten largely by imports and investments originating from the United States. It was centered principally in Havana but had also expanded into the provincial capitals. The effects were stunning.

Cuba boasted one of the highest standards of living in Latin America. In 1957, the island enjoyed the second highest per capita income in Latin America, estimated at $374, following Venezuela's of $857. Only Mexico and Brazil exceeded Cuba in the number of radios (one radio for every 6.5 inhabitants). The island ranked first in television sets (one unit per 25 inhabitants). Daily average food consumption was surpassed only by Argentina and Uruguay. Cuba was first in telephones (one for every 38 people), newspapers (one newspaper copy per 8 inhabitants), private motor vehicles (one per 40 persons), and rail mileage per square mile (one to four). An estimated 58.2 percent of all housing units possessed electricity. By 1953, 76.4 percent of the population was literate, the fourth highest literacy rate in Latin America after Argentina (86.4 percent), Chile (79.5 percent), and Costa Rica (79.4 percent).

The apparent affluence enjoyed by Cuba, however, concealed tensions and frustrations that extended both vertically and horizontally through the society. The fluctuations of the export economy continued to create uncertainty and insecurity and affected all classes. The structural ties to the U.S. economy, no less than the psychological ones, served to create among Cubans expectations that were as unattainable as they were unrealistic. Indeed, the apparent Cuban success contained a large built-in element of frustration. It simply was not reasonable for most Cubans to sustain a consumer economy of this magnitude within the dependent capitalist structures of an export economy. These expectations worked their way virtually across Cuban class lines. "The worker in Cuba," the U.S. Department of Commerce reported in 1956, "is . . . ambitious enough to respond to incentive, he has wider horizons than most Latin American workers and expects more out of life in material amenities than many European workers." The conclusion was nothing short of remarkable. "His goal is to reach a standard of living comparable with that of the American worker."[46] This goal was neither attainable nor realistic.

A boom-bust economy created a consumption logic of its own, obedient to market forces that Cubans could neither predict nor control but that nonetheless shaped the standard by which they continued to measure their material well-being. No less important, and certainly no more controllable, was the yearly announcement by the

U.S. secretary of agriculture fixing the annual quota for Cuban sugar. On this allocation depended the fate and fortune of countless thousands of Cubans. Good times let loose an outburst of consumption, conspicuous and excessive, all of which served to make hard times that much more unbearable. Prosperity after World War I was characterized by vast imports of North American luxury items.[47] Expectations raised during times of prosperity were necessarily dashed during periods of adversity. These volatile conditions created enormous uncertainty and insecurity and often assumed the proportions of a national neurosis. The good life increasingly was defined through the acquisition of material goods, for which standards were set by North Americans. And, indeed, under the circumstances, how could it be otherwise? Cuban familiarity with North American consumer goods, explained Cuban ambassador Guillermo Patterson y de Jauregui as early as 1936, had created an insatiable demand for North American products. The Cuban "will not resign himself," suggested Patterson, "to surrender the comforts and material pleasures of a more enjoyable life of higher standard." Lack of prosperity "prevents him from satisfying the desire for a better life; but the desire is there just the same, alive, imperious, latent, under constant strain, awaiting the opportunity to be satisfied."[48]

Economic stagnation in the 1950s exacerbated uncertainty in Cuba and together with an unstable economy contributed to eroding the security of the middle class. Cubans found little comfort in statistical compilations that touted their high level of material consumption and placed the island near the top of the scale of per capita income in Latin America. The social reality was quite different. Cuba was integrated directly into the larger U.S. economic system and its concomitant consumption patterns. Although Cubans enjoyed a remarkably high per capita income in Latin American terms, they lived within a North American cost-of-living index. Cuba enjoyed a material culture underwritten principally by a vast import component from the United States. Cuban currency and wages remained comparatively stable through the 1950s, but consumption of foreign imports, in the main North American products, increased dramatically from $515 million in 1950 to $649 million in 1956 and $777 million in 1958. Cubans paid North American prices at a time when the purchasing power of the U.S. dollar was declining and the U.S. consumer price index was rising. Indeed, in most instances, Cubans were paying higher prices. In addition to a 4 percent customs duty, a variety of other taxes, consular fees, and even a tax on the total tax, as well as local distribution markups, raised prices in Cuba an average 35 percent. A sale in Havana was announced with telling assurance: "at Miami prices." Indeed, this was one of the appeals of weekend shopping trips to Florida. The International Bank for Reconstruction and Development examined the prices of selected U.S. farm equipment imports and discovered a number of startling differentials: a $1,290 Ford tractor cost $1,750 in Cuba; a $119 hammer mill increased to $249; a milking machine that cost $76 in the United States sold for $134 in Cuba.[49] The expanded use of North American credit cards during the late 1950s added still more to prices in the form of interest and service fees. By the late 1950s, Cubans in growing numbers had resorted to credit purchases as a short-term response to maintain living standards. Nine out of ten cars, seven out of ten televisions, radios, phonographs, and refrigerators, as well as a high proportion of air conditioners, electric and gas ovens, dishwashers, and clothing were purchased on credit.[50]

Under any circumstances, economic conditions would have caused distress and discontent. That the Cuban economy was so thoroughly integrated into the North American system, and, further, that so many Cubans were an integral part of a consumer economy that they could not keep up with all but guaranteed to raise Cuban frustration. The phenomenon of relative deprivation worked powerfully to undermine Cuban morale and heighten discontent. Proximity to the United States had a powerfully debilitating effect. The comparatively high per capita income, by Latin American standards, was increasingly unsatisfactory because it was not improving. This was especially intolerable for a society so close to Florida and so susceptible to images of the good life in the United States, including easy travel, as well as television, movies, radio, and such widely circulated publications as *Life en Español*, *Colliers*, *Vogue*, and *Selecciones del Readers Digest*. The United

States—not Latin America—served as the Cuban frame of reference. And against this measure, the Cuban per capita income of $374 paled against the United States per capita of $2,000, or even that of Mississippi, the poorest state, at $1,000. Life in Havana was considerably more expensive than in any North American city. Havana ranked high among the world's most expensive cities—fourth after Caracas, Ankara, and Manila. Few Cubans could keep up, at least for long. Thus at the height of years of presumed affluence and prosperity, as national per capita income continued to stay well ahead of Latin American figures, Cubans were actually experiencing a decline in living standards and an increase in the cost of living.

Resentment was on the rise. Economist Levi Marrero expressed dismay in 1954 that though Cuba's per capita income was twice as high as any other in Latin America, it was five times lower than North American levels, and he asked rhetorically: "Why this Cuban poverty?" Three years later, writer Antonio Llano Montes expressed a similar complaint: "Although one hears daily of the prosperity that Cuba is now experiencing, the fact is that the workers and the middle class find it more difficult each day to subsist owing to the scarcity of articles of basic necessity." [51]

Cubans participated directly in and depended largely on the U.S. economic system, in very much the same fashion as North Americans but without access to comparable U.S. social service and public assistance programs and at employment and wage levels substantially lower and prices higher than their North American counterparts. Cuba had an unemployment rate three times that of the United States and lacked comparable unemployment subsidies. More than half the wage labor force, not including rural workers and domestics, were without disability compensation, unemployment insurance, and retirement pensions. By the late 1950s, moreover, an estimated 665,000 Cubans, more than 30 percent of the labor force, were unemployed or underemployed. Of the balance working population of 1.5 million, almost 62 percent earned less than $75 monthly. [52]

This disparity was keenly felt in Cuba and was a source of rising frustration and pressure. Middle-class Cubans in the 1950s perceived their standard of living to be in decline as they fell behind income advances in the United States. These perceptions were not without substance, for even the much acclaimed Cuban per capita income represented a standard of living in stagnation. Prices were increasing, and wages and salaries were not. Food increased as much as 25 percent. The food cost index based on the year 1937 as 100 increased from 218.9 in January 1950 to 238.5 in September 1950.[53] Between 1952 and 1954, the decline in the international sugar market precipitated the first in a series of recessions in the Cuban economy during the 1950s. Per capita income declined by 18 percent, neutralizing the gains of the postwar prosperity.[54] In 1956, the National Bank of Cuba estimated that the gross national product increased sufficiently from 1948 to 1954 to permit the maintenance of the 1947 standard of living in only five of the seven years; only in two years (1951 and 1952) was it sufficient to permit a 2 percent increase over the 1947 level. At that rate, the National Bank predicted grimly, the sugar harvest of 1965 would have to reach 8.2 million tons and obtain a value of nearly $800 million to guarantee the 1965 population the same living standard enjoyed by the 1947 population.[55] The purchasing power of Cuban exports between 1952 and 1956 remained approximately at levels reached thirty years earlier. "The increment in net per capita income registered in the last 25 years," reported the U.N. Economic Commission in 1955, "and particularly during the post-war period, constitutes, in large measure, a mere return to the income levels already attained by Cuba in the past."[56] In fact, the Cuban per capita income in 1958 was at about the same level as it had been in 1947.

Increasingly, middle-class Cubans were losing ground, as well as the ability to sustain the consumption patterns to which they had become accustomed. "Cuba's present standard of living, therefore," the International Bank for Reconstruction and Development observed as early as 1951, "depends mainly on an industry which stopped growing many years ago." And at another point: "Cuba is living in—and on—the past and weakened by events beyond her control." Five years later, the U.S. Department of Commerce arrived at a similar conclusion: "The decade ahead should witness a substantial increase in the tempo of economic diversification. It would be foolhardy, however, to gloss over or underestimate the extent of the problem confronting Cuba in its efforts to maintain, let alone increase, the standard of living of its people." Cuba existed in a world, the National Bank warned, that "does not offer sufficient markets to absorb all that the country can produce today and tomorrow."[57]

Middle-class frustration was rising through the mid-1950s, as crisis was overtaking Cuban society. Malaise was settling in, and the reaction assumed some predictable forms. Writing in 1956 Mario Llerena denounced Cuba for its problems: air pollution, poor public services, gambling, prostitution, "erratic electrical services from companies whose bills arrive punctually," poor garbage collection. "In Cuba we have at hand everything that modern civilization can offer together with everything that denies and invalidates it."[58]

The breakdown was in the mind. An uncertainty existed and was increasing, and its principal element was loss of confidence in the future. In no small way, this loss was itself the product of close ties with the United States, as the realization took hold among Cubans that they could not keep up with North Americans and that their national identity was succumbing slowly to North American material culture and commercial vice. Revolution was widely anticipated, and when it came it was initially welcomed, with the expectation of individual fulfillment and national redemption.

Also during the 1950s the long-term effects of the 1934 reciprocity treaty took their final toll. Industrial development during these years had not occurred in Cuba as it had in other Latin American countries. That local industry had to face strong foreign competition with little or no tariff protection discouraged the expansion of new enterprises. That Cuba was so near to the principal industrial supply centers of the United States, moreover, linked by rapid and relatively cheap transport facilities, served further to discourage local industrial development. There was little incentive to expand manufactures. What factories were operating produced principally light consumer goods, largely food and textiles.

Cuban investment patterns reflected these conditions and were symptomatic of the larger malaise of the economy—and of a state of mind. The uncertainty in the sugar economy and the persisting specter of a sudden end to prosperity reverberated across the upper reaches of the economy. Few Cuban capitalists were unaffected by this insecurity, and it figured prominently in their investment strategies. The emphasis fell on the distribution of existing wealth and unemployment rather than the creation of new wealth. Investment in industry did not keep up with the availability of domestic savings. Instead, considerable sums of capital were transferred abroad, by way of profits on foreign investments in Cuba and through Cuban investments outside the island. Cubans rarely invested in government securities or long-term stocks. Long-term investments made by Cubans were principally in U.S. stocks.

VIII

The Auténtico party under the leadership of Ramón Grau San Martín swept into power in 1944 on a swell of national enthusiasm that was surpassed only by national expectations. First under Grau (1944–48) and subsequently under Carlos Prío Socarrás (1948–52), the reformers of 1933 returned to power, and the belief took hold across the nation that the same high purpose that had characterized the provisional government ten years earlier had returned to public life. The letdown was enormous, and disappointment was compounded by disillusionment. Graft and corruption were pervasive. Political competition became armed confrontation as partisan disputes were settled by assassinations and thuggery. In 1947, the ruling party split when the popular Eduardo Chibás broke with the Auténticos and organized a new opposition party. Chibás was a powerful critic of Auténtico government and raised popular expectations anew. In 1951, however, Chibás committed suicide, delivering one more blow to national morale. A year later Fulgencio Batista led an army coup against the constitutional government of Carlos Prío Socarrás.

In the course of the following six years, political conflict deepened and spread across the island. As resistance increased, so did repression. Shoot-outs in the cities, ambushes in the countryside, strikes and demonstrations, and abductions and assassinations became only the more visible expressions of a nation at war with itself. In the mountains of eastern Cuba a full-scale guerrilla war was expanding and gaining support; in the cities of the west, the urban resistance launched a systematic campaign of violence and sabotage.

Of the several revolutionary groups opposed to Batista, the 26th of July Movement led by Fidel Castro soon gained the ascendancy. The revolutionary struggle attracted adherents from all sectors of Cuban society and none more than from those quarters of historical proximity with North Americans. Funds and supplies originated from Cuban communities in Key West, Tampa, and New York. Young Cuban Protestants were especially active in the armed struggle. Almost all the students at the Agricultural and Industrial School at Preston were in active collaboration with the local guerrilla column led by Raúl Castro. The leader of the 26th of July underground in Santiago de Cuba, Frank País, was the son of a Baptist minister. Liberated young women of the Havana Country Club formed part of a vast underground network in the capital. The degree to which North American influences in Cuba served to release the forces that would eliminate the North American influence in Cuba was not then apparent. That was still a few years away.

By the late 1950s, *fidelistas* operated in every province and with widespread support. The insurgency expanded in a fashion reminiscent of armed protest in the early republic. The destruction of property, especially foreign property, increased across the island. In February 1958, the 26th of July leadership announced plans to cripple sugar mills, tobacco production, public utilities, railroads, and oil refineries. The disruption of the sugar harvest emerged as an integral part of the guerrillas' "definitive plan." "Either Batista without the *zafra* or the *zafra* without Batista," vowed the 26th of July. By March 1958 the insurgents reported having applied a torch to every cane-producing province on the island, destroying an estimated 2 million tons of sugar.

The effects of this campaign were felt immediately, both in and out of Cuba. Opposition spread—within labor, among peasants, from students, and within the middle class. The failure of the Cuban economy to sustain expansion and accommodate the growing expectations of the upwardly mobile middle class disillusioned the class initially most disposed to support Batista. But in 1958 it was no longer simply an issue of economic disarray—the economy was approaching collapse. Public works programs came to a halt, and inevitably unemployment increased. Unemployment and underemployment were approaching desperate proportions.

In 1958, Batista acquired one more adversary: the United States. Impatience increased in Washington over Batista's inability to restore political order and, as in 1933, the United States took the first steps to ease Batista out of office. On March 14, the United States imposed an arms embargo on Cuba. The embargo came as a jolt to the Batista government. Politically the embargo was tantamount to a withdrawal of U.S. support and further undermined the government's internal position. The State Department also protested the internal use of U.S. military aid, provided to Cuba for hemispheric defense projects. The State Department asked Havana to withdraw from operations an infantry battalion trained and equipped by the Military Defense Assistance Program and requested Cuban authorities to discontinue the use of MDAP bombers against rebel-held cities.[59]

The arms embargo and the subsequent protest over the use of army units trained and equipped by the United States delivered a body blow to the morale of the Cuban armed forces. Hundreds of Cuban officers had received training in the United States. The military establishment had been created, trained, provisioned, and armed by the United States; its most prestigious military honors emanated from Washington, and for almost half a century it had enjoyed North American support.

The arms embargo was followed in May by the recall and resignation of U.S. Ambassador Arthur Gardner. There was no mistaking the portents. Gardner had been an unabashed defender of the Cuban regime, and on such a scale as to be a source of embarrassment to

President Batista himself.[60] Gardner's departure confirmed the suspicion raised initially by the arms embargo, and the opposition and supporters alike were not slow to draw the obvious moral: the days of the regime were numbered.[61] Indications that the United States no longer supported Batista, Ambassador Earl E. T. Smith later suggested, "had a devastating psychological effect," adding that the embargo "was the most effective step taken by the Department of State in bringing about the downfall of Batista." Batista himself later conceded that U.S. policy "weakened the faith and will to fight of our men."[62]

By late 1958, Washington had lost all confidence in Batista's ability to restore order. Political stability on the island had collapsed. Increasingly, Cuban disorders had placed the lives and property of foreigners in jeopardy and paralyzed business and commerce. Guerrilla operations against property had cost millions of dollars. The government was simply unable to prevent the destruction of property. In a cable to the *New York Times*, Ruby Hart Phillips reported that commerce, industry, and capital, "which have wholeheartedly supported President Batista since he took over the Government in 1952, are growing impatient with the continued violence in the island."[63]

In the autumn of 1958, Batista attempted to recover U.S. support by holding long-deferred elections. Batista sought to demonstrate to Washington that democratic processes were still capable of functioning effectively, civil war notwithstanding. To the surprise of few, the government candidate, Andrés Rivero Agüero, won the election.

Rather than strengthening the regime, the November electoral hoax further weakened the government's position both at home and abroad. The imposition of the official candidate disillusioned many, who, placing their hopes in the election to provide a pacific denouement to the political crisis, had earlier supported the government. Army officers personally loyal to Batista, disheartened by the prospect of an imminent transfer of executive power, lost some enthusiasm in the fight to defend a leader scheduled to retire in several months.[64]

Nor did the election enhance Batista's prestige in the United States. On the contrary, Washington rejected the results of the rigged election and announced in advance plans to withhold diplomatic recognition of the Rivero Agüero government. Ambassador Smith informed the Cuban president-elect that Washington "would not give aid and support to [his] . . . government when installed because we did not feel he could maintain effective control of the country."[65]

In fact, Washington had already determined to ease Batista out of office, in ways reminiscent of the removal of Machado in 1933. In early December, the State Department dispatched William D. Pawley, a North American financier in Cuba, to undertake a covert mission to Havana to persuade Batista "to capitulate to a caretaker government unfriendly to him, but satisfactory to us, whom we could immediately recognize and give military assistance to in order that Fidel Castro not come to power."[66] On December 9, Pawley held a three-hour conference with Batista, offering him an opportunity to live unmolested in Daytona Beach with his family. The North American envoy informed the Cuban president that Washington "would make an effort to stop Fidel Castro from coming into power as a Communist, but that the caretaker government would be men who were enemies of his, otherwise it would not work anyway, and Fidel Castro would otherwise have to lay down his arms or admit he was a revolutionary fighting against everybody only because he wanted power, not because he was against Batista." Ambassador Smith also informed Batista that Washington believed him incapable of maintaining effective control and that he should retire.[67] Batista refused.

9   Revolution and Response

The end of the Batista regime came amid a revolutionary general strike on January 1, 1959, summoning hundreds of thousands of Cubans to dramatic action against the old order, demanding nothing less than unconditional surrender to the new. The success of Cuban arms carried the island over a threshold never before crossed. Not since the nineteenth century had Cubans employed arms with such effect, and never before had the effects of Cuban arms been so complete. An unpopular government was displaced, its political allies discredited, and its armed forces defeated. Cubans had challenged a repressive regime on its own terms and succeeded—unconditionally and unassisted. This was a Cuban solution, one from which North Americans had been largely excluded and hence one over which the United States had little control.

The deed of revolution awakened the popular imagination, creating a vast constituency for radical change. It raised expectations of revolution. Pressure for immediate, deep, sweeping change was building from below, and the invocation of revolution encouraged it to rise to the top. Reform decrees in early 1959 provided immediate material relief to vast numbers of people. In March, the government enacted the first Urban Reform Law. One of the more popular early reforms, the law decreed a 50 percent reduction of rents under $100 monthly, 40 percent reduction of rents between $100 and $200, and 30 percent reduction of rents over $200. Other measures soon followed. The new government reduced telephone rates and drastically cut electricity rates. Virtually all labor contracts were renegotiated and wages raised. Cane cutters' wages were increased by a flat 15 percent. Health reforms, educational reforms, and unemployment relief followed in quick order. The Agrarian Reform Law of May 1959 restricted land titles to 1,000 acres, with the exception of property engaged in the production of sugar, rice, and livestock, for which the maximum limit was fixed at 3,333 acres. Properties exceeding these limits were nation-alized and compensation provided in the form of twenty-year bonds bearing an annual interest rate of 4.5 percent.

II

The revolution had succeeded unconditionally and because it had, it could proceed to make revolutionary change uncompromisingly. What was perhaps not immediately apparent during the early months of 1959 was that the United States was being shorn of much of its tra-ditional power to influence the course of events on the island. Social structures were in disarray, the political system was in crisis, the econ-omy was in distress. National institutions were in varying degrees of disintegration and disrepute, and because they had not served Cubans well, if at all, they were vulnerable. The old army had been defeated and dissolved, and it was replaced by one created from the ranks of the victorious guerrilla columns. The Batista administration had been dislodged; many *bastistianos* were brought to trial, and the assets of all were confiscated.

But more than an unpopular ruler had been removed. In fact, almost all government, all its branches and at all levels, was stigmatized by association with the discredited regime: congressmen and senators, cabinet members and army commanders, judges and governors, pro-vincial councillors and municipal aldermen, mayors and policemen. Nor were only those who held office stigmatized. Banished from the political life of the republic were all politicians who had participated in the 1958 elections. And gradually, too, there was mounting popu-lar animus toward all politicians of the previous two decades, whose malfeasance and misconduct had contributed to the rise of the *batistato*.

That the United States played so prominent a part in this discredited past all but guaranteed a day of reckoning. And, indeed, many of the early reform measures were designed as much to reduce the capacity of the United States to continue to function as a power contender as they were to improve Cuban living conditions. This meant necessarily reducing the prominence of the North American role in the Cuban economy. Imports from the United States were among the first items reduced, declining from $543 million in 1959 to $224 million in 1960.[1] At the same time, Cuba expanded its search for alternative markets and new suppliers. The traditional privileged position long enjoyed by North American capital was challenged. That was the meaning of the reduction of telephone and electricity rates and the renegotiation of labor contracts. It was especially the point of the Agrarian Reform Law, which with one stroke deprived some of the most powerful North American enterprises in Cuba of property and power in local affairs. There was substance to these decrees, of course, but there was even more powerful symbolic content, as the new regime embarked purposefully to modify property relations and readjust power capabilities in favor of Cubans.

Cuban reforms did indeed cause alarm in the United States. Washington reacted with a mixture of suspicion and consternation at the enactment of each new revolutionary decree. International Telephone and Telegraph protested the reduction of its rates, as did the Cuban Electric Company. The Agrarian Reform Law strained relations even further. North American sugar companies and cattle enterprises denounced the measure as confiscatory. The 3,333-acre limit reduced the Pingree ranch in Oriente to one-sixteenth of its size. The King ranch in Camagüey lost nine-tenths of its holdings. By the end of the summer, four hundred of the largest Cuban and North American ranches, an estimated 2.5 million acres of land, had been nationalized. The State Department expressed its "concern" at the rush of events in Cuba and insisted upon "prompt, adequate, and effective compensation" for all property nationalized by the Cuban government. As early as mid-1959, U.S. officials made increasing allusions to the possibility of cutting the Cuban sugar quota in retaliation.[2] Into this highly charged setting was introduced one more volatile issue. Members of the Cuban Communist party, the Partido Socialista Popular (PSP), in increasing numbers, were moving into government positions —not high positions but certainly visible ones: in the armed forces, in the administration of the agrarian reform, at subcabinet levels, in the provinces and municipalities.

III

By autumn of 1959 despair spread among liberals and old-line political leaders in Cuba, who were, in any case, already on the defensive and in disarray. The emerging prominence of the PSP did nothing to calm their misgivings. The participation of the PSP in the government confirmed the worst fears of property owners in Cuba and the United States. Opposition to government programs, in part spontaneous, in part organized, had a sobering effect on Fidel Castro and his closest advisers. Resistance to the agrarian reform program in particular, both within Cuba and from the United States, served to draw sharply the ideological battle lines. Revolutionary leaders stood at a crossroad. "The great landowners," Ernesto Che Guevara recalled later, "many of them North Americans, immediately sabotaged the law of Agrarian Reform. We were therefore face-to-face with a choice . . . a situation in which, once embarked, it is difficult to return to shore. But it would have been still more dangerous to recoil since that would have meant the death of the Revolution. . . . The more just and the more dangerous course was to press ahead . . . and what we supposed to have been an agrarian reform with a bourgeois character was transformed into a violent struggle."[3] The revolution had reached the limits of what it could accomplish through collaboration with liberals and countenance from the United States. To advance further required a fundamental realignment of social forces no less than a reordering of Cuban international relations.

Relations with the United States deteriorated quickly thereafter. Attacks against Cuba from exiles in the United States prompted denunciations from Havana. In February 1960, a Soviet trade delegation headed by Deputy Premier Anastas Mikoyan arrived in Havana. According to the terms of the 1960 economic agreement, the Soviets agreed to purchase 425,000 tons of sugar immediately and 1 million tons in each of the following four years. In addition, the Soviet Union offered Cuba $100 million in the form of low-interest credit, technical assistance, and crude and refined petroleum. In April, Cuba and the Soviet Union resumed diplomatic relations, suspended since 1952. At the same time, the Soviet Union agreed to sell Cuba crude oil at prices considerably lower than those charged by the oil companies to their Cuban refineries, thereby providing immediate savings in foreign exchange for the island. In April 1960, President Dwight D. Eisenhower authorized the Central Intelligence Agency to proceed with the arming and training of Cuban exiles.

The guarantee of alternative markets for sugar exports, no less than the promise of economic assistance, undoubtedly strengthened the government's position against internal opponents and foreign opposition. Cubans were assured at least of the capacity to survive economic warfare with the United States. The North American threat to cut the sugar quota now lost some of its potency. At the same time, these developments also increased the vulnerability of liberals and moderates, for as the influence of the United States waned in Cuba, Washington lost the capacity to protect and promote the interests of those social groups that had long been both agents and beneficiaries of North American hegemony.

The Cuban-Soviet oil agreement in particular had immediate consequences. In May the Cuban government ordered Standard Oil, Texaco, and Shell to refine Soviet petroleum. On June 7 the companies refused. Three weeks later Cuba nationalized foreign refineries. Up to this point, Cuban expropriations had been confined principally to land, mostly sugar estates and cattle ranches, within the larger framework of the agrarian reform project. More than one year had elapsed between these two expropriation decrees. After June 1960, there was no going back. The United States retaliated. On July 6, Eisenhower cut Cuban sugar imports by seven hundred thousand tons, the balance of the Cuban quota for 1960. The quota was thereafter fixed at zero.

The Cuban reaction was not long in coming. On August 5 Cuba expropriated additional North American properties on the island, including two utilities, thirty six sugar mills, and petroleum assets. A month later, the government nationalized the Cuban branches of North American banks. On October 13, the United States responded with an economic embargo on Cuba, a ban on all U.S. exports except medicines and some foodstuffs. Cuba reacted the same day, now in almost predictable fashion, by nationalizing additional properties. Later that month, Cuba nationalized another 166 North American enterprises, including insurance companies, import firms, hotels, casinos, textile firms, metal plants, tobacco export firms, chemical companies, and food processing plants, and in one last stroke all but totally eliminated U.S. investments in Cuba. In January 1961 the United States severed diplomatic relations with Cuba.

IV

The United States sought initially to use economic coercion first to force Fidel Castro into moderation and subsequently to remove him from power. Ambassador Philip Bonsal later suggested that the suspension of the sugar quota in July 1960 was undertaken less in reprisal against Fidel Castro than to remove him. So, too, was the decision by the oil refineries. The petroleum companies were prepared to process Soviet oil until the Eisenhower administration intervened and informed Texaco and Standard Oil that "a refusal to accede to the Cuban government's request would be in accord with the policy of the United States government toward Cuba." The Treasury Department urged the companies "to refuse to refine the Soviet crude oil." The purpose, Bonsal later wrote, was to "hamper the functioning of important units of the island economy" as a way "to achieve the fall of Castro."[4]

North American efforts failed and in so doing actually contributed to the consolidation of the regime at home and enhanced its prestige among socialist regimes abroad. By 1960, Cuban policy assumed an internal logic of its own. The revolution's commitment to an egalitarian order required changing more than the internal structures that had sanctioned privilege. It required, too, redefining the terms of its relations with the North Americans, the most privileged participants in the old order. Confrontation with the United States could not but accelerate the radicalization of the revolution. It aroused powerful nationalist sentiments, revived historic grievances, and in the end promoted a national unanimity of purpose perhaps unimaginable and certainly unattainable through any other means. Cuba's initial alignment with the Soviet Union was a response to this dispute. Confrontation with the United States necessitated that realignment, and realignment further deepened confrontation. The revolution had challenged the fundamental premises of U.S. hegemony in Cuba, and as the Cuban leadership moved implacably to eliminate U.S. influence in Cuba, the United States moved with equal determination to remove the Cuban leadership. It is not certain that anyone could have anticipated where this would all end, not the Cubans, not the North Americans. But it required no prophetic gift for Cubans to realize that this was a confrontation they could not hope to win, at least not alone.

Confrontation with the United States had important internal consequences, for which Cubans had neither planned nor prepared. So central was the presence of North American property in the national economy that its expropriation suddenly thrust upon Cubans responsibility for managing production, allocating resources, and supervising distribution on a vast scale. The Cuban government found itself assuming an increasingly larger role in the management of the economy. Once this process was under way, it was all but impossible to arrest and reverse.

The confiscation of North American property resulted in more than the expulsion of the United States from the Cuban economy. It facilitated the seizure of Cuban property. Cuban landowners, cattle ranchers, and property owners were dislodged with relative ease. The rupture, moreover, shattered the basis of the historic collaboration between the Cuban middle classes and the United States. For the nearly 150,000 Cuban employees of North American enterprises, including managers, clerks, technicians, accountants, and attorneys, the expropriations were traumatic. Many suffered an immediate decline in their standard of living, for Cubans in the employ of foreigners had traditionally enjoyed higher salaries. Conditions were now set for final expulsion of all U.S. influence.

Once the elimination of the U.S. presence was in process, and its influence as an economic force and political power broker inside Cuba began to wane, those classes economically dependent on and ideologically allied to the United States were doomed. Those groups with the greatest resources and resolve to oppose the radicalization of the revolution found themselves vulnerable, without the institutional position or the organizational resources with which to oppose the regime. Not without some irony, the exercise of U.S. authority on such a scale and for so long had stunted the development of independent structures capable of countering from within the appeal of radical change.

The North American response was too little too late. The Central Intelligence Agency organized Cuban exiles for an invasion of the island, and when it arrived in April 1961, at the Bay of Pigs (Playa Girón), the only surprise was the ease and speed with which it was crushed. The survival of the revolution was all but guaranteed a year later when the United States, as part of the negotiations to remove Soviet missiles from Cuba, agreed to suspend direct military operations against the island.

These events set the stage for one of the critical developments central to the consolidation of the revolution. Unable to devise effective means with which to oppose the revolution internally, disaffected Cubans emigrated by the tens of thousands. Planeload after planeload of Cubans left the island. The loss of population in the early years was stunning: sixty two thousand in 1960, sixty-seven thousand in 1961, sixty-six thousand in 1962.

Departing Cubans were acting out the final scene of a century-long drama. For almost three generations, Cubans of means, owners of property, holders of positions and power, had looked to the United States for protection against the forces of radical change that periodically challenged the status quo. Cuban elites had historically shown themselves ill-prepared to defend their interests on their own. This

was not the first time local elites were challenged by popular forces—
it had happened in 1895–98 and again in 1931–33. On both occasions,
they were saved by North American intervention.

Decades of North American hegemony, institutionalized earlier in
the century by the Platt Amendment, were now working to facilitate the expulsion of the U.S. presence in Cuba. For so long Cubans
had become accustomed to expect salvation from the United States.
This attitude encouraged passivity to the point of immobility. Decades
earlier Jorge Mañach had written of this phenomenon, whereby the
Cuban sense of responsibility for affairs of the nation was undermined
and all but extinguished. "Tutelage favored the growth of general civic
indolence," Mañach argued, "a tepid indifference to national dangers.
Should the nation be threatened, the intervention of Washington was
always there as a last resource, or a last hope."[5]

Few Cubans who departed during the 1960s could have even
vaguely foreseen that their expatriation would become permanent.
Many believed their absence would be a short one, that the United
States would step into the breach and return them and the island to
the way it used to be, as in 1898 or 1933. There was no need to be unduly exercised or overly alarmed, emigrating Cubans reassured themselves. The United States would not tolerate a communist government
ninety miles from its shores. "The passivity of the former possessing
classes was startling," Philip W. Bonsal commented later. "The Revolution was vastly encouraged by the demonstrated impotence of the
old order. The dispossessed and their friends believed that the United
States would soon set things in order again." Bonsal wrote:

> A conviction that the U.S. would take care of the situation sapped the
> activism of much of the opposition. Many of Castro's opponents had a
> predisposition (often inherited) to look to the United States rather than
> to their own efforts to correct their situation. . . . Why should the Cuban
> opposition take the risks and undergo the dangers and the sacrifices of
> counter-revolution in Cuba if the United States could be relied upon to
> take the leadership, the responsibility, and the onus of the ejection of
> Castro? . . . Many of those who departed did so in the conviction that
> they would soon return to find their country and their way of life restored
> to them without the need to exert serious effort on their part.[6]

Wayne Smith recalled a similar phenomenon. "Many Cubans were convinced that the U.S. would intervene as Castro moved further toward the Communists," Smith wrote. "Hence the best thing to do, many reasoned, was to sit things out in Miami until the U.S. got rid of Castro."[7]

This emigration represented nothing less than the exportation of the counterrevolution and all but foreclosed any possibility of a sustained and extensive internal challenge to the regime. The flight of the opposition served also to strengthen the revolutionary consensus within the island, thereby contributing in another fashion to the consolidation of the government. Henceforth, organized opposition to the revolution developed outside of Cuba, largely in the United States. But even in this instance, the possibilities of Cubans organizing independent and autonomous opposition capabilities were severely limited by the circumstances of their expatriation. Almost entirely dependent upon funding and support from the Central Intelligence Agency, Cuban exiles became instruments of North American policy, without the means of organizing into a genuine opposition force, unable to articulate autonomous strategies, and incapable of developing objectives independent of U.S. policy needs. Their ultimate demise was a function of their original ascendancy.

Once the source of political opposition was transferred from within the island to abroad, the defense of the revolution became synonymous with the defense of national sovereignty. And once the question of sovereignty was invoked, a deep wellspring of national sentiment was tapped in behalf of the revolution. Nothing was as central to the character of Cuban nationality as this notion of struggle for self-determination and sovereignty. The national memory was long. It could, and did, recall times before when the quest for nationality was thwarted or otherwise compromised and subdued. The revolution was thus transformed at one and the same time into the means and the end of a historic process. The hour of redemption of *patria* was at hand. The United States could not have adopted a more ill-conceived approach through which to attack the revolution. Ignorance of the backlog of Cuban historic grievances blinded the United States to the reality that it was challenging the revolution at its strongest point—

the point at which the past and present converged in the defense of *patria*.

North American opposition to Fidel Castro was also in part encouraged both in its form and function by the belief that the radicalization of the revolution had alienated vast, and maybe most, sectors of the Cuban population. Certainly the political and social groups with which North Americans were in most constant contact, its traditional local allies, reinforced this impression. Bonsal later acknowledged that the U.S. embassy was unduly influenced by "our largely anti-Castro informers."[8] But U.S. opposition was not without symbiotic aspects. Internal opposition to the regime was also in part an effect of outside opposition to it. Indeed, North American hostility toward the revolution served to sustain internal discontent. The belief in the United States that the revolution had fallen into disfavor, moreover, was the result of a mixture of self-deception and an instance of North Americans believing their own propaganda. "Wholesale social and economic change was needed—indeed, long overdue—in Cuba," acknowledged Adolf A. Berle, an adviser to John F. Kennedy, in 1960. Fidel Castro had "betrayed" the legitimate aspirations of the Cuban people when he sacrificed "Cuban national safety and Cuban national interests," when he made the island and its people "part of the Soviet empire and its regime a client government of Moscow." Berle charged that Cuba had become an instrument by which all of Latin America would be aligned "with the Soviet or the Chinese Communist bloc in a cold war aimed directly against the national existence of the United States."[9] This thesis appeared fully developed in the State Department "white paper" of April 1961, timed to appear coincident with the Bay of Pigs invasion. The character of the Batista regime, the State Department conceded, "made a violent popular reaction almost inevitable" and "constituted an open invitation to revolution." But the leaders of the revolutionary regime "betrayed their own revolution, delivered that revolution into the hands of powers alien to the hemisphere, and transformed it into an instrument employed with calculated effect to suppress the rekindled hopes of the Cuban people for democracy and to intervene in the internal affairs of other American republics." [10]

The "revolution betrayed" argument was advanced early and repeated often. It was the linchpin of the North American propaganda campaign against Cuba. Washington acknowledged the validity of Cuban revolutionary aspirations, if only as a way to claim credibility to oppose the Castro government and establish the basis upon which to proclaim the betrayal of those aspirations.

Certainly this was a correct assessment, as far as it went. But it did not go far enough. North Americans inferred certain universal political truths from a tenet that was derived principally from bourgeois opposition and confined during the early years largely to the city of Havana. The United States failed either to gauge accurately or appreciate fully both the depth of popular support for the revolution and the appeal of Fidel Castro. Strategies designed to humble the regime instead strengthened popular resolve and released deep stirrings of historic nationalism. North American opposition provided final validation to the authenticity of the revolutionary experience and aroused vast sectors of the Cuban population to its defense. "We underestimated," Bonsal wrote later of those days, "the degree to which pre-Castro Cuba in most of its manifestations had been rejected by the great majority of the people." [11]

Central to the thinking and planning of the Bay of Pigs was the belief that disaffection in Cuba was widespread and that the landing of an expedition of a mere twenty-five hundred U.S.-trained exiles would be the signal for countless tens of thousands of Cubans on the island to rise in solidarity and join the expeditionaries against the regime. In fact, the exact opposite occurred. The shadowy identity of the United States with the ill-starred enterprise all but guaranteed its failure: those who supported the revolution were especially motivated to defend the homeland against North American aggression; those who opposed the regime were encouraged to passivity in the belief that the United States, in defense of its own prestige and security interests, would not allow the invasion to fail even if it had to use its own armed forces.

V

The end of diplomatic relations between Cuba and the United States in January 1961 did not mean that the island was free of its past. On the contrary, for years thereafter Cubans struggled to overcome the consequences of historic ties to the United States.

The disengagement of the Cuban economy from North American capitalism caused considerable disruption and dislocation. It was a disengagement, moreover, to which the United States refused to acquiesce. After 1961, one of the key elements of U.S. policy was to isolate Cuba economically as a way to disrupt the Cuban economy, increase domestic distress, and encourage internal discontent—all designed to weaken the regime from within. More than two-thirds of Cuban trade with Western Europe ended. All nations receiving U.S. Mutual Security Act economic assistance were informed that continued foreign aid was contingent on an end of all purchases of Cuban sugar. Particular pressure was applied on Japan and Canada to reduce commercial relations with the island. Between 1962 and 1963, the number of "Free World" ships calling on Cuban ports declined from 352 to 59. Air traffic to Cuba was reduced to Iberia Airline from Spain and Cubana Airline to Mexico. Virtually all financial transactions between Cuba and Western Europe and international lending institutions were suspended.

But it was the rupture of trade ties with the United States that hurt Cuba the most and the longest. Cubans were especially vulnerable to this pressure. For the better part of the previous one hundred years, virtually all the machinery, equipment, and supplies used in Cuban industry, agriculture, mining, transportation, communications, and utilities—more than 70 percent of Cuban total imports—had come from the United States. Cuban dependence on North American spare parts was almost total, a corollary condition of dependence on North American capital stock and the proximity of North American suppliers. The economy had long operated on the basis of quick supply and low inventory. Orders were placed by telephone, obviating the need for large inventories of spare parts and replacement stock. Inventories of most spare parts were traditionally low. Shipments were frequent and small. Replacement goods were purchased as needed, often directly out of catalogs, over the telephone, and delivered within days.

The U.S. trade embargo after 1961 had jolting effects in Cuba. By the early 1960s, conditions in many industries had become critical because of the lack of replacement parts. Virtually all industrial structures were dependent on supplies and parts no longer available: hundreds of thousands of parts, large and small, simple and complex, expensive and cheap, were denied to Cuba. Many plants were paralyzed. Havoc followed. Transportation was especially hard hit. The Ministry of Transportation was reporting more than seven thousand breakdowns a month. Nearly one-quarter of all Cuban buses were inoperable by the end of 1961 because of lack of spare parts. One-half of the fourteen hundred passenger rail cars were out of service in 1962. Almost three-quarters of the Caterpillar tractors stood idle for lack of replacement parts. [12]

No less important was the flight of almost all of the sixty-five hundred North American residents, many of whom had worked in important technical and managerial capacities in both U.S. and Cuban enterprises. The historic Cuban dependence on North American technicians was ruptured, with far-reaching and long-lasting consequences. Foreigners directed the oil refineries, operated the Nicaro nickel plant and Matahambre copper mine, supervised the sugar mills, serviced the airline industry, and otherwise occupied an assortment of strategic positions in manufacturing, industry, agriculture, transportation, and communications.

The high import component of Cuban industry created vulnerabilities of other kinds. Many Cuban industries depended heavily on raw materials, processed products, and component parts previously imported from the United States. Without access to these vital supplies, Cuban production slowed and in some instances stopped altogether. A lack of bottles interrupted beer and soft drink production; denied rubber and petrochemicals, the manufacture of automobile tires halted; without ready access to pancreatic enzymes and tannin, Cuban tanneries suffered; paint factories depended on imports of oils, pig-

ments, and solvents; pharmaceuticals on imported serums and anti-
biotics; the manufacture of soaps and detergents relied on imported
caustic soda and tallow.

These were years, too, during which Cuba suffered the greatest
effects from U.S. covert operations designed to cause further economic
havoc by disrupting production and destroying property. Through
the 1960s, the Central Intelligence Agency conducted punitive economic sabotage operations against Cuba, the principal aim of which
was to foster popular disaffection with government policies. Paramilitary missions were organized to destroy sugar mills, sugar and
tobacco plantations, farm machinery, mines, oil refineries, lumber
yards, water systems, warehouses, and chemical plants. Communication facilities were attacked; railroad bridges were destroyed and
trains derailed. The United States was also successful in disrupting
Cuban trade initiatives with Western Europe, activities that included
blocking credit to Cuba, thwarting the sale of sugar products, and con-
taminating Cuban agricultural exports. European manufacturers were
discouraged from trading with Cuba. Cargoes were sabotaged: cor-
rosive chemicals were added to lubricating fluids, ball bearings were
manufactured deliberately off-center, and defective wheel gears were
manufactured. During these years, too, the United States developed
a number of plots to assassinate the top Cuban leaders, including
eight separate plots to murder Fidel Castro. [13]

VI

The departure of disaffected Cubans had far-reaching consequences
both on the island and in the United States. Discontent continued
to find expression principally through emigration. The flight of the
middle class during the early years was in part spontaneous, in part
sponsored. For the Cuban government, emigration was a relatively
cost-effective means of eliminating vast sectors of the opposition, and
it therefore facilitated their departure. For the United States, the spectacle of tens of thousands of Cubans fleeing the island made good propaganda, and it encouraged their arrival. That the emigration included

a disproportionate number of technicians and professionals provided the United States with an opportunity to cause Havana hardship by draining the island of trained personnel. Washington eased visa requirements and subsequently dropped them altogether. Cubans were henceforth free to enter the United States in unlimited numbers.

The Cuban revolution set in motion a vast emigration to the United States that approached 1 million Cubans by the end of the 1980s. Almost one hundred years after the last great emigration of the 1880s, once again nearly 10 percent of the Cuban population had come to reside in the United States. Of the 1 million émigrés, more than half live in urban centers in southern Florida, principally in the Dade County region, followed by New Jersey (eighty thousand), California (sixty thousand), Illinois (twenty thousand), and Texas (fifteen thousand).

In many important ways, the Cuban migration after 1959 was unlike any previous immigration to the United States. It passed through several phases, each with distinct socioeconomic characteristics. The early waves consisted principally of political exiles, originally ousted *batistianos* and later opponents of the revolutionary government. Through the early 1960s, hundreds of thousands of Cubans from the disaffected middle classes emigrated in numbers well out of proportion to their relative size in the general population. They were largely white and educated, in possession of a range of skills, professional expertise, entrepreneurial backgrounds, and often capital resources. The composition of the Cuban emigration underwent significant change during the 1970s and 1980s, involving generally more socially and economically representative sectors of the population with greater racial heterogeneity, lower educational preparation, and limited occupational skills. The Cuban émigrés of the 1970s and 1980s shared many features with other Latin American migrants, including Puerto Ricans, Dominicans, Haitians, Mexicans, and Central Americans. They tended to fall victim to racial discrimination, unemployment or low-paying jobs, and a lack of educational and social services.

In contrast, vast numbers of Cuban exiles during the 1960s enjoyed a privileged emigration. That the exodus occurred against a larger backdrop of deteriorating Cuba-U.S. relations and within a pervasive anticommunist culture provided a distinct political environment for

Cuban emigration. Indeed, through these years, the United States used the emigration as simply one among many means to pressure the revolution and cause dislocation on the island. That this population included Cubans with professional and managerial abilities promised to deprive the new regime of vital skills at a time of maximum need. It was, further, a population most susceptible to North American importunings to migrate. The CIA-operated Radio Swan alternated strident anticommunist broadcasts with more seductive allusions to the abundance of the "American way of life."

The political context of this migration facilitated the Cuban transition to North American society in other ways. Public assistance and entitlement programs were designed to induce still more emigration. In December 1960, the U.S. government established the Cuban Refugee Emergency Center. This was subsequently expanded into the Cuban Refugee Program, which between 1961 and 1971 accounted for $730 million in the form of direct subsidies from the Department of Health, Education, and Welfare. In addition, a wide array of federal, state, and municipal agencies provided émigrés with a variety of services and programs, including educational opportunities in English-language programs, scholarship aid and low-interest loans for college tuition, job-training programs, and for resettling families, maintenance allotments, health services, and for care of unaccompanied children, surplus food distribution, and business credit and loans. The Small Business Administration did its part through generous distribution of low-interest loans to Cuban applicants. The state of Florida and county agencies provided Cubans with support and assistance of other types. The Florida legislature provided generous cash allotments to Cuban families. The Dade County council opened local civil service positions to noncitizens. Early in the 1960s, the University of Miami medical school, with federal and state support, inaugurated special programs to prepare Cuban physicians to meet state licensing requirements. Many who either did not enroll in the program or failed to complete the requirements were often employed anyway by state and federal institutions that did not require such licenses.

The new Cuban presence in the United States had far-reaching effects, particularly in the communities in which émigrés resided, and perhaps nowhere more than Dade County, Florida. By the mid-1980s, Cubans represented nearly $1 billion in the local economy. They owned an estimated twenty thousand businesses, including grocery stores, restaurants, drugstores, jewelry stores, furniture factories, bakeries, garment factories, private schools, cigar factories, phonograph record plants, publication houses, and radio stations. An estimated forty-five hundred physicians and five hundred attorneys in the Miami–Dade County area were Cuban. In addition, Cubans owned 30 percent of the local construction industry, accounted for four bank presidents, thirty-three vice-presidents, and hundreds of banking officials.[14] Cubans occupied the ranks of successful merchants, newspaper publishers, owners of radio and television stations, and contractors. They counted among their numbers an estimated seven hundred millionaires.

The Cuban impact was not confined to the economy. No less dramatic effects were registered in state, county, and municipal politics. Cubans emerged as a voting bloc of formidable proportions and by the 1980s represented more than a quarter of the Dade County electorate. They held the office of mayor in Hialeah (Raúl Martínez) and Miami (Javier Suárez), city commissioners in Hialeah and Miami, state assembly seats from Dade County, and thousands of civil service positions that ranged from police officers to public administration to appointive office. The Cuban electorate similarly played a decisive role in the outcome of congressional contests and statewide elections. In 1989, Cuban-born Ileana Ros-Lehtinen was elected to the House of Representatives. By the 1980s, Cubans had played a major role in the growth of the Republican party in Florida.

Increasingly, the Cuban influence expanded in other spheres. In ever-growing numbers, Cubans moved into administrative and teaching positions in education. These included university presidents, provosts and deans, members of the state board of regents, county and municipal school administrators and principals, and members of the teaching staff and faculty of elementary and secondary schools as well as community colleges and four-year institutions.

In large measure, the success enjoyed by many Cubans in the United States was a direct function of their antecedents and experiences in Cuba. Tens of thousands of Cubans were already familiar with North American structures and institutions. Many had been educated in the United States and were formerly employed by North American corporations. They possessed prior and extensive knowledge of U.S. managerial and administrative methods. They arrived in the United States with professional and business contacts, and for many employment in the United States represented little more than a job transfer.

Not all Cubans, of course, participated equally in these successes. Many did not. But enough achieved sufficient well-being to live comfortably in the United States and exercise a continuing influence in Cuba. For vast numbers of Cubans who remained on the island and within an economy of increasing scarcity, the material success of Cubans in the United States, if only modest by North American standards, stood in sharp contrast. Fully thirty years after disengagement from the United States, Cuba remained as susceptible to the appeal of the North American consumer economy as it did during prerevolutionary times. Indeed, one source of the Mariel exodus of 1980 was the flood of U.S. consumer goods introduced into the island with the inauguration of family visits after 1977. The Cuban government had sought to improve relations with the exile community and at the same time generate foreign exchange through Cuban-American tourism. To this end, the government charged exorbitant fees for air fares and hotel accommodations. The government also established special shops in which visitors with dollars could purchase for their families such consumer items as toasters, televisions, radios, fans, and a wide assortment of appliances and consumer staples.

The plan succeeded beyond Cuban expectations. The dollar stores were a great success. Between 1979 and 1980, Cuba earned over $100 million from returning exiles. In 1979 alone, more than one hundred thousand Cuban-Americans traveled to Cuba loaded down with U.S. consumer goods. The sudden appearance of this consumer abundance at a time when Cuba was able to offer little more than a minimum quantity and almost no variety of consumer goods, together with stories of success and affluence, highlighted with photographs of the bounty of life in the United States, could not have but aroused among many the desire to migrate to the United States. "Their complaints against Cuba rarely touched on political issues," commented one observer of the subsequent Mariel exodus. "These are consumer refugees. The freedom they want is the freedom to buy. They want *things;* they feel desperately deprived. The revolution was an incidental pain in the ass—a lot of work, a lot of study and little material reward."[15] Recalled Wayne Smith of those years: "At a time when most Cubans were asked to tighten their belts and face more years of hard work for little return, relatives from Miami and New Jersey were flooding back into the country with tales of the good life in the U.S. To hear them tell it, everyone had a mansion, three cars, an unlimited number of TV sets, and more food than anyone could eat. Life was easy! More and more Cuban citizens began to yearn for a piece of that vision. Pressure for emigration inexorably increased."[16]

The lure of things North American continued thereafter to operate at other levels. The return of Cuban family members was accompanied by a revival of North American tourism, with comparable effects. During the late 1970s, and until the Reagan administration suspended U.S. travel to the island, tens of thousands of travelers from the United States visited Cuba. Once more Cubans came into close contact with North Americans.

VII

The emphasis of North American policy through the 1970s and 1980s continued to center on the political and economic isolation of the island. In part, U.S. pressure was motivated by a general concern that the Cubans would indeed succeed and emerge as something of a model for economic development.[17] North American efforts were designed to create in Cuba conditions as difficult as possible, principally in the form of shortages and scarcities of spare parts, the denial of markets, the rupture of trade relations, and the withholding of needed imports. These conditions were expected to increase internal discontent and perhaps produce from within the changes that North Americans had failed to obtain from without.

At a more fundamental level, the Cuba policy of the United States was possessed of powerful symbolic content. That the revolution would survive with Soviet support was never very much in doubt. What the United States sought to demonstrate, however, was the high cost of socialism in the Americas. The policy was fundamentally a punitive one, predicated on pushing to the limit the cost of Marxism-Leninism in the Western Hemisphere. It was to serve as an object lesson to other Western Hemisphere nations. Cuba was thus to become an example of the cost of revolution: a state of siege in the form of political, economic, and technical isolation, approaching the dimensions of an embargo, to make the cost of revolution so unbearable as a way to deter and discourage others from emulating the Cuban model. The North American refusal to accommodate itself to the Cuban revolution underscored the inadmissibility of socialism in Latin America. To normalize relations with Cuba would have served to "legitimitize" a Marxist-Leninist government in Havana. Washington's renewal of diplomatic ties with China and not Cuba underscored this distinction. Indeed, it was not that the logic of normal relations with Cuba was any less compelling, but rather to have recognized the Cuban government was perceived as sending the wrong "message" elsewhere in Latin America, namely that the United States would eventually reconcile itself to Marxist-Leninist regimes in the New World—it was only a question of time. No doubt, too, that Fidel Castro continued to preside over the Cuban government, representing in his person and policies an anathema to a generation of North American officials, made the prospect of reconciliation even more unpalatable in Washington. To have resumed diplomatic ties with Fidel Castro would have symbolically if not in substance represented a triumph for the revolution. History would have again absolved Fidel.

Other factors worked against the normalization of relations. The presence of nearly 1 million Cuban exiles in the United States represented a potent political force working against rapprochement with Cuba. Powerful economic interests in the United States, most notably the sugar lobbies of Florida, Louisiana, and Hawaii and the citrus industries of Florida, Texas, and California, also resisted normalization, fearful that the resumption of trade with Cuba would reduce their share of the domestic market. Larger U.S. policy in the circum-Caribbean would also be affected by a resumption of Cuba-U.S. trade. Cuban exports competed directly with products from Mexico, Central America, and the Caribbean islands. The Reagan Caribbean Basin Initiative was predicated on opening further U.S. markets to these countries as a way both to promote U.S. investments in the Caribbean and to provide the region with new sources of foreign exchange. Resumption of trade with Cuba would have required readjustment of key trade elements of the Caribbean Basin Initiative.

North American policy was directed as much against the Soviet Union as it was against Cuba and other would-be socialist regimes. If indeed Moscow was prepared to play the role of protector and provider of New World socialism, it would be charged dearly for the privilege and perhaps in the process encourage future second thoughts in the Kremlin. Through the 1960s and 1970s, the Soviet Union was spending an estimated $1 million per day in Cuba and was no doubt becoming wary of further commitments to new socialist governments in Latin America. "In its essentials," Assistant Secretary of State Edwin M. Martin asserted as early as 1963, "the isolation policy is designed to deny to the Castro regime the wherewithal and the plaudits of success that it requires to consolidate itself. And by increasing the costs to the Soviets in Latin America, we are determined to convince Moscow that it is backing a sure loser, and an expensive one at that." Under-Secretary of State George W. Ball spoke in similar terms of the policy of "economic denial" one year later: as a way "to demonstrate to the peoples of the American Republics that Communism has no future in the Western Hemisphere" and "to increase the cost to the Soviet Union of maintaining a Communist outpost in the Western Hemisphere." [18]

Washington moved early to isolate the island totally. In January 1962, the Organization of American States (OAS) voted to expel Cuba. Two years later, under pressure from the United States, the OAS endorsed comprehensive economic and political sanctions against Cuba. All Latin American countries except Mexico voted to sever diplomatic relations with Cuba and observe a trade boycott.

For the better part of the following decade the United States maintained unremitting pressure on Cuba. During the early 1970s, relations between the two countries improved slightly, if only briefly. In 1973, Havana and Washington signed an antihijacking agreement. In the following years, both countries inaugurated a series of high-level secret meetings to negotiate the terms for normalization of relations. The United States ended these negotiations in late 1975 in protest of the Cuban decision to dispatch combat troops to Angola.

During these years, Cuban interest in pursuing normal relations with the United States were frustrated by North American efforts at linkages, establishing conditions to normal relations that included Cuba distancing itself from the Soviet Union and a withdrawal of Cuban armed forces from Africa. The Cuban government rejected these conditions as infringements upon national sovereignty.

Diplomatic relations improved in the late 1970s during the Carter years. In 1977, Havana and Washington signed a fishing agreement and established a provisional maritime boundary in the Florida Straits. Later that year, Cuba and the United States moved toward a resumption of limited formal, diplomatic contact with the establishment of interests sections in each other's capitals. These efforts at rapprochement ended abruptly, again over Cuban involvement in Africa. In early 1978, Havana dispatched combat forces to Ethiopia in its conflict with Somalia. Washington denounced the Cuban intervention and charged Cuba with playing a surrogate role on behalf of Soviet strategic objectives.

During the 1980s, Cuba-U.S. relations remained unchanged. The United States continued to insist upon linkages, and Cuba continued to resist. The Reagan administration increasingly adopted a hard line against Cuba, charging Havana with subversion and mischief in Central America, threatening to "take it to the source" to end conditions of instability in the region. In 1981, Secretary of State Alexander Haig was reported to be considering a sea and air blockade of Cuba and an invasion of the island. Cubans responded with invasion alerts and full-scale mobilization of all regular military and civilian militia forces. The limited normalization process of the previous decade was arrested and reversed. The Reagan administration increased restrictions on North American travel to Cuba, suspending U.S. tourism to deprive the island of a source of foreign exchange. At the time of the renewed restrictions, an estimated forty thousand North Americans were traveling to Cuba annually. The restrictions prohibited all general and business travel to Cuba by persons under U.S. jurisdiction, permitting travel only by diplomats, journalists, persons engaged in professional research, and for family visits. At the same time, the State Department routinely denied visas to Cubans to participate in international meetings in the United States. In 1985 the United States inaugurated Radio Martí broadcasts to Cuba. A year later, the United States tightened still further the trade and financial embargo against Cuba. The Reagan administration also maneuvered behind the scenes to make Cuban foreign debt negotiations as difficult as possible. New pressure was added on U.S. corporations operating in third countries to curtail trade with Cuba. New limits were placed on cash and gifts Cubans in the United States were able to send to family members on the island, reducing the $2,000 a year per relative to $1,200. New regulations also limited the shipment of food and gifts to Cuba from Cubans residing in the United States.

Bilateral relations took a curious turn in 1987, with dramatic consequences in the United States. In November, Havana and Washington reached a formal immigration agreement, whereby the United States agreed to accept as many as twenty thousand Cuban émigrés annually. In return, Cuba accepted the return of twenty-five hundred refugees of the Mariel exodus classified by the U.S. Immigration and Naturalization Service as "excludable aliens" by virtue of previous criminal behavior or severe mental illness. News of the accord precipitated rioting at detention centers in Oakdale, Louisiana, and Atlanta, Georgia, as thousands of Mariel detainees protested the agreement that would send them back to the island.

Through the 1980s, relations between the countries were reminiscent of the worst times of the early 1960s. Both countries settled on a similar strategy, if with different objectives. United States policy seemed prepared to wait until "after Fidel" to resume normal relations; Cuba adopted an "after Reagan" policy in the hope of obtaining a more favorable political climate to settle outstanding differences with the United States.[19] The Reagan administration refused to work toward accommodation with the Cubans. On the contrary, it continued to increase pressure on Havana and often in ways that seemed at once gratuitous and provocative. When asked in August 1988 about possible talks with Fidel Castro about normalizing relations, Secretary of State George Shultz responded: "Well, he doesn't deserve it. He hasn't done anything for his people, and he is part of the problem . . . in Central America. We would love to have a better relationship with the people of Cuba and the Government of Cuba. But in order to, in a sense, qualify themselves they have to change their behavior."[20]

The Cuban government survived three decades of U.S. harassment, awaiting the propitious moment to settle outstanding differences with the United States and establish something approaching normal relations with a nation that even in a period of nonrelations continued to exercise a profound impact on the island. That Cuba prevailed over North American pressure was in no small way the result of its close and cordial relations with the Soviet Union. Cuban-Soviet relations, however, experienced new tensions during the late 1980s, and these difficulties had growing implications for Cuban-U.S. relations. Cuban leadership looked upon *glasnost* and *perestroika* with a mixture of distrust and disdain. Nor did a thaw in U.S.-Soviet relations bode well for Cuba. At a time of liberalization in the Soviet Union, Cubans were reaffirming the old ways; at a time of growing Soviet reliance on material incentives, Cubans proclaimed the "rectification" and recommitted themselves to moral incentives. As pressure for liberalization policies in socialist bloc countries mounted, Cuba moved to distance itself from the reform impulse. Cuba's boycott of the summer Olympic games of 1988 was as much a gesture of solidarity with North Korea (another socialist outcast) as it was an affirmation of independence from the Soviet Union.

VIII

Through the 1980s and early 1990s U.S. sanctions against Cuba increased. Commando raids resumed. The passage of the Torricelli Bill ("Cuban Democracy Act") in 1992 further tightened the trade embargo and prohibited subsidiaries of U.S. corporations in Third World countries from trading with Cuba. Other features of the law authorized the president to withhold U.S. foreign aid, debt relief, and free trade agreements with countries that provided assistance to Cuba. All ships trading with Cuba were denied access to U.S. port facilities for a period of 180 days after having visited the island. Even before the Torricelli Bill passed, President George Bush issued an executive order banning all ships trading with Cuba from making port calls in the United States. In September 1992, U.S. authorities refused a Greek freighter carrying Chinese rice for Cuba permission to enter Long Beach for repairs. The same executive order also limited the humanitarian aid packages residents in the United States could send to Cuba.

Sanctions assumed a new meaning after the late 1980s, and indeed, the timing of the Torricelli Bill was not without significance. The 1980s were years of retrenchment and reversal in Cuba, a time during which Cuban relations with the Soviet Union deteriorated, the Sandinistas were defeated in Nicaragua, the guerrilla war in El Salvador ended, and Cuban presence in Africa diminished. They were the years of the disintegration of the socialist bloc in Eastern Europe and, of course, the collapse of the Soviet Union. By the end of 1992, Cuban trade with the former socialist bloc had plunged to 7 percent of its former value. Imports fell from an estimated $8.1 billion in 1989 to $2.2 billion in 1921.[21]

By the early 1990s, Cuba faced unprecedented difficulties. For the second time in three decades, Cuban commercial relations with its principal trading partners were interrupted, causing widespread dislocation and disruption. Cuba found itself increasingly isolated and beleaguered, faced with dwindling resources, confronting the necessity of rationing scarce goods and reducing declining services. Survival seemed to preoccupy the Cuban leadership. Authorities resorted to strategies conceived years earlier as measures to be adopted in case of war, first with severe rationing of the "Special Period" followed by even more drastic reductions of the "Zero Option." At the precise moment that Cuba faced a new and perhaps more serious round of difficulties at home as well as reversals abroad, the United States revived the embargo, expanding the scope and increasing the severity of sanctions.

The anomaly of the embargo stood in sharp relief in the 1990s. The collapse of the Soviet Union and the end of the Cold War had eliminated the security concerns that had so decisively driven the rationale of U.S. policy sanctions; however, a strategy designed for threats that were no longer present, against adversaries that no longer existed, continued to dominate policy formulations.

It was clear that the function of sanctions had undergone some important changes. After the 1980s, sanctions were related less to international conditions than to domestic considerations. Political circumstances had transformed the character of public discourse on Cuba in the United States. The policy designed first as a response to a regional dispute, and subsequently expanded to meet security concerns in the context of the Cold War, found renewed vitality as a strategic factor in U.S. electoral politics. U.S. policy toward Cuba had become the special interest of the Cuban-American community in vote-rich Florida. No doubt conditions in Cuba invited the conclusion that the time seemed right to deliver the coup de grâce to the faltering Cuban government and eliminate once and for all the existence of a regime that had so bedeviled eight successive administrations.

Thus by the early 1990s, the meaning and function of sanctions had been transformed. Domestic political factors increasingly acted to shape the course and content of the U.S. policy. No longer could policy planners plausibly invoke security concerns as the rationale for sanctions. The security imperative that had justified the embargo, based on the proposition that Cuba was an instrument of Soviet policy, to be contained and countered at every turn and at every opportunity, no longer possessed either credibility or validity.

The renewal and expansion of sanctions during the early 1990s seemed particularly harsh, both in timing and in kind. The Torricelli Bill, enacted on the eve of presidential elections in 1992, was designed to inflict new hardships on Cuba at a time when Cubans were already reeling from scarcities in goods and the disruption of services in the wake of the Soviet collapse. In the context of events in Eastern Europe, the new round of sanctions seemed especially punitive, for they struck directly at the flow of goods by way of people to people, principally through friends and family. Sanctions in this instance seemed deliberately designed to inflict unrelieved punishment on the Cuban people, to make daily life in Cuba as difficult and as grim as possible, and to increase suffering in measured but sustained increments at every turn, at every opportunity. Pressure was thus applied directly on the population, who faced a new round of shortages, increased rationing, declining services, and growing scarcities, where the needs of everyday life in their most ordinary and commonplace forms could be met only by Herculean efforts. The new emphasis of U.S. policy seemed designed to deepen discontent in the hope that, driven by distress and despair, Cubans would organize politically against the government, to foment political change from within the island. The expectation was that discontent thus obtained would find expression in political opposition, and that Cubans thus wearied would act to produce inside Cuba the changes desired by the United States.

Sanctions designed to increase hardships and add further to distress were not without effects, of course. Cuban discontent did indeed deepen. Scarcities increased, in some instances in frightful proportions. Hardships and difficulties confronted Cubans every day.

Hopes that deepening economic distress would produce significantly increased political dissent, however, remained substantially unfulfilled. Certainly many Cubans raised their voices in protest, to ask for change and demand reforms. To be sure, too, the call for reforms increased in number and persistence, and in some instances gained credibility and consideration. But it was clear that expressions of dissent were greeted harshly by government authorities, who were ill-disposed to tolerate political opposition in the midst of a deepening economic crisis and growing social tensions. Cuban authorities were aware of the implications and intent of U.S. policy. They were not slow — or unwilling — to apply harsh measures to maintain an internal consensus. The government moved swiftly and severely to contain political dissent. Terms of imprisonment, house arrests, and harassment were only some of the most common responses to the first signs of open political protest.

Increased sanctions did indeed contribute to raising the level of political disaffection, but they also created new issues of contention between Washington and Havana, making the resolution of old ones all the more difficult. Increasingly the issue of human rights violations in Cuba assumed greater importance in the U.S. case against Cuba, a condition that U.S. policy had, in fact, by design, acted to exacerbate. Indeed, the policy of sanctions contributed to further Cuban intransigence and all but precluded the possibility of negotiations and compromise. Perhaps even more insidious, however, sanctions served further to reduce space for dialogue and debate inside Cuba. If indeed the survival of the nation was deemed at stake, what mattered most was unanimity of purpose and an unyielding course of action, neither of which easily admitted debate. Dissent was perceived as both pernicious and perilous to the survival of the nation.

The issue of space was indeed a matter of central importance: space to adjust, space to adapt — space, in short, for Cuba to accommodate itself to the logic of changing international realities, to which everyone on the island acknowledged that Cuba had to acquiesce. U.S. pressure may well have served to impede change in Cuba. The Cuban willingness to pursue reform — and the signals were mixed — could not occur in an environment in which the central preoccupation of the national leadership was framed in terms of the survival of the nation. These were perceptions to which even the most active critics of the Castro government inside Cuba subscribed. "No government is likely to negotiate or to liberalize under pressure," human rights activist Elizardo Sánchez affirmed as early as 1991. "Thus, if the United States wants to help the cause of democracy and human rights in Cuba, the best thing it could do is to drop its efforts to pressure and isolate Cuba and instead begin a process of engagement."[22]

It was indeed arguable that the Cuban government was obliged to make reforms, precisely to survive, and that the effect, if not perhaps the purpose, of U.S. policy was to deny Cuba the space within which to pursue transformation. The United States, in the end, did not seek a government reformed, but a government removed. On those occasions when the Cuban government indicated a willingness to implement reforms or negotiate outstanding differences with the United States, it was interpreted as weakness, and provided the rationale to continue if not increase U.S. pressure. When Cubans offered in June 1993 to discuss reparations for U.S. properties nationalized during the 1960s, Representative Ileana Ros-Lehtinen (R-Miami) proclaimed that it was "proof that the U.S. embargo was working, so we must continue with our embargo."[23] These responses left the Cubans with little space within which to pursue change, for even their disposition to make concessions to the United States served only to increase the intransigence of those who defended sanctions.

The implications of U.S. policy, however, went far beyond reducing further the already too small space for dialogue inside Cuba. Indeed, the policy of political isolation and economic sanctions produced exactly the opposite effects sought. The embargo succeeded in creating the desired conditions but without obtaining the desired objectives. U.S. policy was predicated on the proposition that sanctions offered a means to obtain and sustain economic distress, principally through shortages and scarcities, which would deepen popular discontent with the government of Cuba and eventually generate sufficient pressure to force a change of policies, if not a change of governments.

Sanctions did indeed contribute to creating economic hardship and, from time to time, even produced political confrontations. The failure of sanctions to obtain the larger political objectives, however, was due to the cross-purposes of U.S. approaches.

The pressures created by almost four decades of sanctions—and these pressures were at times real and substantial—were in fact relieved by Cuban immigration. The use of economic distress as a means of producing political change could not have reasonably succeeded as long as Cuban discontent was able to find an alternative expression, and this was made possible early through the readily available option of immigration. Confronting increasing hardships and deteriorating living conditions, vast numbers of Cubans sought relief from difficulties of daily life through emigration to the United States rather than risk even greater difficulties by engaging in political opposition — a wholly reasonable and eminently rational decision, made all the more compelling by the presence of a community of friends and families in Florida and the support of friendly state and federal agencies. No less important, the Cuban government itself used emigration as a relatively cost-effective and convenient means through which to dispose of discontented people. As long as Washington persisted both in applying sanctions and keeping its doors open to Cuban refugees, the main effect of the embargo was to increase pressure to emigrate.

The result was predictable. By the early 1990s, the U.S. Interests Section in Havana had accumulated a backlog of hundreds of thousands of visa applications. The Interests Section was called upon daily to decide to whom it would grant visitors' visas, judgments based principally on a determination that only those Cubans who would return to the island should be permitted to visit the United States. Countless numbers were rejected, for fear that they would have remained illegally even though they would have qualified for legal residence. Many who did receive permission to visit did not return. An estimated 13,000 Cubans per year gained permanent U.S. residency by entering on a visitor's visa and remaining. Many arrived by way of third countries. Still others arrived illegally, aboard rafts (balseros) or hijacked boats and planes. The increasing number of balseros arriving in the United States — from 467 in 1990 to 2,203 in 1991, then 2,548 in 1992, and 3,656 in 1993 — was as much a result of the apparent decision of Cuban authorities to refrain from interception as to deteriorating economic conditions.

Developments reached a crisis in the summer of 1994 as conditions on the island continued to deteriorate. Illegal seizures and hijacking increased. In August 1994, a series of ferries hijacked in Havana harbor resulted in the death of some Cuban officials and a riot on the Havana waterfront. Official Cuban protests notwithstanding, few persons implicated in these acts were arrested in the United States or returned to face prosecution in Cuba. The Cuban government alleged that the U.S. government was engaged in deliberate provocation by denying most Cubans legal entry but welcoming them as *balseros* or aboard hijacked ships and planes. In mid-August, the Cuban government announced that it would no longer interdict or in any other way hinder the departure of Cubans wishing to leave for the United States.

The effects were immediate. Hundreds of Cubans boarded boats, constructed rafts, and almost anything else capable of floating, to leave for the United States. Washington reacted immediately and rescinded the thirty-five-year-old policy of automatic asylum, a measure to "demagnetize the United States," one U.S. official commented. Henceforth, Cubans could enter the United States only through visas formally issued by the U.S. Interests Section in Havana. To this end, the U.S. government established a naval cordon outside Cuban territorial waters to prevent Cubans from reaching the United States. Persons thus intercepted were taken to Guantánamo Naval Station for internment. In fact, the U.S. naval presence served to make a bad situation worse, for the United States had actually succeeded in "magnetizing" the Florida Straits. Cubans had to journey only twelve miles — instead of ninety   to reach U.S. authorities. In the days that followed, the number of Cubans departing the island reached more than 1,000 per day. By the end of September more than 21,000 Cubans had been interned at the U.S. Naval Station. The crisis ended in mid-September, when both countries negotiated an immigration pact. Cuban authorities pledged to prevent illegal departures in exchange for which Washington agreed to allow 20,000 Cubans per year to emigrate to the United States legally. In addition, the U.S. government also committed itself to returning to the island all Cubans who managed to elude Cuban coast guard patrols and reach the United States illegally. Eventually almost all Cubans interned at the Naval Station in 1994 were permanently resettled in the United States.

The 1994 crisis passed but not without permanent effects. Measures adopted by the Bill Clinton administration as immediate responses to the Cuban exodus remained in place and were never rescinded. Family support remittances to Cubans on the island were prohibited. The value of gift packages of food, medicines, medical supplies, and vitamins was limited to $200 monthly. In an effort to reduce the source of badly needed foreign exchange, Clinton prohibited all general family and research travel to Cuba. Only travelers who obtained a "specific license" from the Department of the Treasury were exempted from the travel ban.

Crisis and a turn for the worse in Cuba-U.S. relations occurred again in 1996. In February, the Cuban air force downed two civilian aircraft near or in Cuban air space flown by the exile Cuban-American organization "Brothers to the Rescue" (*Hermanos al Rescate*). Their previous flights into Cuban territory were not disputed, including one occasion when planes dropped antigovernment leaflets directly over Havana. Repeated Cuban protests to Washington and warnings to Brothers to the Rescue went unheeded.

The February 1996 incident set the stage for the next round of confrontation. Like 1992 when the Torricelli Bill was passed, 1996 was a presidential election year, and the Republican-controlled congress moved quickly to enact the Helms-Burton Bill. Only months earlier, the Clinton administration had publicly opposed the proposed legislation, but in March 1996 the administration acquiesced to congressional pressure and signed the bill into law.

Helms-Burton sought to internationalize the U.S. embargo by coercing other countries into suspending trade relations with Cuba and halting investments on the island. The bill threatened with lawsuits any foreign companies that "trafficked" in property previously owned by the United States. Foreign executives of those companies, and members of their immediate family, were also to be denied visas to enter or study in the United States. Another provision of the law required the United States to reduce aid to Russia by the same amount that Moscow paid Cuba for the use of intelligence facilities on the island, estimated at approximately $200 million dollars. Perhaps most important, the Clinton administration relinquished executive authority over foreign policy with regard to Cuba. Helms-Burton codified all existing executive orders relating to Cuba in effect as of March 1, 1996. The Cuba policy of the United States was thus transferred from the executive branch to the control of Congress. Not perhaps since the early 1960s had relations between the two countries been as dismal as they were after March 1996.

IX

Through the late 1990s and into the early years of the twenty-first century, political relations between Washington and Havana remained what they had been through much of the preceding four decades. Certainly, both countries found specific areas of cooperation and collaboration. Migration accords signed originally in 1994 were subsequently renegotiated and ratified. In 1998, after a two-year hiatus of direct air traffic, charter flights between Miami and Havana resumed. In the years that followed, U.S. departure cities expanded to include New York and Los Angeles, while destination cities in Cuba increased to include Cienfuegos, Holguín, and Santiago de Cuba. At the same time, Washington permitted the resumption of cash remittances to Cuba from families resident in the United States up to a legal limit of $1,200 annually. By 2002, the total estimated sum of cash remittances to Cuba—both legal and illegal—approached $1 billion annually. Cooperation between Cuba and the United States on drug interdiction expanded with improvement of communication links between the coast guards of both countries and the posting of an antinarcotics agent at the U.S. Interests Section in Havana.

On the whole, however, political relations between Cuba and the United States remained largely unchanged through the end of the 1990s and into the new century. Changes such as had occurred, most notably in the form of the Torricelli Law (1992) and the Helms-Burton Law (1996), remained in force, accompanied by confident predictions in the United States that the continued application of such sanctions would deliver the desired results—but always with the same results as before.

More than forty years after the triumph of the Cuban revolution, the United States showed no disposition to reach an understanding with the government of Fidel Castro. The policy bore the traces of the trauma by which its purpose was fixed after 1959 and derived sustenance in the umbrage that Fidel Castro had visited upon the United States. Castro had deeply offended North American sensibilities. For more than four decades he haunted the United States: a constant reminder of the inability of the United States to will the world in accordance with its own interests, made all the more egregious by the fact that this was a part of the world in which the United States had routinely imposed its will. He had challenged long-cherished notions about national well-being and upset prevailing notions of the rightful order of things. The U.S. response was exorcism in the guise of policy, an effort to purge Fidel Castro as an evil spirit who tormented North American equanimity.

Cultures cope with the demons that torment them in different ways, and indeed the practice of exorcism assumes many forms. Castro continued to occupy a place of almost singular distinction in that nether world to which the United States banished its demons. Fidel Castro remained a man North Americans loved to hate: political conflict personalized, loaded with Manichaean insinuations, the frustration of decades of unsuccessful attempts to force Cuba to bend to the U.S. will vented on one man. The policy of the United States possessed a punitive aspect to its purpose, a determination to punish Castro, a way to avenge past wrongs, which in this instance meant vanquishing Fidel Castro once and for all. *New York Times* foreign affairs columnist Thomas Friedman was entirely correct in suggesting in 1999 that the U.S. position on Cuba was "not really a policy. It's an *attitude*—a blind hunger for revenge against Mr. Castro."[24]

The United States refused to deal with Fidel Castro in any mode other than a repentant one. Indeed, reconciliation with an unrepentant Castro seemed almost inconceivable. Fidel Castro was unwilling to submit to the demands that President Ronald Reagan had earlier made to the *sandinistas:* to say uncle. When asked in 1982 under what conditions the United States would consider normalization of relations with Cuba, Reagan responded, "What it would take is Fidel Castro, recognizing that he made the wrong choice quite a while ago, and that he sincerely and honestly wants to rejoin the family of American nations and become a part of the Western Hemisphere." President George Bush similarly encouraged Castro "to lighten up," vowing, "Unless Fidel Castro is willing to change his policies and behavior, we will maintain our present policy toward Cuba."[25] Kenneth Skoug, former chief of the Cuba desk at the State Department, made the same point. Fidel Castro "has never been prepared to change his principles or his politics," Skoug affirmed. "While Castro holds power, genuine rapprochement between the United States and Cuba is difficult to contemplate. . . . Cuba is no longer a danger to the United States, but it will not be turned around. After the Castro era, rapprochement is all but inevitable."[26]

That Fidel Castro had endured at all, that he had survived scores of U.S.-sponsored assassination attempts, one armed invasion, and more than four decades of economic sanctions and diplomatic isolation, had produced no small amount of confoundment and consternation in Washington. Only the total and unconditional vanquishment of Fidel Castro could vindicate the policy to which the United States had so fully committed itself. By the end of the 1990s, U.S. policy assumed a life of its own. Its very longevity served as the principal rationale for its continuance. It proved increasingly difficult to abandon a policy to which twelve presidential administrations had dedicated themselves, even if the policy had failed utterly to achieve its purpose. On the contrary, its failure served as the last and only rationale for continued enforcement. That the policy had not yet accomplished what it set out to do simply meant that more time was required.

Central to the difficulty with Cuba in the United States was that North American officials were in large part confronting the contradictions and consequences of years of past U.S. policy. Sanctions were less a source of a solution than a cause of the problem. The Cuban condition was in varying degrees historically a function of its relations with the United States. It could be not be otherwise. U.S. policy had consequences: it was designed to. That these consequences were often not the ones intended— or perhaps even the ones desired—should not obscure the fact that they were nevertheless consequences of U.S. policy.

For more than forty years the United States pursued unabashedly a policy designed to destroy the Cuban government. Not surprisingly, internal security developed early into an obsession in Cuba. It was the height of cynicism for the United States to condemn Cuba for the curtailment of civil liberties and political freedoms, on one hand, and, on the other, to pursue policies variously employing assassination, subversion, sabotage, and threatened invasions as means to topple the Cuban government. North American policy did nothing to contribute to an environment in which civil liberties and political freedoms could have flourished.

So too with the failures of the Cuban economy. The embargo certainly must be factored as one source of Cuban economic woes—indeed, that was its overriding objective. The degree to which deteriorating economic conditions were the result of internal factors, on one hand, and the effect of external pressures, on the other, may never be knowable, but neither relationship is disputable.

All through the 1990s, control over the Cuba policy of the United States passed from the White House to Congress, where it was far more susceptible to the sway of Cuban-American lobbying pressures. Under the terms of Helms-Burton, the substantive elements of U.S. policy were appropriated by Congress, enacting into law the prohibition of normal diplomatic relations with Cuba as long as Fidel Castro or Raúl Castro remained in power. The final vestiges of executive prerogative over the Cuba policy, namely, the authority of the president to regulate the travel of U.S. citizens to Cuba, was preempted by Congress in an amendment to the agricultural appropriations bill in 2000. Fearful that President Clinton would lift the travel ban to Cuba in the final weeks of his administration, anti-Castro legislators and their allies in Congress acted to codify in law existing travel restrictions pertaining to Cuba. By 2002, virtually all discretionary authority over the Cuban policy of the United States had been appropriated by Congress.

The 2000 presidential campaign, with the vote count in Florida determining the outcome of the national election, set in further relief the domestic political considerations of U.S. foreign policy. The Cuban-American community was not slow to claim a decisive role in the electoral victory of George W. Bush, thereby positioning itself to claim even greater voice in the formulation of the Cuba policy of the United States. That the brother of President Bush was the incumbent Republican governor of the state of Florida seeking reelection in 2002 provided still further incentive for the administration in Washington to maintain trade and travel sanctions against Cuba. Indeed, the implications for Florida of an end to the embargo went far beyond the immediate politics of the 2002 gubernatorial election. At stake, too, was the very future of the Florida economy, for a normalization of relations between Cuba and the United States could not but have far-reaching repercussions on Florida's economic well-being, including tourism, citrus, sugar, winter vegetables, fruits, and fisheries.

But the call for a change of policy slowly gained new support, and often from the most unlikely sources. Largely in response to the collapse of Cuban trade relations with the former socialist bloc and the onset of difficult economic times in the United States, an ever-widening cross section of representatives of North American business interests were drawn to the prospects of Cuba as a market for U.S. exports. New voices thus joined the debate on the continued efficacy of the forty-three-year-old embargo. In 1997, some four hundred U.S. corporations, including AT&T, Boeing, Proctor and Gamble, and Pepsico, among others, organized USA Engage, an organization designed to lobby Congress to end trade sanctions on Cuba. In the following year, the U.S. Chamber of Commerce organized a broad coalition of civic and corporate entities called Americans for Humanitarian Trade with Cuba. Other specific trade and lobbying organizations also joined the call for a relaxation of trade sanctions against Cuba, including the U.S. Feed Grain Council, the American Soybean Association, the National Barley Grower Association, the National Association of Wheat Growers, the U.S. Rice Producers Association, the National Council of Farmer Cooperatives, and the U.S. Cane Sugar Refiners Association. Increasingly, too, trade and business delegations, including the American Farm Bureau Federation and the U.S. Chamber of Commerce, were organized to visit Cuba to explore market possibilities for U.S. exporters in anticipation of a relaxation of trade sanctions. Between 1998 and 2002, a number of states organized trade missions to visit Cuba, including Illinois, Texas, Arkansas, Kentucky, and North Carolina. The congressional delegations of several farm states, including Indiana, North Dakota, Iowa, and Kansas, sought to enact in Washington the necessary legislation to sell foodstuffs and farm supplies to Cuba.

These lobbying efforts were not without some measure of success. In 2000, Congress provided for the limited commercial exports of foodstuffs to Cuba, on a cash-only or third-country financing basis. The measure provided, however limited, the first trade arrangement between both countries in nearly forty years. In 2001, Cuba purchased $30 million worth of agricultural products from the United States, including corn, rice, soybeans, and poultry.

The debate on U.S. policy was further enlivened with the visit of former President Jimmy Carter to Cuba in May 2002. In a live broadcast address in Cuba, Carter urged the United States to relax the trade and travel restrictions and asked Cuba to permit greater exercise of civil liberties.

These stirrings were short lived. Even before Carter had departed for Cuba, the Bush administration had denounced Cuba for posing a threat in its capacity to mount biological warfare, a charge designed to have particular resonance in an atmosphere of the U.S. war against terrorism. That the Bush administration retained Cuba on the list of rogue terrorist nations further complicated any discussion of modification of the existing relations. Hopes for any shift in policy were dashed in May 2002, on the occasion of the centennial commemorating the end of the U.S. military occupation of Cuba and the establishment of the republic, when President Bush reiterated U.S. hostility to the government of Fidel Castro and proposed new initiatives designed to foment internal political opposition in Cuba. The new initiatives included aid to the families of political prisoners and dissidents, the modernization of Radio and TV Martí, and direct assistance to Cubans through religious and other nongovernment organizations—more changes that reaffirmed the changelessness of U.S. policy.

X

If political relations between the governments of Cuba and the United States remained unchanged, if not unchangeable, during the 1990s, scientific, cultural, and academic relations between the peoples of both countries continued to improve. Perhaps nothing served more to bring Cuba to the attention of a larger American public than the controversy surrounding the status of Elián González in late 1999 and early 2000. Having survived the death of his mother in the perilous crossing of the Florida Straits, the unaccompanied five-year-old arrived in the United States in November 1999 and was immediately the subject of competing claims of custody between his cousins in Miami and his father in Cuba. The highly publicized controversy lasted more than six months and was resolved only with a predawn armed recovery of the boy from the Miami relatives and his eventual return to Cuba.

The drama of Elián González set in relief the politics of Miami and the policies of the United States and in many ways served to bring the matter of Cuba and U.S. relations with Cuba into full public view with a new a sense of immediacy. Indeed, all through the 1990s interest in Cuba had expanded across the United States. Things Cuban assumed a certain fashionableness and vogue—what Bonnie Raitt suggested in her song title "Cuba Is Way Too Cool." Cuban recorded music once again claimed its place as a dominant presence in the North American market. Such musical groups as Irakere, Los Van Van, Cubanismo, and Los Muñequitos de Matanzas, among many others, played to sold-out venues across the United States.[27] The success of the Grammy-winning album *Buena Vista Social Club* (Nonesuch) was nothing short of remarkable. In mid-November 1999, *Billboard* magazine placed *Buena Vista Social Club* at the top of the pop catalog album sales. In 2000, Los Van Van also won a Grammy award for its album *Llego . . . Van Van / Van Van Is Here* (Asin). American musicians performed in Cuba with increasing frequency. One collaborative Cuba-U.S. project called Music Bridge organized a concert in Havana and included American live performances by Jimmy Buffett, Gladys Knight, Burt Bacharach, and Bonnie Raitt. "Cuba is an island no more, musically speaking," pronounced *Time* magazine in 1998.[28]

Awareness of Cuba as a site of cultural innovation was at an all-time high. Art shows in Boston, New York, Chicago, Los Angeles, and Portland exhibited the works of Carlos Estévez, Fernando Rodríguez, Manuel Mendive, and Salvador González. Cuba became the stock-in-trade of mainstream media, not as a topic of political reporting but as the subject of cultural news: *Art News* published a feature piece on Cuban plastic arts; *National Geographic* and *Architectural Digest* marveled at the restoration of prerevolutionary architecture; *Newsweek* published a feature article in 2002 on the restoration project of Old Havana; *Time* magazine published a euphoric feature piece about the innovations of Cuban jazz.[29]

Interest in travel to Cuba soared. The Travel Cable Channel dedicated one program to the charms of Cuba as a tourist destination. A 1998 issue of *Motor Boat and Sailing* extolled the delights of sailing and fishing in Cuban waters, and *Esquire* provided a cycling account of the island "from tip to tip."[30] In August 1999, the Sunday *New York Times* travel section published a front-page feature article on Cuba. One year later, *Travel Holiday* featured Cuba as a tourist venue.[31] In June 1999, the monthly *Cigar Aficionado* published "a complete travel guide for Americans." In the June 2001 issue, *Cigar Aficionado* again published a guide to "the best resort hotels, nightclubs, and restaurants" in Cuba.[32] Cuba travel Web sites proliferated at a bewildering rate and offered information on private apartment rentals, chauffeur services, restaurants, and beach resorts. The publication of Cuba travel guides and tour books developed fully into a growth industry.[33] Travel books addressed specific tourist interests and included guides for driving across Cuba; cycling in Cuba; snorkeling, diving, and sailing in Cuban waters; and retiring and investing in Cuba.[34]

What made these developments all the more remarkable, of course, was that the readership for which this expanding literature was intended, the American public, could not legally undertake vacation travel to Cuba. It did not seem to matter. "It is illegal to travel to Cuba," *Cigar Aficionado* acknowledged in 1999 but hastened to add, "There are tens of thousands who each year make the trip via third countries, most commonly Canada, the Bahamas and Mexico. . . . Prosecuting American tourists is not high on the U.S. government's list of priorities."[35] This was Prohibition all over again, where the law was routinely disregarded and defied. According to U.S. Interests Section sources in Havana, during the late 1990s more than 100,000 Americans were traveling to Cuba annually, and most were doing it illegally.

Colleges and universities across the United States, largely in response to undergraduate curiosities, established exchange programs with Cuban counterpart institutions. Study-abroad programs in Cuba, including semester-long curricula and summer school courses, as well as organized group tours, proliferated and included such diverse study themes as Afro-Cuban religion, Spanish colonial architecture, performing arts, education, and rural health care. Thousands of North American undergraduates annually visited Cuba to study in programs of varying lengths of time.[36] Scientific collaboration and academic cooperation between scholars of both countries increased in number and type; institutional ties between colleges and universities, libraries, and archives of both countries expanded and included ties between Cuban institutions and Harvard, Johns Hopkins, Wisconsin, Tulane, Florida International University, and Wake Forest, among many others. These ties contributed in important ways to promoting interchanges that fostered the development of relations between both peoples, relations that approached the condition of "normal."

Cubans and North Americans came together in other ways. The Baltimore Orioles and the Cuban national baseball team exchanged visits to each other's ballparks. In December 1999, the Milwaukee Symphony performed in Havana. A cultural exchange project called Tail Light Diplomacy represented an initiative bringing together owners and *aficionados* of old American cars in Cuba and the United States. Sister-city programs continued to expand and included Mobile-Havana, Oakland–Santiago de Cuba, Madison-Camagüey, Pittsburgh-Matanzas, Richmond (California)–Regla, Tacoma-Cienfuegos, and Bloomington–Santa Clara.

The larger implications of these developments were not difficult to decipher. As the governments of both countries remained hopelessly stalled on the issue of "normalization" of relations, people on both sides of the Florida Straits took matters into their own hands. These exchanges represented important connections and, in the aggregate, fashioned— often imperceptibly—the larger cultural context in which the politics and policies of both governments had to perforce function. Engagement could not but have fostered the kinds of familiarities that heightened an appreciation for the benefits of "normal" relations. At some point, each government would have to act on the better instincts of its people and put into effect those policies that reflected the best interests of both countries.

XI

The connections between Cuban relations with the United States and Cuban domestic policy have been noteworthy and constant. Much in the Cuban-U.S. relationship has had to do with both countries learning to coexist as neighbors on vastly unequal terms. From the Cuban perspective, to be at the subordinate end of this equation has created a host of obvious difficulties, many of which have served to shape the character of national narratives. From the North American perspective, Cuban sensibilities seem to have mattered little, if at all. What has mattered most has been U.S. interests, broadly and openly defined. Together these countervailing forces have acted to influence decisively the character of relations between the countries. Much of what has served as logic of the Cuban-U.S. relationship during the last century, and certainly during much of the last forty years, has been derived and defined out of a complex set of interactions. These may not have always been understandable actions, or even wholly rational ones, but they have been accurate reflections of the anomalies and ambiguities of Cuba-U.S. relations. It seems to be consistent that the logic of historic and geographic factors that for so long have provided the context for singular intimacy will one day dictate anew the resumption of relations on terms satisfactory to both Cuba and the United States. The same logic of both historical experiences suggests the inevitability of rapprochement on terms far different than the way they have been—perhaps far better.

The only certainty in an otherwise wholly unpredictable relationship is that relations between both countries will resume some day: perhaps sooner, but certainly later. The logic of geography and history simply provides for no other alternative. Cubans and North Americans cannot escape each other.

The important questions, hence, are driven not by "if" but by "when" —and under what circumstances and with what enduring legacies—will relations resume, for when relations do become "normal" again, the people of each country will carry memories of the last four decades for years to come. How these memories will shape the future can be considered only in the realm of conjecture, of course, but it requires no gift of prophecy to understand that the deeper the wounds the more difficult the healing. Cubans and North Americans will long be affected by these years of "nonrelations." It is in the nature of long-standing close ties between both nations, in those realms of shared vulnerabilities, that falling-outs tend to be particularly acrimonious, and that the negotiation of reconciliation and the renewal of trust must be considered among the most difficult transactions to complete.

Notes

1. The Origins of Relations

1. See H. E. Friedlaender, *Historia económica de Cuba* (Havana, 1944), pp. 26–36, 59–73.

2. María Encarnación Rodríguez Vicente, "El comercio cubano y la guerra de emancipación norteamericana," *Anuario de Estudios Americanos* (Seville), 11 (1954): 61–106.

3. James A. Lewis, "Anglo-American Entrepreneurs in Havana: The Background and Significance of the Expulsion of 1784–1785," in Jacques A. Barbier and Allan J. Kuethe, eds., *The North American Role in the Spanish Imperial Economy, 1760–1819* (Manchester, Eng., 1984), pp. 112–126.

4. *American State Papers, 1789–1809: Commerce and Navigation* (Washington, D.C., 1832), 1:33.

5. George Clark Morton to James Madison, April 21, 1801, Despatches from U.S. Consuls in Havana, 1783–1906, General Records of the Department of State, Record Group 59, National Archives, Washington, D.C. (hereafter cited as Despatches/Havana).

6. *American State Papers, 1789–1809*; 1:489, 507, 514–515, 521, 558–570, 576–579, 721, 749–769.

7. See Hubert A. Aimes, *A History of Slavery in Cuba, 1511–1868*, 2d ed. (New York, 1967), p. 264; and Alexander von Humboldt, *The Island of Cuba*, trans. John S. Thrasher (New York, 1856), pp. 218–219.

8. José R. Alvarez Díaz et al., *A Study on Cuba* (Coral Gables, 1965), pp. 81, 83.

9. Susan Schroeder, *Cuba: A Handbook of Historical Statistics* (Boston, 1982), p. 260.

10. *American State Papers 1789–1809*, 1:33, 431.

11. See Kenneth F. Kiple, *Blacks in Colonial Cuba, 1774–1899* (Gainesville, 1976), pp. 25–58.

12. José García de Arboleya, *Manual de la isla de Cuba* (Havana, 1859), p. 241.

13. Anthony Trollope, *The West Indies and the Spanish Main* (London, 1862), p. 136; Basil Rauch, *American Interest in Cuba, 1848–1855* (New York, 1948), p. 182.

14. Richard B. Kimball, *Cuba and the Cubans* (New York, 1850), pp. 196–197.

15. James E. Alexander, *Transatlantic Sketches*, 2 vols. (London, 1833), 1:368–369; Edward Sullivan, *Rambles and Scrambles in North and South America* (London, 1852), p. 279.

16. See Fe Iglesias, "La explotación del hierro en el sur de Oriente y la Spanish American Iron Company," *Santiago*, no. 17 (March 1975), pp. 59–105.

17. Roland T. Ely, *Cuando reinaba su majestad el azúcar* (Buenos Aires, 1963), pp. 515–516; S. M. L. Jay, *My Winter in Cuba* (New York, 1871), p. 85; Richard Henry Dana, Jr., *To Cuba and Back: A Vacation Voyage* (Boston, 1859), p. 60.

18. Cuba, Centro de Estadística, *Noticias estadísticas de la isla de Cuba, en 1862* (Havana, 1864).

19. William T. Minor to William Seward, February 16, 1886; see also Minor to William Hunter, June 15, 1865, Thomas Sauvage to William Seward, July 19, 1865, all in Despatches/Havana. See also Eliza McHatton-Ripley, *From Flag to Flag* (New York, 1889), pp. 132, 149–269.

20. Herminio Portell Vilá, *La decadencia de Cárdenas. (Estudio económico)* (Havana, 1929), pp. 34–36.

21. George W. Williams, *Sketches of Travel in the Old and New World* (Charleston, S.C., 1871), p. 8; Richard R. Madden, *The Island of Cuba: Its Resources, Progress, and Prospects* (London, 1849), p. 83; R. W. Gibbes, *Cuba for Invalids* (New York, 1860), p. 109; John Glanville Taylor, *The United States and Cuba: Eight Years of Change and Travel* (London, 1851), p. 165.

22. J. G. L. Wurdermann, *Notes on Cuba* (Boston, 1844), pp. 271–272. For one account of the celebration of George Washington's birthday see the anonymous *A Winter in the West Indies and Florida* (New York, 1839), pp. 99–101.

23. Charles J. Helm to Lewis Cass, June 14, 1859, May 5, 1860, Despatches/Havana.

24. Maturin M. Ballou, *History of Cuba: Or Notes of a Traveller in the Tropics* (Boston, 1854), pp. 145–146; Dana, *To Cuba and Back*, p. 60; Carlton H. Rogers, *Incidents of Travel in the Southern States and Cuba* (New York, 1862), p. 110.

25. José Ahumada y Centurión, *Memoria histórico-política de la isla de Cuba* (Havana, 1874), pp. 268–270.

26. José G. de la Concha, *Memorias sobre el estado político, gobierno y administración de la isla de Cuba* (Madrid, 1853), pp. 64, 242–243.

27. Tesifonte Gallego García, *Cuba por fuera* (Havana, 1892), p. 139.

28. Madden, *Island of Cuba*, pp. 83–84.

29. Samuel Hazard, *Cuba with Pen and Pencil* (Hartford, Conn., 1871), pp. 402–403; Frederic A. Eustis, *Augustus Hemenway, 1805–1876: Builder of the United States Trade with the West Coast of South America* (Salem, Mass., 1955), p. 102; Williams, *Sketches of Travel*, p. 38; Arthur P. Whitaker, *The United States and the Independence of Latin America, 1800–1830* (New York, 1964), p. 129. For an account of a visit to the Jenks estate see Julia Ward Howe, *A Trip to Cuba* (Boston, 1860), pp. 138–140.
30. Williams, *Sketches of Travel*, p. 38.
31. Quoted in Herminio Portell Vilá, *Historia de Cuba en sus relaciones con los Estados Unidos y España*, 4 vols. (Havana, 1938–41), 1:310.
32. Richard Davey, *Cuba, Past and Present* (London, 1898), p. 19.
33. Fredrika Bremer, *The Homes of the New World; Impressions of America*, 2 vols. (New York, 1854), 2:421.
34. Dionisio A. Galiano, *Cuba en 1858* (Madrid, 1859), p. 21.
35. Abiel Abbot, *Letters Written in the Interior of Cuba* (Boston, 1829), p. 132.
36. Ahumada y Centurión, *Memoria histórico-política*, pp. 262–264.
37. De la Concha, *Memorias sobre el estado político*, pp. 341–342, 348–349.

2. A Convergence of Interests

1. Ramiro Guerra y Sánchez et al., *Historia de la nación cubana*, 10 vols. (Havana, 1952), 3:30–31.
2. See George Coggeshall, *Voyages to Various Parts of the World Made between the Years 1802 and 1841* (New York, 1852), pp. 170–185; James M. Phillippo, *The United States and Cuba* (London, 1857), p. 410; José Luciano Franco, "Comercio clandestino de esclavos en el siglo XIX, *Islas* 11 (January–April 1970): 43–58.
3. See Herminio Portell Vilá, *Historia de Cuba en sus relaciones con los Estados Unidos y España*, 4 vols. (Havana, 1938–41), 1:148–149.
4. William Shaler to James Monroe, December 6, 1810, Despatches from U.S. Consuls in Havana, 1783–1906, General Records of the Department of State, Record Group 59, National Archives, Washington, D.C. (hereafter cited as Despatches/Havana).
5. Ibid.
6. Emilio Roig de Leuchsenring, *Cuba y los Estados Unidos* (Havana, 1949), pp. 118–123.

7. John Quincy Adams to Hugh Nelson, April 28, 1823, U.S. Congress, House of Representatives, 32d Cong., 1st sess., House Document No. 121, Ser. 648, p. 7 (hereafter cited as House Document No. 121).

8. *Congressional Record*, vol. 2, pt. 2, 1826, pp. 2268–2270.

9. John Quincy Adams to Hugh Nelson, April 28, 1823, in Worthington C. Ford, ed., *The Writings of John Quincy Adams*, 7 vols. (New York, 1913–17), 7:372–379.

10. Thomas Jefferson to James Monroe, October 24, 1823, U.S. Congress, Senate, Senate Document No. 26, 57th Cong., 1st sess., Ser. 4220, pp. 3–4; James Buchanan to Romulus M. Saunders, June 17, 1848, in William R. Manning, ed., *Diplomatic Correspondence of the United States: Inter-American Affairs, 1831–1860*, 12 vols. (Washington, D.C., 1932–39), 11:87.

11. For a discussion of U.S.-British rivalry in the Caribbean see Lester D. Langley, *Struggle for the American Mediterranean* (Athens, Ga., 1976), pp. 38–50.

12. John Quincy Adams to Hugh Nelson, April 28, 1823, House Document No. 121, p. 7.

13. Charles Francis Adams, ed., *Memoirs of John Quincy Adams*, 12 vols. (Philadelphia, 1874–77), 6:70–74.

14. Thomas Jefferson to James Monroe, June 11, 1823, in Paul L. Ford, ed., *The Writings of Thomas Jefferson*, 10 vols. (New York, 1898), 10:293; John Forsyth to Secretary of State, November 20, 1822, House Document No. 121, p. 4.

15. Thomas Jefferson to James Monroe, October 24, 1823, U.S. Congress, Senate Document No. 26, 57th Cong., 1st sess., Ser. 4220, pp. 3–4; Alexander H. Everett to the president, November 30, 1825, in Everett, *The Everett Letters on Cuba* (Boston, 1897), p. 6; John Forsyth to John Quincy Adams, February 10, 1823, and Forsyth to Aaron Vail, July 15, 1840, House Document No. 121, pp. 5, 36–37; John M. Clayton to Daniel M. Barringer, August 2, 1849, in Manning, ed., *Diplomatic Correspondence*, 11:70.

16. Lester D. Langley, *The Cuban Policy of the United States* (New York, 1968), p. 5.

17. Henry Clay to Middleton, May 10, 1825, Despatches from United States Ministers to Spain, 1792–1906, General Records of the Department of State, Record Group 59, National Archives, Washington, D.C.; Martin Van Buren to Cornelius P. Van Ness, October 2, 1829, House Document No. 121, p. 26.

18. John Quincy Adams to Hugh Nelson, April 28, 1823, Henry Clay to Alexander H. Everett, April 26, 1825, House Document No. 121, pp. 8, 17–18.

19. For the full text of the Ostend Manifesto see U.S. Congress, House of Representatives, *House Executive Documents*, No. 93, 33d Cong., 2d sess., pp. 127–132.

20. See José García de Arboleya, *Manual de la isla de Cuba*, 2d ed. (Havana, 1859), p. 58. These themes are well treated in Robert E. May, *The Southern Dream of a Caribbean Empire, 1854–1861* (Baton Rouge, 1973).

21. For a detailed account of the López expeditions see Herminio Portell Vilá, *Narciso López y su época*, 3 vols. (Havana, 1930–58).

22. Quoted in Philip Foner, *A History of Cuba and Its Relations with the United States*, 2 vols. (New York, 1963), 2:19.

23. John S. C. Abbott, *South and North, or, Impressions Received during a Trip to Cuba and the South* (New York, 1860), p. 57.

24. John Warner to C. A. Rodney, February 20, 1822, James Monroe Papers, Ser. I, Manuscript Division, Library of Congress, Washington, D.C.

25. Forbes Lindsay, *Cuba and Her People To-day* (Boston, 1911), p. 162.

26. Richard Henry Dana, Jr., *To Cuba and Back: A Vacation Voyage* (Boston, 1859), p. 113; see Antonio Saco, *Ideas sobre la incorporación de Cuba en los Estados Unidos* (Havana, 1845).

27. Ulysses S. Grant, "Annual Message to Congress," December 7, 1875, in James D. Richardson, ed., *A Compilation of the Messages and Papers of the Presidents, 1789–1902*, 10 vols. (Washington, D.C., 1896–1902), 11:4293–4294.

28. Allan Nevins, *Hamilton Fish*, 2 vols. (New York, 1957), 1:180.

29. Hamilton Fish Diary, April 6, 1869, Box 314, Hamilton Fish Papers, Manuscript Division, Library of Congress, Washington, D.C.

3. At the Crossroads

1. H. E. Friedlaender, *Historia económica de Cuba* (Havana, 1944), p. 545. See also Gastón Descamps, *La crisis azucarera y la isla de Cuba* (Havana, 1885).

2. Adam Badeau, "Report on the Present Condition of Cuba," February 7, 1884, Despatches from U.S. Consuls in Havana, 1783–1906, General Records of the Department of State, Record Group 59, National Archives, Washington, D.C. (hereafter cited as Despatches/Havana).

3. William P. Pierce to Secretary of State John Davis, August 10, 1883, Despatches from United States Consuls in Cienfuegos, 1876–1906, General Records of the Department of State, Record Group 59, National Archives, Washington, D.C.

4. See Edwin F. Atkins, *Sixty Years in Cuba* (Cambridge, Mass., 1926), pp. 30–137; Hugh Thomas, *Cuba, the Pursuit of Freedom* (New York, 1971), p. 290.

5. James W. Steele, *Cuban Sketches* (New York, 1881), pp. 78–79.

6. Henry C. Hall to Assistant Secretary of State John Hay, April 13, 1881, Adam Badeau to Assistant Secretary of State John Davis, December 19, 1882, Despatches/Havana.

7. Manuel Moreno Fraginals, *El ingenio: El complejo económico social cubano del azúcar*, 3 vols. (Havana, 1978), 3:71–72; Maturin M. Ballou, *Due South, or Cuba Past and Present* (Boston, 1891), p. 58.

8. Ramon O. Williams to J. C. Bancroft Davis, February 23, 1882, Williams to Assistant Secretary of State James N. Porter, December 18, 1886, Despatches/Havana.

9. Jean Stubbs, *Tobacco on the Periphery: A Case Study in Cuban Labour History, 1860–1958* (Cambridge, Eng., 1985), p. 19; Gloria Garcia, "Papel de la crisis económica de 1857 en la economía cubana," *Universidad de La Habana* 32 (October–December 1968): 25–33.

10. José García Arboleya, *Manual de la isla de Cuba*, 2d ed. (Havana, 1859), p. 178; José R. Alvarez Díaz et al., *A Study on Cuba* (Coral Gables, 1965), pp. 107–108; Stubbs, *Tobacco on the Periphery*; p. 18.

11. *Diario de la Marina*, August 16, 1882.

12. Fernando Portuondo del Prado, *Historia de Cuba*, 6th ed. (Havana, 1957), p. 438.

13. See Rolando Alvarez Estévez, *La emigración cubana en los Estados Unidos, 1868–1878* (Havana, 1986); Louis A. Pérez, Jr., "Cubans in Tampa: From Exiles to Immigrants, 1892–1901," *Florida Historical Quarterly* 56 (October 1978): 129–140; José Rivero Muñiz, "Los cubanos en Tampa," *Revista Bimestre Cubana* 74 (First Semester 1958): 5–140.

14. Richard Henry Dana, Jr., *To Cuba and Back: A Vacation Voyage* (Boston, 1859), p. 79.

15. See Roland T. Ely, *Cuando reinaba su majestad el azúcar* (Buenos Aires, 1964), pp. 355, 404–408.

16. José G. de la Concha, *Memorias sobre el estado político, gobierno y administración de la isla de Cuba* (Madrid, 1853), pp. 63, 242; Nicolás Tanco Armero,

Viaje de Nueva Granada a China (Paris, 1861), p. 27; Ballou, *Due South*, p. 94.

17. L. de Hegermann-Lindencrone, *In the Courts of Memory* (New York, 1912), p. 342.

18. See Carlos Ripoll, *Cubans in the United States* (New York, 1987), pp. 15–20.

19. William Cullen Bryant, *Letters of a Traveller* (New York, 1850), p. 373.

20. Eliza McHatton-Ripley, *From Flag to Flag* (New York, 1889), p. 147.

21. George Lester, *In Sunny Isles* (London, 1897), p. 75.

22. Eddy Martín, "Cien años de vida del beisbol cubano," *Juventud Rebelde*, December 22, 1974, p. 5; Angel Torres, *La historia del beisbol cubano, 1878–1976* (Los Angeles, 1976), p. 7.

23. Ricardo Agacino, "Beisbol de ayer y de hoy," *Cuba Internacional*, July 1987, pp. 64–67; Eric A. Wagner, "Baseball in Cuba," *Journal of Popular Culture* 18 (Summer 1984): 113–120.

24. See Gerald E. Poyo, "Cuban Revolutionaries and Monroe County Reconstruction Politics, 1868–1876," *Florida Historical Quarterly* 55 (April 1977): 407–422, and Poyo, "Key West and the Ten Years War," *Florida Historical Quarterly* 57 (January 1979): 289–307.

25. Interview with Tomás Mayet, February 20, 1973, West Tampa, Florida.

26. See Evelio Tellería Toca, "Los tabaqueros cubanos y sus luchas en Cayo Hueso y Tampa," *Bohemia* 59 (April 28, 1967): 18–23, 113.

27. Pulaski F. Hyatt to Secretary of State, October 12, 1894, Despatches from U.S. Consuls in Santiago de Cuba, 1799–1906, General Records of the Department of State, Record Group 59, National Archives, Washington, D.C. (hereafter cited as Despatches/Santiago de Cuba).

28. *La Lucha*, December 19, 1894.

29. Ibid., January 3, 1895.

30. Pulaski F. Hyatt to Secretary of State, October 12, 1894, Despatches/Santiago de Cuba.

31. *La Lucha*, January 3, 1895.

32. José Martí, "El Partido Revolucionario Cubano," April 3, 1892, in Martí, *Obras completas*, ed. Jorge Quintana, 5 vols. (Caracas, 1964), vol. 1, pt. 2, pp. 303–307.

33. José Martí, "Un drama terrible," November 13, 1897, ibid., 2:799–800.

34. José Martí, "La Conferencia Monetaria de las Repúblicas de América," May 1891, ibid., 3:262.

35. José Martí, "La crisis y el Partido Revolucionario Cubano," August 19, 1893, ibid., vol. 1, pt. 2, p. 665.

36. José Martí, "A la raíz," August 26, 1893, ibid., p. 669; Martí to Manuel Mercado, May 18, 1895, ibid., p. 271.
37. José Martí to Serafín Bello, November 16, 1889, ibid., p. 392.

4. Intervention and Occupation

1. Máximo Gómez, "A los señores hacendados y dueños de fincas ganaderas," July 1, 1895, Fondo de Donativos y Remisiones, Legajo 257, Número 14, Archivo Nacional de Cuba, Havana, Cuba. See also "Manuscrito del acuerdo del Consejo de Gobierno en sesión 13 de julio de 1896 en relación a la prohibición de la zafra de 1896 a 1897," July 30, 1896, Fondo de Donativos y Remisiones, Legajo 624, Número 34, ibid.
2. "To the President of the Republic of the United States of America," enclosure in Fitzhugh Lee to Richard Olney, June 24, 1896, Richard Olney Papers, Library of Congress, Manuscript Division, Washington, D.C.
3. A Planter in Cuba, "The Argument for Autonomy," *Outlook* 58 (April 23, 1898): 1012.
4. *New York World*, March 22, 1897.
5. William J. Calhoun to William McKinley, June 22, 1897, Special Agents, General Records of the Department of State, Record Group 59, Vol. 48, National Archives, Washington, D.C.
6. Richard B. Olney to Enrique Dupuy de Lome, April 4, 1896, U.S. Department of State, *Foreign Relations of United States, 1897* (Washington, D.C., 1898), p. 543 (hereafter cited as *FRUS, 1897*).
7. See Lyman J. Gage, "Work of the Treasury Department," in *The American-Spanish War: A History by the War Leaders* (Norwich, Conn., 1899), pp. 367–391, and John E. Wilkie, "The Secret Service in the War," ibid., pp. 423–436.
8. Richard B. Olney to Grover Cleveland, September 25, 1895, Grover Cleveland Papers, Library of Congress, Manuscript Division, Washington, D.C.
9. Richard B. Olney to Enrique Dupuy de Lôme, April 4, 1896, *FRUS, 1897*, p. 541.
10. Grover Cleveland, "Fourth Annual Message," December 7, 1896, in James D. Richardson, ed., *A Compilation of the Messages and Papers of the Presidents, 1789–1902*, 10 vols. (Washington, D.C., 1896–1902), 9:720.
11. Richard Olney to Enrique Dupuy de Lôme, April 14, 1896, *FRUS, 1897*, pp. 543–544.

12. Duke of Tetuán to Enrique Dupuy de Lôme, May 22, 1896, in Spain, Ministerio de Estado, *Spanish Diplomatic Correspondence and Documents, 1896–1900, Presented to the Cortes by the Minister of State* (Washington, D.C., 1905), pp. 10–11.

13. Fitzhugh Lee to William R. Day, November 17, 1897, Despatches from U.S. Consuls in Havana, 1783–1906, General Records of the Department of State, Record Group 59, National Archives, Washington, D.C. (hereafter cited as Despatches/Havana).

14. Alexander C. Brice to William R. Day, November 17, 1897, Despatches from U.S. Consuls in Matanzas, 1820–89, General Records of the Department of State, Record Group 59, National Archives, Washington, D.C.

15. Pulaski F. Hyatt to William R. Day, March 24, 1898, U.S. Congress, Senate, *Consular Correspondence Respecting the Conditions of the Reconcentrados in Cuba, the State of the War in That Island, and the Prospects of the Projected Autonomy*, 55th Cong., 2d sess., Senate Document No. 230, p. 44.

16. Fitzhugh Lee to William R. Day, November 23, 1897, Despatches/Havana.

17. *Washington Post,* December 22, 1897.

18. *New York Herald,* December 14, 1897.

19. Máximo Gómez to John R. Caldwell, December 5, 1897, *New York Herald,* December 29, 1897.

20. *New York World,* February 10, March 6, 1897.

21. *New York Journal,* February 24, 1898.

22. Calixto García to Editor, December 18, 1897, *New York Journal,* January 5, 1898.

23. Máximo Gómez to Gonzalo de Quesada, March 10, 1898, *New York Daily Tribune,* April 10, 1898.

24. *New York World,* August 17, 1897.

25. William R. Day to Stewart L. Woodford, March 26, 1898, U.S. Department of State, *Foreign Relations of the United States, 1898* (Washington, D.C., 1901), p. 704 (hereafter cited as *FRUS, 1898*).

26. William R. Day, "Recognition of Independence," n.d., William R. Day Papers, Library of Congress, Manuscript Division, Washington, D.C.

27. Stewart L. Woodford to William McKinley, March 17, 1898, Despatches from United States Ministers to Spain, 1792–1906, General Records of the Department of State, Record Group 59, National Archives, Washington, D.C.

28. Stewart L. Woodford to William McKinley, March 17, 1898, Private Correspondence, General Woodford to the President, August 1897 to May 1898,

John Bassett Moore Papers, Library of Congress, Manuscript Division, Washington, D.C.

29. See William R. Day to Stewart Woodford, March 27, 1898, *FRUS, 1898*, pp. 711–712.

30. Luis Polo de Bernabé to Secretary of State, April 10, 1898, in Spain, Ministerio de Estado, *Spanish Diplomatic Correspondence*, p. 121; William R. Day, "Interview with Spanish Minister," April 10, 1898, Day Papers; Charles G. Dawes, *A Journal of the McKinley Years* (Chicago, 1950), p. 149.

31. Ramón Blanco, "Suspension of Hostilities," April 10, 1898, in *FRUS, 1898*, p. 750.

32. Horatio S. Rubens, *Liberty: The Story of Cuba* (New York, 1932), pp. 326–327. Tomás Estrada Palma later wrote that "enormous pressure was brought to bear on the Delegation to persuade the Cubans to accept an armistice." See Tomás Estrada Palma, "The Work of the Cuban Delegation," in *The American-Spanish War*, pp. 419–420.

33. Calixto García to Mario G. Menocal, April 18, 1898, in García, *Palabras de tres guerra* (Havana, 1942), pp. 143–144; Máximo Gómez, *Diario de campaña del mayor general Máximo Gómez* (Havana, 1940), p. 354.

34. Richardson, ed., *Messages and Papers*, 10:63–64.

35. Alvey A. Adee to William R. Day, April 7, 1898, Day Papers.

36. "Borrador relacionado con la Resolución Conjunta," April 1898, in Gonzalo de Quesada, *Documentos históricos* (Havana, 1965), p. 409.

37. *State* (Columbia, S.C.), April 8, 1898. See also *Washington Evening Star*, April 6, 1898.

38. *Congressional Record* 31 (April 16, 1898): 3988–3989.

39. Calixto García to Tomás Estrada Palma, April 26, 1898, in Felipe Martínez Arango, *Cronología crítica de la guerra hispano-cubano-americano* (Santiago de Cuba, 1946), p. 44.

40. *New York Times*, August 5, 1898.

41. See *Washington Evening Star*, July 19, 1898.

42. Calixto García to Pedro Pérez, August 12, 1898, in Juan J. E. Casasús, *Calixto García (el estratega)* (Havana, 1942), p. 284.

43. Calixto García to William R. Shafter, July 17, 1898, in García, *Palabras de tres guerras*, pp. 107–110.

44. Ibid. See also Cuba, Ejército Libertador, *Parte oficial del lugarteniente general Calixto García al General en Jefe Máximo Gómez, 15 de julio de 1898, sobre la campaña de Santiago de Cuba* (Havana, 1953), pp. 22–23.

45. Lieutenant Colonel Clinton Smith to Colonel Augustus R. Francis, July 31, 1898, *New York Times*, August 12, 1898.
46. *State* (Columbia, S.C.), July 20, 1898.
47. *New York Times*, August 23, 1, 1898; *State* (Columbia, S.C.), July 30, 1898, p. 4.
48. Burr McIntosh, *The Little I Saw of Cuba* (New York, 1899), p. 74.
49. *New York Times*, July 29, 1898. See also *State* (Columbia, S.C.), July 20, 1898, and Charles Morris, *The War with Spain* (Philadelphia, 1899), p. 312.
50. *New York Times*, July 29, 1898.
51. Ibid., December 24, 1898.
52. *State* (Columbia, S.C.), December 19, 1898, and *New York Times*, December 19, 1898.
53. Quoted in Walter Millis, *The Martial Spirit: A Study of Our War with Spain* (Boston, 1931), p. 362.
54. Quoted in George Kennan, "Cuban Character," *Outlook* 63 (December 23, 1899): 1021–1022.
55. Leonard Wood to William McKinley, February 6, 1900, Elihu Root Papers, Manuscript Division, Library of Congress, Washington, D.C.
56. Leonard Wood to William McKinley, September 26, 1899, William McKinley Papers, Manuscript Division, Library of Congress, Washington, D.C.; Herbert P. Williams, "The Outlook in Cuba," *Atlantic Monthly* 83 (June 1899): 835–836.
57. Elihu Root to Paul Dana, January 15, 1900, Root Papers.
58. Leonard Wood to Elihu Root, January 1900, in Hermann Hagedorn, *Leonard Wood, A Biography*, 2 vols. (New York, 1931), 1:267.
59. Leonard Wood to William McKinley, August 31, 1900, Wood Papers; Wood to Adjutant General, September 1, 1900, File 340125/B, Records of the Adjutant General's Office, 1780s–1917, Record Group 94, National Archives, Washington, D.C.
60. Leonard Wood to Orville H. Platt, December 6, 1900, Wood Papers.
61. Leonard Wood to Elihu Root, March 4, 1901, in Hagedorn, *Leonard Wood*, 1:359; Wood to Elihu Root, September 26, 1900, January 12, 1901, Wood Papers.
62. Quoted in Louis A. Coolidge, *An Old-Fashioned Senator: Orville H. Platt of Connecticut* (New York, 1910), p. 331.
63. Orville H. Platt, "The Pacification of Cuba," *Independent* 53 (June 27, 1901): 1466.

64. U.S. Congress, Senate, Committee on Relations with Cuba, *Conditions in Cuba* (Washington, D.C., 1900), pp. 17–18.

65. Leonard Wood, "The Future of Cuba," *Independent* 54 (January 23, 1902): 193.

66. Elihu Root to Leonard Wood, January 9, 1901, Root Papers.

67. Elihu Root to John Hay, January 11, 1901, Root Papers.

68. Ibid.

69. Elihu Root, *Military and Colonial Policy of the United States*, ed. Robert Bacon and James Brown Scott (Cambridge, Mass., 1916), pp. 172–173.

70. Elihu Root to Albert Shaw, February 23, 1901, Root Papers; Orville H. Platt, "The Solution of the Cuban Problem," *World's Work* 2 (May 1901): 730–731.

71. Leonard Wood to Elihu Root, January 19, 1901, Wood Papers.

72. *U.S. Statutes at Large*, 21:897–898.

73. *Washington Evening Star*, June 1, 1901, p. 1.

74. Leonard Wood to Elihu Root, March 20, 1901, Root Papers.

75. Orville H. Platt, "Cuba's Claim upon the United States," *North American Review* 175 (August 1902): 146.

5. Context and Content of the Republic

1. In Rafael Martínez Ortiz, *Cuba: Los primeros años de independencia*, 2 vols., 3d ed. (Paris, 1929), 1:41.

2. See Tomás Estrada Palma to Máximo Gómez, January 26, 1899, in Gonzalo de Quesada, *Documentos históricos* (Havana, 1965), p. 8.

3. *New York Times*, December 19, 1898.

4. U.S. War Department, Oficina del Director del Censo de Cuba, *Informe sobre el censo de Cuba, 1899* (Washington, D.C., 1899), pp. 44–45.

5. *Cuba Bulletin* 2 (February 1904): 12.

6. *Commercial and Financial World* 9 (April 7, 1906): 10.

7. Pulaski F. Hyatt and John T. Hyatt, *Cuba: Its Resources and Opportunities* (New York, 1898), p. 95.

8. James L. Hitchman, "U.S. Control over Cuban Sugar Production, 1898–1902," *Journal of Inter-American Studies and World Affairs* 12 (January 1970): 90–106; Atherton Brownell, "The Commercial Annexation of Cuba," *Appleton's Magazine* 8 (October 1906): 409; Zona Fiscal de Manzanillo, "Re-

lación de las fincas que han adquirido en compra los no residentes en la isla de Cuba desde la fecha de la ocupación americana," March 25, 1901, File LMC 1902/31, Records of the Military Government of Cuba, Record Group 140, National Archives, Washington, D.C.

9. Jean Stubbs, *Tobacco on the Periphery: A Case Study in Cuban Labour History, 1860–1958* (Cambridge, Eng., 1985), pp. 22–23; Leland H. Jenks, *Our Cuban Colony* (New York, 1928), p. 157; Brownell, "Commercial Annexation of Cuba," p. 410; Enrique Barbarrosa, *El proceso de la república* (Havana, 1911), pp. 59–61.

10. See Antonio Calvache, *Historia y desarrollo de la minería en Cuba* (Havana, 1944), p. 64; Lisandro Pérez, "Iron Mining and Socio-Demographic Change in Eastern Cuba, 1884–1940," *Journal of Latin American Studies* 14 (November 1982): 390–395; William J. Clark, *Commercial Cuba* (New York, 1898), pp. 402–419.

11. See Jules R. Benjamin, *The United States and Cuba: Hegemony and Dependent Development, 1880–1934* (Pittsburgh, 1974), p. 19.

12. Harry F. Guggenheim, *The United States and Cuba* (New York, 1934), pp. 110–131. Jenks, *Our Cuban Colony*, pp. 164–165; Oscar Pino Santos, *El asalto a Cuba por la oligarquía yanqui* (Havana, 1973), pp. 33–69.

13. See U.S. Congress, Senate, *Cuban Sugar Sales: Testimony Taken by Committee on Relations with Cuba*, 57th Cong., 1st sess., pp. 332, 339–341.

14. U.S. Department of Commerce, *Investment in Cuba* (Washington, D.C., 1956), p. 137.

15. See "Developing Oriente," *Cuba Magazine* 1 (September 1909): 4–7; George Reno, "Oriente, the California of Cuba," *Cuban Review* 25 (August 1927): 14–20; George Fortune, " 'What's Doing' in Cuba for the Younger American," *Cuba Magazine* 3 (February 1912): 336–340; Thomas J. Vivian and Ruel P. Smith, *Everything about Our New Possessions* (New York, 1899), pp. 112–119.

16. Isaac N. Ford, *Tropical America* (New York, 1893), p. 279; Edward Marshall, "A Talk with General Wood," *Outlook* 68 (July 20, 1901): 670.

17. T. Philip Terry, *Terry's Guide to Cuba*, 2d ed. (Boston, 1929), p. 324.

18. See Rolando Alvarez Estevez, *Isla de Pinos el tratado Hay-Quesada* (Havana, 1972), pp. 31–35.

19. Irene Wright, *Cuba* (New York, 1910), p. 322.

20. Sydney A. Clark, *Cuban Tapestry* (New York, 1936), pp. 146–148.

21. Leonard Wood, "The Need for Reciprocity with Cuba," *Independent* 52

(December 12, 1901): 2929; Wright, *Cuba*, pp. 502–504; Lindsay Forbes, *Cuba and Her People of To-day* (Boston, 1911), p. 161.

22. Charles M. Pepper, *Tomorrow in Cuba* (New York, 1899), p. 335, Robert P. Porter, "The Future of Cuba," *North American Review* 153 (April 1899): 420; *New York Tribune*, August 28, 1899; James H. Wilson to Andrew Carnegie, March 16, 1899, Letterbooks, James H. Wilson Papers, Manuscript Division, Library of Congress, Washington, D.C.

23. Alexis E. Frye, *Manual para maestros* (Havana, 1900), pp. 80–86.

24. Carlos Loveira, *Los inmorales* (Havana, 1919), p. 11.

25. William Joseph Showalter, "Cuba—the Sugar Mill of the Antilles," *National Geographic Magazine* 38 (July 1920): 21.

26. Leonard Wood, "Report of Brigadier General Leonard Wood," July 5, 1902, in U.S. War Department, *Civil Report of Brigadier General Leonard Wood, Military Governor of Cuba, for the Period from January 1, to May 20, 1902*, 6 vols. (Washington, D.C., 1902), 1:18.

27. Sylvester Baxter, "The Cuban Teachers at Harvard University," *Outlook* 65 (August 4, 1900): 778; and Medardo Vitier, "En torno a la enseñanza en Cuba durante la República," *Diario de la Marina: Siglo y cuarto* (Havana, 1947), p. 78.

28. Gilbert K. Harroun to F. P. Machado, September 16, 1899, Harroun to John Van R. Hobb, March 22, 1900, General Correspondence, Cuban Educational Association Papers, Manuscript Division, Library of Congress, Washington, D.C. See also Harroun, "The Cuban Educational Association of the United States," *Review of Reviews* 20 (September 1899): 334.

29. Howard B. Grose, *Advance in the Antilles* (New York, 1910), p. 100.

30. Henry L. Moorehouse, *Ten Years in Eastern Cuba* (New York, 1910), p. 11.

31. Richard Aumerle Maher, "Protestanism in Cuba," *Catholic World* 100 (November 1914): 207.

32. Grose, *Advance in the Antilles*, p. 130. See also Sylvester Jones, "Religious Conditions in Cuba," *Missionary Review of the World* 30 (March 1907): 182–188.

33. J. Milton Greene, "What Americans Have Done in Cuba," *Missionary Review of the World* 30 (August 1907): 597.

34. Moorehouse, *Ten Years in Eastern Cuba*, pp. 22–23.

35. Ibid.

36. Grose, *Advance in the Antilles*, p. 112.

37. D. W. Carter, "Cuba and Its Evangelization," *Missionary Review of the World* 25 (April 1902): 257.

38. Margaret E. Crahan, "Religious Penetration and Nationalism in Cuba: U.S. Methodist Activities, 1898–1958," *Revista/Review Interamericana* 8 (Summer 1978): 205–207.

39. Grose, *Advance in the Antilles*, p. 118.

40. Irene A. Wright, "Nipe Bay Country—Cuba," *Pan American Union Bulletin*, June 1911, p. 986; Interview with Edgar G. Nesman, October 27, 1988, Tampa, Florida. Nesman taught at the Agricultural and Industrial School at Preston between 1950 and 1960 and served as its director between 1957 and 1959.

41. U.S. War Department, *Censo de la república de Cuba, 1907* (Washington, D.C., 1908), pp. 572–574.

42. Terry, *Terry's Guide to Cuba*, p. 344.

43. Clark, *Cuban Tapestry*, p. 98.

44. Carlos Martí, *El país de la riqueza* (Madrid, 1918), pp. 110–111.

45. Ariel James, *Banes: Imperialismo y nación en una plantación azucarera* (Havana, 1976), pp. 227–236.

46. Hugh Bradley, *Havana, Cinderella's City* (Garden City, N.Y., 1941), pp. 413–414.

47. Basil Wood, *When It's Cocktail Time in Cuba* (New York, 1928), p. 28.

48. Clark, *Cuban Tapestry*, p. 98.

49. Bruce Bliven, "And Cuba for the Winter," *New Republic* 54 (February 1928): 61.

50. Loveira, *Los inmorales*, p. 12.

51. Harry A. Franck, *Roaming through the West Indies* (New York, 1920), p. 37.

52. Joseph Hergesheimer, *San Cristobal de La Habana* (New York, 1920), p. 145.

53. Quoted in Michael Channan, *The Cuban Image* (Bloomington, 1986), p. 52.

54. Terry, *Terry's Guide to Cuba*, p. 35.

55. Harry F. Guggenheim to Secretary of State, August 9, 1931, 837.00 General Conditions 43, General Records of the Department of State, Record Group 59, National Archives, Washington, D.C.

56. Robert W. Woolley, "America's Bad Faith toward Cuba," *Pearson's Magazine* 13 (June 1910): 716.

57. Herbert G. de Lisser, *In Jamaica and Cuba* (Kingston, 1910), pp. 62, 70.

58. Enrique Collazo, *Los americanos en Cuba* (Havana, 1906); Julio César Gandarilla, *Contra el yanqui* (Havana, 1913).

59. See Manuel Sanguily, "Contra la venta de tierras a los extranjeros," in Hortensia Pichardo, ed., *Documentos para la historia de Cuba*, 2 vols. (Havana, 1965–69), 2:261–263; and Emilio Roig de Leuchsenring, *Tradi-*

ción anti-imperialista de nuestra historia, 2d ed. (Havana, 1977), pp. 115–122; Waldo Frank, *Cuba: Prophetic Island* (New York, 1961), p. 113.

60. Enrique José Varona, *De la colonia a la república* (Havana, 1919), pp. 258–260.

61. Alejo Carpentier, *El recurso del método,* 3d ed. (Madrid, 1976), pp. 251–252.

6. The Purpose of Power

1. Miguel de Carrión, "El desenvolvimiento social de Cuba en los últimos veinte años," *Cuba Contemporánea* 9 (September 1921): 19–20.

2. Manuel Márquez Sterling, *Doctrina de la república* (Havana, 1937), p. 123.

3. Elihu Root, *Military and Colonial Policy of the United States,* ed. Robert Bacon and James Brown Scott (Cambridge, Mass., 1916), p. 100.

4. See Jacob Sleeper to Elihu Root, September 4, 1906, U.S. Department of State, *Foreign Relations of the United States, 1906* (Washington, D.C., 1909), p. 467.

5. Frank Steinhart to William Loeb, Jr., September 8, 1906, Steinhart to Robert Bacon, September 13, 1906, Theodore Roosevelt Papers, Manuscript Division, Library of Congress, Washington, D.C.

6. Hipolito Aranguren et al. to Arthur M. Beaupré, March 22, 1912, 837.00/578, General Records of the Department of State, Record Group 59, National Archives, Washington, D.C. (hereafter cited as DS/RG 59).

7. See José Miguel Gómez to William E. Gonzales, February 19, 1917, in Matias Duque, *Ocios del presidio, 1917* (Havana, 1919), pp. 68–69; Orestes Ferrera and Raimundo Cabrera to Secretary of State, February 16, 1917, 837.00/1239, DS/RG 59.

8. Faustino Guerra to Secretary of State, April 2, 1920, 837.001/1625, DS/RG 59.

9. William Howard Taft to Helen Taft, September 20, 21, 1906, William Howard Taft Papers, Manuscript Division, Library of Congress, Washington, D.C.

10. Ross E. Holaday to Arthur M. Beaupré, June 13, 1912, 837.00/763, DS/RG 59.

11. Ibid.

12. See Arthur M. Beaupré to Secretary of State, June 4, 1912, 837.00/731, DS/RG 59.

13. William E. Gonzales to Secretary of State, October 28, 1914, 837.00/1011, Gonzales to Secretary of State, November 3, 1914, 837.00/1012, DS/RG 59.

14. Philander Knox to Arthur M. Beaupré, June 15, 1912, 837.00/690a, DS/RG 59.

15. Arthur M. Beaupré to Secretary of State, June 6, 1912, 837.00/731, DS/RG 59.

16. Arthur M. Beaupré to Secretary of State, May 4, 1912, 837.5041/22, DS/RG 59.

17. Rutherford Bingham to Secretary of State, January 19, 1919, 837.504/90, DS/RG 59.

18. Harold E. Stephenson to Enoch H. Crowder, December 8, 1920, Correspondence, File 276, Enoch H. Crowder Papers, Western Historical Manuscript Collection, University of Missouri, Columbia.

19. James J. Davis, Secretary, Department of Labor, to Enoch H. Crowder, March 3, 1922, 837.504/235, DS/RG 59.

20. Enoch H. Crowder to Secretary of State, March 3, 1922, 837.504/235, DS/RG 59.

21. William E. Gonzales to Secretary of State, March 9, 1919, 837.504/118, DS/RG 59.

22. Josephus Daniels to Secretary of War, February 2, 1920, 837.504/85, DS/RG 59.

23. Paul W. Beck, "Report on Cuban Strikes since January 1, 1919," April 14, 1919, 837.504/147, DS/RG 59.

24. Consular District of Santiago de Cuba, "Monthly Report on Economic and Political Conditions," January 31, 1919, File (1919) 850, Miscellaneous Correspondence, U.S. Consulate, Santiago de Cuba, Records of the Foreign Service Posts of the Department of State, Record Group 84, National Archives, Washington, D.C.

25. U.S. Army, Department of Santiago and Puerto Príncipe, *Annual Report of Colonel Samuel M. Whitside, 10th U.S. Cavalry, Commanding Department of Santiago and Puerto Príncipe, 1900* (Santiago de Cuba, 1900), pp. 152–153.

26. See "Memorandum on Proposed Legislation Fixing a Minimum Wage for Labor, as Affecting Contracts of American Concerns," July 14, 1910, 837.5041/2, DS/RG 59.

27. F. M. Huntington Wilson to John B. Jackson, July 21, 1910, 837.5041/–, DS/RG 59.

28. "Conversation between Leland Harrison, Assistant Secretary of State,

and John H. Edwards, Consolidated Railroads of Cuba," March 24, 1927, 837.504/308, DS/RG 59.

29. Bainbridge Colby to Woodrow Wilson, July 28, 1920, 837.00/1860s, DS/RG 59; Colby to Francis White, August 25, 1920, 836.00/1737, DS/RG 59; Orestes Ferrara, "Supervisión electoral o intervención permanente," *La Reforma Social* 13 (March 1919): 201–210.

30. Enoch H. Crowder to Secretary of State, March 25, 1922, 837.51/746, DS/RG 59.

31. See Enoch H. Crowder to Alfredo Zayas, April 21, 1922, 837.51/764, DS/RG 59. See also Division of Latin-American Affairs, "Synopsis of General Crowder's 13 Memoranda," November 14, 1923, 123 c 8812/51, DS/RG 59.

32. Enoch H. Crowder to Secretary of State, June 9, 1922, 837.51/786, DS/RG 59.

7. Stirrings of Nationality

1. See Enoch H. Crowder to Secretary of State, August 5, 1924, 837.00/2533, General Records of the Department of State, Record Group 59, National Archives, Washington, D.C. (hereafter cited as DS/RG 59). For a discussion of Machado's views on the Platt Amendment see "Cuba's Dislike of the Platt Amendment," *Literary Digest* 85 (June 6, 1925): 21–22, and Rafael Rodríguez Altunaga, "Cuba's Case for the Repeal of the Platt Amendment: The Views of President Machado," *Current History* 26 (September 1927): 925–927.

2. Gerardo Machado, *Por la patria libre* (Havana, 1926), pp. 14–16; Machado, *Memorias: Ocho años de lucha* (Miami, 1982), p. 11.

3. *The Visit of the President-Elect of Cuba General Gerardo Machado to the United States in April, 1925* (Washington, D.C., 1925), p. 36.

4. José R. Alvarez Díaz et al., *A Study on Cuba* (Coral Gables, 1965), p. 217.

5. See Robert F. Smith, *The United States and Cuba: Business and Diplomacy, 1917–1961* (New Haven, 1960), p. 70.

6. "General Survey of Wages in Cuba, 1931 and 1932," *Monthly Labor Review* 35 (December 1932): 1403–1404, 1409–1411.

7. Smith, *United States and Cuba*, pp. 124–132.

8. Fabio Grobart, "The Cuban Working Class Movement from 1925 to 1933," *Science and Society* 39 (Spring 1975): 89–90.

9. Harry F. Guggenheim to Frank L. Stimson, December 17, 1930, 711.37/ 146, DS/RG 59.
10. See Edward L. Reed to Francis White, September 10, 1930, Francis White Papers, National Archives, Washington, D.C.
11. R. Morgan, "Dr. Fernando Ortiz: Political Situation in Cuba," April 29, 1927, 837.00/2657, DS/RG 59.
12. *Washington Daily News*, April 6, 1929.
13. Lionel Soto, *La revolución del 33*, 3 vols. (Havana, 1977), 2: 98–99.
14. See Henry L. Stimson to Noble Brandon Judah, April 23, 1929, 837.00/ 2730, DS/RG 59.
15. Cordell Hull to Sumner Welles, May 1, 1933, 711.37/178a, DS/RG 59.
16. Manuel Márquez Sterling, "Para la historia del pesimiso en Cuba," August 25, 1916, in Sterling, *Doctrina de la república* (Havana, 1937), pp. 29–34, and Sterling, "Los tres pecados," May 28, 1918, ibid., pp. 294–305.
17. Manuel Douglas, *The Cubans* (New York, 1981), pp. 426, 431; José Soler Puig, *Bertillón 166* (Havana, 1975), pp. 164–165.
18. Sumner Welles to Secretary of State, August 5, 1933, 837.00/3603, DS/ RG 59.
19. *New York Times*, August 7, 1933; Sumner Welles to Cordell Hull, August 7, 1933, 837.00/3606, and August 5, 1933, 837.00/3616, DS/RG 59.
20. Sumner Welles to Cordell Hull, August 8, 1933, 837.00/3616, DS/RG 59; Machado, *Memorias*, p. 125.
21. *New York Times*, August 12, 1933.
22. See Gonzalo de Quesada y Miranda, *¡En Cuba Libre! Historia documentada y anecdótica del machadato*, 2 vols. (Havana, 1938), 2: 243–244; Horacio Ferrer, *Con el rifle al hombro* (Havana, 1950), pp. 321–322; Orestes Ferrara, "Los últimos días del régimen de Machado," *Bohemia* 44 (August 10, 1952): 114.
23. A copy of the proclamation enclosed in Sumner Welles to Cordell Hull, September 5, 1933, 837.00/3753, DS/RG 59. See also Luis E. Aguilar, *Cuba, 1933: Prologue to Revolution* (Ithaca, N.Y., 1972), pp. 163–164.
24. Enrique Lumen, *La revolución cubana, 1902–1934: Crónica de nuestro tiempo* (Mexico, 1934), pp. 149–154; Justo Carrillo, *Cuba 1933: Estudiantes, yanquis y soldados* (Coral Gables, 1985), pp. 267–271, 273–276, 284–288, 343–352.
25. Sumner Welles to Cordell Hull, September 18, 1933, 837.00/3934, Welles to Acting Secretary of State, December 7, 1933, 837.00/4480, DS/RG 59; Welles to Hull, October 16, 1933, U.S. Department of State, *Foreign Rela-*

tions of the United States, 1933, 5 vols. (Washington, D.C., 1952), 5: 487; Welles to Hull, October 13, 1933, 837.00/4193, DS/RG 59.

26. "Memorandum of Telephone Conversation between Secretary of State Hull and Welles," September 5, 1933, 837.00/3757; Welles to Hull, September 5, 1933, 837.00/3756; Welles to Hull, September 7, 1933, 837.00/3778, DS/RG 59.

27. Sumner Welles to Cordell Hull, October 5, 1933, 837.00/4136, DS/RG 59.

28. Lieutenant Colonel T. N. Gimperling, "Army Officers Defy Present Regime," September 11, 1933, File 2012-133(8), Records of the War Department, General and Special Staffs, Record Group 165, National Archives, Washington, D.C. (hereafter cited as WD/RG 165).

29. "Memorandum of Conversation between Secretary Hull at Washington and Ambassador Welles at Habana, by Telephone," September 9, 1933, 837.00/3939, DS/RG 59.

30. *New York Herald Tribune*, September 11, 1933.

31. Lieutenant Colonel T. N. Gimperling, "Army Officers Defy Present Regime," September 11, 1933, File 2012-133(8), WD/RG 165.

32. Quoted in Ruby Hart Phillips, *Cuba: Island of Paradox* (New York, 1959), pp. 90–92. Phillips, the *New York Times* correspondent in Havana, also recalled learning that Welles had promised the officers intervention (ibid., p. 71). See also Alfredo Betancourt to Cordell Hull, November 5, 1933, Cordell Hull Papers, Manuscript Division, Library of Congress, Washington, D.C.

33. Sumner Welles to Cordell Hull, October 4, 1933, 837.00/4131, DS/RG 59. See also Carrillo, *Cuba 1933*, pp. 276–284, 296–302.

34. Sumner Welles to Cordell Hull, October 29, 1933, 837.00/4301, December 5, 1933, 837.00/4475, DS/RG 59.

8. Twilight Years

1. Charles William Taussig, "Cuba–and Reciprocal Trade Agreements," in National Foreign Trade Council, *Official Report of the Twenty-First National Foreign Trade Convention* (New York, 1934), p. 554; Harry F. Guggenheim, "Changes in the Reciprocity Treaty Which Would Probably Benefit the United States Export Trade with Cuba," March 30, 1933, 611.3731/390, General Records of the Department of State, Record Group 59, National Archives, Washington, D.C. (hereafter cited as DS/RG 59).

2. Sumner Welles, *Two Years of the "Good Neighbor" Policy* (Washington, D.C., 1935), p. 7.

3. Susan Schroeder, *Cuba: A Handbook of Historical Statistics* (Boston, 1982), p. 433.

4. International Bank for Reconstruction and Development, *Report on Cuba* (Washington, D.C., 1951), p. 7.

5. "Some Aspects of the Recent Evolution of Cuba's Economy," in United Nations, Economic Commission for Latin America, *Economic Review of Latin America* (Bogotá, 1955), p. 52.

6. U.S. Department of Commerce, *Investment in Cuba* (Washington, D.C., 1956), p. 15.

7. Pablo Armando Fernández, *Los niños se despiden* (Havana, 1968), pp. 294, 298.

8. *Newsweek*, July 4, 1949, p. 36. See also Great Britain, Overseas Economic Survey, *Cuba: Economic and Commercial Conditions in Cuba, 1954* (London, 1954), p. 44.

9. Guillermo Cabrera Infante, *Tres tristes tigres*, 2d ed. (Barcelona, 1971), pp. 157–158, 176.

10. Erna Fergusson, *Cuba* (New York, 1946), p. 104.

11. Consuelo Hermer and Marjorie May, *Havana Mañana: A Guide to Cuba and the Cubans* (New York, 1941), p. 71.

12. Ruby Hart Phillips, *Cuba: Island of Paradox* (New York, 1959), pp. 357–358.

13. See two articles by Roberto Segre, "Continuidad y renovación en la arquitectura cubana del siglo XX," *Santiago* 4 (March 1981): 9–35, and "Contenido de clase en la arquitectura cubana de los años 50," *Revista de la Biblioteca Nacional "José Martí"* 17 (September–December 1975): 97–126.

14. Quoted in Warren Miller, *90 Miles from Home* (New York, 1961), p. 33.

15. Fergusson, *Cuba*, p. 104.

16. Hermer and May, *Havana Mañana*, pp. 44–45.

17. For a complete roster of Cuban ball players in the major leagues see Angel Torres, *La historia del beisbol cubano, 1878–1976* (Los Angeles, 1976), p. 143.

18. Earl Leaf, *Isles of Rhythm* (New York, 1948), p. 40.

19. Marshall W. Stearns, *The Story of Jazz*, 4th ed. (New York, 1962), p. 252.

20. Federal Writers' Project, Tampa, Florida, "Social-Ethnic Study of Ybor City," vol. 2, Unpublished Manuscript, Special Collections, University of South Florida Library, Tampa.

21. See Robert P. Ingalls, *Urban Vigilantes in the New South: Tampa, 1882–1936*

(Knoxville, 1988), and Gene Burnett, "Death and Terror Scar Tampa's Past," *Florida Trend* 18 (December 1975): 76–80.

22. Quoted in Studs Terkel, *Hard Times: An Oral History of the Great Depression* (New York, 1970), p. 125.

23. See the partly autobiographical novel by José Yglesias, *The Truth about Them* (New York, 1971).

24. Federal Writers' Project, Tampa, Florida, pp. 283–284, 177–178, 180, Unpublished Manuscript, Special Collections, University of South Florida Library, Tampa.

25. Rogelio Llopis, "A Horrible Man," in J. M. Cohen, ed., *Writers in the New Cuba* (London, 1967), pp. 140–149; Juan Arcocha, *A Candle in the Wind* (New York, 1967), p. 32; Miller, *90 Miles from Home*, p. 94.

26. The visit of Fidel Castro to Tampa is covered in the *Tampa Tribune*, November 28, 1955.

27. José Yglesias, "The Radical Latino Island in the Deep South," *Nuestro* 1 (August 1977): 6.

28. International Bank for Reconstruction and Development, *Report on Cuba*, pp. 160, 162.

29. U.S. Department of Commerce, *Investment in Cuba*, pp. 5–7, 182; Theodore Draper, *Castroism: Theory and Practice* (New York, 1965), p. 114.

30. José R. Alvarez Díaz et al., *A Study on Cuba* (Coral Gables, 1965), p. 508; U.S. Department of Commerce, *Investment in Cuba*, pp. 104, 107–108, 115, 124.

31. See U.S. Department of Commerce, *Investment in Cuba*, pp. 10–11, 139; Robert F. Smith, *The United States and Cuba: Business and Diplomacy, 1917–1960* (New Haven, 1960), pp. 166–167.

32. International Bank for Reconstruction and Development, *Report on Cuba*, p. 744; U.S. Department of Commerce, *Investment in Cuba*, pp. 140, 143.

33. Phillips, *Cuba*, p. 338.

34. Tad Szulc, "Cuba on Our Mind," *Esquire*, February 1974, p. 91.

35. Fernández, *Los niños se despiden*, p. 229.

36. See Harold B. Quarton, "Cuban Protest American Musicians," December 18, 1929, 837.4038/3, DS/RG 59.

37. Hank Messick, *Lansky* (New York, 1971), p. 89.

38. Martin A. Gosch and Richard Hammer, *The Last Testament of Lucky Luciano* (Boston, 1975), p. 311.

39. Dennis Eisenberg, Uri Dan, and Eli Landau, *Meyer Lansky, Mogul of the Mob* (New York, 1979), pp. 173–175, 226–234, 253–260.

40. Ernest Havemann, "Mobsters Move in on Troubled Havana and Split Rich Gambling Profits with Batista," *Life* 55 (March 10, 1958): 34; *Havana Post*, January 19, 1956.

41. Harry J. Anslinger and Will Oursler, *The Murderers* (New York, 1961), p. 106; Messick, *Lansky*, pp. 135–136.

42. Messick, *Lansky*, pp. 197–198.

43. Ibid., p. 123. A slightly different version of Meyer's mission to Havana is found in Eisenberg, Dan, and Landau, *Meyer Lansky*, pp. 227–228.

44. Arthur M. Schlesinger, Jr., *One Thousand Days* (New York, 1965), p. 165; Antonio Llano Montes, "Tras la noticia," *Carteles*, 38 (May 5, 1957): 32; *Time* 59 (April 21, 1952): 38.

45. Norman Lewis, *Cuban Passage* (New York, 1982), p. 5.

46. U.S. Department of Commerce, *Investment in Cuba*, p. 24.

47. Carlton Bailey Hurst, *The Arms above the Door* (New York, 1932), p. 278.

48. Guillermo Patterson y de Jauregui, "Commercial Relations between Cuba and the United States," *Annals of the American Academy of Political and Social Science* 186 (July 1936): 189.

49. International Bank for Reconstruction and Development, *Report on Cuba*, p. 99.

50. Oscar Pino Santos, "El auge en Cuba de la ventas de plazos," *Carteles* 39 (August 24, 1958): 30–31, 85.

51. Levi Marrero, "¿Por que somos pobres?" *El Mundo*, March 7, 1954, p. A-8; Antonio Llano Montes, "Tras la noticia," *Carteles* 38 (March 24, 1957): 32.

52. Oscar Pino Santos, "665,000 cubanos sin trabajo," *Carteles* 39 (February 16, 1958): 38–40, 100.

53. *New York Times*, January 3, 1951.

54. United Nations, Department of Economic and Social Affairs, *Economic Survey of Latin America for 1954* (New York, 1955), p. 161.

55. Banco Nacional de Cuba, "Temas sobre cuestiones económicas generales: El desarrollo económico de Cuba," *Revista*, March 1956, p. 276.

56. United Nations Economic Commission for Latin America, "Some Aspects of the Recent Evolution of Cuba's Economy," p. 48.

57. International Bank for Reconstruction and Development, *Report on Cuba*, pp. 6–8; U.S. Department of Commerce, *Report on Cuba*, p. 7; Banco Nacional de Cuba, "Temas sobre cuestiones económicas generales," p. 273.

58. Mario Llerena, "Los dos caminos: Política y educación," *Carteles* 37 (April 22, 1956): pp. 14–15, 102.

59. Earl E. T. Smith, *The Fourth Floor* (New York, 1962), pp. 116–118.

60. Phillips, *Cuba*, pp. 324–325.
61. José Suárez Núñez, *El gran culpable* (Caracas, 1963), p. 56.
62. Smith, *Fourth Floor*, pp. 48, 107; Fulgencio Batista, *Respuesta* (Mexico City, 1960), p. 37.
63. *New York Times*, September 15, 1957.
64. See Batista, *Respuesta*, p. 112.
65. U.S. Congress, Senate, *Hearings before the Subcommittee to Investigate the Administration of the Internal Security Act and Other Internal Security Laws of the Committee on the Judiciary: Communist Threat to the United States through the Caribbean*, 86th Cong., 2d sess., pt. 9, p. 687 (hereafter cited as *Hearings*).
66. *Hearings*, pt. 10, p. 739. The Pawley mission is also discussed in Lyman B. Kirkpatrick, Jr., *The Real CIA* (New York, 1968), pp. 178–179, and Dwight D. Eisenhower, *Waging Peace, 1956–1961* (Garden City, N.Y., 1965), p. 521.
67. *Hearings*, pt. 9, p. 687; pt. 10, p. 739.

9. Revolution and Response

1. Susan Schroeder, *Cuba: A Handbook of Historical Statistics* (Boston, 1982), p. 433.
2. For a detailed first-person account of U.S. responses see Philip W. Bonsal, *Cuba, Castro, and the United States* (Pittsburgh, 1972), pp. 70–128.
3. Rolando E. Bonachea and Nelson P. Valdés, eds., *Che: Selected Works of Ernesto Guevara* (Cambridge, Mass., 1969), pp. 246–256.
4. Bonsal, *Cuba, Castro, and the United States*, pp. 145, 149, 151, and Philip W. Bonsal, "Cuba, Castro, and the United States," *Foreign Affairs* 45 (January 1967): 272.
5. Jorge Mañach, "Revolution in Cuba," *Foreign Affairs* 12 (October 1933): 51.
6. Bonsal, *Cuba, Castro, and the United States*, pp. 112, 164.
7. Wayne S. Smith, *The Closest of Enemies: A Personal and Diplomatic History of the Castro Years* (New York, 1987), p. 58.
8. Bonsal, *Cuba, Castro, and the United States*, p. 141.
9. Adolf A. Berle, "The Cuban Crisis," *Foreign Affairs* 39 (October 1960): 46, 47.
10. U.S. Department of State, *Cuba* (Washington, D.C., 1961), pp. 1–3.
11. Bonsal, *Cuba, Castro, and the United States*, p. 141.
12. For a general discussion of the effects of U.S. trade sanctions see Donald

Losman, "The Embargo of Cuba: An Economic Appraisal," *Caribbean Studies* 14 (October 1974): 95–119.

13. See U.S. Congress, Senate, *Alleged Assassination Plots Involving Foreign Leaders* (Washington, D.C., 1975), pp. 71–180; Philip Brenner, "The Assassination Report: Congress and the Investigation of Intelligence," *Cuba Review* 6 (June 1976): 3–15.

14. *Business Week*, May 1, 1971, pp. 88–89; *Cuban Resource Center Newsletter* 2 (July 1972): 10–11; Lourdes Casal, "Cubans in the United States: Their Impact on U.S.-Cuban Relations," in Martin Weinstein, ed., *Revolutionary Cuba in the World Arena* (Philadelphia, 1979), pp. 109–36. See also special supplement, "The Cuban Success: A Realization of the American Dream," *New York Times*, February 9, 1986.

15. Paul Heath Hoeffel, "The Right to Buy," *In These Times*, August 27–September 2, 1980, p. 11. See also Robert L. Bach, "Socialist Construction and Cuban Emigration: Explorations into Mariel," in Miren Uriarte-Gastón and Jorge Canas Martínez, eds., *Cubans in the United States* (Boston, 1984), pp. 36–37.

16. Smith, *Closest of Enemies*, p. 199.

17. Morris H. Morley, *Imperial State and Revolution: The United States and Cuba, 1952–1986* (New York, 1987), p. 195.

18. Edwin M. Martin, "Cuba, Latin America and Communism," September 20, 1963, press release, copy in author's possession; George W. Ball, *U.S. Policy toward Cuba* (Washington, D.C., 1964), pp. 12–13, 18.

19. See Philip Brenner, "Cuba after Fidel," *NACLA: Report on the Americas* 22 (March–April 1988): 4–6, 11.

20. U.S. Department of State, Bureau of Public Affairs, "U.S. Cuban Relations," *GIST*, September 1988.

21. *New York Times*, January 12, 1993, p. A-4.

22. Wayne Smith, "Cuba after the Cold War," *International Policy Report* (March 1993), pp. 4–5.

23. *Tampa Tribune*, June 16, 1993, p. 2.

24. Thomas L. Friedman, "Give That Man a Cigar," *New York Times*, September 29, 1999, p. 9. Emphasis in original.

25. Ronald Reagan, *Reagan on Cuba* (Washington, D.C., 1986), p. 21; George Bush, *Bush on Cuba* (Washington, D.C., 1991), pp. 46, 60.

26. Kenneth N. Skoug, Jr., *The United States and Cuba under Reagan and Shultz: A Foreign Service Officer Reports* (Westport, Conn., 1996), pp. 207, 212.

27. See Phil Johnson, "Hot from Havana," *New Statesman* 127 (August 7, 1998): 38–40; Peter Watrous, "Cuban Bands Find U.S. Fans as Curbs Relax," *New York Times*, April 20, 1998, p. E1.

28. "¡Viva la música cubana!" *Time*, June 22, 1998, p. 67.

29. J. J. Putnam, "Cuba: Evolution in the Revolution," *National Geographic* 195 (June 1999): 2–35; E. L. Rodríguez, "Cuba Golden Era," *Architectural Digest* 56 (November 1999): 78; Cathleen McGuigan, "Saving Havana," *Newsweek*, July 15, 2002, pp. 52–55; Joseph Judge, "The Many Lives of Old," *National Geographic* 176 (August 1989): 278–300; "¡Viva la música cubana!" *Time*, June 22, 1998, pp. 66–68.

30. R. Attaway, "The Old Man and the Boat," *Motor Boat and Sailing* 182 (October 1998): 51–52; W. S. Hylton, "Cuba from Tip to Tip," *Esquire* 133 (April 2000): 56–63.

31. N. Singer, "Cuba: The Taboo Next Door," *Travel Holiday* 183 (October 2000): 77–81.

32. *Cigar Aficionado*, May–June 1999, pp. 62–282; *Cigar Aficionado*, June 2001, pp. 68–152.

33. See Beate Schumann, Paul Fletcher, and Glyn Genin, *Cuba* (Maspeth, N.Y., 2001); Kirsten Ellis, *Cuba Traveler's Companion* (Old Saybrook, Conn., 1999); Stephen Fallon, *Cuba: The Bradt Travel Guide*, 3rd ed. (Guilford, Conn., 2000); Fiona McAuslan et al., *The Rough Guide to Cuba* (New York, 2000); Andy Gravette, *Globetrotter Travel Guide: Cuba*, 2nd ed. (London, 2000); Sarah Cameron, *Footprint Cuba Handbook*, 3rd ed. (Chicago, 2002); Fred Mawer, *Berlitz Cuba Pocket Guide* (Princeton, 2000); Richard Sale, *Essential Cuba*, 2nd ed. (Lincolnwood, Ill., 2000); Neil E. Schlecht and Eliot Grennspan, *Frommer's Cuba* (New York, 2002); Laura M. Kidder, *Fodor's Cuba* (New York, 2000); Paula Diperna, *The Complete Travel Guide to Cuba* (New York, 1988); DK Travel Writers, *Eyewitness Travel Guide to Cuba* (New York, 2002); Christopher Baker, *Moon Handbooks: Cuba*, 2nd ed. (Chico, Calif., 2000).

34. Carlo Gebler, *Driving through Cuba* (New York, 1990); Rosa Jordan and Derek Choukalos, *Lonely Planet Cycling Cuba* (Oakland, Calif., 2002); Wally Smith and Barbara Smith, *Bicycling Cuba: Fifty Days of Detailed Ride Routes from Havana to El Oriente* (Woodstock, Vt., 2002); Diana Williams, *Diving and Snorkeling Cuba* (Oakland, Calif., 1999); Nigel Calder, *Cuba: A Cruising Guide* (Dunedin, Fla., 2000); Simon Charles, *The Cruising Guide to Cuba*, 2nd ed. (Dunedin, Fla., 1997); David Schaefer, *Sailing to Hemingway's Cuba* (Dobb's Ferry, N.Y., 2000); Christopher Howard, *Living and Investing in the "New"*

Cuba: A Guide to Inexpensive Living and Making Money in the Caribbean's Most Beautiful Tropical Paradise (Miami, 1998).

35. *Cigar Aficionado*, May–June 1999, p. 109.

36. See Carolyn Mooney, "Socialism, Salsa and Santería: American Students Have a Rare Encounter with Cuba," *The Chronicle of Higher Education* 42 (June 21, 1996): A43.

Bibliographical Essay

One result of two centuries of the Cuba-U.S. connection has been the accumulation of an extraordinarily rich body of literature on the relations between Cubans and North Americans. This bibliographical essay does not include general histories of Cuba but concentrates instead on works that explicitly address issues derived from the Cuban–North American connection. Nor does it include general studies that treat Cuba in a larger context of U.S. relations with Latin American and / or the Caribbean. Readers interested in the larger regional and policy context should consult David F. Trask, Michael C. Meyer, and Roger R. Trask, eds., *A Bibliography of United States–Latin American Relations since 1810* (Lincoln, 1968). This volume was subsequently augmented by the *Supplement to a Bibliography of United States–Latin American Relations since 1810*, compiled by Michael C. Meyer (Lincoln, 1979). Also useful in this regard is the succinct historiographical summary provided in Carmen Almodóvar Muñoz, "¿Cómo analizan los historiadores cubanos en la 'República' las relaciones surgidas en el 98 entre Cuba y EUA?" *Debates Americanos* 4 (July–December 1997): 157–65.

II

Several noteworthy attempts have been made to provide a comprehensive historical overview of Cuban-U.S. relations. At the time of its appearance, Herminio Portell Vilá, *Historia de Cuba en sus relaciones con los Estados Unidos y España*, 4 vols. (Havana, 1938–41), was unrivaled. Based on prodigious research in Cuba and the United States, the work stood as a model study spanning the period between the late eighteenth and early twentieth centuries. Although it has been surpassed in many ways, it nevertheless remains a standard study and necessary reference work. Also useful is Philip S. Foner, *A History of Cuba and Its Relations with the United States*, 2 vols. (New York, 1962–65), which spans the years between 1492 and the end of the nineteenth century. Emphasis is given to internal Cuban developments and the ways U.S. policy affected the course of events on the island. Michael J. Mazarr, *Semper Fidel: America and Cuba, 1776–1988* (Bal-

311

timore, 1988), is a survey of political relations between the countries. A useful study of U.S. policy toward Cuba, concentrating on the nineteenth and twentieth centuries, is Lester D. Langley, *The Cuban Policy of the United States* (New York, 1968). Jane Franklin, *The Cuban Revolution and the United States: A Chronological History* (Melbourne, 1992), offers a useful chronology of key points in the history of Cuba-U.S. relations up through 1990. Miguel A. D'Estéfano Pisanti, *Dos siglos de diferendo entre Cuba y Estados Unidos* (Havana, 2000), provides a general survey of Cuba-U.S. relations from the colonial period through the 1990s. Half the book is dedicated to the forty years of Cuba-U.S. relations since the triumph of the Cuban revolution in 1959.

Contacts between the countries in the eighteenth century have received increasing attention in recent years. Eduardo J. Tejera, *La ayuda cubana a la lucha por la independencia norteamericana/The Cuban Contribution to the American Independence* (Miami, 1972), is slightly panegyric but provides useful data about the role of Cubans in 1776. By far one of the most comprehensive accounts of trade and commerce during these years is found in María Encarnación Rodríguez Vicente, "El comercio cubano y la guerra de emancipación norteamericana," *Anuario de Estudios Americanos* (Seville) 11 (1954): 66–106. Other useful surveys of eighteenth- and nineteenth-century trade and commerce between Cuba and the United States include René Alvarez Ríos, "Cuba: Desarrollo interno y relaciones con los Estados Unidos de Norteamérica," *Política Internacional* 2 (1964): 59–135; and Roland T. Ely, "The Old Cuba Trade: Highlights and Case Studies of Cuban-American Interdependence during the Nineteenth Century," *Business History Review* 38 (Winter 1964): 456–78. The literature dealing with the nineteenth century offers the reader a vast selection from many different vantage points. One of the more useful surveys of nineteenth century, Emilio Roig de Leuchsenring, *Cuba y los Estados Unidos, 1805–1898* (Havana, 1949), provides a critique of U.S. policy and defense of Cuban efforts at self-determination with emphasis on politics and diplomacy. The critical middle decades of the nineteenth century, the years of peak annexationist conspiracies and filibustering activities, are well treated in the literature. Although somewhat dated and in many ways surpassed by Cuban scholarship, Basil Rauch, *American Interests in Cuba, 1848–1855* (New York, 1948), remains one of the most detailed accounts in English for these years. Emeterio S. Santovenia, *El presidente Polk y Cuba* (Havana, 1936), is a useful study of U.S. policy during midcentury, with specific attention to North American efforts to acquire the island in 1848. Still unrivaled in the sweep of interpretation and thoroughness of the research is Herminio Portell Vilá, *Narciso López y su época*, 3 vols. (Havana, 1930–58). Not all will agree with the liberating role in which Portell Vilá casts López, but the arguments are thoughtful and suggestive. Perhaps the most useful and complete account of the López expeditions is found in the thoroughly researched account by Tom Chafin, *Fatal Glory: Narciso López and the First Clandestine U.S. War against Cuba* (Charlottesville, 1996).

III

Perhaps at no other point did Cuban and North American interests reach as much parity—as measured by the sheer volume of scholarship—as in the events of 1895 to 1902. These were the decisive years of the Cuban struggle for independence and nationality. In the United States, the period has been associated with the war with Spain and a newfound sense of international importance. Older useful works include French Ensor Chadwick, *The Relations of the United States and Spain: The Spanish-American War*, 2 vols. (New York, 1911); Andrew S. Draper, *The Rescue of Cuba* (New York, 1899); Walter Millis, *The Martial Spirit: A Study of Our War with Spain* (Boston, 1931); Albert G. Robinson, *Cuba and the Intervention* (London, 1905); and Richard N. Titherington, *A History of the Spanish-American War of 1898* (New York, 1900).

One of the better recent studies is David F. Healy, *The United States in Cuba, 1898–1902* (Madison, 1963). Healy's approach is balanced and his assessments judicious. He examines the genesis and evolution of U.S. policy during the critical occupation years. James H. Hitchman, *Leonard Wood and Cuban Independence, 1898–1902* (The Hague, 1971) and "The American Touch in Imperial Administration: Leonard Wood in Cuba, 1898–1902," *Americas* 24 (April 1968): 394–403, presents a sympathetic view of the North American military occupation and especially of the role of Leonard Wood. In contrast, Philip S. Foner, *The Spanish-Cuban-American War and the Birth of American Imperialism, 1895–1902*, 2 vols. (New York, 1972), and Jack C. Lane, "Instrument for Empire: The American Military Government in Cuba, 1899–1902," *Science and Society* 36 (Fall 1972): 314–30, are critical of U.S. policy toward Cuban independence. Louis A. Pérez, Jr., *Cuba between Empires, 1878–1902* (Pittsburgh, 1983), examines the way the North American presence influenced the course of events in Cuba during the late nineteenth century.

Among the most representative of the older Cuban literature are Raúl Cárdenas, *Cuba no puede invocarse en testimonio del imperialismo norteamericano* (Havana, 1917); Tiburcio P. Castaneda, *La explosión del Maine y la guerra de los Estados Unidos contra España* (Havana, 1925); Alvaro Catá, *Cuba y la interven-*

ción (Havana, 1899); Severo Gómez Muñiz, *La guerra hispano-americana*, 5 vols. (Madrid, 1899–1902); the two studies by Rafael Martínez Ortiz, *Cuba: Los primeros años de independencia*, 2 vols., 3d ed. (Paris, 1929) and *General Leonard Wood's Government in Cuba* (Paris, 1920); Jorge H. Piloto, *Mayor General James Harrison Wilson, el buen amigo de los cubanos* (Matanzas, 1934); Enrique Piñeyro, *Como acabó la dominación de España en América* (Paris, 1908); and Cosme de la Torriente, *Fin de la dominación de España en Cuba* (Havana, 1948) and *Calixto García cooperó con las fuerzas armadas de los Estados Unidos en 1898, cumpliendo órdenes del gobierno cubano* (Havana, 1950).

A significant historiographical shift in Cuba began during the 1930s and 1940s, as a new generation of scholars challenged existing interpretations. Revisionist historiography rejected the role of the United States as liberator and portrayed the Cubans as already having defeated Spain in 1898 and therefore owing nothing to the North Americans. The best single account of these shifting historiographical currents is Duvon C. Corbitt, "Cuban Revisionist Interpretations of Cuba's Struggle for Independence," *Hispanic American Historical Review* 43 (August 1963): 395–404.

Perhaps no one is more closely associated with revisionist historiography than Emilio Roig de Leuchsenring. Roig addressed many of the most critical issues bearing on the Cuba-U.S. connection. Among the most important are *Cuba no debe su independencia a los Estados Unidos*, 3d ed. (Havana, 1960); *Los Estados Unidos contra Cuba Libre* (Havana, 1960); *La guerra hispano-cubano-americana fué ganada por el lugarteniente general del ejército libertador Calixto García Iñiguez* (Havana, 1955); *La lucha cubana por la república, contra la anexión y la enmienda Platt, 1899–1902* (Havana, 1952); *Por su propio esfuerzo conquistó el pueblo cubano su independencia* (Havana, 1957); and *El presidente McKinley y el gobernador Wood, máximos enemigos de Cuba Libre* (Havana, 1960).

The centennial observation of 1898 stimulated a new interest in the Cuban war for independence and the North American military intervention in Cuba, Spain, and the United States. Louis A. Pérez, Jr., *The War of 1898: The United States and Cuba in History and Historiography* (Chapel Hill, 1998), examines the multiple interpretations and historiographical forms associated with representations of the war. Oscar Luis Abdala Pupo, *La intervención militar nortamericana en la contienda independentista cubana: 1898* (Santiago de Cuba, 1998), provides thoughtful attention to the military aspects of joint Cuban and U.S. operations in eastern Cuba. Jorge Ibarra Cuesta, *Máximo Gómez: Frente al imperio, 1898–1905* (Havana, 2000), provides a detailed examination of the relationship between General Gómez and military and civil authorities of the United States. Some of the racial dimensions of the U.S. presence and policy in Cuba are explored in Eliades Acosta Matos, *Los colores secretos del imperio* (Havana, 2002). The publication of the proceedings of three academic conferences address a wide range of issues pertaining to the social, economic, political, and military aspects of 1898: Consuelo Naranjo Orovio, Miguel A. Puig-Samper, and Luis Miguel García Mora, eds., *La nación soñada: Cuba, Puerto Rico y Filipinas ante el 98* (Madrid, 1996); Angel Smith and Emma Dávila-Cox, eds., *The Crisis of 1898: Colonial Redistribution and National Mobilization* (New York, 1999); and Virginia M. Bouvier, ed., *Whose America? The War of 1898 and the Battles to Define the Nation* (Westport, Conn., 2001). Articles of interest published in the larger context of the centennial observations of 1898 include Enrique Baltar Rodríguez, "El contexto internacional del 98: Imperialismo y reparto colonial," *Debates Americanos* 4 (July–December 1997): 7–20; and José Tabare del Real, "Estados Unidos, la sociedad política norteamericana y el '98," *Debates Americanos* 4 (July–December 1997): 21–32. Participants in "Significación del 98: Mesa redonda entre historiadores acerca de un centenario de entre siglos," *Debates Americanos* 4 (July–December 1997): 179–94, include María del Carmen Barcia, Francisco Pérez Guzmán, Pedro Pablo Rodríguez, and Oscar Zanetti Lecuona. Other articles include Oscar Zanetti Lecuona, "Nación y modernización: Significados del 98," *Debates Americanos* 5–6 (January–December 1998): 3–18; Pedro Pablo Rodríguez, "Modernidad y 98 en Cuba: Alternativas y contradicciones," *Temas* 12–13 (October 1997–March 1998): 13–18; Jorge Ramírez Calzadilla, "Impactos de los 98 en el campo religioso cubano," *Temas* 12–13 (October 1997–March 1998): 34–41; and Louis A. Pérez, Jr., "Incurring a Debt of Gratitude: 1898 and the Moral Sources of United States Hegemony in Cuba," *American Historical Review* 104 (April 1999): 356–98.

IV

Nothing preoccupied Cubans more or engaged their attention for ao long a time as the Platt Amendment. Indeed, no single aspect of relations with the United States so offended Cuban sensibilities as the Platt Amendment. Until its final abrogation in 1934, Cubans pondered the circumstances of its conception and the intent of its imposition, disputed interpretations of its application, and otherwise challenged its provisions on legal, political, and moral grounds. Among the most prominent Cuban works in the first category are Enrique Gay, "Génesis de la enmienda Platt," *Cuba Contemporánea* 60 (May–August 1926): 47–63; Manuel Sanguily, "Sobre la génesis de la enmienda Platt," *Cuba Contemporánea* 30 (October 1922): 117–25; Emilio Roig Leuchsenring, *Historia de la enmienda Platt*, 2 vols., 2d ed. (Havana, 1961) and "La enmienda Platt, consecuencia y ratificación de la inalterable política seguida por el estado norteamericano contra Cuba desde 1805," *Universidad de La Habana* 7 (January–February 1935): 119–47. Works in the second category are Luis Machado y Ortega, *La enmienda Platt, estudio de su alcance e interpretación y doctrina sobre su aplicación* (Havana, 1922), and Emilio Roig de Leuchsenring, "La enmienda Platt: Su interpretación primitiva y sus aplicaciones posteriores," *Cuba Contemporánea* 29 (1922): 197–224, 305–336. Among the latter works are Ambrosio López Hidalgo, *Cuba y la enmienda Platt* (Havana, 1921); Manuel Márquez Sterling, *Proceso histórico de la enmienda Platt (1897–1934)* (Havana, 1934); Pedro Capo Rodríguez, "The Platt Amendment," *Current History* 26 (September 1927): 925–27; and Cosme de la Torriente, *La enmienda Platt* (Havana, 1930) and "The Platt Amendment," *Foreign Affairs* 8 (April 1930): 364–78. Interest in the Platt Amendment increased in the United States after 1959. Lejune Cummins, "The Formulation of the 'Platt Amendment,'" *Americas* 23 (April 1967): 370–89, examines in detail the origins and authorship of the amendment. Louis A. Pérez, Jr., *Cuba under the Platt Amendment, 1902–1934* (Pittsburgh, 1986), looks at the changing interpretations of the amendment over its life and the consequences in Cuba of its application. Florence Hellman, *List of References on the Platt Amendment* (Washington, D.C., 1934), and James H. Hitchman, "The Platt Amendment Revisited: A Bibliographical Survey," *Americas* 33 (April 1967): 343–69, provide useful bibliographical compilations of the vast Platt Amendment literature.

V

The discussion of the Platt Amendment has served as background to another important theme in the Cuba-U.S. historiography, the issue of North American intervention. A large part of this inquiry has focused on intervention as a military phenomenon, that is, the landing of North American armed forces to occupy the island, as in the "second intervention" (1906–9), and localized armed landings to protect North American lives and property during political disorders in 1912 and 1917–22. Politico-diplomatic intervention occurred during the 1933 crisis. The second intervention has been treated in both countries, not, of course, with similar interpretations but with equal interest. David A. Lockmiller, *Magoon in Cuba: A History of the Second Intervention, 1906–1909* (Chapel Hill, 1938), has been superseded by Allan Reed Millett, *The Politics of Intervention: The Military Occupation of Cuba, 1906–1909* (Columbus, Ohio, 1968). Both emphasize the formulation and implementation of U.S. policy and draw largely from North American manuscripts and archival sources. José M. Hernández, *Cuba and the United States: Intervention and Militarism, 1868–1933* (Austin, 1993), deals principally with the years between 1898 and 1909.

Cuban works on the events of 1906–9 see the second intervention from an entirely different perspective. Greater emphasis is given to the dynamics of local politics and the Cuban role in the settlement. As the object of U.S. military intervention and foreign rule, moreover, Cubans have paid greater attention to the consequences of the North American presence. Older works include Enrique Collazo, *La revolución de agosto de 1906* (Havana, 1906), and Rafael Martínez Ortiz, "Juicio acerca de los sucesos políticos de Cuba en 1906," *Cuba Contemporánea* 15 (October 1917): 118–30. Some of the better recent studies include Jorge Ibarra, "Agosto de 1906: Una intervención amañada," *Revista de la Biblioteca Nacional "José Martí"* 64 (January–April 1973): 161–86; and Teresita Yglesia Martínez, *Cuba: Primera república, segunda ocupación* (Havana, 1977). Comparatively little has been written about the U.S. intervention in 1912 except as a peripheral aspect of political disorders. The intervention of 1917–22 (the "sugar intervention") is examined in George Baker, "The Wilson Administration and Cuba, 1913–1921," *Mid America* 46 (January 1964): 48–63; and Louis A. Pérez, Jr., *Intervention, Revolution, and Politics in Cuba, 1913–1921* (Pittsburgh, 1978). Somewhat dated but still useful is Leo J. Meyer, "The United States and the Cuban Revolution of 1917," *Hispanic American Historical Review* 10 (February 1930): 138–66; and Bernardo Merino and F. de Ibarzabal, *La revolución de febrero: Datos para la historia*, 2d ed. (Havana, 1918).

The events of 1933 have also received growing attention in recent years. Among the more useful historical accounts of 1933 are Luis E. Aguilar, *Cuba 1933* (Ithaca, N.Y., 1972); E. David Cronon, "Interpreting the New Good Neighbor Policy: The Cuban Crisis of 1933," *Hispanic American Historical Review* 39 (November 1959): 538–67; and William S. Stokes, "The Welles Mission to Cuba," *Central America and Mexico* 1 (December 1953): 3–21. Irwin F. Gellman, *Roosevelt and Batista: Good Neighbor Diplomacy in Cuba, 1933–1945* (Albuquerque, 1973), traces the events of 1933 through the 1940s. Jorge Renato Ibarra Guitart, *La mediación del 33: Ocaso del machadato* (Havana, 1999), provides a detailed and thoughtful account of the U.S.-sponsored mediations of June–August 1933 leading to the collapse of the government of Gerardo Machado.

During these years, the construct of intervention has undergone considerable change. Scholars have embraced a broader meaning of the notion of intervention, something suggesting considerably more than the landing of armed force and seizure of customs houses. Dependency formulations have opened new avenues of inquiry. New understanding of cultural penetration provides new perspectives. Increasingly, North American intervention is understood as a process, not an event, in which national structures and international relationships are seen as underwriting North American hegemony. In the context of Cuban–North American relations, these formulations are most apparent during the Plattist republic. Indeed, because the exercise of North American hegemony emerged so strongly during these decades, even casual contemporary observers with a critical eye could lay the groundwork for approaches that would follow decades later. Leland H. Jenks, *Our Cuban Colony* (New York, 1928), was among the first to explore the dynamic of U.S. hegemony in a political, economic, and social context. Cuban writers were especially mindful of the immediate impact and long-term consequences of the North American presence. These concerns were very much on the Cuban mind, as indicated in the following works: Fernando Ortiz, *Las responsibilidades de los Estados Unidos en los males de Cuba* (Washington, D.C., 1932); Emilio Roig de Leuchsenring, "La ingerencia norteamericana en los asuntos interiores de Cuba," *Cuba Contemporánea* 30 (September 1922): 36–61; and Leuchsenring, *Análisis y consecuencias de la intervención norteamericana en los asuntos interiores de Cuba* (Havana, 1923). Dependency constructs serve as the explicit analytical framework for Francisco López Segrera, *Cuba: Capitalismo dependiente y subdesarollo* (Havana, 1972), and Julio E. LeRiverend, *La república: Dependencia y república,* 3d ed. (Havana, 1971). A useful survey of U.S. intervention is Oscar Pino Santos, "Intervencionismo en Cuba: De Magoon a Batista," *Casa de las Américas* 14 (September–October 1973): 48–61.

Recent scholarship in the United States has also taken a larger view and a broader perspective on the issue of intervention. One important contribution to this literature is Jules R. Benjamin, *The United States and Cuba: Hegemony and Dependent Development, 1880–1934* (Pittsburgh, 1977). A highly informative examination of U.S. efforts to promote democracy in Cuba in the course of the twentieth century is found in Lars Schoultz, "Blessings of Liberty: The United States and the Promotion of Democracy in Cuba," *Journal of Latin American Studies* 34 (May 2002): 397–425. Carlos Alzugaray, *Crónica de un fracaso imperial* (Havana, 2000), offers a detailed examination of U.S. policy during the years of the government of Fulgencio Batista (1952–1958), with a particular focus on U.S. efforts to prevent the triumph of the revolutionary movement. Other aspects of U.S. intervention have also come under scrutiny. North American electoral machinations have been the object of several essays in both Cuba and the United States, including Theodore P. Wright, Jr., "United States Electoral Intervention in Cuba,"

Inter-American Economic Affairs 13 (Winter 1959): 50–71. An informative account of U.S. migration to Cuba after 1898 is found in Carmen Diana Deere, "Here Come the Yankees! The Rise and Decline of United States Colonies in Cuba, 1898–1930," *Hispanic American Historical Review* 78 (November 1998): 729–65.

Increasingly, too, attention has turned to bilateral cultural relations, on the impact of popular culture, sports, music, religion, and education on the relationship between both people. Louis A. Pérez, Jr., *On Becoming Cuba: Identity, Nationality, and Culture* (Chapel Hill, 1999), examines the multiple facets of these processes during the nineteenth and the first half of the twentieth century. Rafael Hernández, ed., *Mirar el Niagara: Huellas culturales entre Cuba y los Estados Unidos* (Havana, 2000), offers a collection of essays examining Cuban women travelers to the United States, the establishment of North American agricultural colonies in Cuba, U.S. Protestant missionary presence on the island, the study of the sciences and social sciences in Cuba, and the plastic arts in Cuba. The volume edited by Rafael Hernández and John H. Coatworth, *Culturas encontradas: Cuba y los Estados Unidos* (Havana, 2001), includes a number of essays treating variously music, art, literature, religion, and race as factors in relations between Cuba and the United States.

VI

The role of the United States in the Cuban economy has long absorbed the attention of scholars on both sides of the Florida Straits. Several general works provide useful surveys. Robert F. Smith, "Cuba: Laboratory for Dollar Diplomacy, 1898–1917," *Historian* 27 (August 1966): 586–609, and *The United States and Cuba: Business and Diplomacy, 1917–1960* (New Haven, 1960), are highly readable and well-researched accounts of twentieth-century trade and investment. Older but still useful are several essays published in Cuba: Luis Marino Pérez, "Las relaciones económicas entre Cuba y los Estados Unidos," *Cuba Contemporánea* 28 (April 1922): 264–70; and Harold S. Sloan, "Los efectos de las inversiones norteamericanas en Cuba," *Cuba Contemporánea* 44 (June–July–August 1927): 150–61.

North American economic penetration of Cuba received increased attention after 1959, especially in Cuba. The more useful works include Oscar Pino Santos, *El imperialismo yanqui en la economía de Cuba* (Havana, 1960), *El asalto a Cuba por la oligarquía financiera yanqui* (Havana, 1973), and "El imperialismo yanqui y el caso de Cuba," *Casa de las Américas* 10 (May–June 1970): 31–51; Julio E.

LeRiverend, "La penetración extranjera económica en Cuba," *Revista de la Biblioteca Nacional "José Martí"* 3 (January–March 1966): 5–20; and Nelson H. González, "Las relaciones económicas Cuba-EE.UU., 1902–1958," *Economía y Desarrollo* 46 (March–April 1978): 123–36. Cubans have published case studies examining important facets of the U.S. economic presence on the island. Enrique Collazo, *Una pelea cubana contra los monopolios (Un estudio sobre el crac bancario de 1920)* (Obviedo, 1994), examines the role of U.S. finance capital in the "Dance of the Millions" and the subsequent financial collapse between 1920 and 1921. Among the most important studies of the United Fruit Company in Cuba include Alejandro García and Oscar Zanetti, *United Fruit Company: Un caso del dominio imperialista en Cuba* (Havana, 1976); Ariel James, *Banes: Imperialismo y nación en una plantación azucarera* (Havana, 1976); Sergio Guerra and Rosa Pulpeiro, "Política domográfica de la United Fruit," *Universidad de La Habana* 200 (March 1973): 60–92; and Oscar Pino Santos, "Los mecanismos imperialistas de apropriación de la tierra en Cuba (caso de la United Fruit Co.)," *Santiago* 23 (September 1976): 181–90. Other informative case studies include Erasmo Dumpierre, "El monopolio de la Cuban Telephone Company," *Bohemia* 67 (September 12, 1975): 88–92; Dumpierre, "El monopolio de la Standard Oil Company en Cuba," *Bohemia* 66 (November 15, 1974): 88–92; Dumpierre, *La ESSO en Cuba: Monopolio y república burguesa* (Havana, 1984); Jesús A. Chía Garzón, *El monopolio del jabón y el perfume en Cuba* (Havana, 1977); and Fe Iglesias, "La explotación de hierro en el sur de Oriente y la Spanish American Iron Company," *Santiago* 17 (March 1975): 59–106. Antonio Vázquez Galego, *La consolidación de los monopolios en Camagüey en la década del 20* (Havana, 1975), deals principally with sugar and railroads. A collection of case studies published under the auspices of the Cuban Academy of Sciences, *Monopolios norteamericanos en Cuba* (Havana, 1973), deals with soap and perfume manufacturing, petroleum, and utilities. Along similar lines, a collection of essays by Soviet investigators, translated by Félix de la Uz, appeared in Spanish as *Los monopolios extranjeros en Cuba, 1898–1958* (Havana, 1984) and examines banking and finance, sugar, manufacturing, and soap production.

VII

Relations between Cuba and the United States changed dramatically after 1959. A vast literature treats two distinct aspects of relations after 1959: the years of conflict and the break of diplomatic relations (1959–61) and Cuba-U.S. relations thereafter. The literature can be arranged into four distinct groupings: (1) works dealing principally with the first two years of the Cuban revolution and relations during these years; (2) general accounts of relations between the early 1960s and the turn of the century; (3) works treating the Bay of Pigs *(Playa Girón)*; and (4) accounts of U.S. covert activities against Cuba.

The early literature was very much caught up in the debate of the time, unabashedly on one side or the other. Some of it was openly polemical and provocative, and today its principal value is largely as a gauge of the tenor of the times. Accounts sympathetic to Cuba include William Appleman Williams, *The United States, Cuba, and Castro* (New York, 1962), and C. Wright Mills, *Listen, Yankee* (New York, 1960). The literature critical of U.S. policy as insufficiently hard-line includes Mario Lazo, *Dagger in the Heart: American Policy Failures in Cuba* (New York, 1968), and Nathaniel Weyl, *Red Star over Cuba* (New York, 1961).

Among the better recent accounts of the early years are Richard E. Welch, Jr., *Response to Revolution: The United States and the Cuban Revolution, 1959–1961* (Chapel Hill, 1985), and Cole Blasier, "The Elimination of United States Influence," in Carmelo Mesa-Lago, ed., *Revolutionary Change in Cuba* (Pittsburgh, 1971), 43–80. Thomas G. Paterson, *Contesting Castro: The United States and the Triumph of Cuban Revolution* (New York, 1994), is an excellent account of the U.S. response to the Cuban revolution during the final days of the government of Fulgencio Batista and the early months of the Castro government. Some of the better surveys of the years after the revolution include Wayne S. Smith, "U.S.-Cuba Relations: Twenty-Five Years of Hostility," in Sandor Halebsky and John M. Kirk, eds., *Cuba: Twenty-Five Years of Revolution, 1959–1984* (New York, 1985), 333–51; John Plank, ed., *Cuba and the United States: Long Range Perspectives* (Washington, D.C., 1967); Robert D. Crassweller, *Cuba and the United States: The Tangled Relationship* (New York, 1976); Lynn Darrell Bender, *The Politics of Hostility: Castro's Revolution and U.S. Policy* (Hato Rey, P.R., 1975); and Morris H. Morley, *Imperial State and Revolution: The United States and Cuba, 1952–1986* (New York, 1987). A useful survey of U.S. policy toward Cuba during the early years of the revolution is found in Ana Julia Faya, *El despliegue de un conflicto: La política norteamericana hacia Cuba* (Havana, 1996). A survey of forty years of U.S. policy as it responded to the person of Fidel Castro is found in Louis A. Pérez, Jr., "Fear and Loathing of Fidel Castro: Sources of U.S. Policy toward Cuba," *Journal of Latin American Studies* 34 (May 2002): 227–54.

A number of informative works treat various aspects of Cuba-U.S. relations in the post–cold war years. Of particular use is Rafael Hernández, "Frozen Relations: Washington and Cuba after the Cold War," *NACLA: Report on the Americas* 35 (January–February 2002): 21–26. Prepared under the auspices of the Centro de Estudios sobre Estados Unidos (CESEU) at the University of Havana, the volume *El conflicto Estados Unidos–Cuba* (Havana, 1998) examines a variety of aspects about the relations between the two countries principally in the 1990s, including such themes as the Helms-Burton Law, drug policy, Radio Martí, and migration. Another useful general account includes José Cantón Navarro, *Cuba, el desafío del yugo y la estrella: Biografía de un pueblo* (Havana, 1996). Also useful is Olga Mirando Bravo, *Cuba/U.S.A.: Nacionalizaciones y bloqueo* (Havana, 1996). Aspects of new initiatives from Washington are examined in Philip Brenner, "Washington Loosens the Knots (Just a Little)," *NACLA: Report on the Americas* 32 (March–April 1999): 41–47. Relations between both countries during the 1990s are examined expertly by Soraya M. Castro Mariño, "U.S.-Cuban Relations during the Clinton Administration," *Latin American Perspectives* 29 (July 2002): 47–76.

Several accounts of these years treat specific aspects of Cuba-U.S. relations. Donald Losman, "The Embargo of Cuba: An Economic Appraisal," *Caribbean Studies* 14 (October 1974): 95–119, is a thoughtful analysis of North American efforts to overthrow the revolutionary government through economic warfare. Susan Fernández, "The Sanctity of Property: American Responses to Cuban Expropriations, 1959–1984," *Cuban Studies/Estudios Cubanos* 14 (Summer 1984): 21–34, traces the negotiations, formal and informal, between Havana and Washington concerning compensation for expropriated U.S. property. Leland L. Johnson, "U.S. Business Interests in Cuba and the Rise of Castro," *World Politics* 17 (April 1965): 440–59, examines the role played by U.S. investments in the course of relations between Cuba and the United States during the early years of the revolution. Roger W. Fontaine, *On Negotiating with Cuba* (Washington, D.C., 1975), sought to develop an agenda for the normalization of relations. Perhaps the most comprehensive study of Helms-Burton is found in Joaquín Roy, *Cuba, the United States, and the Helms-Burton Doctrine* (Gainesville, 2000). Also of value is Miriam Sofía Quintana Rodríguez, *Cuba, Estados Unidos y la Helms-Burton* (Havana, 1997); William M. Leogrande, "Enemies Evermore: U.S. Policy towards Cuba after Helms-Burton," *Journal of Latin American Studies* 29 (February 1997): 211–22; and Wayne S. Smith, "Our Dysfunctional Cuban Embargo," *Orbis* 42 (Fall 1998): 533–45. The volume edited by Wayne S. Smith and Esteban Morales Domínguez, *Subject to Solution: Problems in Cuban-U.S. Relations* (Boulder, 1988), treats a wide range of topics, including the trade embargo, telecommunications, the Guantánamo naval station, and economic questions. The volume edited by Joseph S. Tulchin and Rafael Hernández, *Cuba and the United States: Will the Cold War in the Caribbean End?* (Boulder, 1991), provides a series of essays examining economic developments, domestic politics, and the process of policy formulation. Of particular value for Soviet perspectives on the missile crisis is A. V. Fursenko, *"One Hell of a Gamble": Khruschev, Castro, and Kennedy, 1958–1964* (New York, 1997).

In recent years, a number of important books have appeared dealing with the October missile crisis of 1962. *Peligros and principios: La Crisis de Octubre desde Cuba* (Havana, 1992) provides perspective and documents from Cuban sources. Two important collections of previously classified U.S. documents, including materials from the State Department, the National Security Council, and the Central Intelligence Agency, are found in Laurence Chang and Peter Kornbluh, eds., *The Cuban Missile Crisis, 1962: A National Security Archive Documents Reader* (New York, 1992), and Mary S. McAuliffe, ed., *CIA Documents on the Cuban Missile Crisis 1962* (Washington, D.C., 1992). Still one other location where the interests of Cuba and the United States clashed head-on was in Africa. The details of the Cuban presence in Africa within the larger framework of global politics are carefully and convincingly examined in Piero Gleijeses, *Conflicting Missions: Havana, Washington, and Africa, 1959–1976* (Chapel Hill, 2002).

Perhaps few aspects of the post-1959 period have attracted as much attention as the ill-fated Bay of Pigs invasion. A distinct if not obvious difference of emphasis and approach characterizes treatments by Cubans and North Americans. Cuban accounts deal principally with operational issues; those by Americans stress policy formulation and implementation. Haynes B. Johnson, *The Bay of Pigs* (New York, 1964), is a useful journalistic account of the invasion based largely on interviews with the members of the U.S.-organized brigade and on published materials. It has been superseded by Peter Wyden, *Bay of Pigs: The Untold Story* (New York, 1979), which relies on interviews with participants on both sides and materials obtained through the Freedom of Information Act. An important document collection is Paramilitary Study Group, *Operation Zapata: The "Ultrasensitive" Report and Testimony of the Board of Inquiry on the Bay of Pigs* (Frederick, Md., 1981). Another important source is E. Howard Hunt, *Give Us This Day* (New Rochelle, N.Y., 1973), a first-person account by a key CIA organizer. Cuban accounts of the Bay of Pigs include Justina Alvarez, *Heroes eternas de la patria* (Havana, 1964); Rafael del Pino, *Amanecer en Girón* (Havana, 1964); Raul González, *Gente de Playa Girón* (Havana, 1962); Lisandro Otero, *Playa Girón, derrota del imperialismo*, 4 vols. (Havana, 1961–62); Sergio Aguirre, "Actualidad de la Bahía de Cochinos," *Universidad de La Habana*, vols. 186–88 (July–December 1967): 59–70; Quintín Pino, *La batalla de Girón: Razones de una victoria* (Havana, 1983); Elio Carré Lazcano, *Girón: Una estocada a fondo* (Havana, 1975); and Jesús Arboleya Cervera, "Playa

Girón: Kennedy ante un dilema," *Debates Americanos* 10 (July–December 2000): 39–45. The volume *Politics of Illusion: The Bay of Pigs Invasion Reexamined*, edited by James G. Blight and Peter Kornbluh (Boulder, Colo., 1998), provides a mixture of declassified documents, narratives, maps, and meeting transcripts involving first-person accounts from all sides of the Bay of Pigs invasion—U.S., Cuban exile, Cuban, and Soviet—thereby offering a highly informative body of information on the events leading to and immediately following April 1961.

Accounts of U.S. covert operations against Cuba during the 1960s and 1970s include Bradley Earl Ayers, *The War That Never Was: An Insider's Account of CIA Covert Operations against Cuba* (Indianapolis, 1976); Warren Hinckle and William W. Turner, *The Fish Is Red: The Story of the Secret War against Castro* (New York, 1981); and Taylor Branch and George Crile, "The Kennedy Vendetta," *Harper's*, August 1975, pp. 172–82. Jon Elliston, *Psywar on Cuba: The Declassified History of U.S.-Anti-Castro Propaganda* (Melbourne, 1999), provides a useful collection of documents chronicling U.S. covert operations and destabilizing projects against Cuba spanning from the early 1960s through the mid-1990s. William B. Breur, *Vendetta! Fidel Castro and the Kennedy Brothers* (New York, 1997), examines U.S.-Cuba relations in the early 1960s, especially after the Bay of Pigs, with a particular emphasis on covert operations undertaken in the Kennedy White House. Also useful for these isses is Tomás Diez Acosta, *La guerra encubierta contra Cuba* (Havana, 1997), and Roberto Orihuela, *Terrorismo made in U.S.A.* (Havana, 2000).

The literature dealing with Cuba-U.S. relations is also rich with first-person accounts by North American diplomats. Unfortunately, nothing similar exists for the Cuban side. Used in conjunction with other materials, these first-person accounts provide useful insights into the formal aspects of policy formation and political relations. The two works by former ambassador Harry J. Guggenheim, "Amending the Platt Amendment," *Foreign Affairs* 12 (April 1934): 445–57, and *The United States and Cuba: A Study of International Relations* (New York, 1934), provide a critical assessment of Cuba-U.S. relations based on Guggenheim's experiences in Havana during the early 1930s. Sumner Welles, *Relations between the United States and Cuba* (Washington, D.C., 1934), deals almost exclusively with political and economic issues between 1933 and 1934. Earl E. T. Smith served as U.S. ambassador in Cuba between 1957 and 1959, and in *The Fourth Floor: An Account of the Castro Communist Revolution* (New York, 1962), he excoriates the State Department for its failure to obstruct the triumph of the revolution. Similarly, Paul Bethel, the press attaché in the U.S. embassy during the late 1950s, condemns U.S. policy in *The Losers* (New Rochelle, N.Y., 1969). A more judicious assessment of Cuba-U.S. relations during these difficult years is found in the works by the last ambassador to Cuba, Philip W. Bonsal, "Cuba, Castro and the United States," *Foreign Affairs* 40 (January 1967): 260–76, and *Cuba, Castro and the United States* (Pittsburgh, 1971). Perhaps the most balanced account of these years, and especially during late Carter and early Reagan administrations, is Wayne S. Smith, *The Closest of Enemies: A Personal and Diplomatic Account of U.S.-Cuban Relations since 1957* (New York, 1987).

VIII

Cuban immigration to the United States has become an important theme in the literature. The material is divided into two parts, one dealing with Cuban emigration between the 1860s and the early 1900s and the other treating the post-1959 period. The subject of Cuban emigration from the island has a long tradition in Cuban studies. One of the better surveys of the early Cuban immigration to the United States is Rolando Alvarez, *La emigración cubana en Estados Unidos, 1868–1878* (Havana, 1986). José Rivero Muñiz, "Los cubanos en Tampa," *Revista Bimestre Cubana* 71 (Primer Semestre 1958): 5–140, is an extensive historical survey dealing with the origins and development of the Cuban cigarworkers' communities in central Florida and their contribution to the struggles for independence. The Rivero Muñiz study was translated into English by Eustasio Fernández and H. Beltrán and published under the title of *The Ybor City Story, 1885–1954* (Tampa, 1976). Juan José E. Casasús, *La emigración cubana y la independencia de la patria* (Havana, 1953), is one of the most complete histories of Cuban emigration in the nineteenth century, examining the relationship between the expatriate communities in the United States and the independence movements in Cuba. The study spans the latter half of the century, with attention to fund-raising activities, propaganda efforts, and politico-military contributions. Manuel Deulofeu, *Heroes del destierro* (Cienfuegos, 1904), examines the émigré communities in Florida, with particular emphasis on the 1890s. Wen Gálvez, *Tampa, impresiones de emigrado* (Tampa, 1897), is a useful first-person account of the Cuban community in Tampa. Louis A. Pérez, Jr., "Cubans in Tampa: From Exiles to Immigrants, 1892–1901," *Florida Historical Quarterly* 57 (October 1978): 129–140, examines the transformation of the Cuban expatriate community in Tampa from political exiles to permanent residents.

The second principal period of Cuban emigration occurred after 1959, and on this subject the literature reaches voluminous proportions. Several bibliographical guides are of considerable value: Lourdes Casal and Andrés R. Hernández, "Cubans in the United States: A Survey of the Literature," *Cuban Studies/Estudios Cubanos* 5 (July 1975): 25–51; Casal, "An Annotated Bibliography on Cuban Exiles," in *The Cuban Minority in the U.S.* (Boca Raton, Fla., 1973), 179–99; Gastón Fernández and León Narváez, "Bibliography of Cuban Immigration/Adaptation to the United States," *Cuban Studies/Estudios Cubanos* 15 (Summer 1985): 61–72; Esther B. González, *Annotated Bibliography on Cubans in the United States, 1960–1976* (Miami, 1977); and Lyn MacCorkle, *Cubans in the United States* (Westport, Conn., 1984). Among the more useful and thematic works in this vast literature are the following: Eleanor R. Rogg, *The Assimilation of Cuban Exiles: The Role of Community and Class* (New York, 1974), a sociological study of the adjustment of Cuban exiles in West New York, New Jersey, to North American norms. José Llanes, *Cuban Americans: Masters of Survival* (Cambridge, Mass., 1982), seeks to categorize Cuban exiles through the use of fifty-eight composite characters created from extensive interviews. Lynn Darrell Bender, "The Cuban Exiles: An Analytical Study," *Journal of Latin American Studies* 5 (November 1973): 271–78, deals with various phases of Cuban immigration to the United States and the occupational/professional strata represented during each phase. The two books by Félix R. Masud-Piloto, *With Open Arms: Cuban Migration to the United States* (Totowa, N.J., 1988) and *From Welcomed Exiles to Illegal Immigrants: Cuban Migration to the U.S., 1959–1995* (Lanham, Md., 1996), serve as indispensable sources for these years. Other studies of value include Miguel González-Pando, *The Cuban Americans* (Westport, Conn., 1998), and Hedelberto López Blanch, *Descorriendo mamparas: La emigración cubana en los Estados Unidos* (San Juan, P.R., 2001). The influence of Cuban-Americans in policy is well developed in María Cristina García, "Hardliners v. 'Dialogueros': Cuban Exile Political Groups and United States–Cuba policy," *Journal of American Ethnic History* 17 (Summer 1998): 3–29. Silvia Pedraza-Bailey, "Cubans and Mexicans in the United States: The Function of Political and Economic Migration," *Cuban Studies/Estudios Cubanos* 11–12 (July 1981–January 1982): 79–97, is a comparative study of Cuban and Mexican migration, with attention to the causes of migration, the role of public assistance, the impact of ideology, and the class origins of émigrés. Myra Max Ferree, "Employment without Liberation—Cuban Women in the United States," *Social Science Quarterly* 60 (June 1979): 35–50, examines the employment of émigré women in the United States. The essay deals with the economic realities confronting Cubans and the effect of these conditions on attitudes toward women's participation in the wage labor force.

Index

Abbott, John S. C., 51

ABC Revolutionary Society: founded, 182–83; and mediations (1933), 186–87, 188, 190; and Gerardo Machado, 189; opposition to provisional government (1933), 195, 199

Adams, John Quincy, 40; advocates annexation of Cuba, 38, 39

Agramonte, Ignacio, 50

Agrarian Reform Act (1959), 238, 240

Agüero, Joaquín de, 47

Aguilera, Francisco Vicente, 50

Alcoy, Conde de, 20

Aldama, Miguel, 46, 49

Alfonso, José Luis, 46, 49

American Mining Company, 18

American Sugar Company, 118

American Sugar Refining Company, 136–37

Amorós, Sandy, 213

Anastasia, Alberto, 223

Anderson, P. B., 120

Annexation: and slavery, 34–35, 47–49; and Cubans educated in United States, 36, 68; Cuban support of, 36–37; U.S. designs for, 38–43; and filibustering expeditions, 43–44, 46–47; and Consejo de Gobierno Cubano, 45–46; and Club de La Habana, 46–47; and Ten Years War, 51, 53; Cuban opposition to, 52–53; opposed by José Martí, 78

Arango, Miguel, 138

Arango y Núñez del Castillo, José de, 36–37

Arcocha, Juan, 213, 216

Armenteros, Isidro, 47

Armstrong, Louis, 214

Arnaz, Desi, 213

Art, 277–78

Arteaga, Emilio, 147

Aspiazu, Don, 214

Atkins, Edwin, 57

Atlantic Sugar Company, 137

Auténtico party, 205, 233

Autonomist party, 55

Baker, J. W., 24

Ball, George W., 259

Ballou, Maturin M., 22, 67

Barbour, George M., 100

Baró, Juan Pedro, 66

Baseball: Cuban adoption of, 71–72; Cuban players in the U.S., 213; Cuban team plays Baltimore Orioles, 279

Batista, Fulgencio, 217, 234; and Sergeants' Revolt (1933), 193; and Sumner Welles, 200–201; removes Ramón Grau San Martín (1934), 201; presidency of (1940–44), 205; and gambling in Havana, 223; and 1944 elections, 224–25; leads 1952 coup, 233; opposed by Fidel Castro, 234; and U.S. arms embargo (1958), 235–36; flees Cuba (1958), 237, 238

Bauza, Mario, 214

Bay of Pigs, 245, 248, 249
Beaupré, Arthur M., 161
Bee, Hamilton P., 19
Benítez Rojo, Antonio, 213
Berle, Adolph A., 248
Bermúdez, Anacleto, 46
Betancourt, Alcides, 115
Betancourt, Alonso, 45, 46
Betancourt, Pedro, 115
Betancourt Cisneros, Gaspar, 45, 46, 68
Bethlehem Steel Corporation, 60, 119, 135
Blakey, Art, 214
Blanco, Manuel, 57
Blanco, Ramón, 87, 92
Bonnano, Joe, 223
Bonsal, Philip W., 243, 246, 248, 249
Boxing, 213
Bradford, Hezekiah, 18
Breckinridge, John C., 19
Bremer, Fredrika, 25–26
Brown, H. T., 141
Brubeck, Dave, 214
Bryant, William Cullen, 69
Buchanan, James, 39
Buenavista School, 136
Buena Vista Social Club, 277
Bush, George, 263, 272–73
Bush, George W., 274–75, 276

Cabrera Infante, Guillermo, 210, 212
Caibarién Electrical Company, 120
Calhoun, William H., 84
Camero, Candido, 214
Campaneris, Bert, 213
Candler School, 134, 136
Cape Cruz Company, 119
Cárdenas Railway and Terminal Company, 120

Carpentier, Alejo, 148
Carrión, Miguel de, 151
Cartaya, José Eliseo, 115
Carter, D. W., 133
Carter, Jimmy, 260, 276
Castillo Duany, Demetrio, 115
Castro, Fidel, 243, 249; in Tampa, 217–18; and 26 of July Movement, 234; insurrection against Fulgencio Batista, 237; and U.S. opposition, 248, 249, 250–52, 258–59, 271–73; and assassination attempts, 252, 273
Castro, Raúl, 234, 274
Central Intelligence Agency, 242; and Bay of Pigs, 245; organizes Cuban exiles, 247; and covert activities against Cuba, 252; and Radio Swan, 254
Central Sugar Company, 139
Céspedes, Carlos Manuel de (1819–74), 50, 51
Céspedes, Carlos Manuel de (1871–1939), 193, 197, 198
Chase Bank, 182
Chibás, Eduardo, 233
Cigar manufacturing, 62; exports to the U.S., 63–65; relocation of factories in Florida, 64–66; cigar workers, 65–66, 72–73, 215, 217–18; and U.S. investments, 119
Cisneros Betancourt, Salvador, 50
Clark, Sydney A., 126, 137, 141
Clay, Henry, 42–43
Clayton, John M., 41–42
Cleveland, Grover, 83–84; and Cuban insurrection (1895), 85–86
Clinton, Bill, 269, 274
Club de La Habana, 46–47
Coggeshall, George, 35

Colby, Bainbridge, 166
Cole, Nat King, 214, 223
Collazo, Enrique, 146
Commercial and Financial World, 118
Communist party, 174; opposition to
 Gerardo Machado, 178–79; and
 mediations (1933), 190; and 1959
 revolution, 240–41, 259
Compañía de Minería Cubana, 18
Concha, José de la, 23, 27–28, 67
Confederación Nacional Obrera de
 Cuba (CNOC), 174; opposition to
 Gerardo Machado, 178–79; and
 1930 general strike, 183
Consejo de Gobierno Cubano, 45–46
Conservative party: supports reelec-
 tion of Gerardo Machado, 180;
 and mediations (1933), 190–91
Cossío Woodward, Miguel, 212
Costello, Frank, 223
Crowder, Enoch H., 175, 187; as
 special representative, 162, 167–
 69; and 1920 elections, 166
Cruger, Alfred, 19
Cuba Cane Corporation, 137
Cuba Company, 119
Cuban-American League, 130
Cuban-American Sugar Company,
 118, 137, 138
Cuban Central Railway, 119
Cuban Copper Company, 120
Cuban Eastern Railway, 120
Cuban Education Association, 130
Cuban Electric Company, 240
Cuban League of Professional
 Baseball, 71
Cuban Railway, 119, 120
Cuban Revolutionary Party (PRC),
 77
Cuban Steel Ore Company, 119

Cuban Telegraph and Telephone
 Company, 120
Cuéllar, Miguel, 213
Cugat, Xavier, 214
Curbelo, José, 214

Dana, Richard Henry, Jr., 22, 52, 66
Davey, Richard, 25
Day, William R., 90
de Lôme, Enrique Dupuy, 85–86
Desvernine, Pablo, 115
Dewolf, George, 24
Diago family, 66
Díaz, Alberto J., 70
Dihigo, Martín, 213
Directorio Estudiantil Universitario,
 193
Dorham, Kenny, 214
Drake, Carlos, 66
Drake Brothers, 18

E. & L. Ponvert Brothers, E. L., 57
Early, Jubal A., 19
Eastern Steel Company, 119
Education: under Spanish govern-
 ment, 23, 67; Cubans in the U.S.,
 36, 67–68, 115; U.S. education in
 Cuba, 127–30, 132, 133–35; U.S.
 exchange programs, 279
Eisenhower, Dwight D., 242, 243
Electric Bond and Share Company,
 195
Eliza Bowman School, 136
Ellington, Duke, 214, 223
England, 5–6, 10; and Seven Years
 War, 3–4; capture of Havana
 (1762), 4; trade with Cuba, 4, 19;
 and slave trade, 4, 30, 32–34, 44;
 and North American colonies, 5–
 6; exports to Cuba, 19; opposition

England (cont.)
to Cuban annexation to the U.S., 36–37, 39–40
Estévez, Carlos, 277
Estrada Palma, Tomás, 115–16, 153–54, 157
Everett, Alexander H., 41

Factoría de Tabacos, 1
Febre, Paul, 35
Federación Obrera de La Habana, 179
Fergusson, Erna, 210, 212
Fernández, Pablo Armando, 208, 211, 222
Fernández Marcané, Luis, 138
Ferrara, Orestes, 138
Ferrer, Horacio, 197–98
Figueredo, Fernando, 115
Figueredo, Pedro, 50, 51
Fish, Hamilton, 53, 54
Forsyth, John, 41
Foster-Cánovas Treaty, 62, 74
Franca, Porfirio, 172
France, 7, 10; and sugar consumption, 9; and revolution in Saint Domingue, 9, 10; shipping, 26
Freeman, Frederick, 24
Frías, Francisco de (Count of Pozos Dulces), 46, 49, 68
Fry, Birkett D., 19
Frye, Alex E., 128
Funston, Frederick, 87

Gandarilla, Julio César, 146
García, Calixto, 90, 93; and U.S. intervention (1898), 96; relations with U.S. command, 97–98
García Ramis, Federico, 115
Gardner, Arthur, 235
Genovese, Vito, 223

Gibbes, R. W., 20
Gillespie, Dizzy, 214
Gómez, José Miguel, 158, 159
Gómez, Máximo, 82–83; and Cuban independence, 90, 93
Gonzales, William E., 158; and railroad strikes, 162–63
González, Elián, 277
González, Luciano, 214
González, Miguel Angel, 213
González, Salvador, 277
Goodman, Benny, 214
Grant, Ulysses S., 51, 53–54
Grau San Martín, Ramón: provisional government (1933), 194–201; presidency (1944–48), 206, 233
Greene, J. Milton, 130, 132
Grillo Frank (Machito), 214
"Grito de Baire," 82
"Grito de Yara," 50. See also Ten Years War
Guantánamo Naval Station, 163, 202
Guantánamo Railroad Company, 120
Guevara, Ernesto Che, 241
Guggenheim, Harry F., 144–45, 183

Haig, Alexander, 260–61
Harris, George, 18
Harris Brothers, 120
Harroun, Gilbert K., 130
Havana Advertising Company, 121
Havana Casino Orchestra, 214
Havana Commercial Company, 119
Havana Electric Railway Company, 120
Hawley, R. B., 118
Haymarket strike, 73, 78
Hay-Quesada Treaty, 126
Helms-Burton Law, 270, 271, 274

Hemenway, Augustus, 24
Herman, Woody, 214
Herrera, Alberto, 190
Hershey Corporation, 134, 136, 137
Holiday, Ross E., 157
Hollins, H. B., 119
Homestead strike, 73
Horne, Lena, 223
Howland, Samuel Shaw, 18
Howland Brothers, 18, 35
Huston Contracting Company, 121
Hyatt, Pulaski F., 88

International Bank for Reconstruction and Development, 206, 218, 231
International Ocean Telegraph Company, 70
International Telephone and Telegraph, 219, 240
Irene Toland School, 136
Isle of Pines, 109; and U.S. colonization, 124–27
Iznaga, Carlos, 57
Iznaga, José Aniceto, 45, 66

Jefferson, Thomas, 39, 40, 41, 91
Jenks, Russell, 24
Joint Resolution (1898), 96, 105, 108. *See also* Teller Amendment
Jones-Costigan Act, 202
J. P. Morgan and Company, 182
Juraguá Iron Company, Ltd., 60, 120

Kennedy, John F., 248
Kenton, Stan, 214
Kid Chocolate, 213
Kid Gavilán, 213
Kitt, Ertha, 223
Knight, Martin, 18
Knox, Philander, 159

Krupa, Gene, 214
Ku Klux Klan, 73, 215

Labor, 159, 163; threat to U.S. property, 160–65; strikes, 160–65, 173, 183, 190–91, 238; U.S. opposition to labor legislation, 162, 163–64; and trade unionism, 173–75; unemployment, 182, 230; and mediations (1933), 190; opposition to government of Ramón Grau San Martin (1933), 194, 195
Lacosta, Perfecto, 115
Lansky, Meyer, 223, 224, 225
La Verdad, 45
Lay, Louis, 20
Leaf, Earl, 213
Lecuona, Ernesto, 214
Lee, Fitzhugh, 89
Lewis, Norman, 225
Liberal party, 176; and 1906 revolution, 153–55; and 1917 revolution, 156, 158; supports reelection Gerardo Machado, 180; and participation in mediations (1933), 190, 191
Lindsay, Forbes, 52
Lisser, Herbert G. de, 146
Llano Montes, Antonio, 225, 230
Llerena, Mario, 232
Llopis, Rogelio, 216
López, Narciso, 46–47
Loveira, Carlos, 128, 142–43
Lucchese, Tommy, 223
Luciano, Lucky, 223, 224

Machado, Gerardo, 184, 199; campaigns against Platt Amendment, 176; and economic reforms, 177–78, 204; attacks labor, 178–79; and U.S. investments, 178–79;

Machado, Gerardo (*cont.*)
   reelected, 180; loans from U.S.
   banks, 179, 182; opposition to,
   181–86; and the U.S., 181, 183;
   and Sumner Welles, 186–93;
   participates in mediations (1933),
   190–92; deposed, 192
Madán, Cristobal, 45, 46
Madden, Richard R., 20, 24
Maffitt, John N., 19
Magruder, John B., 19
Mañach, Jorge, 246
Mann, Herbie, 214
Márquez Sterling, Manuel, 152, 188–
   89
Marrero, Conrado, 213
Marrero Leví, 230
Martí, José, 117, 217, 222; organizes
   Cuban Revolutionary party, 77;
   and independence, 77–78; views
   on U.S., 78–81
Martin, Edwin M., 259
Martínez, Raúl, 255
Masó, Bartolomé, 50, 51, 89–90
Mayet, Tomás, 73
McHatton-Riply, Eliza, 19
McKinley, William, 89; opposition to
   Cuban independence 87, 92–93;
   war against Spain, 94–96; and
   intervention in Cuba (1898), 94–96
Mendieta, Carlos: quits Liberal
   party, 180; appointed president,
   201; and trade with the U.S., 204
Mendive, Manuel, 277
Menocal, Mario G., 115, 138; and
   1917 revolution, 156
Mercantile Weekly Report, 20
Mikoyan, Anastas, 241
Miller, Warren, 216
Mining, 18; U.S. investments in, 60,
   119–20; exports to U.S., 60, 62

Minoso, Minnie, 213
Moderate party, 153
Monroe, James, 37, 40, 41
Monte, Domingo del, 36, 46
Monte, Ricardo del, 68
Moore, Thomas Overton, 19
Moreland & Company, 18
Moret, Segismundo, 91
Morgan and Company, J. P., 182
Morland, J., 35
Morton, George C., 7
Morúa Delgado, Martín, 72
Music, 213–14

New York Ore Dressing Company, 18
Nipe Bay Company, 118
North American Sugar Company,
   136
Núñez, Emilio, 115

O'Farrill, Chico, 214
Oliva, Tony, 213
Olney, Richard, 84–85
Organización Celular Radical
   Revolucionaria (OCRR), 183; and
   mediations (1933), 188, 190;
   opposition to provisional govern-
   ment (1933), 195
Ortiz, Fernando, 184
Ostend Manifesto, 44
O'Sullivan, John L., 45

Pact of Zanjón, 54, 55
País, Frank, 234
Pan American Airways, 207
Partido Comunista de Cuba (PCC).
   See Communist party
Partido Socialista Popular (PSP). *See*
   Communist party
Pascual, Camilo, 213
Pawley, William, 237

Peña, Orlando, 213
Pennsylvania Steel Company, 60, 119
Pepper, Charles M., 127
Peraza, Armando, 214
Pérez Galdós, Juan, 57
Pérez Prado, Dámaso, 214
Perkins, Benjamin, 63
Permanent Treaty (1903), 124, 149, 155, 176, 202. *See also* Platt Amendment
Phillips, Ruby Hart, 211, 236
Phinney family, 21, 24
Pierce, Franklin, 43
Pinson School, 136
Platt, Orville H., 103; and Teller Amendment, 105; and Platt Amendment, 108
Platt Amendment, 109–10, 111, 117, 152, 166, 184–85, 188, 189, 246; and Cuban independence, 108; Cuban opposition to, 111, 112; source of Cuban nationalism, 146, 176–77; and 1906 revolution, 153; as source of Cuban instability, 154–56; and 1912 revolution, 156; and 1917 revolution, 156, 158; and 1920 elections, 156; protection of foreign property, 158–59; and Cuban labor, 160–63; and opposition to Gerardo Machado, 184–85; abrogated by provisional government (1933), 194, 195; abrogated, 202
Polk, James K., 43, 46
Ponupo Manganese Company, 60, 119
Ponvert Brothers, E. & L., 57
Popular party: supports reelection of Gerardo Machado, 180; and mediations (1933), 190, 191

Porter, Robert P., 127
Pozo, Chano, 214
Preston, William, 19
Prío Socarrás, Carlos, 206; overthrown (1952), 233
Prohibition, 223
Protestantism, 25; Cubans convert to, 69; Cuban ministry, 70; missionaries in Cuba, 130–36

Quesada, Gonzalo de, 114
Quintana family, 21
Quitman, John, 44

Raft, George, 222
Railroads, 26, 61, 67; construction of, 19, 71; operated by North Americans, 21–22; U.S. investments in, 119, 120, 160, 219; strikes, 160, 162
Ramos, Pedro, 213
Reagan, Ronald, 257, 259, 260, 261–62, 272
Real Compañía de Comercio, 1
Reciprocity Treaty (1903), 121–22, 144; effects on Cuban industry, 122; source of encouragement to U.S. immigrants, 123; and U.S. cultural penetration, 144
Reciprocity Treaty (1934), 204–5
Red Telefónica de La Habana, 120
Reformist party, 49
Reid, Whitelaw, 91
Rigney, Joseph, 119
Rivero Agüero, Andrés, 236, 237
Rockefeller, John D., 132
Rodríguez, Arsenio, 214
Rodríguez, Fernando, 277
Rogers, Carlton H., 22
Rojas, Carlos M., 115
Rojas, Cookie, 213
Roncali, Federico, 48–49

Roosevelt, Franklin D., 187, 225
Root, Elihu, 102, 104, 153; formulation of Platt Amendment, 106–9, 111, 112
Ros-Lehtinen, Ileana, 255, 267
Royo family, 20
Rubens, Horatio, 92–93, 95–96

Saco, Antonio, 52–53
Safford, Smith and Company, 18
Safford, William F., 20
Sagasta, Mateo de, 87
Saint Domingue: U.S. trade with, 6, 10–11; and sugar production, 9, 10
Sánchez, Bernabé, 37
Sánchez, Diego Julián, 57
Sánchez, Elizardo, 266
Sánchez de Bustamante, Antonio, 138
Sánchez Iznaga, José María, 46
Sanguily, Manuel, 147
San José Copper Company, 120
Sarduy, Severo, 212
Schlesinger, Arthur, Jr., 225
Seguí, Diego, 213
Segura, Francisco, 72
Seigle, Octavio, 184
Selden, Dudley, 18
Sergeants' Revolt, 193
Seven Years War, 3–4
Seward, William, 51
Shafter, William R., 97, 100, 117
Shaler, William, 36, 37
Shearing, George, 214
Shell Oil Company, 242
Sherman, John, 90
Shipping, 18, 19, 22; Cuba-U.S. service, 26–27; post-World War II, 207
Shultz, George, 262

Sigua Iron Company, 60, 119
Sinatra, Frank, 223
Sister-city programs, 279
Skoug, Kenneth, 273
Slavery, 1, 5, 12, 20; slave trade, 2, 4, 8; and U.S. plantations, 24, 25; abolition of slave trade, 30, 44; and sugar production, 30; rebellion, 30–31; Spanish defense of, 32–34; and annexationism, 34–35, 47–49; and U.S. Civil War, 48
Smith, Earl E. T., 236, 237
Smith, Thomas B., 18
Smith, Wayne, 247, 257
Smoot-Hawley Tariff, 181, 202
Snare and Triest Company, 121
Soler Puig, José, 189
Sorondo, Guillermo, 72
Soviet Union, 244, 248; and Cuban revolution, 258, 259, 260, 263, 264
Spain, 3, 7, 10, 19; and Bourbon policies, 1, 2–5, 11; and slave trade, 2, 32–34; commercial relations with Cuba, 6–7, 8–9, 13–17, 29–30, 44–45; tariff policies, 16–17, 49–50, 75–76; response to U.S. activities in Cuba, 23, 27–28; and Ten Years War, 50–53, 54; relations with U.S., 83–96; and colonial reforms, 87, 92; and Cuban insurrection of 1895, 90–91, 83–96; war with U.S., 91–96
Spanish-American Iron Company, 60, 119, 120
Spanish-American Light and Power Company, 70, 120
Stafford, Eaton, 57
Standard Fruit Company, 121
Standard Oil, 220, 242, 243
Steele, James W., 58
Stewart, William, 24

Storey and Company, 18
Suárez, Javier, 255
Sugar production, 1, 82; and Spanish
    policy, 2; exports to U.S., 5, 7, 12–
    14, 16–18, 23–26, 61–63, 206–7,
    242; in Saint Domingue, 6, 9–10;
    and slavery, 8, 11–12; and revolu-
    tion in Saint Domingue, 10–11;
    and U.S. planters, 18, 20, 24–25;
    under U.S. control, 56–58, 62–63;
    after Ten Years War, 56–59; and
    U.S. tariff policy, 74–76; and war
    of 1895, 82–83, 111–19; and World
    War II, 205; disruption during
    1950s, 234

Taft, William H., 156, 157
Tanco Armero, Nicholas, 67
Tarafa, José Miguel, 138–39
Tartabull, José, 213
Taylor, John Glanville, 21
Taylor, Moses, 18
Taylor, Wood, 19
Tejera, Nivaria, 212
Teller Amendment, 96, 98, 113; and
    Cuban pacification, 105
Ten Years War, 50, 55, 56, 70; and
    annexation, 51, 53–54; and Pact of
    Zanjón, 54
Terry, Tomás, 57, 66–67, 119
Tetuán, Duke of, 86
Texaco Oil Company, 220, 242, 243
Thorndike, George K., 24
Tjader, Cal, 214
Tobacco production, 1, 34; exports to
    U.S., 62, 63; and U.S. investment,
    119. *See also* Cigar manufacturing
Toombs, Robert A., 19
Torre family, 57
Torricelli Law, 263, 265, 270, 271
Torriente, Cosme de la, 185

Torriente, Ramón de la, 57
Tourism, 278
Touzet, René, 214
Trade: with U.S., 1, 73–74, 76, 204–5,
    206–7; with England, 4; and
    slavery, 34, 35; and U.S. tariff
    policies, 62–63, 73–74, 76, 204;
    effects of U.S. Reciprocity Treaty
    (1903), 121–22; post–World War II,
    218–19, 226, 228–29, 232, 240; U.S.
    trade embargo, 250–51, 275–76
Trafficante, Santo, 223
Trollope, Anthony, 14
Tropical Engineering and Construc-
    tion Company, 121

Unión Nacionalista: founded, 180;
    opposition to Gerardo Machado,
    184; and mediations (1933), 188;
    opposition to provisional govern-
    ment (1933), 195, 199; as govern-
    ment party, 201
United Fruit Company, 118–19, 121,
    134, 135, 137, 138
Urban Reform Law (1959), 238

Valdés, Miguelito, 214
Valdez, Carlos (Potato), 214
Van Buren, Martin, 42
Varona, Enrique José, 147
Vaughan, Sarah, 223
Verdad, La, 45
Vernon Brothers, 18
Versalles, Zoilo, 213
Vila family, 57
Villaverde, Cirilo, 45

Wald, Jerry, 214
Walker, William, 43–44
Walsh, Osgood, 63
Webster, Daniel, 38–39

Welles, Sumner, 203; and Gerardo
    Machado, 186–93; organizes
    mediations (1933), 186, 190–93;
    and removal of Gerardo
    Machado, 192–93; opposition to
    provisional government (1933),
    193–201; relations with Fulgencio
    Batista, 200–201
Whitside, Samuel M., 164
William, George W., 20, 25
Williams, Herbert P., 101
Williams, Ramon O., 61–62
Wilson, F. M. Huntington, 164
Wilson, James H., 105, 128
Wilson-Gorman Tariff Act, 74
Wood, Leonard, 111; opposition to
    Cuban independence, 100, 101;
    and pro-U.S. political parties, 102;
    and Cuban elections, 103–4; on

U.S. responsibility in Cuba, 105–
    6; and Platt Amendment, 108–9;
    and prospects of U.S. invest-
    ments, 123; support of U.S.
    immigration to Cuba, 126–27;
    and U.S. education, 129
Woodbury, D. B., 20
Woodford, Stewart, 91–92
Wright, Irene, 127

Yglesias, José, 218
Young, Samuel B. M., 100
Young America Movement, 43

Zaldo, Carlos, 115
Zayas, Alfredo, 173; and Enoch
    Crowder, 166–69; and reform, 175
Zayas, Henry Lincoln de, 69

Printed in the United States
138288LV00003B/20/P